DISCIPLINARY CORE IDEAS
— RESHAPING TEACHING AND LEARNING —

DISCIPLINARY CORE IDEAS
— RESHAPING TEACHING AND LEARNING —

Edited by

Ravit Golan Duncan
Joseph Krajcik
Ann E. Rivet

National Science Teachers Association

Arlington, Virginia

National Science Teachers Association

Claire Reinburg, Director
Wendy Rubin, Managing Editor
Rachel Ledbetter, Associate Editor
Amanda Van Beuren, Associate Editor
Donna Yudkin, Book Acquisitions Coordinator

ART AND DESIGN
Will Thomas Jr., Director
Joe Butera, Senior Graphic Designer, cover and
  interior design

PRINTING AND PRODUCTION
Colton Gigot, Senior Production Manager

NATIONAL SCIENCE TEACHERS ASSOCIATION
David L. Evans, Executive Director
David Beacom, Publisher

1840 Wilson Blvd., Arlington, VA 22201
www.nsta.org/store
For customer service inquiries, please call 800-277-5300.

*NSTA is committed to publishing material that promotes the best in inquiry-based science education.
However, conditions of actual use may vary, and the safety procedures and practices described in this book
are intended to serve only as a guide. Additional precautionary measures may be required. NSTA and the
authors do not warrant or represent that the procedures and practices in this book meet any safety code
or standard of federal, state, or local regulations. NSTA and the authors disclaim any liability for personal
injury or damage to property arising out of or relating to the use of this book, including any of the recommendations, instructions, or materials contained therein.*

Library of Congress Cataloging-in-Publication Data
Names: Krajcik, Joseph S. | Rivet, Ann E., 1974- | Duncan, Ravit Golan, 1973-
Title: Disciplinary core ideas : reshaping teaching and learning / Joseph Krajcik, Ann E. Rivet, and Ravit
Golan Duncan.
Description: Arlington, VA : National Science Teachers Association, [2016] |
  Includes bibliographical references and index.
Identifiers: LCCN 2016014730 (print) | LCCN 2016020728 (ebook) | ISBN 9781938946417 (print) | ISBN
9781941316672 (e-book) | ISBN 9781941316672 (epub)
Subjects: LCSH: Science--Study and teaching (Elementary)--United States. |
  Science--Study and teaching (Middle school)--United States. |
  Science--Study and teaching (Secondary)--United States. |
  Interdisciplinary approach in education--United States.
Classification: LCC Q183.3.A1 K73 2016 (print) | LCC Q183.3.A1 (ebook) | DDC 507.1/273--dc23
LC record available at *https://lccn.loc.gov/2016014730*

CONTENTS

CHAPTER 1

INTRODUCTION TO DISCIPLINARY CORE IDEAS:
WHAT THEY ARE AND WHY THEY ARE IMPORTANT

Joseph Krajcik, Ravit Golan Duncan, and Ann E. Rivet

1

PHYSICAL SCIENCES

9

LIFE SCIENCES

95

CHAPTER 2

CORE IDEA PS1: MATTER AND ITS INTERACTIONS

Kristin Mayer and Joseph Krajcik

13

CHAPTER 3

CORE IDEA PS2: MOTION AND STABILITY:
FORCES AND INTERACTIONS

David Fortus and Jeffrey Nordine

33

CHAPTER 4

CORE IDEA PS3: ENERGY

Jeffrey Nordine and David Fortus

55

CHAPTER 5

CORE IDEA PS4: WAVES AND THEIR
APPLICATIONS IN TECHNOLOGIES FOR
INFORMATION TRANSFER

David Fortus and Joseph Krajcik

75

CHAPTER 6

CORE IDEA LS1: FROM MOLECULES TO
ORGANISMS: STRUCTURES AND PROCESSES

Aaron Rogat, Barbara Hug, and Ravit Golan Duncan

99

CHAPTER 7

CORE IDEA LS2: ECOSYSTEMS: INTERACTIONS,
ENERGY, AND DYNAMICS

Charles W. (Andy) Anderson and Jennifer H. Doherty

123

CHAPTER 8

CORE IDEA LS3: HEREDITY: INHERITANCE AND
VARIATION OF TRAITS

Nicole A. Shea and Ravit Golan Duncan

145

CHAPTER 9

CORE IDEA LS4: BIOLOGICAL EVOLUTION:
UNITY AND DIVERSITY

Cynthia Passmore, Julia Svoboda Gouvea, Candice Guy, and Chris
Griesemer

165

FOREWORD

Helen Quinn

This is not a book about disciplinary core ideas (DCIs) in science. This is a book about teaching science organized around DCIs as defined in *A Framework for K–12 Science Education* (*Framework*; NRC 2012) and encapsulated in the performance expectations of the *Next Generation Science Standards* (*NGSS*; NGSS Lead States 2013). As anyone looking at this book knows, the *Framework* and *NGSS* stress three dimensions in science learning: Students are not just learning the DCIs but are also engaging in science and engineering practices and understanding and applying a set of crosscutting concepts. Teachers must meld all three of these dimensions together to build effective science lessons, but before they can do that, they need to understand each dimension and the shifts in emphasis around each that are central to the definition and structure of the *NGSS*.

The *Framework* was developed based on the best available research knowledge on effective science teaching approaches. Central to effectiveness is the recognition that students must build new knowledge by refining and revising prior knowledge (or their preconceptions, if the topic is new to them). Teaching that ignores what has come before and does not capitalize on research into what makes a topic difficult to learn is at best inefficient and at worst ineffective. Hence, it is important not just to have a science curriculum for the current year but to have one that is designed to build knowledge and deepen understanding progressively across multiple years.

This book, then, is about how the *NGSS* are structured with regard to DCIs, how these ideas build across the grade levels, and what aspects are newly emphasized or de-emphasized at each level to achieve continuity and establish a firm base for further learning and use of that knowledge beyond high school. For each DCI, the authors—who are experts in that area of science or engineering learning—discuss how the *NGSS* expectations at each grade band are structured, stressing shifts in emphasis and explaining some of the reasons for these shifts.

Teachers redesigning their instruction to better support the *NGSS* will find that the material in this book provides useful background for that effort, but it will not serve as an instruction manual. As every teacher knows, the art of teaching is the art of making choices, of choosing the right strategy at each moment and combining multiple factors in planning units or lessons to achieve desired outcomes. To make these choices well, a teacher needs both a near view (i.e., what are the goals of today) and a far view (i.e., which goals of today fit into and build toward an overall set of larger and longer-term goals). In the far view, the teacher knows both what came before and what comes after the current lesson, and even the current year. This book helps a teacher engaged in developing or using *NGSS*-oriented curriculum with that view. In combination with other publications that provide a similar overview and perspective on the science and engineering practices and the crosscutting concepts and their development across the K–12 school years, this book provides essential background for those who wish to be effective science teachers in the *NGSS* context.

ACKNOWLEDGMENTS

The editors would like to thank Kevin J. B. Anderson, a science consultant from the Wisconsin Department of Public Instruction, for his insightful and productive comments on various chapters in this book.

ABOUT THE EDITORS

The editors have been listed here and on the cover in alphabetical order.

Ravit Golan Duncan is an associate professor of science education with a joint appointment in the Graduate School of Education and the School of Environmental and Biological Sciences at Rutgers University. She received her PhD in learning sciences from Northwestern University. She currently has two main research strands: (1) the design and study of inquiry-based learning environments in life sciences that engage students with modeling and argumentation and (2) the study of learning progressions in science education, specifically in genetics. She is the recipient of three early career awards from the National Academy of Education/ Spencer Foundation, the National Science Foundation, and the Knowles Science Teaching Foundation. In addition, Duncan also coordinates and teaches in the Certification Program in Life Sciences at Rutgers University and has studied the development of preservice teachers' knowledge and beliefs. Duncan is the recipient of several federal grants that involve the design of instructional materials that support student (and teacher) engagement with scientific inquiry. She has published in both education research journals such as the *Journal of Research in Science Teaching*, *Science Education*, and the National Science Teachers Association (NSTA) practitioner journals *The Science Teacher*, *Science Scope*, and *Science and Children*. Duncan was also one of the reviewers of *A Framework for K–12 Science Education* and has facilitated several NSTA professional development workshops and webinars about the *Next Generation Science Standards* disciplinary core ideas and science practices over the past few years.

Joseph Krajcik, a Lappan-Phillips Professor of Science Education at Michigan State University (MSU), serves as director of the CREATE for STEM (Collaborative Research for Education, Assessment and Teaching Environments for cience, Technology, Engineering, and Mathematics) Institute, which seeks to improve the teaching and learning of science and mathematics in kindergarten through college through innovation and research. During his career, Krajcik has focused on working with science teachers to reform science teaching practices to promote students' engagement in and learning of science. He served as lead writer for developing physical science standards for the *NGSS* and the lead writer for the physical science design team for *A Framework for K–12 Science Education*. He has authored and coauthored curriculum materials, books, and over 100 manuscripts. Krajcik served as president of the National Association for Research in Science Teaching, from which he received the Distinguished Contributions to Science Education Through Research Award in 2010. In 2014, he received the George G. Mallinson Award for Lifetime Achievement in the Field of Science Education from the Michigan Science Teachers Association for overall excellence of contributions to science education over a significant period of time. The University of Michigan, where Krajcik was a faculty member for 21 years, recognized him for his commitment to graduate education by presenting him with the Faculty Award for Distinguished Graduate Mentoring. Krajcik received his PhD in science education from the University of Iowa. Prior to receiving his PhD, Krajcik taught high school chemistry and physical science in Milwaukee, Wisconsin for eight years.

Ann E. Rivet is an associate professor of science education in the Department of Mathematics, Science, and Technology at Teachers College Columbia University. Her research uses learning sciences frameworks to explore the intersections of scientific reasoning, instructional design, and assessment, primarily at the middle and secondary school level. Her current work employs a learning progressions lens to examine students' interpretations and use of representations of large-scale Earth systems and see how their reasoning can be supported and developed through various classroom instructional strategies. She is also actively involved with current efforts to support teachers and instructional leaders with the *Next Generation Science Standards* in collaboration with the National Science Teachers Association. Rivet has extensive experience with the development and evaluation of project-based science curriculum materials, particularly in urban settings. Her prior research looked specifically at the role of contextualizing features of project-based science programs at the middle school level and how the design of those aspects of the curriculum support the activation of students' prior knowledge for learning and lead to more robust understandings of the science content. Her work has been published in several leading journals including *Science*, the *Journal of Research in Science Teaching*, and the *American Education Research Journal*, and she has presented her work in multiple national and international settings. She holds a bachelor's degree in physics from Brown University and a doctoral degree in science education from the University of Michigan.

CONTRIBUTORS

Foreword

Helen Quinn, SLAC National Accelerator Laboratory, Menlo Park, California

Chapter 1

Joseph Krajcik, Michigan State University, East Lansing, Michigan

Ravit Golan Duncan, Rutgers University, New Brunswick, New Jersey

Ann E. Rivet, Teachers College Columbia University, New York, New York

Chapter 2

Kristin Mayer, Michigan State University, East Lansing, Michigan

Joseph Krajcik, Michigan State University, East Lansing, Michigan

Chapter 3

David Fortus, Weizmann Institute of Science, Rehovot, Israel

Jeffrey Nordine, Leibniz Institute for Science and Mathematics Education (IPN), Kiel, Germany

Chapter 4

Jeffrey Nordine, Leibniz Institute for Science and Mathematics Education (IPN), Kiel, Germany

David Fortus, Weizmann Institute of Science, Rehovot, Israel

Chapter 5

David Fortus, Weizmann Institute of Science, Rehovot, Israel

Joseph Krajcik, Michigan State University, East Lansing, Michigan

Chapter 6

Aaron Rogat, Purdue University, West Lafayette, Indiana

Barbara Hug, University of Illinois at Urbana-Champaign, Champaign, Illinois

Ravit Golan Duncan, Rutgers University, New Brunswick, New Jersey

Chapter 7

Charles W. (Andy) Anderson, Michigan State University, East Lansing, Michigan

Jennifer H. Doherty, University of Washington, Seattle, Washington

Chapter 8

Nicole A. Shea, Bio-Rad Laboratories, Hercules, California

Ravit Golan Duncan, Rutgers University, New Brunswick, New Jersey

CONTRIBUTORS

Chapter 9

Cynthia Passmore, University of California, Davis, Davis, California

Julia Svoboda Gouvea, Tufts University, Medford, Massachusetts

Candice Guy, University of California, Davis, Davis, California

Chris Griesemer, University of California, Davis, Davis, California

Chapter 10

Julia D. Plummer, Pennsylvania State University, University Park, Pennsylvania

Chapter 11

Ann E. Rivet, Teachers College Columbia University, New York, New York

Chapter 12

Nancy Brickhouse, Saint Louis University, Saint Louis, Missouri

J. Randy McGinnis, Center for Science and Technology in Education, Department of Teaching and Learning, Policy and Leadership, University of Maryland, College Park, Maryland

Nicole A. Shea, Bio-Rad Laboratories, Hercules, California

Andrea Drewes, School of Education, University of Delaware, Newark, Delaware

Emily Hestness, Center for Science and Technology in Education, Department of Teaching and Learning, Policy and Leadership, University of Maryland, College Park, Maryland

Wayne Breslyn, Center for Science and Technology in Education, Department of Teaching and Learning, Policy and Leadership, University of Maryland, College Park, Maryland

Chapter 13

David E. Kanter, Kanter Learning Design & Research, New York, New York

David P. Crismond, The City College of New York, New York, New York

Chapter 14

Cary Sneider, Portland State University, Portland, Oregon

Chapter 15

Ann E. Rivet, Teachers College Columbia University, New York, New York

Joseph Krajcik, Michigan State University, East Lansing, Michigan

Ravit Golan Duncan, Rutgers University, New Brunswick, New Jersey

CHAPTER 1

INTRODUCTION TO DISCIPLINARY CORE IDEAS

WHAT THEY ARE AND WHY THEY ARE IMPORTANT

Joseph Krajcik, Ravit Golan Duncan, and Ann E. Rivet

A Framework for K–12 Science Education (*Framework*; NRC 2012) paints a new vision for science education that moves classroom teaching from the presentation of numerous disconnected science concepts to the development of learning environments in which students use disciplinary core ideas (DCIs), science and engineering practices, and crosscutting concepts to make sense of real-world phenomena or to design solutions to problems. A phenomenon is anything that can be observed and repeated. The *Framework* focuses on a limited number of core ideas that students draw on to explain and predict phenomena that they encounter in their daily lives. Moreover, these core ideas build a conceptual tool kit that will allow students to continue learning, exploring, and explaining throughout their lives.

In the last 20 years, the fields of science and engineering have progressed rapidly, resulting in knowledge and explanations that have pushed the frontiers of science and engineering in new directions. Consider the changes that have occurred over the past decade just in our ability

to send information wirelessly across the globe. Concurrently, research in cognitive science, the learning sciences, and science education has shown that for knowledge to be useful, students need to learn ideas in greater depth. The *Framework* puts forth a set of DCIs that students learn progressively over the course of schooling. This book presents insights into the meaning of those DCIs and their components, as well as the importance of the DCIs in making sense of phenomena and finding solutions to problems. The authors of the various chapters expand on the ideas presented in the *Framework* to provide a deeper, more comprehensive explanation of the core ideas and further insights into what they mean for teaching and learning at the various grade bands (NGSS Lead States 2013). This book also highlights an important shift in emphasis in the *Framework* compared to prior standards.

The *Framework* identifies three key dimensions for student learning of science: DCIs, science and engineering practices, and crosscutting concepts. Although each of the dimensions is critical on its own, they all work together to support students in explaining phenomena or designing solutions to problems. This knowledge-in-use perspective is one of the most significant changes described in the *Framework* and the *NGSS*. This integration is referred to as three-dimensional learning. This book focuses primarily on the DCIs, but because they work together with crosscutting concepts and science and engineering practices, it makes sense to mention the other two dimensions when discussing these core ideas and strategies for addressing them through instruction.

The DCIs were identified as part of the *Framework* committee's charge. Design teams of national experts for each of the disciplines—physical sciences, life sciences, Earth and space sciences, and engineering—were tasked with identifying a maximum of four core ideas in each area. Imagine how challenging it was for these teams to reduce their field to just four central ideas. Once identified, these ideas were discussed by the *Framework* committee and then vetted publicly by individuals and organizations. In response to the vetting, the DCIs were modified and changed. After the *Framework* committee revised the core ideas, these and the other two dimensions were approved by the National Academy of Sciences.

What Are the Disciplinary Core Ideas?

The *Framework* stresses the importance of a small number of DCIs in science and engineering to support students in explaining and predicting phenomena and in designing solutions to problems that students encounter in their daily lives. These core ideas also form a strong foundation that allows individuals to continue learning throughout their lives. The *Framework* stresses the

importance of building these ideas across time to support deeper and more meaningful understandings and of forming connections between the ideas so that students can apply their knowledge to novel situations. As such, DCIs serve as the major organizer of concepts and allow learners to make connections and further refine and enhance their ideas.

DCIs are critical within and across the various science disciplines. If you think of a discipline in which you have expertise, you can imagine the DCIs for that area because they form the network of understanding that allows you to explain phenomena. Most individuals who have a background in chemistry think of matter and how it changes; those in physics think of energy and force and motion; people in biology think of evolution; and those in the Earth sciences think of Earth systems. Meanwhile, engineers typically think of design processes.

Core ideas are powerful in that they are central to the disciplines of science, provide explanations of phenomena, and are the building blocks for learning within a discipline (Stevens, Sutherland, and Krajcik 2009). For example, electrical interactions (DCI PS2: Motion and Stability: Forces and Interactions) that occur at the molecular level can explain diverse phenomena such as the boiling of water and the folding of proteins. In the Earth and space sciences, the core idea of Earth's dynamic systems (DCI ESS2: Earth's Systems) explains not only the causes of local weather phenomena that we experience every day but also the ways that the environmental conditions combine to create specific ecosystems and how energy is distributed across the globe. In the life sciences, the inheritance of traits (DCI LS3: Heredity: Inheritance and Variation of Traits) can explain diverse phenomena such as the observable differences and similarities of individuals within families and the likelihood of a species becoming extinct.

According to the *Framework* (NRC 2012), a DCI

- has broad importance across multiple sciences or engineering disciplines or is a key organizing principle of a single discipline,

- provides a key tool for understanding or investigating more complex ideas and solving problems,

- relates to the interests and life experiences of students or is connected to societal or personal concerns that require scientific or technological knowledge, and

- is teachable and learnable over multiple grades at increasing levels of depth and sophistication.

The design teams used these characteristics in developing the core ideas for each discipline. Figure 1.1 presents the DCIs. Each area has a maximum of four ideas, which themselves have two or more components associated with them. These components will be discussed in subsequent chapters. The appendix (pp. 283–284) provides the components of each DCI.

Focusing on few powerful ideas allows learners to develop the depth and integration of concepts needed to learn more and use what they know throughout their lives in future learning or for careers. As such, the DCIs are essential. Building understanding of the DCIs is critical because it allows learners to solve real-world problems and further develop understanding in conjunction with the science and engineering practices and crosscutting concepts. Because of their power to explain phenomena, DCIs serve as important

FIGURE 1.1

Disciplinary Core Ideas

Physical sciences

    PS1: Matter and its interactions

    PS2: Motion and stability: Forces and interactions

    PS3: Energy

    PS4: Waves and their applications in technologies for information transfer

Life sciences

    LS1: From molecules to organisms: Structures and processes

    LS2: Ecosystems: Interactions, energy, and dynamics

    LS3: Heredity: Inheritance and variation of traits

    LS4: Biological evolution: Unity and diversity

Earth and space sciences

    ESS1: Earth's place in the universe

    ESS2: Earth's systems

    ESS3: Earth and human activity

Engineering, technology, and applications of science

    ETS1: Engineering design

    ETS2: Links among engineering, technology, science, and society

intellectual tools. This foundation will allow all learners to make civic and personal decisions based on a stronger base of science and engineering knowledge. For some, this will be vital for future careers or further education.

Importantly, DCIs differ from the presentation of science concepts in previous standards in three key ways: First, many of the DCIs are reflective of shifts in *how* the idea is framed, in terms of what and how particular aspects of the concept are emphasized. For example, in the physical sciences core idea of energy (PS3), the *Framework* emphasizes the idea that "interactions of objects can be explained and predicted using the concept of transfer of energy from one object or system of objects to another. The total energy within a defined system changes only by the transfer of energy into or out of the system" (NRC 2012, p. 120). In essence, the focus on energy in the *Framework* is on how it exists in the interactions between objects and that it is conserved and can be accounted for within closed systems as it changes forms. This is a distinctly different kind of understanding of energy than what was included in previous standards and is typically presented in most science classes. These prior presentations of energy conveyed it as existing in different forms (light, heat, motion, etc.), and the focus was on transformation between forms rather than on conservation. Other DCIs across disciplines reflect similar shifts in how a concept is reframed differently from previous learning goals.

A second key adjustment in DCIs is in *what* concepts are central to the discipline. In the Earth and space sciences, for example, the DCI of Earth and Human Activity has been added as an area of emphasis. Specifically, the concept of global climate change related to human activity is now included as a central component of this DCI. This is distinctly different from earlier science standards, in which exploration of human effects on climate was relegated to a "science in personal and social perspectives" discussion (NRC 1996, p. 16) and not included as part of the formal curriculum. Similar shifts within each discipline are found throughout the DCIs in what is now considered a central idea but wasn't before.

A third change is in *when* particular ideas are taught. For example, by the end of 8th grade the DCI LS3.A: Inheritance of Traits involves understanding that "each distinct gene chiefly controls the production of a specific protein, which in turn affects the traits of the individual (e.g., human skin color results from the actions of proteins that control the production of the pigment melanin)," (NRC 2012, p. 159). The prior standards had a similar expectation but for much later, by the end of 12th grade: "The genetic information stored in DNA is used to direct the synthesis of the thousands of proteins that each cell requires" (NRC 1996, p. 184). At the middle school level, the prior standards did not expect students to reason about genes as instructions for making proteins. Rather, they presented genes as units of information for traits without opening up the black box of the underlying mechanism for how genes bring about these traits (i.e., via the proteins they encode). The *NGSS*, with their emphasis on explaining phenomena, envisage that students will understand some of the key aspects of the genetic mechanism earlier. Similar revisions to when specific component ideas of DCIs are discussed occur in the other disciplines as well.

Given the examples shown above about the differences between the old and new standards, when examining the DCIs within a content area it is critical to be aware of the nature of these shifts and to adjust instruction and assessment accordingly.

Three-Dimensional Learning

Although the DCIs are essential, they serve as only one dimension necessary for students to develop usable knowledge. Elements of the science and engineering practices, DCIs, and crosscutting

[handwritten margin notes: "concept change in meaning", "adding/removing subjects"]

concepts work together to support students in three-dimensional learning to make sense of phenomena or design solutions. Research in the teaching and learning of science shows that teaching content in isolation from how to use it results in disconnected ideas that learners find difficult to use and apply (NRC 2007). Similarly, using a science process in isolation of ideas leads to learning how to carry out a procedure without knowing why or when to use it. DCIs and crosscutting concepts work with the science and engineering practices to form understanding that is usable and can be further developed. You cannot learn the ideas of science apart from the doing, and you cannot learn the practices of science apart from the core ideas.

An analogy of preparing a really great meal can help one understand what three-dimensional learning is all about. Joe, one of the editors of this book, loves to cook and has found the following analogy helpful to others: Think of knowing how to do various techniques in the kitchen, such as kneading bread, cutting tomatoes, beating an egg, frying or roasting meat, and so on. These kitchen practices are like the science and engineering practices. You could know how to do all of these and still not be able to prepare a good meal. Now think about picking out great ingredients and knowing how those ingredients work together to form a delicious dish. You want a top-shelf piece of fish or poultry, some fresh vegetables, and well-made pasta. These are like your DCIs. DCIs are essential to explaining a number of phenomena; your main ingredients are essential to preparing a fantastic dinner. But just as the DCIs work with practices to help students make sense of phenomena and design solutions, the main ingredient is not as good if you don't use proper cooking techniques. But, even with these two elements, something

is still missing. The food tastes bland. To make it really stand out, spices and herbs are needed. Crosscutting concepts are like your seasonings because they work across and are essential to all the disciplines. Cooking techniques, quality of the main ingredients, and condiments work together to make a delectable meal. Similarly, to make sense of phenomena and design solutions to problems, all three dimensions need to work together. This builds the type of understanding that will be usable throughout a person's life. Similar to the process of how one learns to do science, Joe learned to cook by working with his mother for a number of years. He discovered the importance of slowly simmering a tomato sauce and the feel of dough when enough flour has been added. Such practices do not happen in isolation. He now tries to pass down this knowledge by having his own children help prepare family meals. Joe also learned to cook by sharing what he does with others, seeing their reactions, and listening to what they have to say about their experiences. Over the years, by engaging with others, Joe has become a better cook. Three-dimensional learning and the process of building knowledge in science are similar: They do not happen in isolation.

An important aspect of three-dimensional learning that bears emphasis is the core aim of science as a knowledge-building endeavor and the critical role that the community of practicing scientists plays in this endeavor. Like the cooking example above, building expertise in science does not happen in isolation. Rather, the process of developing new knowledge in science depends on the presentation and critique of new ideas in the form of explanations and models. These explanations and models are human inventions; we cannot see atoms, genes, or gravity. Our scientific models involve interpretation of data as evidence in support of these explanations. To ensure that the knowledge generated from observations and experiments is valid and reliable, scientists vet these ideas by presenting them to the community for critique. It is through critique, argumentation, and the evaluation of alternative explanations and models that the best ideas rise to the top. With enough evidentiary support, our most robust and productive ideas become established theories. However, this process is only possible within a community that has shared goals and norms about scientific inquiry and how to develop sound scientific knowledge (i.e., what counts as good evidence, models, and arguments). Three-dimensional learning entails creating a similar knowledge-building community in the science classroom. Instead of telling students what the established scientific models are, the goal is for students to develop (with support) these ideas for themselves through exploration of evidence and vetting of ideas, just as scientists do. Engaging students with the *Framework*'s science and engineering practices means having students work together to explore, explain, and understand real-world phenomena, and through critique and argumentation build the concepts captured by the DCIs.

How the Disciplinary Core Ideas Develop Across Grades

An important characteristic of the DCIs reflected in the *Framework* is that they are not stand-alone, individual facts that students come to "know" as the result of one lesson or across one grade. Rather, DCIs develop in ways that become progressively more sophisticated as students use the ideas to make sense of new phenomena or problems across the grade levels. What do we mean by sophisticated? Students' explanations become deeper and broader, allowing them to explain more fully the causes and consequences of a wider array of related phenomena. Sophistication is not the same as accruing more details; rather, it is about opening black boxes and understanding more of the mechanisms that underlie a range of phenomena.

Let's look at a physical science example of how ideas become more sophisticated across time. Students in K–2 first develop a descriptive model of matter. They can describe matter as solid and predict that some solids, such as ice, will melt when heated but that others, such as paper, will burst into flames, while still others will become hot but appear not to change. At the grade 3–5 level, this descriptive explanation begins to give way to a more explanatory model as students develop a particle model of matter that provides a richer explanation of what happens when a substance is heated and changes from a solid to a liquid. They can use the model to describe a substance as being made of invisible particles too small to see and to clarify that in the solid state, the particles are held together in a rigid manner, whereas in the liquid state they can slide past one another. At the grade 6–8 level, students' models of how matter interacts become even richer and can explain a broader set of phenomena. They now develop understanding that these invisible particles are made of atoms, that these atoms can combine in particular ways to form molecules, and that the collection of similar molecules form substances with unique properties. Students can use these ideas of atoms and molecules to explain that in a chemical reaction, the atoms that make up molecules rearrange to form new molecules (but none are lost). The collection of these new molecules exhibits different properties than the initial materials. The formation of these molecules explains the variety of materials that exist in the world. At the grade 9–12 level, students' models of matter become even more sophisticated in that they can now provide reasons for why certain atoms will join together to form a molecule while others will not.

Similarly, in the life sciences, students in the very early grades begin noticing patterns of similarities and differences between parents and offspring and between siblings. At this point, the explanations they form are about these similarities and differences and not about causes beyond noting that parents and offspring share genes. In late elementary school, students come to see genes as having information about traits, which begins to open the black box of how genes bring about our traits. As students progress through middle school, their understandings of the genetic information become more constrained, and they come to view genes as having instructions for proteins. Understanding genes and proteins can help students explain a variety of genetic phenomena, such as the missing insulin proteins in those with diabetes and the misshaped hemoglobin protein in individuals with sickle cell anemia. Lastly, at the high school level, students add to their developing explanations the role of environmental factors in turning genes on and off or altering the genetic instructions. Thus, over the course of schooling, students develop explanations that feature more of the causal mechanism that underlies many of the genetic phenomena they observed in the early grades.

From a developmental perspective, as students progress in their schooling, their understanding of the DCIs needs to become more complex and sophisticated. With this comes a growing depth of the crosscutting concepts and science practices.

This developmental perspective takes into account the initial ideas that students bring with them and leverages these ideas and experiences toward more sophisticated conceptual models as the students progress in schooling. Ideas become more connected and useful as tools for addressing complex real-world problems and phenomena.

The developmental perspective also stresses that teaching more content devoid from the use of those ideas does not allow students to explain or reason about phenomena. Students can memorize the points of the theory while not understanding the phenomena that the theory is trying to explain. Moreover, learning more details about a concept may hinder understanding of the big idea because one loses the forest for the trees. We can all think back to our schooling when we successfully memorized facts to pass a test but had no understanding of why that idea was useful or how to use it to solve real problems. When the *Framework* refers to deepening understanding, it is therefore not simple addition of details but an expanding explanatory power, allowing students to better explain the causes and effects of phenomena in the contexts in which they occur.

The Structure of This Book

This book is divided into four sections. The first focuses on delving deeper into physical sciences core ideas that explain phenomena such as why ice freezes and how information can be sent around the world wirelessly. The second looks at the core ideas in the life sciences that can be used to explain why we look similar to but not identical to our parents, how human behavior is affecting ecosystems around the globe, and how organisms evolved to inhabit every part of our planet. The third section on the Earth and space sciences includes core ideas that center primarily on complex interactions between aspects of the Earth system, examining diverse phenomena such as the big bang and global climate change. The final section covers engineering, highlighting many examples of engineering design and how they are related to developing innovative solutions for society's challenges. We hope readers will find the presentations of DCIs in these sections useful in planning instruction, providing professional development, and preparing new science teachers.

Safety Practices in the Science Laboratory

It is important for science teachers to make hands-on and inquiry-based lab activities as safe as possible for students. Teachers therefore need to have proper engineering controls (e.g., fume hoods, ventilation, fire extinguisher, eye wash/shower), standard operating safety procedures (e.g., chemical hygiene plan, board of education/school safety policies), and appropriate personal protective equipment (sanitized indirectly vented chemical-splash goggles, gloves, aprons, etc.) in the classroom, laboratory, or field during all hands-on activities. Teachers also need to adopt legal safety standards and enforce them inside the classroom. Finally, teachers must review and comply with all safety polices and chemical storage and disposal protocols that have been established by their school district or school.

Throughout this book, safety precautions are provided for each investigation. Teachers should follow these safety precautions to provide a safer learning experience for students. The safety precautions associated with each activity are based, in part, on the use of the recommended materials and instructions, legal safety compliance

standards, and current better professional safety practices. Selection of alternative materials or procedures for these activities may jeopardize the level of safety and therefore is at the user's own risk. We also recommend that students, before working in the laboratory for the first time, review the National Science Teacher Association's safety acknowledgment form in the document *Safety in the Science Classroom, Laboratory, or Field Sites* under the direction of the teacher. This document is available online at *www.nsta.org/docs/SafetyInTheScienceClassroom-LabAndField.pdf*. The students and their parents or guardians should then sign this document to acknowledge that they understand the safety procedures that must be followed during a lab activity. Additional safety compliance resources can be found on the NSTA safety portal at *www.nsta.org/safety*.

REFERENCES

National Research Council (NRC). 1996. *National science education standards*. Washington, DC: National Academies Press.

National Research Council (NRC). 2007. *Taking science to school: Learning and teaching science in grades K–8*. Washington, DC: National Academies Press.

National Research Council (NRC). 2012. *A framework for K–12 science education: Practices, crosscutting concepts, and core ideas*. Washington, DC: National Academies Press.

NGSS Lead States. 2013. *Next Generation Science Standards: For states, by states*. Washington, DC: National Academies Press. *www.nextgenscience.org/next-generation-science-standards*.

Stevens, S., L. Sutherland, and J. S. Krajcik. 2009. *The big ideas of nanoscale science and engineering*. Arlington, VA: NSTA Press.

PHYSICAL
SCIENCES

PHYSICAL SCIENCES

The physical sciences area consists of four disciplinary core ideas (DCIs) that help explain a wide variety of phenomena, from how new materials form, to why some materials stick together and others do not, to why things stop moving, to how information can be sent and stored electronically. Developing usable knowledge of the core ideas in physical science will allow learners to answer important questions such as, "How can we make new materials?" "Why do some things appear to keep going but others stop?" and "How can information be shipped around wirelessly?" The physical sciences core ideas are essential to making sense of phenomena in the other disciplines. Developing understandings of the properties of substances and how matter reacts serves as a building block for making sense of phenomena in the life and Earth and spaces sciences. Making sense of photosynthesis and respiration requires an understanding of the flow and matter and energy. Using elements of PS2: Motion and stability: Forces and interactions and PS3: Energy provides an explanation as to why earthquakes can cause so much damage. As a fourth example, PS4: Elements of waves and their applications in technologies for information transfer can provide insight into how scientists and engineers have contructed instruments to detect signals humans cannot detect directly, such as X-rays and ultrasound. As such, the physical sciences ideas explain many natural and human-made phenomena that occur each day across the disciplines. Each of the core ideas is broken down into

FIGURE PS.1

Physical Sciences Disciplinary Core Ideas and Component Ideas

PSI: Matter and its interactions

  PSI.A: Structure and properties of matter

  PSI.B: Chemical reactions

  PSI.C: Nuclear processes

PS2: Motion and stability: Forces and interactions

  PS2.A: Forces and motion

  PS2.B: Types of interactions

  PS2.C: Stability and instability in physical systems

PS3: Energy

  PS3.A: Definitions of energy

  PS3.B: Conservation of energy and energy transfer

  PS3.C: Relationship between energy and forces

  PS3.D: Energy in chemical processes and everyday life

PS4: Waves and their applications in technologies for information transfer

  PS4.A: Wave properties

  PS4.B: Electromagnetic radiation

  PS4.C: Information technologies and instrumentation

component ideas. Figure PS.1 highlights the core ideas and their components.

In Chapter 2, Kristin Mayer and Joseph Krajcik explore and expand on core idea PS1: Matter and Interactions and its components. This core idea explores the question, "How can one explain the structure, properties, and interactions of matter?" Developing usable knowledge of this core idea helps explain very diverse phenomena in the physical sciences, such as why an ice cube melts and why so many new materials with different properties can be formed from only a few elements. This DCI is also essential to making sense of photosynthesis and respiration in the life sciences and the erosion of riverbanks in Earth science. It consists of three component ideas: Structure and Properties of Matter, Chemical Reactions, and Nuclear Reactions. Each of these components has its own associated questions that develop throughout the grade levels.

In Chapter 3, David Fortus and Jeffrey Nordine expand on core idea PS2: Motion and Stability: Forces and Interactions and its components. This DCI explores the question, "How can one explain and predict interactions between objects and within systems of objects?" and is important for describing and explaining how the motion of objects changes and why objects fall to the ground and for predicting the stability or instability in systems at various scales. The *Framework* describes the forces between objects that arise from a few types of interactions: gravity, electromagnetism, and strong and weak nuclear interactions. The ideas in core idea PS2 are critical for solving many problems related to various fields of engineering, such as how to build a bridge that can withstand the forces against it. As Fortus and Nordine explain, the *Framework* places equal weight on the importance of students understanding electrical interactions as it does on gravitational interactions because the idea of electrical interactions is key in understanding why materials bond. This idea is critical across the various disciplines and consists of three component

ideas: Forces and Motion, Types of Interactions, and Stability and Instability in Physical Systems.

In Chapter 4, Jeffrey Nordine and David Fortus write together again to elucidate core idea PS3: Energy. This DCI addresses the question, "How is energy transferred and conserved?" and allows students to explain phenomena such as how power plants can provide energy to homes and factories, how biofuels can be used to drive engines, and why perpetual motion machines cannot exist. Students must understand from this idea that the total energy within a system changes only by transferring energy into or out of the system with the total amount of energy remaining constant. Energy transfer and transformations are also critical for understanding diverse phenomena such as photosynthesis, respiration, plate tectonics, combustion, and various energy storage devices, such as batteries. This core idea consists of four components: Definitions of Energy, Conservation of Energy and Energy Transfer, the Relationship Between Energy and Force, and Energy in Chemical Processes and Everyday Life.

In Chapter 5, David Fortus and Joseph Krajcik explore core idea PS4: Waves and Their Applications in Technologies for Information Transfer. This DCI helps answer questions such as, "How are waves used to transfer energy and send and store information?" "Why is it that I can turn off my monitor with a remote controller?" "How does that work?" "How is it that I can talk and see someone in real time on my cell phone?" and "How does that information get to me?" Developing usable knowledge of this core idea will help students make sense of how these new technologies work and how information is shipped around and stored wirelessly. It helps learners throughout the grade bands build critical ideas that explain how various forms of light and sound serve as mechanisms for the transfer of energy and transfer of information among objects not in contact with each other. It also helps students build understanding of how electromagnetic radiation can serve both as a carrier of information and a source of energy, depending on its frequency. This core idea consists of three components: Wave Properties, Electromagnetic Radiation, and Information Technologies and Instrumentation. Building usable knowledge of light and sound and their interactions with matter helps explain how many

tools that make use of electromagnetic radiation work.

As a whole, these DCIs help students build usable knowledge that is central to the physical sciences but also across the life sciences, Earth and space sciences, and engineering. As shown in these chapters, these ideas need to develop across the grade bands for students to develop usable knowledge to figure out how phenomena work, find solutions to problems, and have the ability to learn more when needed.

CHAPTER 2

CORE IDEA PS1
MATTER AND ITS INTERACTIONS

Kristin Mayer and Joseph Krajcik

What Is This Disciplinary Core Idea, and Why Is It Important?

How can there be so many different materials in the world? Why does paper burn when lit with a match but iron does not? Why does water boil at 100°C but carbon dioxide at much lower temperature? Why does a piece of iron rust but gold does not seem to change? Why can some materials form new products that have totally different properties when mixed together, yet other materials just seem to mix together without forming new materials? How do snowflakes form intricate and beautiful six-sided patterns? Atomic theory can explain these phenomena and many more. Students can use this theory to explain many observations and phenomena they experience in the science laboratory and in daily life. A rich understanding of atomic theory leads to a deeper understanding of why there are so many different substances in the world and also helps explain biological processes such as protein construction and folding. Richard Feynman (1952), a leading theoretical physicist during the 20th century, famously stated,

*If, in some cataclysm, all of scientific knowledge were to be destroyed, and only one sentence passed on to the next generation of creatures, what statement would contain the most information in the fewest words? I believe it is the **atomic hypothesis** (or the atomic fact, or whatever you wish to call it) that **all things are made of atoms— little particles that move around in perpetual motion, attracting each other when they are a little distance apart, but repelling upon being squeezed into one another.** In that one sentence, you will see, there is an enormous amount of information about the world, if just a little imagination and thinking are applied. (p. 2; emphasis in the original)*

An understanding of atomic theory allows an individual to account for all the different materials observed in our world as well as all the changes those materials can undergo. According to atomic theory, all matter is made of atoms, which are particles too small to be seen. These atoms are made of even smaller charged particles. The attractive and repulsive forces among these smaller charged particles hold the atoms together and govern the interactions between them. A broad range of phenomena can be explained based on an understanding of these particles, their motion, and the forces among them.

Previous standards for science education often emphasized the learning of disconnected ideas. Students learned definitions for various types of reactions and memorized them; for example, in combustion reactions, oxygen is a reactant and carbon dioxide and water are produced. With this piecemeal approach, students often apply ideas they learn through rote memory to inappropriate examples. Continuing with the example of the memorized definition of combustion, a student may predict that a reaction between oxygen and magnesium will also produce water and carbon dioxide. However, this makes no sense: Where did the carbon and hydrogen come from? Instead of learning pieces of information, the new vision for learning science presented in the *A Framework for K–12 Science Education* (*Framework*; NRC 2012) emphasizes helping students develop an integrated understanding of disciplinary core ideas (DCIs), a rich network of connected concepts that build across time (NRC 2007, 2012), as they use these ideas along with crosscutting concepts and science and engineering practices to make sense of phenomena or solve problems. A DCI provides an organizational framework for explaining, learning, and making predictions about a broad range of observations and phenomena. Rather than memorizing definitions of different types of reactions, students can develop the core idea that matter is composed of atoms and that those atoms rearrange during chemical changes. This allows students to explain a much wider variety of phenomena. An additional criterion for DCIs is that they develop over time. Initially, students may start by just observing different types of matter or changes to matter; as they continue to learn, they add details to their explanations,

which enables them to account for more of their observations about these different types of matter and changes. DCIs work along with science and engineering practices and crosscutting concepts to help students make sense of phenomena or to find solutions to problems.

The core idea of Matter and Its Interactions should help students formulate an answer to the question, "How can one explain the structure, properties, and interactions of matter?" Understanding matter and its interaction is a DCI in physical science because it provides an organizational structure that can explain a wide variety of observations.

Below we give a summary of core idea PS1: Matter and Its Interactions and how this idea builds over the K–12 school years. However, a full understanding of matter and interactions cannot occur without also understanding PS2: Motion and Stability: Forces and Interactions and PS3: Energy. For each grade band, we provide an overview of how the core idea builds and describe the commonly held ideas about this DCI that students bring with them to the classroom. Research has shown that directly confronting students' ideas has limited success (Mayer 2011); it is much more powerful to use their ideas as stepping stones to help them revise and develop those ideas (NRC 2007). Therefore, we describe how commonly held ideas can be used as resources to develop a more coherent framework and understanding of the core idea.

PS1: Matter and Its Interactions is made up of three component ideas. The subcomponents focus on how elements and substances have characteristic properties that can be used to identify them. PS1.A: Structure and Properties of Matter builds understanding in response to the question, "How do particles combine to form the variety of substances one observes?" This subcomponent also deals with the substructure of atoms and how the substructure determines how the atoms interact with other atoms. PS1.B: Chemical Reactions provides insights into two questions: "How do substances combine or change (react) to make new substances?" and "How does one characterize and explain these reactions and make predictions about them?" This builds understanding of how only a few elements can account for the great diversity of materials in the universe. PS1.C: Nuclear Processes explores the question, "What forces hold nuclei together and mediate nuclear processes?" Building understanding of this subcomponent allows for understanding of the elements, radioactivity, the release of energy from the Sun and other stars, and the generation of nuclear power.

The atomic structure of matter served as an important idea in the *Benchmarks for Science Literacy* (AAAS 1993). The *Framework* (NRC 2012) and the *Next Generation Science Standards* (*NGSS;* NGSS Lead States 2013) with their focus on energy (PS3: Energy; see Chapter 4, p. 55) and electrostatic forces that govern the interactions between atoms (PS2: Motion and Stability; see Chapter 3, p. 33) emphasize why atoms and molecules attract or don't attract each other rather than the types of bonds that are formed (Levy-Nahumet et al. 2006). Atoms are composed of charged particles. The balance between competing attractive and repulsive forces underlies all atomic interactions, from determining the size of an individual atom to explaining how atoms within one molecule will interact with atoms in a different molecule. Further, because energy is a crosscutting concept as well as a DCI, it is important to help students develop an understanding of how bonding and energy are related. The *Framework* emphasizes

that energy can be understood in terms of the motion of molecules and energy in fields. Bonds will form at the stable point where attractive and repulsive forces are balanced. The stability is created by minimizing the electrostatic potential energy while simultaneously maximizing the freedom of motion at that low energy point. Usable knowledge of the forces and energy that govern the interactions between charges within atoms helps students to account for matter and interactions.

How Does Student Understanding of This Disciplinary Core Idea Develop Over Time?

The enterprise of science and the focus of the *Framework* is on explaining phenomena. Unfortunately, even after studying chemistry, many students have a difficult time connecting ideas about atoms to observable phenomena (Treagust, Chittleborough, and Mamiala 2003). Phenomena do not need to be elaborate, explosive, or unusual. For example, you could simply observe what happens to sand or clay when a container full of this material is held upside down. Or notice that when a drop of food coloring is added to liquid, the whole thing ends up colored. What changes do you notice as a match burns?

In the study of matter and interactions, students must start with systematic observations of matter so that they can then develop increasingly sophisticated models to explain their observations. According to the *Framework* (NRC 2012), students in K–4 should develop descriptive ideas about matter. Students should experience that matter can change from a solid state to a liquid to a gas. By the end of fifth grade, students should have a simple particle model to explain phenomena such as evaporation. In middle school, students can use an atomic–molecular model to explain in more detail changes that don't involve nuclear reactions. For instance, students should be able to give a causal account of why water in the liquid stage and water in the gas stage are the same materials. Finally, students in high school can add interactions between subatomic particles to explain the why atoms bond together to form molecules or why some molecules are attracted to other molecules.

Grades K–2: Systematic Study of Materials

At the early elementary level, the PS1 DCI from the NRC *Framework* (2012) is broken down into two subideas: PS1.A: Structure and Properties of Matter, and PS1.B: Chemical Reactions. In general, at young ages students should focus on making observations of things in the world around them, noting the properties of those objects, describing changes that the objects can go through, and developing a language for describing their observations. The *Framework* identifies several ideas that young students can develop. Students can notice that objects can be made of different kinds of materials; for example, a spoon could be made of plastic, metal, or wood. Objects can be measured and have weight. Students can observe different changes and note that some are easily reversible while others are not. Further, heating and cooling some substances can cause them to change, whereas others remain the same. Finally, pieces can be put together in different ways to build different things. For example, interlocking bricks or building blocks can be used to build a tower, a bridge, a rocket—all kinds of things. These initial ideas are instrumental

in building more sophisticated ideas as students continue the exploration of matter.

PS1.A: STRUCTURE AND PROPERTIES OF MATTER

Initially students see solids and liquids as very different materials and therefore do not have a unifying idea of "matter" (Wiser, O'Connor, and Higgins 1995). Students can start developing ideas about matter by systematically observing and describing different materials and the same materials in different states. For example, students can observe that heating or cooling a material can change it from a solid to a liquid or from a liquid to a solid. Students can also observe that some solids are squishy, some shine, and some crumble. Some liquids are clear, yet others have color. Different liquids also vary in how quickly they can be poured or in their smells (Rogat et al. 2011). While young students see solids and liquids as very different types of materials, they can start to notice similarities, such as how solids and liquids both have mass and take up space (TERC 2011) and that some liquids can become a solid if they get cold, but will become a liquid again when they warm. By observing these changes and properties, students will begin to develop a much richer understanding of matter.

Young students initially do not differentiate objects from materials (Wiser and Smith 2008). For example, students "may understand that a silver spoon is shiny and hard, but do not realize the spoon has these properties because it is made of silver" (Rogat et al. 2011, p. 30). Students need help differentiating the properties that make the spoon a spoon (a small bowl shape with a handle) from the properties associated with the material. To support students in making this distinction, they could compare, for example, plastic, silver, and wooden spoons to identify the properties that make it a spoon versus the properties of the materials.

Finally, at young ages, students can study aggregates (powders) as materials that bridge the ideas of liquids and solids (TERC 2011). For example, in a cup of sand, each individual grain of sand seems like a solid; however, the cup of sand can be poured into other containers or will spread out if poured on a table. These observations can help students link different forms of matter—solids and liquids—into a more unified concept of "stuff" or matter. Additionally, these observations provide a foundation that students can later use when developing a particle nature of matter in fifth grade. At this age, the goal is to get students using observations and developing a language for discussing their observations. The states of matter are an important element of the DCI that elementary students need to develop. In these grades, the study of states of matter are limited to studying solids and liquids; gases are not included. Since gases cannot be observed and are therefore much more difficult to study, students should not be asked to study gases till they are able to use equipment to make observations of gases.

PS1.B: CHEMICAL REACTIONS

Once young students have developed language and techniques for making systematic observations of materials and objects, they can look at what happens to materials during changes. In grades K–2, the changes that are studied should be limited to macroscale, concrete changes such as cutting an object into smaller pieces or reshaping clay (Rogat et al. 2011). These changes do not alter the substance, just the shape or size. Students

can compare these changes with those that do alter the properties of the substance, for example, burning paper or freezing water. Students will explain these different changes in later grades. At this age, the goal is to make careful observations and develop a language for describing materials and changes. Students can make claims about the nature of a change and support those claims with their observations. Heating ice can cause it to become a liquid, and cooling water below 0°C will cause it to become a solid again. However, once paper burns, it cannot become paper again. The observations are important for students to understand the difference between phase changes and chemical reactions in later grades.

Grades 3–5: The Study of Materials and a Particle Model

In the upper elementary grades, the DCI PS1 is again broken into PS1.A: Structure and Properties of Matter and PS1.B: Chemical Reactions. As students get a bit older, it is appropriate to continue focusing on concrete, macrolevel observations of materials, but students can use equipment to make additional observations, including measurements. Students in grades 3–5 may still believe that solids and liquids are different types of matter (Stavy 1991); however, they can develop a more formal definition of matter, which is that matter has weight and takes up space. Further, since gases cannot be seen, students often think of them as nothing instead of as a third form of matter. However, students can measure how solids, liquids, and gases all have mass and take up space and therefore fit the definition of matter (Rogat et al. 2011). Students could also observe a material, such as water, freezing and melting. In earlier grades, students may have observed that heating or cooling a substance can cause it to melt and freeze. At this point, students can note that these changes do not change the material itself and therefore the same material could be both a liquid and a solid (Smith et al. 2006). However, it is important to give students experience with more than just one substance. Students could observe substances such as menthol or bromine in a sealed flask melting and freezing. Helping students understand that matter can exist as a solid and liquid also means supporting them in developing an understanding of volume and mass. In fifth grade, students attain a particle model of matter, which they can use to begin explaining some of their observations of matter. Note that a particle model of matter is different from an atomic model. Students should analyze evidence that supports the idea that all materials are a collection of small particles that can move around. Students can use the movement of these particles to explain some observations, but since they do not yet know what the particles are, they cannot explain all their observations.

PS1.A: STRUCTURE AND PROPERTIES OF MATTER

At this point, students can start using instruments to explore materials in more detail. Students may think that small objects do not have weight, but by using a scale, students can observe that this is not the case. Students can also use microscopes or magnifying glasses to observe smaller objects, noting that things too small to be seen could be matter as well (Smith et al. 2006). Students may also note that some objects seem heavy or light for their size. These ideas can later be built on to develop ideas like a particle model of matter

and density, but at this point students should still focus on observable solids and liquids and building an understanding of weight and volume.

In grade 5, students should begin to develop a model of matter that is particle in nature. This model will be further refined and developed in middle grades. To develop a particle model, students need experience with observations that help motivate the need for a particle model. For example, students could observe that when 50 ml of water is mixed with 50 ml of ethanol, the volume of the mixture will be about 95 ml; the volume is nonadditive. Similarly, mixing marbles and sand is nonadditive. The loss of volume can be explained if water and ethanol are actually made of a collection of particles that are too small to be seen. (A particle model of matter does not provide a complete explanation for why adding equal volumes of water and alcohol is nonadditive. The electrical interactions among the molecules are a critical piece of the explanation. This level of understanding comes in later grades.) Students can build on their earlier observations of aggregates to develop a particle model. At this point, they do not need to learn what the particles are or discuss atoms or molecules; they just need to create a model that all matter is made of small particles. Since students do not have an atomic–molecular model at this point, they are not able to distinguish between physical and chemical changes. In a chemical change, the particles break apart and the pieces rearrange and form new particles; because students are only developing the idea that a material is a collection of small particles, they cannot explain chemical reactions. What students are asked to explain or model should be limited to making mixtures and phase changes. The goal is to get students to use their observations to support the idea that materials that look uniform are actually made of small particles that are too small to be seen.

When first developing a particle model, students may think that the particles are floating or embedded within the material rather than that the particles make up the material with nothing in between the them (Novick and Nussbaum 1978). It is particularly difficult for learners to grasp that there is nothing in between gaseous particles. In grades 3–5, students can begin to study gases, and this may help them develop their particle model to include the idea that nothing is between the particles. We can support students in learning that matter is particulate by making observations of gases. For example, the mass of gas can be measured by keeping the volume of a container constant while more gas is added (Sakar and Frazier 2008). Students often find this surprising, but this helps them realize that gas is also matter and made of particles (Mayer 2011). Students can then further explore the properties of gas: If gas is sealed in a container with a movable piston, the container can be compressed and expanded. Students then need to be challenged to construct a model of matter that explains these observations (Krajcik and Merritt 2012; Merritt and Krajcik 2013). The only way to explain how you could compress and expand a gas would be if nothing were between the particles that make up the gas. Similar logic applies to the example of mixing water and ethanol; if there was something between the particles, then the volume of the particles of the mixture could not be more compact than the individual liquids. Figure 2.1 shows an example of a model a sixth-grade student drew when asked to show what it might look like if you could see the gases that made up an odor.

FIGURE 2.1

A Sixth-Grade Student's Model of an Odor

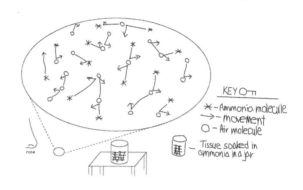

A final important component to the particle model is that the small particles that make up matter are in constant motion. Students have a hard time picturing the particles of matter and therefore may have a difficult time visualizing them moving (Novick and Nussbaum 1978; Lee et al. 1993; Johnson 1998). Observations of smells and mixtures can help students add movement to their particle model. For example, students could observe what happens when a drop of food coloring is added to warm and cool water. This also builds in the crosscutting concept of energy and links to PS2: Energy. The food coloring will spread through the water on its own without stirring and spread faster in the warm water than the cool water because the particles that make up the warm water are moving faster than particles that make up the cool water and colliding with the particles that make up the food coloring. Temperature is essentially measuring the kinetic energy of the particles in the water, albeit this connection is not a notion young students can fully grasp. A strong-smelling perfume placed in one corner of

2

the room provides a similar phenomenon; students can note when they smell the perfume and the pattern for how the smell spreads.

PS1.B: CHEMICAL CHANGES

There are a variety of activities students can use to explore PS1.B: Chemical Changes in elementary school. In third grade, students could note that when paper is cut, the weight does not change and that scraps can be put back together in the same size and shape as the original piece of paper—albeit not into one sheet; importantly, the smaller pieces are still paper. Have students make predictions and compare how the water level changes when a set amount of water is poured back and forth between a tall, skinny cup and short, wide cup.

In fourth and fifth grade, students can make careful observations of changes by, for example, measuring mass before, during, and after a change. Students may think that changes in appearance cause changes in mass. Students often believe that products resulting from changes that produce gases or powders will have less mass after the change (Mohan et al. 2009). Students should observe events in closed systems to note that the total mass is always conserved. When observing the change in mass involving gases, it is important to keep the volume of the container constant. If balloons or bags are inflated, the reading on the scale will be lower than the mass because buoyancy force reduces the pressure of the object on the scale (Sakar and Frazier 2008); two-liter soda bottles can be used to seal in gases without changing the volume (Kavanah and Zipp 1998; Mayer 2011). When trapping gases in a container, make sure the amount of gas that will be produced is reasonable given the volume of the container (for example,

a slightly flat vs. a fully inflated basketball). One activity to examine the question, "Do the numbers of particles change when the material changes?" involves adding some steel wool that has been dampened with water to a sealed flask. The steel wool will rust, but the total mass of the sealed flask will remain the same, even though the mass of the rust is higher than the mass of the original steel wool. Although students can measure mass before and after both phase changes and chemical reactions, students are not able to develop models of chemical reactions until they develop an atomic–molecular model. At this stage, students can develop models that explain their observations of a phase change that creates a gas and show why the mass does not change. For example, the teacher could place a small, pea-sized piece of dry ice in a two-liter soda bottle, which the students can then seal with a cap. The dry ice will turn into a gas. Students then measure the mass of the soda bottle with the dry ice and with the gas to note that the mass does not change (Mayer 2011). Students may also notice that the pressure inside the soda bottle increases. Students can develop models to explain these observations. Their model might show the particles spreading farther apart, in line with their observations that gases can be compressed, but the number of particles inside the soda bottle stays the same. Figure 2.2 shows a high school example of an assessment item based on this lab. After completing the lab as part of a chemistry class, the student was given an image of a bottle with some carbon dioxide molecules represented at the bottom. The student was given the following instructions: "The picture below represents the solid carbon dioxide in the soda bottle. Draw what the soda bottle and carbon dioxide would look like after all the solid sublimed to gaseous carbon dioxide. *Be as accurate as possible.*"

FIGURE 2.2

Student Model to Explain Why the Mass Stayed the Same When Dry Ice Was Sealed in a Two-Liter Bottle

Note: For fifth grade and earlier, the carbon dioxide molecules could be represented as simple particles with a simple shape, rather than as molecules of carbon and oxygen combined. Molecules and atoms are appropriate for middle and high school.

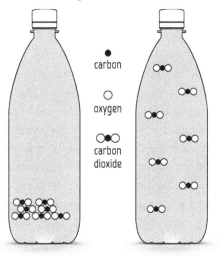

● carbon

○ oxygen

○●○ carbon dioxide

"The mass stayed the same because in the gas state the amount of CO_2 stayed the same. The only difference is that the CO_2 atoms are more spread out."

Safety note: Make sure students have on indirectly vented chemical-splash goggles when working with dry ice and liquids under pressure. Given the risk of potential container explosion and exposure to dry ice pellets, glass, and plastic, if too much dry ice is added to the container, the teacher should dish out an appropriate amount of dry ice for each group.

The model shown in Figure 2.2 is from a high school class where students were instructed to provide an image to explain why mass was conserved; however, younger students can also draw models that represent the conservation of mass. For example, fifth-grade students might use

a simple circle to represent a whole carbon dioxide molecule rather than the combination of three circles. Additionally, the question could be more open-ended by asking students to draw both the before and after diagrams and explain how the two representations account for their observations.

When students begin developing a particle model, they often attribute macroscopic observations to the particles. For example, students may think that individual particles melt when a material changes from a solid to a liquid, or some students have explained that rust is inside iron atoms and water allows it to come out (Kind 2004). At this age, students do not have an atomic or molecular model, so these ideas are developmentally appropriate and should not be judged as wrong. Similarly, these students cannot differentiate physical and chemical changes. However, they can collect systematic observations of changes.

Grades 6–8: An Atomic–Molecular Model

In middle school, the PS1 DCI from the *Framework* (NRC 2012) is broken into three subcomponents: PS1.A: Structure and Properties of Matter, PS1.B: Chemical Reactions, and PS1.C: Nuclear Processes. By the end of middle school, students will be able to apply their understanding that the small particles that make up matter can be atoms or groups of atoms that are tightly collected together, and that these groups are called molecules. It is important to note that this is a simple atomic model. At this grade level, introducing students to subatomic particles such as protons, neutrons, and electrons or atomic structure is not appropriate. Atoms can instead be treated as tiny particles that sometimes stick together. Students will be able to use an atomic–molecular model to explain various changes in matter.

2

In general, students do not have a particle view of matter. Students tend to focus on observations at the macro and tangible level and therefore often have ideas consistent with a continuous view of matter (AAAS 1993; Merritt and Krajcik 2013). By continuous we mean that there are no spaces between particles, even in the gaseous state. For example, students will state their main observation from an experiment is that they observed a color change and will struggle to connect that observation to underlying changes in atomic arrangement. Another example can be seen in students' struggles to understand gases: gases cannot be observed, and therefore students often do not think of gas as the same type of matter that makes up solids and liquids. Students frequently think that if a solid or liquid turns into a gas, then the mass will decrease or vanish (Driver et al. 1994).

Once they have developed a particle view, students are ready to develop an atomic–molecular view. While learners at this level will not be able to explain why atoms bond together, they can develop ideas that the variety of different substances that exist result from atoms of different elements coming together to form molecules and that molecules of the same substance always have the same composition. By observing a variety of chemical reactions and measuring the properties, students can also come to learn that different substances can react together to form new substances with different properties and that the reason for this change is that the atoms of the original materials rearranged to form new molecules (Krajcik, McNeill, and Reiser 2008). Students at the middle school level need support in developing these complex ideas and also in understanding conservation of mass.

PS1.A: STRUCTURE AND PROPERTIES OF MATTER

Atomic theory is difficult for many students. They may memorize definitions such as "atoms are the building blocks of matter" but have a difficult time connecting an atomic model with observations (Treagust, Chittleborough, and Mamiala 2003). When students begin to develop a particle or atomic model, they may ascribe macroscale properties to the particles or atoms; for example, students may think that gold atoms are gold colored (Ben-Zvi, Eylon, and Silberstein 1986; Kind 2004; Nakhleh, Samarapungavan, and Saglam 2005). Understanding that properties observed at the macro scale result from interactions of a collection of particles at the molecular scale is a challenging idea and involves students understanding how light interacts with matter (see Chapter 5, "Core Idea PS4: Waves and Their Applications in Technologies for Information Transfer," p. 75). Students need time to develop a model of atoms and apply their model to explain a variety of observations. Throughout their development of an atomic–molecular model, students should be asked to draw representations that demonstrate how their atomic model accounts for observations from labs and demonstrations.

Understanding the size of an atom creates challenges for learners. Students often think that objects that are too small to be seen are all similarly small. For example, blood cells and atoms are both really tiny, and students may think they are equivalently sized. Developing a sense of relative sizes is an important aspect of the crosscutting concept Scale, Proportion and Quantity in the *Framework* (NRC 2012). Students need support to realize that small objects can vary in relative size just as objects we observe do. A marble and a skyscraper are both at the macroscopic/human level but are significantly different in relative size. Analogies relating the relative sizes of small objects to the relative sizes of macroscopic objects can help students develop a sense of how small the particles of matter are relative to other small objects such as germs and cells. For example, atoms are measured in nanometers, while a red blood cell is about 0.006 cm across; this is about the same ratio as the distance across a sugar sprinkle compared to half the length of a football field.

In addition to helping them comprehend both the scale of atoms and a model of the formation of molecules from atoms, it is also important to help students understand the difference between the individual atoms and the compound formed when those atoms bond together. Students often struggle to differentiate between atoms and molecules (Devetaka and Glazara 2010). A simple activity is to give students samples of several compounds and samples of the elements those compounds are made of. Students can make detailed observations of various compounds and the elements that bond together to make them. For example, students might observe a sample of copper sulfate (blue crystals) and the elements that copper sulfate is made of: copper (metal), sulfur (yellow powder), and oxygen (gas). Properties of molecules differ from the elements that compose the molecule, and molecules that are made of the same elements can differ depending on how the atoms are connected. For example, both ethanol and oleic acid are made of carbon, hydrogen, and oxygen atoms. Ethanol is a clear flammable liquid that easily turns into a vapor and has the chemical formula of C_2H_5OH. Oleic acid has a formula of $C_{18}H_{34}O_2$ and is a yellow, oily liquid with a smell similar to lard. Both these substances are made from carbon (a black solid), oxygen (a highly reactive gas essential for life on Earth), and hydrogen

(an explosive gas). The color we observe results from the light reflected back by the substance. All other wavelengths of light are absorbed. Clearly, the properties of these elements are very different from the compounds that can be made when they bond together.

Students can develop and draw models to represent the difference between individual atoms and atoms that are in a compound. Students should be able to explain their observations using the representations they develop: the different ways atoms are linked together changes the observable properties at the macro scale. It is also important to help students understand common representations used in chemistry. Students may not recognize the difference between H_2O and $H + H + O$. Students often interpret these as the same since they both have two hydrogen atoms and one oxygen atom. However, in chemistry the symbol H_2O is communicating that the two hydrogen atoms and one oxygen atom are all bonded together into a molecule. While developing a model of atoms and bonding, it is also important that students develop an understanding of the common forms of representation. These common representations are critical because they indicate that matter always forms in a particular way. Chemists use the term H_2O to indicate that the matter we call water consists of molecules composed of two atoms of hydrogen bonded to one oxygen atom.

PS1.B: CHEMICAL REACTIONS

Students can use their atomic–molecular model to explain different types of changes. However, to assess a change, it is important to carefully evaluate the materials left after the reaction to the materials at the beginning. "Indicators" of chemical change, such as color change or bubbles, can be misleading. Students often have a difficult time differentiating between phase changes and chemical changes (Ahtee and Varjola 1998). For example, it is well documented that students often predict that the gas produced when boiling water is a mixture of hydrogen gas and oxygen gas (e.g., Gensler 1970; Mayer 2011). Furthermore, boiling water and electrolysis of water both produce bubbles. However, the gas produced from boiling water is water vapor, while electrolysis produces hydrogen and oxygen gases. Instead of relying on indicators of chemical or physical change, students should carefully evaluate the properties of the beginning materials and ending materials. In fact, the *Framework* (NRC 2012) emphasizes describing types of changes and avoids the term "physical changes." Students should compare the properties of the material before and after the change to describe the type of change: chemical reaction, phase change, dissolution, formation of a mixture, and so on. For example, students could collect the vapor from boiling water, allow it to return to room temperature, and then note that the type of material is the same before and after the change. Students could also use cobalt chloride test paper to test water, the gases formed above boiling water, and the liquid that forms when those gases cool. In all these cases, the cobalt chloride paper will turn from blue to pink. These observations indicate that the material stays the same and, therefore, this is an example of a phase change. Students can use their atomic–molecular model to show that the molecules do not change, just the spacing between each molecule. Alternatively, students could collect the gas that is created when an electric current is passed through water. Unlike water vapor, this gas will remain a gas as it cools. Additionally, this gas would explode if ignited. In this case, the properties of the materials after the change are significantly different from those of the material before the reaction, indicating this is a chemical change. Here students would model the reaction by explaining that the atoms rearranged to form new molecules. If students mix sugar and water, the sugar seems to disappear, but the sweet taste is present in the water and the mass of the sweetened water is equal to the mass of the sugar plus the mass of the water. This would be an example of dissolving, and students can model that the molecules of sugar and water do not change but mix with each other. As students use their atomic–molecular model to explain a variety of observations, they need to recognize that atoms only rearrange during changes (Smith et al. 2006).

Note: In middle school, students should learn that atoms can bond together to form molecules, but students do not develop a mechanism for bonding and therefore cannot predict what molecules will form during reactions. Students can determine if atoms rearranged to form new molecules; however, they do not have enough information to predict the ratio in which atoms will bond together to form compounds. To determine, for example, that magnesium will bond with chlorine in a one-to-two ratio making $MgCl_2$, students first need to develop a subatomic model. At this point, students may be able to figure out some products based on their observations of the products. For example, if students test the properties of several known gases, they will learn that carbon dioxide extinguishes flames. Students could then use this information to test if reactions that give off bubbles are forming carbon dioxide gases. However, for other reactions, students may need to be told what the compounds are, or they may make guesses that are reasonable given the atoms involved but are inaccurate.

PS1.C: NUCLEAR PROCESSES

Little research has been done on students' ideas about nuclear processes, particularly at the middle school level. By the end of middle school, the *Framework* (NRC 2012) states that students should understand that nuclear fusion is responsible for the variety of elements in the universe. Fusion occurs in stars, where the nuclei of smaller atoms combine together to form larger atoms. Students often think that the number of protons in the nucleus of an atom can change when atoms form bonds; however, the amount of energy involved in nuclear changes is significantly higher than the energy involved in chemical changes. Students must know that nuclear fusion is not a process that occurs on Earth. More research is needed on how to help students develop these complex ideas.

Grades 9–12: A Subatomic Model

In high school, students develop an explanation for why atoms bond together. For high school, PS1 is broken into three components ideas: PS1.A: Structure and Properties of Matter, PS1.B: Chemical Reactions, and PS1.C: Nuclear Processes. At this point, students develop a model of the atomic theory that includes charged subatomic particles. Students should now develop a model of atomic structure: Atoms are made of smaller positive and negative pieces, and the positives are concentrated in the center of atoms. More importantly, students need to develop an understanding of what evidence there is that supports this model of matter (Mayer, Damelin, and Krajcik 2013). Students should develop this model by analyzing evidence that supports it, such as the results of historically significant experiments. Students can then use the interactions between these charged particles to explain

why atoms bond and how molecules interact with each other. Understanding the competing interactions between these charged subatomic particles makes the core idea of matter and its interactions more powerful for explaining observations and making predictions.

As students progress in their understanding in high school, they are expected to develop understanding of the substructure of atoms and provide more mechanistic explanations of the properties of substances. Chemical reactions, including rates of reactions and energy changes, can be understood by students at this level "in terms of the collisions of molecules and the rearrangements of atoms into new molecules" (NRC 2012, p. 111). Students are able to use the periodic table as a tool to help explain and predict the properties of elements; they can use this expanded knowledge of chemical reactions to explain important biological and geophysical phenomena. Phenomena involving nuclei are also important to understand, as they explain the formation and abundance of the elements, radioactivity, the release of energy from the Sun and other stars, and the generation of nuclear power.

PS1.A: STRUCTURE AND PROPERTIES OF MATTER

At the high school level, students develop models to explain that electrostatic forces govern the behavior and properties of atoms. For example, atoms bond to other atoms because the negative electrons of one atom are attracted to the positive protons of another atom. However, students usually have an incomplete model of the atom that does not include electric interactions (Griffiths and Preston 1992; Stevens, Delgado, and Krajcik 2010). Interactions between atoms are governed, in large part, by the attractive and repulsive forces between positively charged protons and negatively charged electrons. Students need to explore electrostatic interactions to identify patterns in how charged objects interact (similar charges repel, opposite charges attract, the interactions are stronger when objects are closer, etc.) so that they can apply these rules to the subatomic particles as well. Additionally, when collecting systematic observations about how charged objects interact, students should notice that neutral objects are attracted to both positively and negatively charged objects. This observation leads to a natural question about the nature of matter and the atoms that make up matter. Notice how the elements of this core idea are tied to other DCIs. To develop an understanding of the interactions that hold atoms together, students need to have an understanding of how objects interact through forces and the energy transfers that can accompany these interactions. (The Interactions curriculum [*http://interactions.portal. concord.org*] provides interdisciplinary instructional materials to support high school students in developing usable knowledge of forces and energetics involved in interactions that occur between atoms and molecules. Videos of the Interactions project can be seen at *http://ngss.nsta.org/ngss-videos. aspx.*) In this way, their understanding of matter and its interactions is dependent on students also developing understanding of the DCI PS2: Motion and Stability: Forces and Interactions (see Chapter 3, p. 33) and PS3: Energy (see Chapter 4, p. 55).

Since atoms are too small to see, indirect evidence must be used to study them. Students should discuss the benefits and limits of indirect evidence so that they understand that, although we cannot see atoms, we can make some claims about atomic structure. An atom has a dense, positively charged center with negative electrons in constant motion around it. This model was developed in large part based on the results of Ernest Rutherford's gold foil experiment. In this experiment, Rutherford used photoelectric paper to track the trajectory of small, positively charged particles that were shot at a thin sheet of gold foil. The path of a few of these alpha particles changed drastically, indicating that there must be regions with dense positive charges. This experiment is foundational to our understanding of atomic structure, but it is also abstract and difficult to understand. Students have trouble imagining that atoms are mostly empty space. It will take time to help them understand the setup of Rutherford's experiment and what the evidence was and to use that understanding to develop and revise models of atomic structure. A simulation on the Concord Consortium website (*http://concord.org/ stem-resources/rutherford*) provides students with a virtual experience to better understand the Rutherford experiment.

PS1.B: CHEMICAL REACTIONS

Once students have a model of atomic structure, they can start to analyze how atoms interact with each other. It is important for students to develop a model of how atoms link to form molecules. Students should look at how attractive and repulsive forces vary as atoms approach each other (NRC 2012; Stevens, Delgado, and Krajcik 2010). Understanding the involvement of electrostatic interactions in bonding can also help students understand the relationship between bonding and energy. Again, this is where the tight connection with the core idea PS3: Energy is significant (see Chapter 4, p. 55). Students often believe that energy is stored in chemical bonds and will be released when the bond is broken (see Cooper and Klymkowsky 2013). This idea, however, is not scientifically accurate. Bonds will form at the point where attractive and repulsive forces are balanced and therefore the electric potential energy is minimized. Bonds actually form at the distance where energy is at a low point, not at a high point. Energy is needed to break a chemical bond and is released when a new bond is formed. When analyzing reactions, the energy that was used to break the bonds in the system must be compared to the energy that was released when the new bonds were formed to determine if, overall, the reaction absorbs or releases more energy.

Once students have an atomic–molecular model of chemical changes, they can use this model to make sense of a wide range of observations of phenomena. Students can evaluate different types of chemical reactions. They can use their model of energy and bonding to explain reactions that release and absorb energy. They can also explain a variety of physical changes, such as protein folding, a key phenomenon in biology.

PS1.C: NUCLEAR PROCESSES

Again, little research has been done on this area and more research needs to be conducted. However, several important civic issues, such as voting on nuclear energy, are related to an understanding of nuclear reactions. In middle school, students used nuclear fusion to explain how different elements are formed. In high school, students should add nuclear fission to their atomic models. If atoms are unstable, the nucleus can split into smaller atoms. It is important that students understand that nuclear decay is spontaneous. While it is not possible to predict when an individual unstable atom will decompose through nuclear fission, for larger samples of atoms you can predict how many will likely decay in a given amount of time. For a sample of a particular type of unstable atom, half of the sample will decompose in a set amount of time. The decay of atoms is governed by probability. Note the connection to the science practice of using mathematical and computational thinking (NRC 2012).

What Approaches Can We Use to Teach About This Disciplinary Core Idea?
Elementary School

At this grade level, students need to experience numerous phenomena, for example by observing the evaporation of puddles, the burning of wood, the melting and freezing of water, or other simple changes. Students' descriptions of these phenomena lay the groundwork for building causal explanations of them in later grades. In early elementary school, students should make observations, describe materials and objects, and make and support claims about changes they observe. In later grades, students can use instruments to make more precise observations. Students can measure the mass of changes in closed and opened containers. By fifth grade and early middle school, students should begin to develop a particle model of matter. To develop this model, students need to make observations that motivate a need for a particle model, such as observing volume changes when liquids are mixed and observations of gases in sealed containers.

FIGURE 2.3

Concord's Models of Particles in (A) a Gas and (B) a Liquid

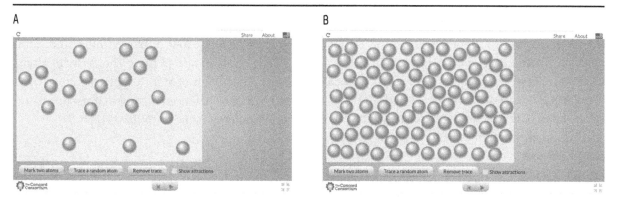

Note: At this grade level, the attraction between the particles needs to be turned off.

The Concord Consortium's Next-Generation Molecular Workbench (*http://mw.concord.org/nextgen*) offers an array of simulations that can support students in building a particle model. Students can observe models of gaseous, liquid, and solid states and use those observations to describe the differences among them. Figure 2.3a shows a model of particles in a gaseous state (*Molecular View of a Gas* simulation, available at *http://mw.concord.org/nextgen/#interactives/chemistry/phase-change/molecular-view-gas*), and Figure 2.3b shows a model of particles in a liquid state (*Molecular View of a Liquid* simulation, available at *http://mw.concord.org/nextgen/#interactives/chemistry/phase-change/molecular-view-liquid*). Students can observe these simulations and describe what they see.

Middle School

In middle school, students develop an atomic–molecular model to show what happens during a chemical change, a phase change, mixing, or dissolving. To support the development of this model, students should make careful observations of materials and changes. They should observe that the properties of materials change in a chemical reaction. For example, students can observe that when solutions of calcium chloride ($CaCl_2$, rock salt) and sodium bicarbonate ($NaHCO_3$, baking soda) are mixed, the result is a gaseous product that puts out flames (CO_2), a precipitate that when dried form a solid you can write on a board with and which also reacts with acid ($CaCO_3$, calcium carbonate or chalk), and sodium chloride (NaCL, table salt) in solution. What is critical is that students collect evidence that the products have different properties than the starting materials; the names and formulas are secondary and unimportant at this level. (Although, this reaction could also be used in high school, and then the formulas should be learned). Students can also develop atomic–molecular models to explain their observations of these changes. For instance, students can draw models of magnesium reacting with oxygen or of hydrogen gas reacting

FIGURE 2.4

Concord's Model of a Gas Allows Students to Observe the Gaseous World and How the Particles Change With Temperature.

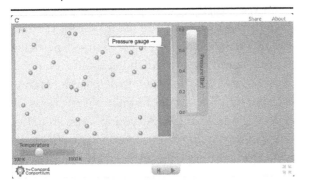

with oxygen gas. Concord's Next-Generation Molecular Workbench can also be used at the middle-grade levels. Figure 2.4 shows Concord's *Temperature-Pressure Relationship* simulation, a model of a gas that allows students to observe the gaseous world and how the particle motion changes with temperature (*http://mw.concord. org/nextgen/#interactives/chemistry/gas-laws/ temperature-pressure-relationship*). Students can note the relationships among the pressure, temperature, and volume of gases and use these to explain their observations of gases that have been sealed in a closed container like a syringe. Students are developing the relationships described by the ideal gas laws—but only as a support for developing a particle and atomic model of matter that can be used to explain various phenomena. The gas laws do not represent a core idea because they can only explain observations involving gases and do not build over time.

High School

In high school, students use interactions between charged particles within atoms to explain why atoms form bonds in molecules. Students can make observations of interactions between charged objects and between charged objects and neutral objects and link those observations to interactions between charged particles within atoms. Michigan State University's and Concord's Interactions project (*http://concord.org/ projects/interactions*) helps build students' understanding toward this important learning goal that aligns with the *Framework* and *NGSS*. Figure 2.5 (p. 30) shows a simulation students can interact with to identify the relationships among energy, the distance between atoms, and the interactions between atoms (*https://concord.org/stem-resources/ energy-bond-formation*).

FIGURE 2.5

Simulation Showing Relationships Among Atomic Interactions, Distance, and Energy

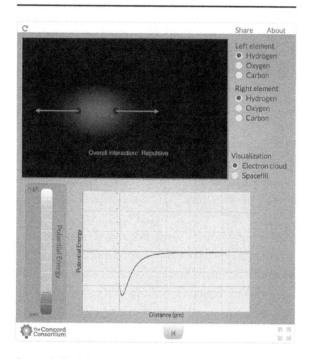

Concord's Next-Generation Molecular Workbench allows students to interact with a simulation to explore the relationships among atomic interactions, distance, and energy. Students can use these relationships to explain observations of changes and make predictions about the outcomes of changes in matter. Concord's Next-Generation Molecular Workbench also includes other simulations (not shown) that allow students to explore how bond breaking and bond formation are dependent on temperature. Students need to use their models of atomic structures to explain observations so they can connect macrolevel observations and atomic-molecular-level explanations.

Conclusion

The atomic model is powerful in making sense of a variety of phenomena. If students understand the structure of atoms and the charges of the particles that atoms are made of, they can use the interactions between these charged particles to explain and make predictions about a range of observations. It is important to help students connect their atomic model to their observations of materials and changes. At young ages, students can start by making careful observations of materials. Students can differentiate between properties of materials and properties of objects. As they grow older, they can use instruments, take measurements of materials, and develop a definition of matter. Then students can develop a particle model of matter to explain some of their observations. It is important that students develop a particle model of matter before being introduced to the atomic model. They need opportunities to use a particle model of matter to explain and make predictions about observations, such as why a puddle evaporates. After they have used a particle model of matter to explain observations, they can develop an atomic–molecular model to explain different types of changes, such as chemical reactions and phase changes. Finally, students develop a model of atomic structure. They can use interactions between charged subatomic particles to further explain various changes in matter. Once students can use interactions between subatomic particles to explain chemical and physical changes, they can then analyze nuclear changes as well. Throughout the development of the core idea of Matter and Its Interactions, it is important that students always connect the ideas they are developing to concrete examples, observations, and experiences. A full understanding of matter and interactions is linked to the other physical sciences core ideas of forces (PS2), energy (PS3) and waves (PS4). Building an integrated understanding of these DCIs will allow learners to explain a host of phenomena they experience in their everyday lives.

REFERENCES

Ahtee, M., and I. Varjola. 1998. Students' understanding of chemical reaction. *International Journal of Science Education* 20 (3): 305–316.

American Association for the Advancement of Science (AAAS). 1993. *Benchmarks for science literacy.* New York: Oxford University Press.

Ben-Zvi, R., B.-S. Eylon, and J. Silberstein. 1986. Is an atom of copper malleable? *Journal of Chemical Education* 63 (1): 64–66.

Cooper, M. M., and M. W. Klymkowsky. 2013. The trouble with chemical energy: Why understanding bond energies requires an interdisciplinary systems approach. *CBE-Life science Education* 12 (2): 306–312.

Devetaka, I., and S. Glazara. 2010. The influence of 16-year-old students' gender, mental abilities, and motivation on their reading and drawing submicrorepresentations achievement. *International Journal of Science Education* 32 (12): 1561–1593.

Driver, R., A. Squires, P. Rushworth, and V. Wood-Robinson. 1994. *Making sense of secondary science: Research into children's ideas.* New York: Routledge.

Feynman, R. P., R. B. Leighton, M. Sands, and E. M. Hafner. 1965. The Feynman lectures on physics, vol. 1. *American Journal of Physics* 33 (9): 750.

Gensler, W. 1970. Physical versus chemical change. *Journal of Chemical Education* 47 (2): 154–155.

Griffiths, A. K., and K. R. Preston. 1992. Grade-12 students' misconceptions relating to fundamental characteristics of atoms and molecules. *Journal of Research in Science Teaching* 29 (6): 611–628.

Johnson, P. 1998. Progression in children's understanding of a 'basic' particle theory: A longitudinal study. *International Journal of Science Education* 20 (4): 3934–12.

Kavanah, P., and A. P. Zipp. 1998. Gas experiments with plastic soda bottles. *Journal of Chemical Education* 75 (11): 1405–1406.

Kind, V. 2004. *Beyond appearances: Students' misconceptions about basic chemical ideas.* 2nd ed. London: Royal Society of Chemistry.

Krajcik, J., K. L. McNeill, and B. J. Reiser. 2008. Learning-goals-driven design model: Developing curriculum materials that align with national standards and incorporate project-based pedagogy. *Science Education* 92 (1): 1–32.

Krajcik, J., and J. Merritt. 2012. Engaging students in science practices: What does constructing and revising models look like in the science classroom? *The Science Teacher* 79 (3): 10–13.

Lee, O., D. C. Eichinger, C. W. Anderson, G. D. Berkeimer, and T. D. Blakeslee. 1993. Changing middle school students' conceptions of matter and molecules. *Journal of Research in Science Teaching* 30 (3): 249–270.

Levy-Nahum, T., R. Mamlok-Naaman, A. Hofstein, and J. S. Krajcik. 2007. Developing a new teaching approach for the chemical bonding concept aligned with current scientific and pedagogical knowledge. *Science Education* 91 (4): 579–603.

Mayer, K. 2011. Addressing students' misconceptions about gases, mass, and composition. *Journal of Chemical Education* 88 (1): 111–115.

2

Mayer, K., D. Damelin, and J. S. Krajcik. 2013. Linked in: Using modeling as a link to other science practices, DCIs and crosscutting concepts. *The Science Teacher* 80 (6): 57–62.

Merritt, J., and J. Krajcik. 2013. Learning progression developed to support students in building a particle model of matter. In *Concepts of matter in science education*, ed. G. Tsaparlis and H. Sevian, 11–45. Dordrecht, the Netherlands: Springer.

Mohan, L., J. Chen, and C. W. Anderson. 2009. Developing a multi-year learning progression for carbon cycling in socio-ecological systems. *Journal of Research in Science Teaching* 46 (6): 675–698.

Nakhleh, M. B., A. Samarapungavan, and Y. Saglam. 2005. Middle school students' beliefs about matter. *Journal of Research in Science Teaching* 42 (5): 581–612.

National Research Council (NRC). 2007. *Taking science to school: Learning and teaching science in grades K–8*. Washington, DC: National Academies Press.

National Research Council (NRC). 2012. *A framework for K–12 science education: Practices, crosscutting concepts, and core ideas*. Washington, DC: National Academies Press.

NGSS Lead States. 2013. *Next Generation Science Standards: For states, by states*. Washington, DC: National Academies Press. *www.nextgenscience. org/next-generation-science-standards*.

Novick, S., and J. Nussbaum. 1978. Junior high school pupils' understanding of the particulate nature of matter: An interview study. *Science Education* 62 (3): 273–281.

Rogat, A., C. Anderson, J. Foster, F. Goldber, J. Hicks, D. Kanter, J. Krajcik, R. Lehrer, B. Reiser, and M. Wiser. 2011. Developing learning progressions in support of the new science standards: A RAPID workshop series. Consortium for Policy Research in Education. *www.cpre.org/developing-learning-progressions-support-new-science-standards-rapid-workshop-series*.

Sakar, S., and R. Frazier. 2008. Conservation of mass and an unsuspected buoyancy effect. *Science Scope* 31 (9): 52–53.

Smith, C. L., M. Wiser, C. W. Anderson, and J. Krajcik. 2006. Focus article: Implications of research on children's learning for standards and assessment: A proposed learning progression for matter and the atomic–molecular theory. *Measurement: Interdisciplinary Research and Perspective* 4 (1–2): 1–98.

Stavy, R. 1991. Children's ideas about matter. *School Science and Curriculum* 91 (6): 240–244.

Stevens, S. Y., C. Delgado, and J. S. Krajcik. 2010. Developing a hypothetical multi-dimensional learning progression for the nature of matter. *Journal of Research in Science Teaching* 47 (6): 687–715.

TERC. 2011. Research overview: The inquiry project: Seeing the world through a scientist's eyes. The Inquiry Project. *http://inquiryproject.terc.edu/ research/inquiry_project*.

Treagust, D. F., G. Chittleborough, and T. Mamiala. 2003. The role of submicroscopic and symbolic representations in chemical explanations. *International Journal of Science Education* 25 (11): 1353–1368.

Wiser, M., K. O'Connor, and T. Higgins. 1995. Mutual constraints in the development of the concepts of matter and molecule. Paper presented at American Educational Research Association, San Francisco, CA.

Wiser, M., and C. L. Smith. 2008. Learning and teaching about matter in grades K–8: When should the atomic–molecular theory be introduced. In *Handbook of research on conceptual change*, ed. S. Vosniadou, 205–239. Mahwah, NJ: Lawrence Erlbaum Associates.

CHAPTER 3

CORE IDEA PS2

MOTION AND STABILITY: FORCES AND INTERACTIONS

David Fortus and Jeffrey Nordine

What Is This Disciplinary Core Idea, and Why Is It Important?

If any idea is a core concept, it is the idea of forces and interactions. Forces affect every single thing in the world, every single second. Every phenomenon involves forces at some level. Sitting, getting up, standing, walking, driving, and brushing your teeth all do. Even things that do not include activity require forces. Your computer is made of substances, your body is made of tissues; everything is made of something. How these materials are formed, what holds them together, why they maintain their shape (and why sometimes they don't), are all to do with forces. The weather, plate tectonics, planetary motion, electricity, you name it—they depend on forces. Indeed, physicists believe that *everything* in the world can be explained as an outcome of the interplay of four fundamental forces: electromagnetic force, gravitational force, strong nuclear force, and weak nuclear force.

Forces are a key concept in most physical, chemical, and engineering contexts. They have played an important role in the development of these disciplines; indeed, much of the history

of science can be described as the development of understanding of the concept of force. The Newtonian revolution was all about the centrality of causation in science, with forces being the main source of causation. Forces play a major role in phenomena and apparatuses that are central to students' lives. Though a truly deep understanding of forces requires some mathematical knowledge, most of the characteristics are very simple and easy to learn at different stages in students' development. Indeed, well before they begin school, students already have an intuitive understanding of forces as pushes and pulls.

PS2: Motion and Stability: Forces and Interactions consists of three component ideas: PS2.A: Forces and Motion explores the question, "How can one predict an object's continued motion, changes in motion, or stability?" PS2.B: Types of Interactions builds understanding of the question, "What underlying forces explain the variety of interactions observed?" And PS2.C: Stability and Instability in Physical Systems provides insight into the question, "Why are some physical systems more stable than others?" Next we describe each component.

FIGURE 3.1

A Bat Hitting a Ball

PS2.A: Forces and Motion

PS2.A focuses on the question, "What are forces?" Forces are entities that cause objects to do one or both of the following things: change their motion and deform. When a bat hits a ball, it applies a force to it, making it change its motion (Figure 3.1). However, the ball is not infinitely hard, so when it is hit (when a force is applied to it) it deforms a little and becomes squeezed or compressed. We don't typically notice this because the impact between the bat and the ball lasts such a short time and because the ball is so hard that it gets compressed just a bit. But if you use a beach ball instead of a baseball, the deformation of the ball during the impact will be very clear. This can also be seen very nicely in slow-motion videos made by Alciatore (2015).

Think of situations in which something changes its motion (e.g., tea being poured out of a teapot, coke spurting out of can, a dog chasing a cat). The possibilities are endless, and they all involve forces. Just because there is no motion doesn't mean that there are no forces at play. For example, my laptop is sitting on a table in a café and is subjected to forces even though it isn't moving. These forces make sure that it is stable and that it won't flip backward every time I touch it. Every time I tap a key on the laptop's keyboard, a few things happen: (1) The key moves. It hadn't moved before, so there is a change in its motion. This is due to the force my finger applies to the key. (2) I sense the key touching my fingertip. This is a result of the force the key applies to my finger. (3) My fingertip gets slightly deformed due to the force the key applies to it. (Actually, the reason I feel the key touching my finger is because my fingertip is deformed by the force the key applies to it—but more about that later.) (4) The key returns to its original position after I remove my finger from it. There's a spring under the key that gets compressed when I push on the key (deformation due to a force), and when I remove my finger, the spring pushes upward on the key (a force), making it change its motion and return to its original position.

A number of ways of thinking about forces are raised here that may create some confusion, so let's deal with them one by one.

FORCES CAN START MOTION, STOP MOTION, AND CHANGE MOTION.

Imagine there is a tennis ball lying stationary on the table in front of you. The tennis ball will remain stationary unless a force is applied to it, which causes it to start moving. So, you tap it on its right side (apply a force to it), and it begins rolling across the table, from right to left. Now you want to stop it so that it won't fall off the left edge of the table, so you put your hand down to block its path. The ball collides with your hand and stops. Your hand applies a force to the ball when the two collide, and it is this force that causes the ball to stop moving.

If we idealized the situation and imagined that the table was infinitely long, the ball would have kept on rolling to the left forever—until a force was applied to it that stopped it or changed its motion. If you had placed your hand differently at the end of the table or tapped on the side of the ball while it was rolling, it probably wouldn't have stopped rolling, but its motion would have changed. So you started, stopped, and changed the ball's motion by applying forces to it. Actually, starting motion is an example of changing motion because before something begins moving, it is motionless, and after it begins moving, it is moving, so its motion changed. The same can be said for stopping motion. So, instead of saying that forces can start, stop, and change motion, it is really enough to say that forces can change motion.

There are two kinds of changes to motion: changing speed and changing direction. Both changes are caused by forces. Physicists combine both when they use the term *velocity*: the velocity of an object is both its speed and its direction of motion, so when either changes, the velocity changes. A change in speed occurs when a force is applied to an object in the direction it is moving (this causes the object to accelerate, or for its speed to increase) or against the direction it is moving (in which case it causes the object to decelerate, or for its speed to decrease). A change in direction of motion occurs when a force is applied to an object perpendicularly to its direction of motion. Try this with the rolling ball: If you tap it from behind or in front while it is rolling, you will change its speed, but if you tap it from the side, you will change its direction. Often, forces are not applied in or against the direction of motion or perpendicular to the direction of motion, but instead at an angle to the direction of motion. In this case, the force will cause both the object's speed and its direction to change.

While these examples may seem so simplistic as to be removed from "real" examples of motion, which are usually very complex, the same principles underlie every example of motion: It is always forces that cause changes in motion, even when there appear to be none, such as when a train is moving on tracks that curve to the left. We say the train turns left because the tracks turn left, but from perspective of the force, the rails apply a sideways force on the train, causing it to change its direction of motion to the left.

Many students hold the conception that whenever an object is moving, a force is being applied to it, that is, motion equals the existence of force (Halloun and Hestenes 1985). This implies that when there is no force, there cannot be any motion, and that when an object slows down, the force that causes its motion slowly dies away as well. This contradicts the Newtonian idea that force leads to changes in motion rather than to motion itself. Galileo identified this commonly held notion. This naïve conception is highly resistant to change and seems to be deeply ingrained in most people.

FORCES CAN MAKE OBJECTS CHANGE THEIR ROTATION.

If an object has a hinge and a force is applied to the object so that the line along which the force is applied does not pass through the hinge, the object will begin to rotate, or if it is already rotating, its rotation will change. If the line along which the force is applied passes through the object's hinge, the force will have no effect on the object's rotation.

3

FIGURE 3.2

Rotation Caused by a Force

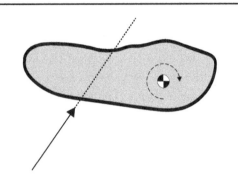

This is true for an object without a hinge as well. Every object has a center of gravity (we chose to use the term *center of gravity* because it is probably known to many readers; the more precise term is *center of mass*). If a force is applied to an object without a hinge so that the line along which the force is applied does not pass through the object's center of gravity, in addition to making the object change its motion, the force will also make the object change its rotation (Figure 3.2). On the other hand, if the line along which the force is applied passes through the object's center of gravity, the force will only cause the object to change its motion, not its rotation. Thus, forces can cause changes to rotation just as they can cause change to motion, but only if the line along which the force is applied does not pass through the object's center of gravity or through its hinge, if there is a hinge.

ONLY THE EXTERNAL FORCES ACTING ON AN OBJECT INFLUENCE ITS CHANGE IN MOTION.

If you push your chest with your hands, no matter how hard you push, you will not move. As hard as you may try, you cannot lift yourself by pulling at your boots. This is because the force your hand applies to yourself is an internal force: It is not applied by something outside of you, and so it cannot influence your motion. Imagine you just jumped off a diving board at a swimming pool, only to realize midair that there's somebody beneath you on whom you are about to land. Try as hard as you want, you won't be able to change your trajectory and land somewhere else, because you can apply only internal forces to yourself.

FORCES ALWAYS COME IN EQUAL AND OPPOSITE PAIRS.

When you pound your hand on the table, clearly you are applying a force to the table. However, it is also clear that your hand changed its motion (it stopped moving), so a force external to your hand must have been applied to it. This is the force that the table applied to your hand during the impact. So actually, when your hand strikes the table, two forces are involved: one is the force your hand applies to the table, and the other is the force the table applies to your hand. They are equal in strength but opposite in direction. Notice that although there are two forces, each object (your hand and the table) applies only one and is subjected to only one.

When you jump, you push downward on the ground with your feet; at the same time the ground pushes up on you (Figure 3.3). When a rocket engine operates, it pushes hot gases out downward through its nozzle, but at the same time the gases push upward on the engine. You feel heavy because you are pulled downward by the Earth (the force of gravity), but actually, at the same time you are pulling upward on the Earth.

This pairing of all forces is described by Newton's third law, named after Sir Isaac Newton, who first recognized this pairing. It is often stated as, "For every action there is an equal and opposite reaction." But we could more precisely say that forces always come in pairs, and that these force pairs always have the same strength and act in opposite directions on different objects.

According to Newton's third law, every force applied *by* an object is paired with an equal and opposite force that is applied *to* the object (sometimes called action and reaction forces). Students often think that there is no distinction between the forces applied to an object and those applied by the object and consider both at the same time, reaching the conclusion that they cancel each other so that there appears to be no total force (Gunstone 1987). Actually, *only* the forces applied *to* an object influence its motions, not any of the forces applied *by* it.

Multiple forces acting on an object can reinforce one another, counteract the effect of one another, or have no joint effect, depending on their relative arrangement. If two people push a washing machine from the same side, it will accelerate (its motion will change) at a greater rate than if only one person had pushed it. This is because each person applies a force to the washing machine in the same direction, reinforcing each other, thus leading to an effect that is greater than each person (force) would have caused on his or her own. On the other hand, if they push the washing machine from opposite sides, it will either stay in its place or move toward one of the sides, depending on which person pushes harder. If both people push it equally hard, it will stay in its place. This is because the two forces, each applied by a different person, counteract each other, and in this case, each one cancels out the effect of the other. If one person pushes harder than the other,

FIGURE 3.3

Pairs of Forces

GROUND PUSHING UP ON MY FOOT

MY FOOT PUSHING DOWN ON THE GROUND

FORCE FROM HOT GASES ON ROCKET

FORCE FROM ROCKET ON HOT GASES

the washing machine will start moving in the direction of the stronger force, but at a smaller acceleration than if the stronger force had been applied to the washing machine by itself. This is because the weaker force diminishes the effect of the stronger force, but not enough to cancel it.

When multiple forces are applied to an object, the resulting motion is identical to the motion that would have occurred if a single, equivalently large force had been applied. Thus, when predicting or explaining the motion of an object, we can simplify the situation by assuming the object is subjected only to a single force, the resultant force, which is the vector sum (a sum that takes into consideration the directions of the forces) of all the individual forces that are applied to the object.

3

Notice that this is true only for understanding the *motion* of the object. The deformation of the object by the applied forces is not canceled by counteracting forces. When the washing machine is pushed from both sides, it may not move, but it is still compressed.

THE INFLUENCE A FORCE HAS ON AN OBJECT'S CHANGE IN MOTION IS INVERSELY RELATED TO THE OBJECT'S MASS.

If you tap a Ping-Pong ball, a tennis ball, and bowling ball with about the same force, the Ping-Pong ball will go flying, the tennis ball will roll gently away, and the bowling ball will barely start moving. This is because the Ping-Pong ball has substantially less mass than the tennis ball, which has less mass than the bowling ball. Put mathematically,

$$a = F/m,$$

where a is the object's acceleration or rate of change in motion, F is the force applied to the object, and m is the object's mass. If an identical force is applied to multiple objects (in our case, three different balls), the greater the object's mass, the smaller its acceleration. This is traditionally known as Newton's second law, which can be described qualitatively as follows: "The acceleration of an object depends directly on the net force acting on the object, and inversely on the mass of the object. If the force acting on an object increases, the acceleration of the object decreases, and if the mass of an object increases, the acceleration of the object decreases.

THE FORCE DURING AN IMPACT IS INVERSELY PROPORTIONATE TO THE DURATION OF THE IMPACT.

When two objects collide, they apply forces to each other during the collision. The briefer the collision, the greater the forces they apply. The duration of the collision is often determined by the rigidity of the colliding objects: The more rigid they are, the shorter the duration of the impact. Why does it hurt more when you fall on a concrete floor than on a mattress? Because the mattress is padded (soft) and you do not stop suddenly when you fall on it but instead slow down gradually as the mattress deforms. By lengthening the time it takes you to stop (the duration of the impact), the force you apply to the mattress (and the mattress to you) becomes much smaller—small enough to keep you from getting hurt. Why do you bend your knees when landing after jumping? By bending your knees, you are instinctively lengthening the duration of the interaction between you and the ground, thereby decreasing the force of the impact and protecting your body. You can also apply these ideas to explain why we should wear seat belts when driving in a car or bicycle helmets when riding a bike.

NEWTON'S LAWS OF MOTION ARE APPLICABLE ONLY TO MACROSCOPIC OBJECTS AND AT SPEEDS THAT ARE MUCH LOWER THAN THE SPEED OF LIGHT.

Newton's laws were developed before scientists became aware of the existence of the microscopic world and learned that the behavior of objects changes as they approach the speed of light. For most macroscopic objects, knowledge of an object's velocity and all the forces to which it is subjected allows one, using Newton's laws, to predict the object's velocity in the future. However, in the nanoscopic domains, quantum behaviors become pronounced, and they are fundamentally probabilistic in that one can only predict what is *likely* to occur. When analyzing the behavior of submicroscopic systems, one must use principles drawn from quantum mechanics.

Newton's laws assume that an object's mass is independent of its speed. Einstein demonstrated that this is correct only for speeds much smaller than the speed of light. When an object's speed approaches that of the speed of light, Newton's laws no longer hold and one must use principles drawn from the theory of special relativity.

THE TOTAL MOMENTUM IS CONSERVED IN ISOLATED SYSTEMS.

Although forces are not conserved, they are directly related to the conservation of another property called momentum. Momentum is a property of an object; it is defined as an object's mass multiplied by its velocity. The momentum of an object or a system is conserved as long as no external forces are applied to the object or system. When two objects apply a force to each other, one object's momentum decreases while the other increases. Thus, the interaction between objects can be seen as a process of momentum transfer between them. The total or combined momentum of the two objects remains constant during the interaction. For a system of multiple objects interacting with each other but not with any object outside the system (an isolated system), the total momentum is conserved. Thus, the sum of the momentum of the solar system remains constant even though the Sun, planets, moons,

and asteroids all apply gravitational forces to one another because these are all forces internal to the solar system.

FORCES AND ENERGY ARE NOT THE SAME THING.

Let's summarize the differences between forces and energy (see Chapter 4, p. 55, for a more detailed discussion):

- Forces have directions. Energy does not.

- Energy cannot be created or destroyed. We say that energy is transferred and conserved. This is not so for forces.

- Forces always come in pairs. This is not so for energy.

- Forces are especially useful to explain changes to motion on a moment-to-moment basis; energy is especially useful for describing beginning-to-end changes.

Every type of potential energy (e.g., gravitational, elastic, electrical, chemical) is associated with a force. Gravitational potential energy is associated with the gravitational force. Elastic energy is associated with the elastic forces within a substance. Chemical energy is associated with the electric force between the atoms that make up molecules. As an object moves in a force field, the potential energy of the object associated with the force field changes. When an object moves against the direction of the force, its potential energy increases. For example, when a spring is stretched, its ends move against the direction of the elastic force pulling the spring back to its original shape. For this reason, as a spring stretches, its elastic energy increases (Figure 3.4). When a spring is compressed, its ends move against the direction of the elastic force, pushing it back to its original shape, so again its elastic energy increases. When an object moves up and away from Earth's surface, it moves against the direction of the gravitational force pulling it down, so its gravitational energy increases. However, when it moves down, it moves in the same direction as the gravitational force, so its gravitational energy decreases.

PS2.B: Types of Interactions

All forces between objects arise from a few types of interactions: gravity, electromagnetism, and strong and weak nuclear interactions. Forces are typically described as either contact forces or forces that act at a distance.

CONTACT FORCES AND FORCES THAT ACT AT A DISTANCE

Examples of contact forces are my hand pushing or pulling you, the friction between you and the air as you ride your bike, and a hammer striking a nail. In each of these cases, one thing is in contact with a second thing, and due to this contact, there is a force between them. Examples of forces that act at a distance are Earth's gravity pulling the Moon and me down (and the Moon and me pulling the Earth up), the repulsion or attraction between two magnets, and the electric force between my hairs that makes them stand out after I comb my hair on dry days.

FIGURE 3.4

Metal Spring

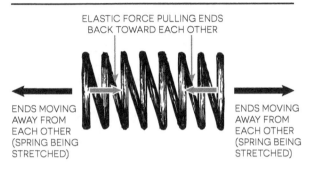

ELASTIC FORCE PULLING ENDS BACK TOWARD EACH OTHER

ENDS MOVING AWAY FROM EACH OTHER (SPRING BEING STRETCHED)

ENDS MOVING AWAY FROM EACH OTHER (SPRING BEING STRETCHED)

ALL FORCES ARE ACTUALLY FORCES THAT ACT AT A DISTANCE.

When you push the table with your hand, you bring the molecules in your skin near the molecules that make up the table's surface. These molecules are made of atoms, which are made of charged particles (protons and electrons) and are held together by electric forces. When your hand and the table begin "touching," the molecules in your skin exert a repulsive electric force on the molecules in the table's surface; you interpret this as your hand pushing the table. However, the molecules in your skin don't always exert a repulsive force on other objects; they can also exert an attractive force (think of touching something sticky). Whether attractive or repulsive forces result from the proximity between molecules depends on the types of molecules involved. Every case of contact forces can be shown to actually be macroscopic instantiations of electric forces at the atomic level.

FORCES ARE MEDIATED BY THE FOUR FUNDAMENTAL FORCE FIELDS.

As mentioned above, there are only four fundamental forces in the universe: gravitational force, electromagnetic force, strong nuclear force, and weak nuclear force. Each of these forces is mediated by a field that transfers energy and momentum to the participating objects.

Every mass is a source of a gravitational field and is affected by the gravitational field generated by all other masses. The gravitational force is always attractive. The force of gravity explains why we are attracted to the Earth, why moons orbit planets and planets orbit stars, and the evolution and motion of all astronomical systems.

The electric and magnetic forces are different aspects of the same underlying electromagnetic field. Every charged particle generates an electromagnetic field and is affected by the electromagnetic field generated by all other charged particles. The bonds holding all atoms together into molecules and molecules together into substances are the outcomes of the interplay of electromagnetic forces. As mentioned before, all "contact" forces are actually the result of electromagnetic forces acting on the microscopic scale.

The nucleus of an atom is made up of positively charged particles and neutral particles packed extremely tightly together. Have you ever wondered why the nucleus of an atom doesn't just fly apart, since similarly charged particles repel each other? Strong and weak nuclear forces are relevant only inside nuclei, where they play a central role in holding nuclei together and causing them to decay. The strong nuclear force holds the nucleus together by counteracting the repulsive electric force among all the protons in the nucleus. The weak nuclear force is involved in many types of nuclear decay that lead to the emission of beta particles and neutrinos.

Electric forces are dependent on the magnitudes of the charges involved and the distance between them. Electric forces can be either attractive or repulsive. Assume you have two electric charges, one with a charge A and the other with a charge B. There are four possible configurations: (1) both charges are positive, (2) both charges are negative, (3) A is positive and B is negative, and (4) A is negative and B is positive. In configurations 1 and 2, when both charges have the same sign, the electric force between them will be repulsive, meaning they push each other apart. In configurations 3 and 4, when the charges have opposite signs, the electric force between them will be attractive, meaning they pull each other together. Put mathematically, when the product of $(A \times B)$ is positive, the force is repellent, and when the product is negative the force is attractive. Note that regardless of the configuration, there are two forces, one that charge A applies to charge B, and one that charge B applies to charge A. These two forces are identical in magnitude but act in opposite directions (see Forces Always Come in Equal and Opposite Pairs, p. 36).

As the distance between the charges increases, the magnitude of the forces they apply to one another decreases by the square of the distance. This means that if the distance between them increases threefold, the forces between them decrease ninefold, and if the distance is increased by 4 times, the forces between them decrease by 16 times.

Electric forces are typically not recognized as forces that affect everyday life because most positive and negative charges are spread out symmetrically and in identical numbers, so at large scales the influence of one tends to cancel out that of the other. However, even though typically not thought of as force, electric forces are actually omnipresent; every contact force is actually an

3

electric force, and electric forces hold every substance or object together.

Magnetic forces are dependent on the strength of the magnets involved and the distance between them. Magnetic forces can be attractive or repellent, similar to electric forces. Assume you have two magnets. Each magnet has two poles: a north pole and a south pole. Consider four possible configurations: (1) the north poles of both magnets are facing each other, (2) the south poles of both magnets are facing each other, (3) the north pole of one magnet is facing the south pole of the other magnet, and (4) the poles are not facing each other but are aligned at an angle to each other. In configurations 1 and 2, when the same poles of the magnets are facing each other, there will be a repulsive magnetic force between them, meaning they will push each other apart. In configuration 3, when the opposite poles of the magnets are facing each other, the magnetic force between them will be attractive, meaning they will pull each other together. In configuration 4, forces that do not pass through the magnets' center of gravity will be applied to both magnets, making them turn around their center of gravity (see Figure 3.2) so that opposite poles will be facing each other and then they will attract each other. Again, the forces applied by each magnet to the other are identical in magnitude but act in opposite directions.

Gravitational forces are dependent on the masses of the objects involved and the distance between them. Gravitational forces are always attractive. Gravitational forces are almost identical to electric forces, with three big differences: They are dependent on masses rather than charges, they are always attractive, and they are much weaker than electric forces. Yet, we typically think of gravitational forces as being much stronger than electric force. This is because we typically only apply the idea of gravity to the Earth, and we feel its massive gravity all the time. All objects with mass have gravity, but compared to the Earth, objects with much smaller masses (e.g., two pencils) have very little gravitational attraction between them.

Assume you have two objects, one with a mass of A and the other with a mass of B. The gravitational force between these two objects will always be attractive, meaning they will always pull each other together. Note that there are always two forces, the one that A applies to mass B, and the one that mass B applies to mass A. These two forces are identical in magnitude but act in opposite directions (see Forces Always Come in Equal and Opposite Pairs, p. 36)

As the distance between the objects increases, the magnitude of the gravitational forces they apply to one another decreases by the square of the distance, so that if the distance between them increases threefold, the forces between them decrease ninefold.

Gravitational forces are extremely weak. To be felt, at least one of the objects involved has to be extremely massive. While there are gravitational forces acting between my laptop and me, they are so utterly small as to be totally negligible. That is why we never notice that these forces exist. However, the Earth is extremely massive, and so the gravitational forces between the Earth and me are significant—enough to be very noticeable and make me feel heavy.

FORCES ACT AT A DISTANCE THROUGH THE MEDIATION OF FIELDS.

An earlier section presented the idea that there are actually no contact forces, only forces that act at a distance. How can two objects that are not in contact apply forces to each other? Remember that there are really only four forces in the universe: gravitational force, electric force, strong nuclear force, and weak nuclear force. Any object that has an electric charge can apply and be subjected to electric and magnetic forces (the magnetic force is actually a result of the electric force, but it affects charges differently). The electric charges create an electric field around them. This field stretches out to great distances but gets weaker very rapidly as one gets farther from the charges that created it. Every charge can "sense" the existence of electric fields generated by other electric particles but not its own field. Thus, even though two electric charges are not in contact with each other, they sense the electric field generated by each other, and as a result of the interaction between the field and their charge, a force is generated that is applied to them whose magnitude and direction depend on the characteristics of the field between them and the magnitude of the charges.

Similarly, two magnets that are not in contact apply a force to each other because each of them generates a magnetic field that the other magnet senses, leading to each magnet being subjected to a force. Likewise, any object that has mass can apply and be subjected to gravitational forces because every object with mass generates a gravitational field around it and senses the gravitational fields generated by other objects. Finally, nucleons (particles that are found in the nuclei of atoms) can apply and be subjected to the nuclear forces (strong and weak).

THERE ARE SEVERAL KINDS OF FRICTION.

Friction is the force that resists the relative motion of objects or fluids. When you push your cell phone and then let go, it slides across the table and slows down until it stops. Since it slows down, its motion is changing, so it must be subjected to a force. This force is the friction between the cell phone and the table. This kind of friction, which occurs when two objects are in contact with each other and slide relative to each other, is called kinetic friction.

Friction can exist even when there is no relative motion between two objects. When you push the table in front of you horizontally and not too strongly, nothing happens. You might have expected the table to change its motion, but since it didn't, it must be subjected to another, counteracting force that cancels out the effect of the force your hand applied to the table. This counteracting force is the friction between the table and the floor, and is known as static friction because there is no relative motion between the table and the floor. Static friction has an interesting characteristic: Its magnitude and direction are automatically adjusted to counteract and cancel other forces acting on the object. Once again, think of yourself pushing the table. You start pushing really weakly, and then harder and harder, and still the table doesn't move. To keep the table from moving, the static friction between the table and the floor must be increasing as you push the table harder. If you push still harder, at a certain stage the table will suddenly start moving. This is because there is a maximum magnitude the static friction can have. If the equivalent of all the forces acting on the table, not including the static friction, is greater than the maximum magnitude of the static friction, the static friction will not be able to counteract and cancel the other forces and the table will start moving anyway.

3

FIGURE 3.5

Pendulum

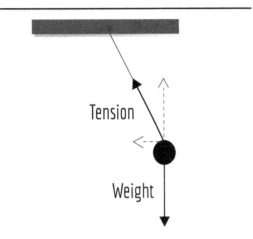

Tension

Weight

PS2.C: Stability and Instability in Physical Systems

PS2.C: Stability and Instability of Physical Systems focuses on why some physical systems are more stable than other. This subcomponent of the PS2 DCI has many connections with the crosscutting concept of systems and system models. Below we discuss important ideas related to this subcomponent.

A STABLE SYSTEM IS ONE IN WHICH SMALL PERTURBATIONS LEAD TO FORCES THAT RETURN THE SYSTEM TO ITS FORMER STATE.

Think of a weight hanging from a string (a pendulum) at rest. If the weight is lightly tapped, it will swing back toward its original position. When the weight moves to the side, the tension in the string has a sideways component that pulls the weight back to its position of equilibrium. A rocking chair also returns to its position of equilibrium. When a basketball bounces, it gets compressed but then returns to its fully inflated shape because the pressure inside the ball increases and pushes the surface of the ball back outward.

An unstable system is one in which small perturbations lead to forces that move the system even further from its prior state. For example, consider a ball lying at the top of a hill. If the ball is lightly tapped, it will roll down the hill, away from its initial position. Many explosives are unstable in that a small spark can cause them to explode.

A SYSTEM DOES NOT NEED TO BE STATIC TO BE STABLE.

A system can have a stable repeating cycle of changes, such as a planet orbiting the Sun, or a fluorescent lamp flickering at a constant rate. Stability here means that if the system is subjected to a small perturbation, it will tend to return to the repeating pattern of behavior that it had before.

A SYSTEM WILL BE STABLE OR INSTABLE DEPENDING ON THE BALANCE OF COMPETING EFFECTS.

A pendulum is subjected to two competing forces: the bob's weight and the string's tension. When the bob moves upward and sideways, the string's tension develops a horizontal component that opposes the pendulum's sideways motion. The vertical component of the tension decreases so that the bob's weight is greater than it, creating a net downward force on the bob, opposing its upward motion (Figure 3.5).

How Does Student Understanding of This Disciplinary Core Idea Develop Over Time?

One of the key features of DCIs is that they can be taught and learned over multiple grades at increasing levels of depth and sophistication. Let's see how this progression can be played out for motion and stability and what kind of simple activities that require no special equipment can support them. What students should know related to a subcomponent of the core idea is written in italics. This is followed by various potential learning tasks that could support developing this understanding. At the high school level, learning tasks are described only for those ideas that can be experienced without the use of special equipment.

By the End of Grade 2

PS2.A: FORCES AND MOTION

- *Objects push or pull each other when they collide or connect (see PS2.C).*

- *Pushes and pulls can vary in strength and direction (see PS2.C).*

- *An object can be pulled or pushed to change the speed or direction of its motion and to start or stop it (see PS2.C).*

- *When sliding on a surface or sitting on a slope, an object experiences pull because of friction between the object and the surface.*

Possible tasks: Have children push their hands across the table with their palms down, push a heavy container across the floor, and slide down a slide while keeping the soles of their shoes flat on the slide. In each case, they will sense a force (friction) generated by the surface that opposes the motion (of their hand across the table, the container across the floor, and their body down the slide). *Safety note:* Make sure all fragile and potentially sharp objects are removed from the paths used in moving hands across the table and pushing the heavy container across the floor.

PS2.B: TYPES OF INTERACTIONS

- *Objects that touch or collide push on each other and can change motion or shape (see PS2.C).*

PS2.C: STABILITY AND INSTABILITY IN PHYSICAL SYSTEMS

- *Whether an object is stationary or moves usually depends on the effects of several pushes and pulls on it.*

Possible tasks: Students can experience these PS2 ideas (except for that dealing with friction) with the use of two tetherballs. Hang one tetherball from a pole. By pushing on the tetherball from different sides with varying strengths, one can demonstrate that forces can have different directions and strengths, that these forces cause the ball to change its speed or direction of motion—whether or not the ball was stationary when the force was applied—and that stronger pushes cause a greater change in the ball's speed and/or direction of motion. This can be repeated by pulling on the rope rather than pushing the ball, demonstrating the same things for pulls rather than pushes.

By having two children push the ball at the same time they can see that the way the ball moves (or doesn't move) depends on the relations between the pushes.

Holding two tetherballs by their ropes and allowing them to swing and collide will demonstrate that the impact between them causes them to change their motion just like forces, implying that they apply a force to one another. *Safety note:* Make sure students wear eye protection (safety glasses or goggles) for this task.

By the End of Grade 5
PS2.A: FORCES AND MOTION

- *A force has both strength and direction.*

Possible task: Have the students think of a force, any kind, and then consider whether this force could be stronger or weaker or act in a different direction. Experience this by pushing and pulling each other (but not too roughly!). *Safety note:* Make sure all fragile and potentially sharp objects are removed from the path in which this activity is done.

- *An object at rest typically has multiple forces acting on it, but they counterbalance one another.*

Possible tasks: Look at any object at rest in the classroom. This object is always subjected to at least two forces: its weight (the downward force of gravity) and the upward force of the surface on which it rests or to which it is attached that counteracts the object's weight and keeps it from falling. Ask the students to think of an example that doesn't follow this behavior.

- *Forces that are not counterbalanced can change an object's speed or direction.*

Possible tasks: Hold any object in the palm of your hand. Using the logic from the prior activity, if the object is held motionless, the upward force exerted by your hand on the object must be identical to the weight of the object. However, by increasing or decreasing the upward force applied by your palm, you create a situation in which the two forces applied to the object (its weight and the force your hand applies) are not counterbalanced, and the object changes it vertical speed. As another example, take a string and attach two equal weights to its ends. Hang the weights by looping the string over a broomstick. The two weights will hang motionless. Increase one of the weights and the system will begin moving and accelerate, the greater weight downward and the lighter weight upward, because the forces applied to them (their weights and the tension of the string) are not counterbalanced. *Safety note:* Make sure students wear eye protection (safety glasses or goggles) for this task. Also remind students to use caution in working with weights and to prevent them from falling and causing injury to feet.

- *Patterns in an object's motion in different circumstances can be observed, and when a regular pattern is shown, future motion can be predicted.*

Possible tasks: Many objects move in a regular way: When pushed, a swing moves back and forth at a regular pace, the plate in a microwave goes around at a regular pace when power is applied, and a spring with a weight hanging from it goes up and down at a regular pace when it is agitated. Because of this regular pace, we can predict where the objects will be in the future. Thus, if there's a cup of water sitting on the microwave plate and we know that the plate takes five seconds to complete a revolution, students can be asked to predict what the orientation of the cup of water will be at any time as long as the microwave plate spins. *Safety note:* To prevent an explosion from steam in the microwave, make sure the cup of water is not capped.

PS2.B: TYPES OF INTERACTIONS

- *Objects in contact exert forces on each other, including pushes, pulls, friction, and pressure.*

- *Electric, magnetic, and gravitational forces between a pair of objects do not require that the objects be in contact.*

Possible tasks: Have the students experience how a magnet can push and pull another a magnet without touching it. Rub a rubber rod or comb with fur, then attract small pieces of paper to the rod. Electric forces attract the pieces of paper to the rod even though the two aren't touching. Drop any object. Why does it fall? Does it have to be in contact with the Earth for it to be subjected to Earth's gravitational pull? *Safety note:* Make sure students wear eye protection (safety glasses or goggles) for this task. Use caution when dropping objects so as not to injure feet.

- *The properties of objects and their distances apart dictate the sizes of forces in any situation. For two magnets, the forces between them are affected by their orientation relative to each other.*

Possible tasks: Have students "mess around" with four bar magnets, two of which are stronger.

Direct them to investigate how the force between any two magnets depends on the magnets' strength, the distance between them, and their orientations relative to each other. The force of gravity of the Earth acting on an object near Earth's surface pulls that object toward the planet's center. When objects are dropped, they fall directly down to the Earth's surface; they do not fall sideways. By drawing a circle on the board, one can show that "down" anywhere near Earth's surface corresponds with a line toward Earth's center. *Safety note:* Make sure students wear eye protection (safety glasses or goggles) for this task. Use caution when dropping objects so as not to injure feet.

PS2.C: STABILITY AND INSTABILITY IN PHYSICAL SYSTEMS

- *A system can appear unchanging when processes within it have opposite effects at equal rates.*

Possible tasks: Imagine a swimming pool that is filled with water from one pipe and emptied through another pipe. If water enters the pool through the first pipe at the same rate as the pool is emptied through the other pipe, the level of water in the pool will remain unchanged and the pool will appear to be unchanging, even though the actual water in the pool is being replaced. Likewise, as you eat, go to the toilet every day, and breathe in and out, you may appear unchanged with your weight constant, even though the stuff from which you are made is changing.

- *Changes can be very quick or slow and are sometimes difficult to see.*

3

Possible tasks: A tree (or a person, for that matter) grows so slowly that you cannot see it grow; only when you compare photos of it weeks or months apart can you see any change. On the other hand, a bullet moves so quickly that its motion cannot be seen. Only with special cameras can you track its motion.

- *Conditions and properties of objects influence how quickly or slowly a process occurs in a system.*

Possible tasks: It takes longer for a pot with lots of water in it to boil than the same pot with less water in it, even though they are both placed above the same flame. A spring with a heavy weight attached to it bobs up and down more slowly than the same spring with a light weight attached to it. Frozen things take longer to melt when placed in cold water than in hot water. *Safety note:* Make sure students wear eye protection (safety glasses or goggles) for these tasks. Use caution when working around boiling water and heated pots because they can cause severe skin burns.

By the End of Grade 8
PS2.A: FORCES AND MOTION

- *Any two interacting objects exert forces of equal magnitude on each other in opposite directions (Newton's third law).*

Possible tasks: Connect two force probes together. Fix one of the force probes so that it cannot move. Have a student pull and push on the other force probe, with two other students making simultaneous readings from both probes. Regardless how one force probe is pulled or pushed by

FIGURE 3.6

Experiment Setup

the student, the readings from both will be identical. Repeat this with both force probes being held by two students rather than having one of them fixed. Challenge the students to make a reading of 2N on one probe and 5N on the other, at the same time. They won't succeed! *Safety note:* Make sure students wear eye protection (safety glasses or goggles) for this task.

- *The sum of the forces acting on an object determine its change in motion; if the total force is not zero, the object's motion will change.*

Possible tasks: Build the object shown in Figure 3.6. A wooden block with two eye screws inserted into it is set on a table at its center. Long threads are tied to the eye screws, passed over opposite edges of the table, and connected to weights, with one hanging from each thread. Measure on the table two points, about 18 in. in either direction from the center of the wooden block. When identical weights are hung from each thread, the block will not move. When one weight is heavier than the other, the wooden block will accelerate in the direction of the heavier weight. Measure the time required for the center of the block to reach the point 18 in. away from its starting position.

Change the weights several times, and each time record the weights, the difference between them, the direction of motion, and the time required to travel 18 in. When the hung weights are identical, the block remains motionless. The greater the difference between the hung weights, the faster the block passes the mark, meaning that its acceleration is greater. *Safety note:* Make sure students wear eye protection (safety glasses or goggles) for this task. Use caution when dropping objects so as not to injure feet.

- *The heavier the object, the greater the force needed to achieve a change in motion.*

Possible tasks: Repeat the above experiment but add weights on top of the block and compare the results with those from when there were no weights on the block. *Safety note:* Make sure students wear eye protection (safety glasses or goggles) for this task. Use caution when dropping objects so as not to injure feet.

- *A larger force will cause a larger change in motion, whatever the object.*

Possible tasks: See prior activity with wooden block and weights.

- *Forces can also change an object's shape or orientation.*

Possible tasks: Demonstrate this with multiple objects: bend a ruler, model with clay, rotate any object by pushing on it, watch a slow-motion video of a basketball bouncing or a soccer ball being kicked, and so on. *Safety note:* Make sure students wear eye protection (safety glasses or goggles) for this task.

PS2.B: TYPES OF INTERACTIONS

- *Forces that are electric and magnetic (electromagnetic) can be attractive or repulsive. The size of the force is related to the magnitudes of the charges, currents, or magnetic strengths of the objects and the distances between them.*

Possible tasks: Give students a table of data in four columns: the first column gives the distance between two charged objects. The second, third, and fourth columns give the forces between the two charged objects for different magnitudes of charges. Have them identify trends in the data: If there's a difference when either charge is larger than the other, what happens when the magnitudes of the charges increase? And what happens to the forces when the charges get farther away from each other? Do the same with a table depicting the magnetic forces resulting from two magnets of varying strengths situated at varying distances from each other when their poles are lined up. (Unit 1 of the Concord Interactions materials provides a number of tasks and simulations to help students build understanding of electrical interactions. See *http://concord.org/ projects/interactions#curriculum.*)

- *Gravity is always attractive. Any two masses will have gravitational force between them, but the force is quite small unless at least one of the object has a very large mass, like a planet or the Sun.*

Possible tasks: Show a model of the planets orbiting the Sun. Deduce from change in the planets' direction of motion that they must be subjected at all times to a force inclined into their orbit, directed toward the Sun. Given the relative positions of the Sun and any of the planets,

3

conclude that the force between the Sun and each of the planets is attractive.

- *Gravitational, electric, and magnetic forces act at a distance and therefore involve fields that can be mapped by their effect on an object (e.g., mass, charge, or magnet).*

Possible tasks: Demonstrating this idea for electric or gravitational fields requires a computer-based simulation. Unit 2 of the Interactions curriculum *(http://concord.org/projects/interactions# curriculum)* contains several simulations to demonstrate an electric field. Figure 3.7 shows the *Electric Charge Simulation* from Concord's Unit 2, Investigation 2. The simulation shows the force field (triangles) generated from two charged objects, the force (arrows) between the objects, and potential energy associated with the interacting objects. Because this is a simulation, students can drag objects to see how fields change and how the force and potential energy change.

For magnetic fields, place a bar magnet under a sheet of paper and sprinkle a small amount of iron filings onto the paper. Shake the paper a bit and a pattern will appear; the filings will line up with field lines of the magnetic field generated by the magnet. Notice how this pattern is similar in the simulation of the electric field and the field generated from the magnetic and iron fillings.

PS2.C: STABILITY AND INSTABILITY IN PHYSICAL SYSTEMS

- *In a stable system, any small change leads to forces that return the system to its previous state.*

FIGURE 3.7

A Simulation Showing the Force Field Generated by Two Charged Objects and the Force Between the Objects

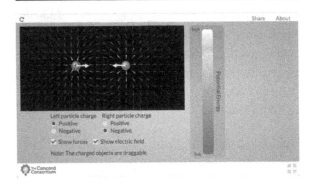

Possible tasks: Hang a weight from a string and tap it lightly. The weight will swing back toward its position of equilibrium. When moved from equilibrium, the tension in the string has a sideways component that pulls on the weight back to its position of equilibrium. *Safety note:* Make sure students wear eye protection (safety glasses or goggles) for this task. Also remind students to use caution in working with weights and to prevent them from falling and causing injury to feet.

- *A system can be static and unstable. When a system is static, it is in equilibrium but not necessarily stable.*

Possible tasks: A ball lying motionless at the top of a hill is in equilibrium, but any small perturbation will cause it to roll down the hill, away from its position of equilibrium, meaning it was not stable. Try to balance a meterstick on your finger or a pencil on its eraser. If you succeed, it may be in equilibrium, but it definitely will not be stable! *Safety note:* Make sure students wear eye protection (safety glasses or goggles) for this task.

- *Stable repeating cycles of change can occur in a changing system, allowing for the prediction of the system's future.*

Possible tasks: Discuss and observe various phenomena, including the planets revolving about the Sun, four seasons in a year, many plants following the Sun as it moves across the sky (heliotropism), the Moon's regular phases, and pendulums swinging back and forth. Demonstrate the pendulum phenomenon. These are examples of systems that change, but with a regular, repeating cycle. Therefore, predictions can be made about the system's state at any given time. *Safety note:* Make sure students wear eye protection (safety glasses or goggles) for the pendulum task.

- *A system in an unstable state will change until it becomes stable.*

A ball rolling down a hill will continue to roll until it reaches a low spot in which the ball can be in equilibrium and be stable. When an hourglass is turned over, an unstable situation is created. The sand flows until all of it reaches the bottom part of the hourglass, which is a stable situation.

By the End of Grade 12
PS2.A: FORCES AND MOTION

- *Although Newton's second law predicts changes in the motion of macroscopic objects, it is not accurate for subatomic scales or for speeds close to the speed of light.*

Possible tasks: Use the setup in Figure 3.6 (p. 48) and measure the time that passes until the block crosses one of the dotted lines. Assuming constant acceleration, calculate the block's acceleration between its starting position and the dotted line. Multiply this acceleration by the block's mass and compare it to the theoretical value of the net force on the block, which can be obtained by setting up a system of equations by writing an expression for Newton's second law for every mass in the system (the block's mass and each hanging mass) and combining them using the fact that the acceleration of each mass must be the same. It is not possible to demonstrate the limitation of Newton's second law at microscopic scales or near the speed of light without availability of special equipment typically not found in schools. *Safety note:* Make sure students wear eye protection (safety glasses or goggles) for this task.

- *Total momentum is always conserved in a system. When outside objects are introduced, the total momentum can change, but the momentum of objects outside the system also changes to balance that change.*

Possible tasks: Have two billiard balls or air-hockey pucks collide with each other in various ways. Video-record each collision from above. Analyze the resulting videos to calculate the momentum of each ball or puck before and after the collisions. Using vector algebra, calculate the change in each ball's (or puck's) momentum during each collision and show that these changes are of identical magnitude but opposite in direction. *Safety note:* Make sure students wear eye protection (safety glasses or goggles) for this task.

PS2.B: TYPES OF INTERACTIONS

- *Newton's law of universal gravitation and Coulomb's law are mathematical models*

3

FIGURE 3.8

A Simulation Showing Why Substances Boil at Different Temperatures

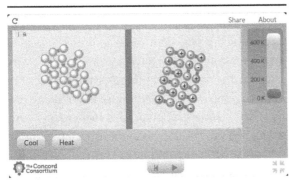

The *Boiling Point* simulation from the Next-Generation Molecular Workbench helps explain why substances boil at different temperatures because of electrical interactions between molecules.

that describe and predict gravitational and electrostatic forces and their effects between distant objects.

Possible tasks: Using data from an ephemeris, analyze the motion of various planets around the Sun and calculate each planet's average acceleration. Show that these accelerations are proportional to $1/R^2$, where R is the distance between the Sun and the planet as predicted by Newton's law of gravitation. A similar demonstration for Coulomb's law requires the availability of specialized equipment.

- *The structure, properties, and transformations of matter and the contact forces between material objects are explained by the atomic-level attraction and repulsion of electric charges.*

Possible tasks: Concord's Next-Generation Molecular Workbench provides a number of simulations that allow students to explore how electrical interactions at the atomic scale explain the structure and properties of matter. Go to *http://mw.concord.org/nextgen/#interactives*, select "Browse Interactions," and then "Intermolecular Attractions" under the Chemistry heading. The simulations will allow students to explore how electrical interactions affect phenomena such as boiling points, why water and oil don't mix, and the folding of protein molecules. Figure 3.8 shows the simulation *Boiling Point* (available at *http://mw.concord.org/nextgen/#interactives/chemistry/intermolecular-attractions/boiling-point*) from the Next-Generation Molecular Workbench and helps explain why substances boil at different temperatures because of electrical interactions between molecules.

The Interactions online materials allow students to explore familiar but somewhat curious aspects of the everyday world that require electrostatic forces for explanation. Students explore questions such as the following: Why do clothes stick together when they come out of the dryer? How is it that a tiny spark can trigger an explosion? What powers a hurricane? Students ask their own related questions, observe phenomena, engage in firsthand experiences, and use online simulations to collect evidence to support claims. From their evidence, they construct models of the forces that drive explanations of the phenomena. Through these experiences, students develop and use models of interactions taking place at the atomic and molecular scale to explain things they can observe in the world around them, and develop a model that can explain the flow of energy and cycles of matter for things taking place on both the macroscopic and submicroscopic scales. Learn more about the Interactions curriculum at *http://concord.org/projects/interactions* and *http://create4stem.msu.edu/project/forces*. You can see videos of students and teachers using the Interactions curriculum materials at *http://ngss.nsta.org/ngss-videos.aspx*.

Conclusion

It is important for all students to construct a deep understanding of forces, motion, and stability because they are involved in *every* phenomenon and *every* technology. Even when there is no apparent motion involved, as in an electric or chemical phenomenon, on a microscopic level, motion and forces are ubiquitous. Many of the central issues facing society today, such as fracking or interstate highway bridge repair, cannot be fully appreciated without an understanding of forces, motion, and stability. For example, a new coal-fired power station is being built near the town where you live. Should you be concerned? Does this power station pose a health hazard? One cannot understand many aspects of this issue, such as how the hot air and smoke released by the power station affect the air currents near his or her town, without having a deep understanding of forces,

motion, and stability. With global warming, sea levels are expected to rise worldwide. For a country like the Netherlands, which uses dikes to keep the sea out of much of its territory (much of which is below sea level), this raises a major question: Are the existing dikes strong enough to protect the Netherlands from a rising sea? A 21st-century scientifically literate person who can make sense of issues such as this will have a basic understanding of forces, motion, and stability.

REFERENCES

Alciatore, D. G. 2015. Untitled video, 0:15. *http://high_speed_video.colostate.edu/Sports%20Equipment/basketball_bounce.wmv*.

Gunstone, R. F. 1987. Student understanding in mechanics: A large population survey. *American Journal of Physics* 55 (8): 691–696.

Halloun, I. A., and D. Hestenes. 1985. Common-sense concepts about motion. *American Journal of Physics* 53 (11): 1056–1065.

National Research Council (NRC). 2012. *A framework for K–12 science education: Practices, crosscutting concepts, and core ideas.* Washington, DC: National Academies Press.

CHAPTER 4

CORE IDEA PS3

ENERGY

Jeffrey Nordine and David Fortus

nergy is perhaps the most important idea in all of science. It is used by every scientific discipline and applies to all known natural phenomena. Biologists, chemists, engineers, geoscientists, and physicists all use the principle of conservation of energy to make sense of natural phenomena and construct human-made devices. Energy is also a central idea in modern society. Politicians discuss and vote on laws concerning energy resources, families are constantly looking for ways to lower their monthly energy bills, and we all know the feeling of "lacking energy" when we are tired. The notion of energy pervades scientific and everyday life. However, it is discussed differently in everyday contexts than in school contexts, and students often struggle to understand how the everyday meanings of energy map onto the scientific ideas they encounter in school (Solomon 1983). To complicate matters further, scientists from different disciplines often employ the energy concept differently and even communicate using different sets of terminology. It is perhaps no wonder that, in schools, students often fail to see how the energy they learn about in physics class is the exact same thing as the energy they learn about in biology class. The purpose of this chapter is to clarify why energy is such a useful concept, to expand on energy as a disciplinary core idea (DCI) in *A Framework for K–2 Science*

Education (*Framework*; NRC 2012), and to illustrate some example teaching strategies that may be useful for energy instruction across grade levels.

What Is This Disciplinary Core Idea, and Why Is It Important?

Believe it or not, the scientific concept of energy is relatively new. Although scientists had been working for hundreds of years to make sense of how objects moved and thermodynamic systems behaved, it wasn't until the late 19th century (just a few decades before Einstein published his theory of special relativity) that the conservation of energy was an accepted scientific idea.

The conservation of energy is a scientific *law*, which means that it is not something derived from other principles. Rather, it is a statement that summarizes a very large number of empirical observations. The law of conservation of energy can never be proven, though it seems present in every system we have investigated. So accepted is the conservation of energy that virtually all scientists have simply stopped investigating alternative explanations. By 1930, the idea of energy conservation was so ingrained as a scientific idea that Wolfgang Pauli suggested the existence of an undiscovered particle (which we now know as

4

the neutrino) to account for an apparent violation of the conservation of energy during experiments.

Today, energy is such a central scientific principle for one reason: it is conserved. Armed with the knowledge that any process that increases energy must be coupled with another process that decreases energy by the exact same amount, scientists can set limits on the behavior of systems or speculate that some previously undetected process must be occurring. Because the law of energy conservation applies to every single system scientists have ever investigated, scientists from every field rely on the concept of energy to make sense of the phenomena they study.

How Scientists Use the Energy Concept in Different Disciplines

While the principle of conservation of energy is about as simple a mathematical principle as can be (for any isolated system, initial energy = final energy), the application of this principle to real systems usually involves some pretty sophisticated thinking and complex mathematical equations. For example, a physicist may be interested in calculating the energy in a system of two colliding objects, like two pucks on an air-hockey table. She may calculate the total energy of the system before the collision by summing the kinetic energy (calculated by $\frac{1}{2} \times mass \times speed^2$, or $\frac{1}{2}mv^2$) of each puck as they move toward each other. If she uses the same strategy to calculate the total energy after the collision, she will always find that her value is a little bit lower than it was before! This is because, although there might have been only kinetic energy due to the speed of the pucks before the collision, lots of things happened as the collision unfolded. For one, when

the pucks struck each other, this made a sound, and the sound wave transferred energy out of the two-puck system. Also, as each puck traveled along the air-hockey table, it was constantly colliding with air molecules, both from the air blowing out of the table and from the air in the room. Overall, these collisions slowed down the puck and sped up the air molecules, which also transferred energy out of the two-puck system. (Molecules move in random directions, and it will happen that some moving air molecules happen to hit the puck from behind and actually help the puck keep moving! But, overall [assuming nobody blows on the puck from behind], there are far more collisions that slow down the puck than help it along, and the puck eventually slows down.) Further, one or both pucks may start to rotate slightly, and just as there is kinetic energy associated with the back and forth (translational) motion of an object, there is kinetic energy associated with the rotation of an object, but rotational kinetic energy is calculated differently than translational kinetic energy. The rotational kinetic energy is still in the system, but it won't show up if she only calculates the translational kinetic energy. Finally, the collision will cause molecules inside the pucks to vibrate faster than before, and this increase in molecular speed has an energy associated with it that we call thermal energy. To calculate the exact conservation of energy for this system, the physicist's "after-collision" energy calculations will have to include equations for the energy transferred to the surroundings via the sound and air molecule collisions, the energy still in the system as rotational kinetic energy of the pucks, and the energy still in the two-puck system as thermal energy of the faster-vibrating molecules in each puck. All this is to say that tracking the exact conservation of energy within a real

system can get really complicated really quickly, even for a relatively simple system of two colliding air-hockey pucks!

Imagine, then, how tough it can be for a chemist to use the physicist's equations to calculate the energy changes occurring in a system with trillions upon trillions of interacting molecules. It is so tough that it's pointless to even try. Instead, the chemist relies on a different set of equations that are specially formulated to calculate the energy associated with systems that contain too many particles to track individually. These are the equations of thermodynamics. Thermodynamic equations make it possible to describe the behavior of large numbers of microscopic objects (e.g., molecules) by measuring the macroscopic characteristics of a system. Rather than calculate the translational kinetic energy of single molecules (by using the same equation that our physicist did) and add them all up, a chemist instead relies on a single number that describes the average kinetic energy of all of the molecules in a system; this number is called temperature. Thus, when tracking kinetic energy changes within systems, a physicist may use one set of equations and terms while a chemist uses another. Ecologists, seismologists, and electrical engineers also use different energy terminology and equations that are more appropriate and convenient for the systems they study. It is important to note that no matter the term or equation, they are expressions of the same fundamental idea—that energy is conserved. The energy discussed by astronomers, mineralogists, and dieticians is all the same thing; as far as we know, there is absolutely nothing different about the energy we get from our food and the energy released in a distant supernova.

The *Framework* (NRC 2012) makes an important set of recommendations aimed at helping students understand that "energy is energy is energy." That is, whether we call it kinetic, potential, chemical, nuclear, or thermal, all energy is fundamentally identical. The *Framework* stresses that the idea of different energy forms is misleading because it implies that each is a physically distinct quantity, when in fact all are macroscopic expressions of the same microscopic phenomena involving particle motion, fields between particles, and radiation.

Any phenomenon can be interpreted through the lens of a relatively small set of ideas about the behavior of energy at the microscopic level. Energy is fundamentally a physical science idea, but the wide-ranging applicability of a small set of ideas about energy make it a crosscutting concept as well (Nordine 2016).

By focusing on a small number of key ideas about energy and building a more sophisticated understanding over the course of years, students will be better positioned to see connections between the energy ideas they encounter across subjects, which in turn promotes an "integrated" understanding of energy—that is, an understanding that enables them to connect related ideas together to make sense of phenomena they encounter both in and out of school (Linn 2006). The *Framework* presents four component ideas about energy and describes how students might build an understanding about them over time. In the next sections, we explore how energy is presented within the *Framework* and the *Next Generation Science Standards* (*NGSS*; NGSS Lead States 2013).

Energy in the *Framework* and the *NGSS*

Researchers have known for decades that students often have a great deal of difficulty understanding the energy concept (see Chen et al.

4

2014). Several key standards documents have attempted to help clarify what students need to know about energy, and when they need to know it, to support them in constructing ideas about energy that correspond with scientific consensus. The *Benchmarks for Science Literacy* (AAAS 1993) and *National Science Education Standards* (NRC 1996) both aimed to identify ideas that should be the focus of energy instruction across grade bands. While these documents were instrumental in clarifying key energy ideas for each grade level as students build toward understanding energy conservation, recent research has indicated that many students fail to develop an understanding of energy conservation by the end of 12th grade (Liu and McKeough 2005; Neumann et al. 2013).

A key difference between the *Framework* and *NGSS* and previous documents is the inclusion of energy as both a DCI in the physical sciences and a crosscutting concept that spans all scientific disciplines. The *Framework* stresses the importance of explicitly and consistently connecting key energy principles to disciplinary investigations of phenomena. For example, in biology class, students discuss energy in the context of living systems, and energy in this context typically means the amount of energy that becomes available to an organism through the digestion of food resources; in physics class, students discuss energy in the context of physical systems, and energy in this context typically means the sum of a system's kinetic energy and potential energy. While students in a biology class learn that about 90% of energy is "lost" when going from one trophic level to the next, students in physics class are often asked to assume that energy is quantitatively conserved during phenomena such as a mass bobbing on a spring or a pendulum swinging. By focusing on energy as a crosscutting concept, the *Framework*

and *NGSS* advocate for making explicit what we mean by energy being lost in a biological context (i.e., the transfer of energy to the surrounding environment and its subsequent dissipation) and for intentionally exploring in physics class why a pendulum does not, in fact, conserve energy within the system (because energy is transferred out of the system into the surrounding environment and subsequently dissipated). As students learn to consistently apply a small set of key ideas across disciplinary contexts, they will be in a better position to develop an integrated understanding that applies across disciplinary boundaries and better prepares them for continued energy-related learning (Fortus et al. 2015; Nordine, Krajcik, and Fortus 2011).

While the emphasis on energy as a crosscutting concept is new, another major difference between the *NGSS* and preceding standards documents is the emphasis on connecting key energy ideas to science practices. By specifying what students should focus on at each grade level and linking this to specific science practices, students are supported in developing an increasingly sophisticated evidence base for understanding the behavior of energy over grades K–12. As a DCI, energy appears within the physical sciences strand and includes four component ideas:

- PS3.A: Definitions of energy

- PS3.B: Conservation of energy and energy transfer

- PS3.C: Relationship between energy and forces

- PS3.D: Energy in chemical processes and everyday life

In the next section, we expand each of these component ideas by considering common student conceptions, discussing key scientific principles that are connected to each component idea, and describing the "storyline" for how energy ideas and science practices should be combined in elementary, middle, and high school as students develop their understanding of energy over time.

How Does Student Understanding of This Disciplinary Core Idea Develop Over Time?

To develop an integrated understanding of energy that is useful for making sense of natural phenomena and establishing the groundwork for future learning, instruction must be coherent (Fortus and Krajcik 2012). To be coherent, instruction should be organized around a small set of the most important disciplinary ideas and involve students in the process of scientific investigation. The four component ideas about energy identified by the *NGSS* form a foundation on which scientific investigations can be designed. Each energy component idea discussed below takes years to fully develop through students' participation in coherent curriculum and the development of an increasingly sophisticated evidence base over time.

PS3.A: Definitions of Energy
COMMON PRIOR CONCEPTIONS

Long before students are formally introduced to the concept of energy in school, they hear and use the term in their everyday lives. During these everyday experiences, students develop their own set of ideas about energy that correspond with their experience but are often not consistent with a scientific view of energy. Michael Watts (1983) was among the first to categorize students' alternative ideas about energy. Among these conceptions was the belief that energy was only associated with living organisms, only related to overt displays of action, a by-product of certain actions, or associated mainly with technical devices. Watts's findings provided early insight into how students may come to "define" energy through their own experiences.

DEFINING ENERGY AS A SCIENTIFIC IDEA

Although energy is ubiquitous in our lives and we all seem to have an intuitive sense of energy as an everyday idea, it is very difficult to define in a rigorous and self-consistent way. Commonly, textbooks will define energy as "the capacity to do work" or "the ability to cause a change," but each of these definitions is flawed. In the first, saying that energy is a capacity to do work is circular, since work is a process of energy transfer between systems. Thus, this definition essentially says "energy is the ability to transfer energy." This is hardly helpful for defining what energy is. The second definition is not circular, but it is so broad that it fails to give students specific direction regarding energy as a distinct scientific idea. Richard Feynman, one of the great physicists of the twentieth century, described the challenge of defining energy:

> It is important to realize that, in physics today, we have no knowledge of what energy is. We do not have a picture that energy comes in little blobs of a definite amount. It is not that way. However, there are formulas for calculating some numerical quantity, and when we add it all together it

gives … always the same number. It is an abstract thing in that it does not tell us the mechanism or the reasons for the various formulas (Feynman, Leighton, and Sands 1965, p. 4-2).

According to Feynman, it is far more important to be able to describe how energy *behaves* in physical systems than it is to define what energy *is*. Though a definition of energy eludes us, we can say very precisely how energy is calculated. For example, kinetic energy is associated with motion and can be calculated by the formula $\frac{1}{2}mv^2$ (when objects are moving much slower than the speed of light) where m is the mass of an object and v is its speed. Potential energy due to gravity is associated with height and can be calculated as mgh (for objects close to the surface of the Earth), where m is the mass of the object, g is the acceleration of gravity, and h is the height of an object above some reference height.

BY THE END OF GRADE 5

In elementary school, it is not important to operationally define the term energy. Rather, it is critical for teachers (and eventually students) to use the word in consistent and correct ways when exploring energy-related phenomena. Since students will already have an intuition for the term energy from their everyday lives as associated with action or vitality, the important thing in elementary school is to hone this intuition by intentionally exploring energy-related phenomena in such a way that students begin to identify how energy is manifested in various phenomena (e.g., light, motion, sound) and to gather evidence for energy transfers between objects and systems. For example, students should be able to connect the idea of energy to the speed of moving objects or to the operation of electric circuits. By focusing on building an intuition for how observable variables are connected to various energy-related phenomena, elementary students will be well positioned to progress in their understanding during middle school.

BY THE END OF GRADE 8

Middle school students should begin to use more precise terms for the ways that energy is manifested in phenomena. Instead of using "motion energy" to describe energy associated with motion, they should use "kinetic energy." Further, they should be able to use the idea of energy to connect related phenomena, for example, the speed of a falling object to its height above the Earth and the temperature of an object and its surroundings. These students should recognize that kinetic energy is related to the mass and the speed of an object and that speed indicates whether an object can be considered to have kinetic energy. They should recognize that gravitational potential energy is associated with the distance between two mutually attracting masses. Though we cannot define what energy is, it is possible to pretty clearly delineate ways that energy is manifested in phenomena, and students at this age should focus on relating these manifestations to each other. Rather than performing simple calculations of energy or merely learning to name various energy "forms" (e.g., kinetic energy, gravitational potential energy), middle school students should connect qualitative descriptions of observations of phenomena (e.g., faster/slower, higher/lower, hotter/colder) to each other using the idea of energy transfer between objects and systems.

BY THE END OF GRADE 12

Just as in previous grade levels, the focus in high school is on what energy does, not what it is. In high school, students should begin to more formally identify and measure various energy changes both in terms of qualitative descriptions of variables and in quantitative terms by using data gathered during investigations to calculate changes in the magnitude of energy. Further, students should use a microscopic perspective to interpret the role of energy in phenomena. For example, while a middle school student may connect changes in temperature to changes in thermal energy, a high school student should be able to explain changes in thermal energy in relation to changes in random (as opposed to bulk) molecular motion.

As students become more able to connect energy phenomena in terms of interactions between atoms and molecules, they move toward a more unified understanding of energy across disciplines. In doing so, they become more able to explain energy flow in biology in terms of chemical interactions and to explain chemical reactions in terms of changes in the potential energy stored in a system of interacting particles and the kinetic energy associated with their motion. With a more unified understanding of energy, students become more capable of applying energy ideas consistently to a wide range of Earth and space science, life science, physical science, and engineering problems.

PS3.B: Conservation of Energy and Energy Transfer

COMMON PRIOR CONCEPTIONS

While students will usually agree that energy can never be created nor destroyed, a deep understanding of energy conservation eludes most K–12 students (Liu and McKeough 2005; Neumann et al. 2013). For example, students commonly believe that when energy is used, it is "used up" and no longer exists (Driver et al. 1994). When asked to explain the law of conservation of energy, many students confuse the scientific and everyday meaning of these terms and report that energy conservation is not a law of nature but a choice or policy put in place by human beings (Boyes and Stanisstreet 1990). In problem-solving situations, many students will resist applying the principle of energy conservation and choose instead to use other reasoning strategies that might be less suited to the situation (Driver and Warrington 1985), and it seems that a quantitative problem-solving approach for idealized situations (e.g., frictionless roller coasters) may actually be a source of misunderstanding about when and where the energy conservation law applies (Bryce and MacMillan 2009).

Although students have plenty of trouble understanding the law of energy conservation, they also often struggle to understand the idea of energy transfer. Many students conceptualize energy as some sort of physical fluid that flows or transfers between places and systems (Trumper 1993; Watts 1983). When considering a device such as a battery-powered flashlight, it is not uncommon for students to combine incorrect ideas about energy; for example, they may believe that energy is some sort of fluidlike substance that is stored in a battery and flows through the wires to the light bulb, where it powers the bulb and is used up in the process. It is important to note that while these ideas do not correspond to scientific ideas, they generally do a nice job of explaining why the light from a flashlight dims over time. Though students' alternative ideas about energy

4

may not be complete, students often fail to see a reason for revisiting their ideas in the face of traditional instruction. When helping students build ideas related to energy conservation and transfer, the *NGSS* stress the importance of building an evidence base over time that makes it apparent to students that a scientific conception of energy can give a more complete picture of the world.

CONSERVATION OF ENERGY AND ENERGY TRANSFER

As a scientific idea, energy is essentially an accounting system. The law of conservation of energy tells us that the total energy of an isolated system cannot change. If we determine a value for the total energy of an isolated system, this value cannot change as events unfold within the system. If we observe that the value does change, then the system is not actually isolated—energy must have been transferred into or out of our system of interest. Thus, energy conservation is inextricably connected with the ideas of energy transfer and systems. To empirically validate the law of conservation of energy, it is essential to investigate very carefully defined "isolated" systems, that is, systems in which energy is not transferred in or out. Before we can apply the conservation of energy, we must carefully define our system of interest and consider whether it is reasonable to assume that energy transfers across system boundaries are negligible or zero.

For example, a swinging pendulum can be an excellent example of energy conservation because carefully designed pendulums can swing almost as high as their release point, but never higher. (Among others, retired Massachusetts Institute of Technology professor Walter Lewin is the subject of several YouTube videos in which he uses a finely crafted pendulum to demonstrate just how well a pendulum can conserve energy [that is, minimize transfers to its surroundings as it swings].) From the pendulum's height above the ground at any point in its swing, we can determine the gravitational potential energy in the pendulum–Earth system (using the formula mgh). Suppose we raise the pendulum to a height such that the system has 10 joules (J; a unit for measuring energy) of gravitational potential energy when it is at rest. As we release the pendulum and it swings downward, the system has less gravitational potential energy due to the decreasing separation between the pendulum and the Earth. If we assume that the pendulum–Earth system conserves energy (has no transfers into or out of it), the total energy of the system will remain 10 J. Thus, at a point when there are 7 J of gravitational potential energy (due to the height of the pendulum above the ground), there must be 3 J of kinetic energy (due to the speed of the pendulum). Knowing this, it is possible to predict the speed of the pendulum using the equation for calculating kinetic energy ($\frac{1}{2}mv^2$). The problem is that the calculated value of the speed of the pendulum is always lower than what we measure. If we have a very good pendulum, it will only be a little bit lower; if the pendulum is not very well designed (e.g., the hanging mass catches a lot of air as it moves), the speed will be way off. Applying the law of conservation of energy to the pendulum–Earth system will give us very good predictions for the pendulum's motion if it transfers a negligible amount of energy to the surroundings as it moves. However, if the pendulum transfers a substantial amount of energy to its surroundings, then the predictions will be so bad that they may actually make it seem as if energy is not conserved at all. In virtually all everyday systems, energy is not obviously conserved because substantial energy transfers are taking place across their boundaries.

Energy transfers occur through a variety of mechanisms: mechanical processes (forces acting on an object or system), electrical processes (moving charges), conduction (collisions between particles), convection (bulk movement of particles), electromagnetic radiation (light and other electromagnetic waves), and sound (vibrations in physical media). Energy transfer mechanisms carry energy from one place to another within a system and across system boundaries. As these transfers occur, systems tend toward more stable and uniform states.

Consider a metal spoon that is heated at one end and then removed from the heat source. As it is heated, the atoms at the end being heated will begin to move faster, and these atoms will collide with those adjacent to them, which will result in the initially faster-moving atom slowing down and the initially slower-moving atom speeding up. As these random collisions continue, the most statistically likely scenario is the one in which faster-moving molecules are distributed evenly throughout the spoon. This energy transfer process is called conduction, and it always happens such that energy is transferred from hotter areas to colder areas until fast-moving molecules are evenly distributed—that is, until all areas of the spoon reach the same temperature. Of course, we know from experience that a hot spoon does not stay hot for long, so what happens to this energy? If we are in the kitchen, most of the energy is transferred from the spoon to the surrounding air via molecular collisions (and some is also transferred to the surroundings as infrared radiation, which is emitted as the molecules vibrate) until

the spoon and the air reach the same temperature. This transfer happens because the spoon is not an isolated system: It interacts with its surroundings. If the spoon is in a big enough room, we are unlikely to ever notice the very slight increase in air temperature that occurred during this transfer of energy. Thus, it is easy to think that the energy contained within the hot spoon simply disappeared over time. In fact, we say that the energy has dissipated as it becomes more spread out.

The dissipation of energy can make energy conservation quite difficult to notice, especially if there are transfers occurring between a relatively small system (like our spoon) and a relatively large one (like the entire Earth's atmosphere). In most cases, when it seems like some stored energy is "used up," the culprit is energy dissipation. In the battery-powered flashlight discussed above, the bulk of the energy stored in the battery is ultimately transferred to the surrounding environment as faster-moving air molecules (i.e., thermal energy) and light waves (i.e., electromagnetic radiation) traveling through space (which will eventually transfer their energy to another system when they impinge on it).

When teaching about energy conservation in real systems (such as a swinging pendulum that will eventually slow down and stop), it is tempting to ask students to take it on faith that the missing energy was transferred to the surroundings; the evidence for quantitative conservation can be very subtle indeed. Thus, the *Framework* and the *NGSS* do not introduce quantitative conservation until the high school level, when students are capable of gathering and interpreting the evidence for it. In the earlier grades, students should be building a set of experiences in which they recognize evidence for energy changes and transfers.

4

BY THE END OF GRADE 5

At the elementary level, students should focus on gathering evidence of energy transfers, for example, when objects collide such that one slows down as the other speeds up. Phenomena such as electric circuits, heating by light, or the generation of sound by vibrating objects can also provide rich and comprehensible evidence for energy transfers. The main objective of energy instruction at the elementary level is to provide intentional experiences in which students observe phenomena with an energy perspective in mind. Rather than formally tracking energy transfers, students should focus on connecting energy transfer processes such as electricity, light, sound, or forces to changes in objects and systems. This sets the stage for more explicitly tracking energy transfers in middle school.

BY THE END OF GRADE 8

At the middle school level, students should begin to qualitatively track energy transfers in familiar phenomena and define appropriate system boundaries. By connecting changes in energy-related variables across systems (e.g., the speed of an object, the amount of stretch or compression in a spring), students should be able to identify increases and decreases in the energy of systems and objects as phenomena occur and to recognize that when the energy of one object or system decreases, the energy of at least one other must increase. Further, students should begin to identify appropriate system boundaries (e.g., what set of objects should be included in a system) to understand when energy is transferred into or out of the system of interest. By qualitatively tracking energy transfers between familiar systems, students begin to build a sense of conservation that will be further developed in high school.

BY THE END OF GRADE 12

By the end of high school, students should be able to quantitatively model energy conservation within systems in which energy transfers into and out of the system are known. By calculating the total energy available within a system, students should be able to identify limits on its behavior, for example, the maximum speed of a pendulum or the maximum temperature change possible in a sample of water by burning organic matter.

Students should also quantitatively model how energy moves within a system as it spreads out toward a more stable state in which energy is uniformly distributed. For example, students should be able to predict the final temperature of a cup of room temperature water when an ingot of aluminum is taken from an ice bath and placed in the water.

PS3.C: Relationship Between Energy and Forces
COMMON PRIOR CONCEPTIONS

It is very common for students to confuse the concepts of energy and force by associating each with a general type of impetus that is responsible for causing things to happen (Lacy et al. 2014). For example, students often think that a thrown object will carry some sort of "force energy" with it that gradually fades away until the object comes to rest again. Indeed, the concepts of force and energy are inextricably linked, but they are distinct scientific ideas.

FORCES AND ENERGY TRANSFER PROCESSES

Forces are responsible for changing the speed of an object, and anytime this happens, energy is transferred. When forces act between objects, they are mediated by a "field."

Students are typically familiar with fields in their everyday lives if they have ever noticed that one magnet can exert a force on another even if the two are not in contact with each other. The magnetic fields surrounding the magnets interact such a way that each magnet experiences a push that is equal in magnitude and opposite in direction compared with the other. Similarly, the Earth pulls downward on all of us, and we pull upward on it—even if we are not touching it—via a gravitational field that mediates the force of gravity between each of us and the Earth. For both magnets and gravity, the farther the interacting objects are from each other, the weaker the field becomes. This is why we cannot detect the magnetic force between magnets if they are very far from each other and why the Earth has a much larger effect on our Moon's orbit than does Venus.

It turns out that *every* force is mediated by a field. Even our everyday "contact" forces (e.g., friction, normal force) are really macroscopic manifestations of the electromagnetic fields acting between atoms and molecules. (The reader should notice the connection of this DCI to PS2: Forces and Interactions.) When, for example, one billiard ball collides with another, the molecules of each never actually touch; rather, they get very close until the electromagnetic fields surrounding the molecules are strong enough to result in a repulsive force between the two billiard balls that is strong enough to suddenly alter their motion. In fact, every force in the known universe is one of four fundamental forces, and each is mediated by a field (see Chapter 3, p. 33).

Energy is transferred between objects and systems because of fields. Mechanical transfer processes, conduction/convection, and sound all transfer energy via forces between particles or objects, and these forces are mediated by fields between the interacting objects. Electromagnetic radiation and electrical processes are mediated by electromagnetic fields that propagate through space and through materials to move energy from one place to another.

POTENTIAL ENERGY AND FORCES

When a brick is lifted above the ground and dropped, the kinetic energy with which it will strike the ground will increase as the height of the drop is increased. That is, the gravitational potential energy of the brick–Earth system will increase as the separation of the brick and Earth increases. The gravitational potential energy of this system depends on the arrangement of the objects in it: The closer the brick and the Earth are to each other, the less potential energy is in the system. Further, the gravitational potential energy is due to the force acting between the brick and the Earth, so we can think of this gravitational potential energy as being "stored" in the gravitational field between the Earth and the brick.

Every potential energy is connected to a particular force. (Note that though every potential energy is associated with a force, not every force is associated with a potential energy. Only "conservative" forces store potential energy. A conservative force is one that transfers energy to an object if it moves in one direction and from the object if it moves in the other, such that if the object begins and ends in the same place, the total

4

energy transferred to the object by the force will be zero.) Gravitational potential energy is associated with the gravitational force that is mediated by a gravitational field. Elastic potential energy is associated with the electromagnetic forces between atoms and molecules. Nuclear energy is associated with the "strong" force acting between nucleons. Chemical energy is associated with the electromagnetic forces within and between atoms. Chemical energy is determined not only by electromagnetic forces that exist between protons and electrons within an atom (which hold atoms together), but also the electromagnetic forces between atoms that result in atomic bonding (which hold molecules together). For each example of potential energy listed above, the way to change its magnitude is to change the arrangement of the interacting objects or particles. To change the potential energy associated with a molecule, the arrangement of the molecule must change. During chemical reactions that release energy, atoms rearrange from a high potential energy arrangement to a lower potential energy arrangement, and the difference in the potential energy is typically manifested as an increase in kinetic energy of the newly formed molecules and/or as light emitted into the surroundings.

BY THE END OF GRADE 5

At this level, students are just beginning to build their understanding of energy and force. Though these ideas are connected by the notion of fields, the idea of fields should not yet be introduced. Instead, students should predict and describe energy transfers when a contact force acts between objects. (Note that students at the elementary level should learn that there can be forces between objects that do not touch, for example, magnetism and gravity. However, students are not yet ready to use fields to explain how this happens. Thus, fields should not be discussed in the context of energy transfers either.) Though phenomena under investigation should include forces, the emphasis here is on the energy changes, not the forces acting between objects. It is a good idea to avoid the term potential energy in elementary school when discussing devices such as batteries or fuel; rather, the term stored is more appropriate at this age level because it more clearly illustrates that the energy associated with those devices exists at all times. The term potential may indicate to students that the devices have the potential to have energy.

BY THE END OF GRADE 8

In middle school, students begin to more formally investigate forces and Newton's laws. By the end of middle school, students should be able to connect transfers of energy to the equal and opposite forces acting between two colliding objects. As students begin to discuss the idea of potential energy in middle school, they should start to recognize that some changes in the energy of systems are observed as changes in the arrangement of objects or particles that exert forces on each other via fields (i.e., potential energy), whereas other changes are related to the motion of objects or particles (i.e., kinetic or thermal energy). Students should also be able to identify various mechanisms for transferring energy between systems, such as light (radiation), electricity, and collisions between objects or particles.

BY THE END OF GRADE 12

By the end of high school, students should be able to connect changes in energy to forces acting between objects and calculate the magnitude of these changes. Further, they should connect changes in potential energy to changes in the forces and fields between objects that interact at a distance. For example, students should be able to calculate the electric potential energy changes between two charged particles that change position relative to each other. Additionally, they should be able to connect the energy released or absorbed in chemical reactions to changes in the electric fields acting between particles.

PS3.D: Energy in Chemical Processes and Everyday Life

COMMON PRIOR CONCEPTIONS

Students commonly think that energy conservation is a daily lifestyle choice rather than a physical law of nature and believe that the energy stored in fuels is used up and released over time. Students often think that in chemical and biological processes, chemical bonds store energy and that energy is released when these bonds are broken (Cooper and Klymkowsky 2013).

ENERGY IN CHEMICAL PROCESSES AND EVERYDAY LIFE

When fuel is burned to release energy, fuel molecules and oxygen molecules in the air collide with enough speed (because the temperature is high enough) that they break apart. Because these free atoms are close to each other, they begin to attract one another again in such a way that they form the lowest available potential energy arrangement. The difference in potential

energy from the end state to the beginning state is typically manifested in even faster motion of the molecules, that is, an even higher temperature and even more average kinetic energy per molecule. This increase in kinetic energy can be harnessed to make things happen; for example, the hot gases can be trapped in the piston of a car engine and used to turn a crankshaft, or the hotter molecules can be forced to interact with water thereby heating it into steam, which can then be forced through pipes to turn the blades of a turbine in an electric generator. In fact, most of the electric energy in the world is generated when coal is burned such that the energy released in the burning reaction is used to heat water into steam, which can be forced through a turbine to generate electricity. Nuclear power works in a similar way way: A nuclear reaction (as opposed to a chemical reaction) heats water into steam, which turns an electric turbine.

Most of the time, using energy resources involves the transfer of energy from natural systems (e.g., energy stored in fields between atoms in fossil fuels, thermal energy in rocks deep underground, gravitational potential energy in water in a reservoir) so that the kinetic energy of water or steam increases. This fast-moving water or steam is then forced to turn an electric turbine to generate electricity. There are exceptions such as wind turbines, which turn an electric turbine using moving air, and photovoltaic cells, which capture energy in transit from the Sun (light) to excite electrons that can then be forced to travel through an electric circuit.

Regardless of the energy resource, it is impossible to capture 100% of the stored energy (this is known as the second law of thermodynamics). Invariably, some of the stored energy is transferred to thermal energy in the device (e.g.,

4

engine, photovoltaic cell) and the surroundings. Eventually, this thermal energy spreads out, or dissipates. This thermal energy still exists, but is difficult to use because it is so spread out. Scientists refer to this energy as "lost."

When energy resources are exploited such that the energy stored in them is used to run devices, the released energy is transferred to useful work (i.e., what we wanted to make happen) and to energy lost to the surroundings as thermal energy. In fact, in virtually all of our powered devices, *most* of the energy transferred from energy resources is lost to the surroundings. A car engine is typically about 25–30% efficient, meaning that roughly three quarters of the energy released from burning gasoline is not available for making the car move. In a car engine, even energy used to turn the crankshaft is eventually transferred to the surroundings in the form of thermal energy as the car slows down and stops. Thus, scientists often refer to the energy transferred from energy sources as "used" because it is not easy to recover and use again. While it still exists (i.e., is not "used up"), it is for all practical purposes gone. Energy is always conserved, but nature makes no guarantee that it will be easy for us to use it.

Luckily for us, the plants on Earth have evolved to be capable of capturing and concentrating energy so that it is readily available for later use. Living plants absorb energy from sunlight and use it to rearrange water and air atoms from a relatively low potential energy state to a higher potential energy state. This process is called photosynthesis, and it is how plants make food (glucose). This process is far from being 100% efficient (most plants transfer less than 5% of the light that hits their leaves to the food molecules they construct), but photosynthesis is critical for all life on Earth. Plants and animals rely on the energy stored by plants in glucose to carry on their life functions, such as moving, constructing tissues, or staying warmer than their surroundings. When these plants and animals die, their tissues are an energy resource because the atoms in them continue to be arranged in a relatively high potential energy configuration.

Fossil fuels, such as coal, oil, and natural gas, are energy resources formed from the tissues of once-living plants and animals. These are valuable energy resources because they are highly concentrated, that is, they contain a lot of available energy per unit mass. These fuels are so energy dense because they contain hydrocarbons (molecules consisting entirely of hydrogen and carbon, which burn very easily and efficiently) that were synthesized over millions of years from the energy-rich tissues in once-living plants and animals. Fossil fuels are highly convenient and useful energy resources because of this energy density and because they can be burned easily at any time. However, as a part of the burning process, fossil fuels also release carbon dioxide (burning reactions *always* require oxygen and release carbon dioxide and water) and other chemicals, which are considered pollutants that contribute to environmental problems such as global warming. Further, it takes a very long time for fossil fuels to be formed; most of the fossil fuels we find on Earth have existed for hundreds of millions of years.

Scientists and policymakers are concerned with finding and using energy resources that are renewed on a much faster timeline than fossil fuels and/or resources that can be considered inexhaustible (such as sunlight and wind). While using these nonfossil fuel resources is scientifically possible, making practical and economical

devices to do it is an important engineering problem for the 21st century.

BY THE END OF GRADE 5

In elementary school, students should become familiar with the idea that energy in plants and animals was once energy carried to Earth in the form of sunlight. While many students investigate light as a necessary ingredient for plant growth, the focus of this investigation is often not on the energy stored in plants. In elementary school, students can close the loop between sunlight and energy resources by considering how, after plants grow, plant-made tissues can provide energy to animals when they are consumed as food or can be used in other ways (i.e., burned) to make things happen. Further, students in elementary school can design and test devices such as rubber band–powered propeller airplanes, windmills, or solar cookers. When building these devices, students should be encouraged to identify evidence for the energy transfers that are taking place (e.g., sound, light, heat, and changes in the speed of objects).

BY THE END OF GRADE 8

At this level, students should develop a more sophisticated understanding of photosynthesis and be able to connect this process to energy changes both during the photosynthesis reaction and during processes such as cellular respiration and burning, in which the energy stored by photosynthesis is released. In addition to exploring photosynthesis and cellular respiration as chemical processes that store and release energy, students should investigate energy changes that take place in other chemical reactions, for example,

reactions that result in temperature changes or can be used to construct a simple battery.

In addition to gathering evidence of energy changes in chemical reactions, students should also design and test devices to perform a particular function and track energy changes that occur as these devices operate. For example, students could be challenged to construct a Rube Goldberg machine that uses an energy input to initiate a chain of connected events that illustrate as many different mechanisms of energy transfer as possible (e.g., electricity, heating, collisions between objects). By tracking evidence of energy inputs and outputs within systems and subsystems, students should qualitatively consider the apparent energy efficiency of the devices they construct and recognize that some devices are more efficient than others based on the amount of energy that is transferred out of the system as thermal energy.

BY THE END OF GRADE 12

In high school, students are ready to conduct a more quantitative analysis of the efficiency of devices and to explain efficiency differences in terms of increases in thermal energy of the device and its surroundings. For example, students can burn a marshmallow to heat a sample of water and use temperature changes in the water and nutritional information for the energy content of a marshmallow to evaluate the efficiency of their devices and to construct a quantitative model of the energy flow as the marshmallow burns.

Students should also recognize that the arrangement of mutually interacting atoms in foods and fuels, which can be burned to release energy, stores energy that was transferred from the Sun via light. Students should be able to construct the chain of events that connects the energy

released by nuclear fusion in the Sun to the energy released when food and fuels are burned on Earth, and they should be able to connect energy transfers in this chain of events to changes in potential energy associated with the arrangement of particles during chemical reactions.

Students should recognize the importance of chemical reactions, especially between organic materials and oxygen (as in cellular respiration and burning), in transferring energy through living and designed systems. By focusing on energy changes in chemical reactions, high school students should be well positioned to compare the use of energy resources based on efficiency, energy density, waste products, and sustainability. At these grades, students should be able to design and test devices, such as simple calorimeters, electric motors, or compound pulley systems with different mechanical advantages, and gather data from them to quantitatively compare their efficiency.

What Approaches Can We Use to Teach About This Disciplinary Core Idea?

By the End of Grade 5

A group of educators from TERC (Tissue Engineering Research Center) and Tufts University has been working on how to lay a foundation for energy learning among upper elementary students that is aligned with the recommendations of the *NGSS* (Crissman et al. 2015; Lacy et al. 2014). In their approach, they focus on helping students develop an "energy lens" by prompting students to consider a consistent set of questions

FIGURE 4.1

A Student Represents the Energy Transfers That Occur When Marbles Collide.

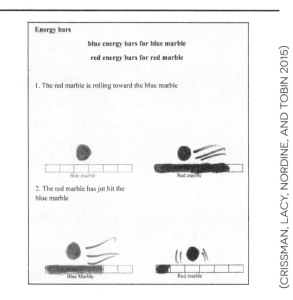

(CRISSMAN, LACY, NORDINE, AND TOBIN 2015)

across a range of energy-related phenomena. The questions are as follows:

- What is the system of interest?

- What observable or measurable changes or other interesting behaviors are taking place?

- Where in the system are energy changes occurring?

- Where does the energy come from?

- Where does the energy go?

- What is the evidence for our answers?

By focusing students on these questions, the educators prompt students to consider the notions of systems, measurable changes, energy transfers, and evidence as they explore everyday devices

FIGURE 4.2

Example of an Energy Conversion Diagram as Used in the IQWST Curriculum

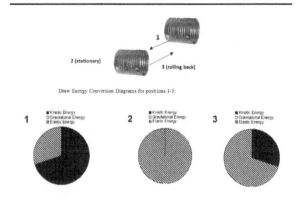

Note that the can starts rolling at position I because the rubber band inside the can is already twisted up when the can is released.

FIGURE 4.3

Example of Combining an Energy Conservation Diagram and an Energy Transfer Diagram From the IQWST Curriculum

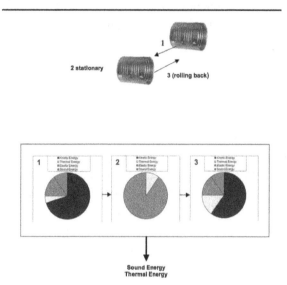

and phenomena. Among these phenomena are rubber band–powered propellers, simple battery-powered circuits, colliding marbles, and hand-cranked electric generators. When considering the role of energy in these examples, Lacy and her colleagues ask students to represent energy changes and transfers through simple semiquantitative representations. Figure 4.1 shows how upper elementary students can represent the energy transfers that occur when a red and blue marble collide.

By the End of Grade 8

A group of educators from several universities collaborated to create a middle school curriculum known as IQWST, which stands for Investigating and Questioning Our World Through Science and Technology (Krajcik et al. 2012). In this curriculum, students learn about energy by tracking

energy transformations (e.g., gravitational potential energy transforming into kinetic energy as a ball falls) in everyday phenomena. (Although IQWST emphasizes the importance of energy transformations in making sense of phenomena, the *Framework* emphasizes the role of energy transfers between systems and the "unitary" nature of energy [i.e., that all energy is fundamentally the same]. The effect of a transformation-based vs. a transfer-based perspective on energy learning in middle school is a subject of ongoing research.) Students track energy changes by using a set of factors and indicators to identify changes in energy forms as phenomena occur. Factors are measurable variables that affect the amount of an energy form (i.e., mass and speed for kinetic energy), and indicators are the observable variables that determine whether an energy form is involved in a particular phenomenon (i.e., speed

4

for kinetic energy). Students construct energy conversion diagrams to track energy changes within systems and energy transfer diagrams to track energy flow between systems. Figure 4.2 (p. 71) shows how students can draw an energy conversion diagram to track energy forms as they change with a special "rollback" can moves back and forth on a table. (A "rollback" can has a hanging mass in it that twists up a rubber band as it rolls, which causes it to slow down, stop, and turn around.)

Figure 4.3 (p. 71) shows how, as instruction continues, an energy conversion diagram and energy transfer diagram can be combined to explain why a rollback can slows down and eventually stops.

By using a set of factors and indicators to construct representations of energy conversions and transfers in everyday systems, students advance beyond an elementary school understanding of energy and become better prepared to develop a quantitative understanding of energy conservation when they enter high school.

By the End of Grade 12

Roberta Tanner, a physics teacher from Colorado, teaches a lesson sequence to her students in which they investigate and compare the performance of incandescent light bulbs, compact fluorescent (CFL) bulbs, and light-emitting diode (LED) bulbs. The lessons come at the end of a physics unit on energy. Prior to investigating the bulbs, students are prompted to consider proposed legislation to phase out incandescent bulbs and are asked to consider pros and cons of such a law. During the investigation, students directly measure the light intensity from different types of bulbs at a given distance and use these data, along with the nominal power rating

of each bulb, to compare the energy efficiency of the bulbs. After the lab, students explore energy production in their region and use this information to calculate the carbon dioxide produced in a household using each type of bulb over time. Finally, students are prompted to assume the role of a political leader and investigate other bulb factors (e.g., cost, expected life) so they can make a recommendation for legislation.

In her lesson, Roberta involves her students in gathering data and performing energy calculations for real devices, exploring important chemical reactions for the production of electricity, and considering implications for energy policy. In doing so, her students must reach beyond what is traditionally taught in a physics classroom to make connections to other scientific disciplines and to the social sciences.

Conclusion

Students hear and use the word "energy" from a very early age, but developing an understanding of energy as a scientific concept requires careful instruction over the course of many years. The *Framework* (NRC 2012) and *NGSS* (NGSS Lead States 2013) call for a new approach to energy instruction that builds an increasingly sophisticated evidence base over time to support students' development of more integrated understandings of energy. By focusing on building an evidence base to support the introduction of new ideas about energy over time, this approach mirrors the scientific process and puts students in a stronger position to see how the scientific concept of energy can be useful in their everyday lives. If students develop a deep understanding of a small set of fundamental energy ideas over time by exploring real-world phenomena, then they

are well positioned to continue using the concept after they finish school as they reason about energy-related decisions in their everyday lives and participate in energy policy discussions that affect our environment and social systems.

REFERENCES

American Association for the Advancement of Science (AAAS). 1993. *Benchmarks for science literacy.* New York: Oxford University Press.

Boyes, E., and M. Stanisstreet. 1990. Misunderstandings of "law" and "conservation": A study of pupils' meanings for these terms. *School Science Review* 72 (258): 51–57.

Bryce, T. G. K., and K. MacMillan. 2009. Momentum and kinetic energy: Confusable concepts in secondary school physics. *Journal of Research in Science Teaching* 46 (7): 739–761.

Chen, R., A. Eisenkraft, D. Fortus, J. S. Krajcik, K. Neumann, J. C. Nordine, and A. Scheff, eds. 2014. *Teaching and learning of energy in K–12 education.* New York: Springer.

Cooper, M. M., and M. W. Klymkowsky. 2013. The trouble with chemical energy: Why understanding bond energies requires an interdisciplinary systems approach. *Cell Biology Education* 12 (2): 306–312.

Crissman, S., S. Lacy, J. C. Nordine, and R. Tobin. 2015. Looking through the energy lens. *Science and Children* 52 (6): 26–31.

Driver, R., A. Squires, P. Rushworth, and V. Wood-Robinson. 1994. *Making sense of secondary science: research into children's ideas.* New York: Routledge.

Driver, R., and L. Warrington. 1985. Students' use of the principle of energy conservation in problem situations. *Physics Education* 20 (4): 171–176.

Feynman, R. P., R. B. Leighton, M. Sands, and E. M. Hafner. 1965. The Feynman lectures on physics, vol. 1. *American Journal of Physics* 33 (9): 750.

Fortus, D., and J. S. Krajcik. 2012. Curriculum coherence and learning progressions. In *The international handbook of research in science education*, 2nd ed., ed. B. Fraser, K. Tobin, and C. McRobbie. Dordrecht, the Netherlands: Springer-Verlag.

Fortus, D., L. M. Sutherland Adams, J. Krajcik, and B. Reiser. 2015. Assessing the role of curriculum coherence in student learning about energy. *Journal of Research in Science Teaching* 52 (10): 1408–1425.

Krajcik, J. S., B. J. Reiser, L. M. Sutherland, and D. Fortus. 2012. *IQWST: Investigating and questioning our world through science and technology, (Middle School Science Curriculum Materials).* Greenwich, CT: Activate Learning.

Lacy, S., R. Tobin, M. Wiser, and S. Crissman. 2014. Looking through the energy lens: A proposed learning progression for energy in grades 3–5. In *Teaching and Learning of Energy in K–12 Education*, ed. R. Chen, A. Eisenkraft, D. Fortus, J. S. Krajcik, K. Neumann, J. C. Nordine, and A. Scheff, 241–266. New York: Springer

Linn, M. C. 2006. The knowledge integration perspective on learning and instruction. In *Cambridge handbook for the learning sciences*, ed. R. K. Sawyer, 243–264. New York: Cambridge University Press.

Liu, X., and A. McKeough. 2005. Developmental growth in students' concept of energy: Analysis of selected items from the TIMSS Database. *Journal of Research in Science Teaching* 42 (5): 493–517.

National Research Council (NRC). 1996. *National science education standards.* Washington, DC: National Academies Press.

National Research Council (NRC). 2012. *A framework for K–12 science education: Practices, crosscutting*

4

concepts, and core ideas. Washington, DC: National Academies Press.

Neumann, K., T. Viering, W. J. Boone, and H. E. Fischer. 2013. Toward a learning progression of energy. *Journal of Research in Science Teaching* 50 (2): 162–188.

NGSS Lead States. 2013. *Next Generation Science Standards: For states, by states.* Washington, DC: National Academies Press. *www.nextgenscience. org/next-generation-science-standards*.

Nordine, J. 2016. *Teaching energy across the sciences, K–12.* Arlington, VA: NSTA Press.

Nordine, J., J. Krajcik, and D. Fortus. 2011. Transforming energy instruction in middle school to support integrated understanding and future learning. *Science Education* 95 (4): 670–699.

Solomon, J. 1983. Messy, contradictory, and obstinately persistent: A study of children's out-of-school ideas about energy. *School Science Review* 65 (231): 225–233.

Trumper, R. 1993. Children's energy concepts: A cross-age study. *International Journal of Science Education* 15 (2): 139–148.

Watts, M. 1983. Some alternative views of energy. *Physics Education* 18 (5): 213–217.

CHAPTER 5

CORE IDEA PS4

WAVES AND THEIR APPLICATIONS IN TECHNOLOGIES FOR INFORMATION TRANSFER

David Fortus and Joseph Krajcik

What Is This Disciplinary Core Idea, and Why Is It Important?

Although you may not realize it, and they cannot always be detected without special instruments, waves are *everywhere*. As you read this chapter, there are radio waves going through your body. Stop reading for a minute, close your eyes, and concentrate on your surroundings, your breathing, and your heartbeat. Can you hear anything, or is it completely silent? Most likely there is something you can hear, evidence that you are immersed in a sea of sound waves. Start reading again. How can you read this text? Light waves are being scattered by the page (if you're reading this on paper) or being generated by a screen (if you're reading this on an electronic device) and reaching your eyes. Are there electric apparatuses near you? Every electric device generates electromagnetic waves. Think about cell phones, GPS devices, heat lamps, x-rays, microwave ovens, police radars, lasers, antennas, stereo systems, computer networks, ultrasound imaging devices, and MRI scanners. Think about contact lenses, sunburns, sunglasses, earthquakes, optical fibers, surfing, telescopes, and microscopes. Are these apparatuses and phenomena relevant to you and your students' lives? Is it important that students have some understanding of how they work? If yes, then waves are important, because waves play a key role in each of these apparatuses and phenomena and in many, many others things as well. In fact, many of the technologies developed in the 20th century and those under development now are dependent on waves. For example, stealth technology is based on waves and uses ideas such as reflection, transmission, absorption, and superposition (which will be described in detail later in this chapter) to render stealth planes nearly invisible to radars. Understanding wave properties and the interactions of electromagnetic radiation with matter is critical to the investigation of nature at all scales, including the invisible world of atoms and molecules and the far away world of stars and galaxies. Wave properties and interactions of electromagnetic radiation with matter explain how information can be transferred over long distances and stored as digital information.

In contrast to the *National Science Education Standards* (NRC 1996) and the AAAS *Benchmarks for Science Literacy* (AAAS 1993), *A Framework for K–12 Science Education* (*Framework*; NRC 2012) emphasizes the dependence of modern technologies, especially communications technologies, on

5

waves. It also highlights the role waves play in transferring energy and information from one location to another. The concepts of wave properties and the interaction of electromagnetic waves with matter explain many important phenomena in our world. We now present the components of the disciplinary core idea (DCI) in the *Framework* that deals with waves.

PS4: Waves and Their Applications in Technologies for Information Transfer provides answers to the question, "How are waves used to transfer energy and information?" This DCI is made up of three component ideas. PS4.A: Wave Properties examines the question, "What are the characteristic properties and behaviors of waves?" PS4.B: Electromagnetic Radiation provides insights into three questions: "What is light?" "How can one explain the varied effects that involve light?" and "What other forms of electromagnetic radiation are there?" Finally, PS4.C: Information Technologies and Instrumentation builds understanding of answers to the question, "How are instruments that transmit and detect waves used to extend human senses?"

PS4.A Wave Properties

PS4.A: Wave Properties describes the properties of waves. It provides an answer to the question, "What are waves?" Think of a simple example that many of us have experienced: a stone thrown into a pond of water. Before the stone hits the pond, the water's surface is relatively flat and smooth. After the stone hits the water and disappears below the surface, circles centered where the stone hit spread out and away from where they were created (Figure 5.1). These spreading circles and the area between them on the surface of the water are an example of a wave.

FIGURE 5.1

Waves in a Pond

The definition of a wave is a disturbance that propagates—that is, moves or spreads—through space. In the case that we just imagined of a stone being thrown into a pond, the disturbance was the deformation of the water's surface caused by the entrance of the stone into the water (the stone applied a force to the water, which caused a change in the water's motion; the water started to move down and away from the stone; see Chapter 3, p. 33, on PS2: Motion and Stability: Forces and Interactions). The spreading out of the circles was the propagation of the disturbance. Because the wave is moving, it has energy (see Chapter 4, p. 55, on PS3: Energy).

Let's see how this definition works in another case. If you knock on one end of a table with your knuckle, you can feel the knock with your other hand if you place it at the other end of the table, or you can hear the knock if you place your ear on the table. What does this have to do with waves? When your knuckle hits the table, it pushes down on the table, making a small deformation in the table's surface. Although you can't see it, this deformation expands out through the table, which is why you can feel and hear it at a distance. The spreading out of the deformation in the table's surface is a wave.

FIGURE 5.2

Stadium Wave

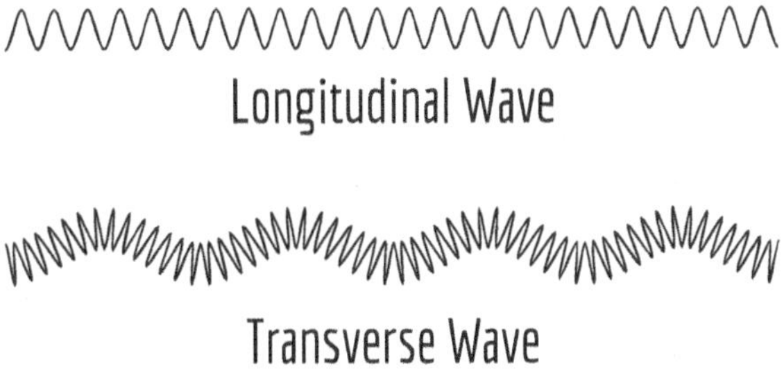

LONGITUDINAL AND TRANSVERSE WAVES

When you throw a stone into a pond, the water's surface bobs up and down. (Actually, the movement of any water particle near the surface is a combination of up and down and back and forth motions.) However, the wave generated by this up-down movement of the water's surface moves horizontally. That is, the direction in which the wave moves is perpendicular to the direction in which the disturbance was made. This is called a transverse wave. There are many kinds of transverse waves. All electromagnetic waves are transverse waves. Think about a human wave in a football stadium. People get up and sit down in their seats, but the wave moves horizontally across the stadium (Figure 5.2). This is an example of a transverse wave.

Now imagine a Slinky that is stretched and lying on the floor. One end is held stationary, and the other end is shaken sideways. A wave is generated and propagates through the toy. Try it! Is this a transverse wave? (A demonstration of transverse waves in a Slinky can be found at

FIGURE 5.3

Waves in a Slinky

Longitudinal Wave

Transverse Wave

www.teachertube.com/viewVideo.php?video_id=75927.) Now instead of shaking the Slinky's end sideways, move it back and forth in the direction in which the Slinky is stretched. Once again, a wave is generated in the Slinky; however, this time the direction of the disturbance is the same as the direction in which the wave travels (Figure 5.3). This is called a longitudinal wave (for a demonstration of longitudinal waves in a Slinky, visit *www.youtube.com/watch?v=y7qS6SyyrFU*). Sound waves traveling through the air are longitudinal waves, with the air molecules moving back and forth in the direction in which the sound wave is traveling. Sound waves moving through solids (like when you knocked on the table with your knuckle) can be both transverse and longitudinal.

WHAT MOVES WHEN A WAVE MOVES?

Above we mentioned that a wave is a moving disturbance. In a pond wave, the disturbance is a depression of the surface of the water. When the wave spreads outward, does the water in the pond move outward with it? The answer is no, because otherwise there would be less water left in the area where the wave originated. The water near the top of the pond moves up and down in a coordinated manner so that the water appears to be moving outward when it is actually only moving up and down. So no water really moves away from the wave's source. You may have seen humans create a wave in a football stadium. As the wave moves across the stadium, do the spectators making the wave actually move horizontally with the wave? No. Every spectator moves up and down in a coordinated manner, but each spectator stays in the place where she began—sitting.

This idea that no material moves permanently from its original location is true for all waves. In a sound wave, for example, the air molecules move a bit back and forth around their original location, but they stay on average where they were before the wave was generated and do not move with the wave. Flap your hand at your ear. You can feel the air that is being forced at your ear by your hand. The air molecules are being moved from their original location toward your ear. Now hold your hand near your ear and snap your fingers. You can clearly hear the snapping sound but not feel any wind moving toward your ear. So the sound wave generated by the snapping of your fingers does not cause the air molecules to move toward your ear. This can be seen very nicely in a simulation from Pennsylvania State University's acoustics program at *www.acs.psu.edu/drussell/Demos/waves/Lwave-v8.gif*. The simulation shows the propagation of a sound wave. Follow the red particle. You will see that it moves back and forth but does not propagate with the sound wave. Here, too, you can see why sound waves in the air are longitudinal waves: The air particles move back and forth in the same direction in which the wave travels.

Some students consider sound to be an entity that is carried by individual molecules as they move through a medium (Linder and Erickson 1989). Just as particles can have energy, they think

that particles can have sound, that the particle picks up the sound at one place (e.g., a loudspeaker or a tuning fork), carry it from that place to another (e.g., a microphone or an ear), and then release it there. In this view, the more particles that carry the sound, the louder the sound is. This conception of sound is based on the mistaken idea that the particles of the medium actually move along with the wave or that there are special sound particles that differ from the particles that make up the medium. Accordingly, in this scenario, these sound particles are created at the sound's source and destroyed when the sound is heard, which contradicts the law of energy conservation. Another problem with this notion is that there are infinitely different kinds of sound; in what way does the sound carried by the particles in one case differ from the sounds in other cases? Or are there an infinite number of different kinds of sound particles?

A more sophisticated conception than the one above, but still mistaken, is that sound is a physical entity that is transferred from one molecule to another through a medium. In this case, sound is still something carried by the particles of the medium, but instead of moving through the medium, the particles collide with each other and in each collision transfer some sound from one to another.

WAVE DIMENSIONALITY

Some waves spread out in three dimensions throughout space, others spread out in two dimensions over a surface, and others spread out in one dimension. When you speak, you create sound waves. People in front of you, behind you, to your sides, above you, and below you can all hear you. This is lucky because it means that when you are teaching you needn't repeat yourself 30 times while facing every student in your class. The sound waves you generate spread out in all dimensions, so they are three-dimensional (3-D) waves.

When you knocked on the table, you couldn't hear the sound *in* the table unless you pressed your ear to the table because the sound *in* the table spread out only *in* the table (you could hear the sound of the knocking in the air, but that is because the knocking created a sound wave in the air as well as in the table). The table is relatively thin, so you can say that the sound wave spreads out in the table only horizontally and not vertically, so the sound wave in the table is a two dimensional (2-D) wave.

If you take a pipe or a water hose and speak into it, nobody around you can hear you. However, if somebody holds up the other end of the hose to their ear, they can hear you quite well. In this case, the sound wave traveled in only one direction, along the water hose. Since it propagated in only one direction, we say that it is a one dimensional (1-D) wave.

So a sound wave can be a 1-D, 2-D, or 3-D wave, depending on the structure or configuration of the environment in which it propagates.

Why is the dimensionality of a wave important? It turns out that the dimensionality of a wave determines the rate at which the intensity of the wave decreases. The relation between the rate at which a wave's intensity decreases and its dimensionality is a result of the law of conservation of energy. When 3-D waves spread out, like sound waves disseminating from your mouth, the intensity of the waves decrease as the waves get farther from your mouth. This is why your voice sounds weaker the farther the listener is from you. Close up, it may be loud; far away, it sounds faint. It turns out that all 3-D waves decrease in intensity at the same rate, regardless of whether they are sound waves or electromagnetic waves or tectonic waves or any other kind of wave. The intensity of all 3-D waves depends on $1/r^2$, where r is the distance of the wave from its source. Thus, as the distance of a 3-D wave from its source doubles, its intensity decreases fourfold.

When a 2-D wave spreads out, its intensity also decreases as it gets farther away from its source. However, the rate at which it decreases is different from the rate at which a 3-D wave decreases. The intensity of all 2-D waves, regardless of what kind they are, decreases at a rate of $1/r$, meaning that when the distance of the wave from its source doubles, the intensity of the wave is halved.

When a wave's dimensionality is 1-D, it does not spread out; it just moves from one place to another. Its intensity does not decrease but remains the same. So the intensity of the sound from your mouth decreases as it gets farther from you unless the sound waves are channeled into a tube where it can travel long distances without getting weaker.

WAVELENGTH

When a stone is thrown into a pond, not just one ripple is made, but several. We see concentric circles traveling outward from the place where the stone hit the water (see Figure 5.1, p. 76). If we look a bit closer, we will see that the distance between the circles is the same and that this distance is maintained as the ripples move outward. The distance between any two ripples is called the wave's wavelength. The Greek letter λ (lambda) is used to represent the wavelength.

Every wave has a wavelength. If you revisit the simulation of a sound wave mentioned on page 78, you will see that there is a constant distance

5

between the areas of high particle density that move to the right. This distance is the wavelength.

SPEED

Waves also have a speed at which they spread out. Every type of wave has a speed which is dependent on the medium through which the wave is traveling. Thus, the speed of sound is the speed at which sound waves travel through the air. This speed is temperature dependent but is about 300 m/s at room temperature. Look again at the simulation of sound waves—you will see that the air of high density moves to the right at a constant speed. Sound can also travel through other media. The speed of sound in liquids and in most solids is much faster than in air. The speed of sound in helium is different from in air, which is why voices sound funny if one inhales helium and then speaks while exhaling.

FREQUENCY

Waves have a frequency. When a stone is thrown into a pond, the rings that move outward are generated at a certain frequency, that is, every second a certain number of rings are generated. Look again at the simulation of the sound waves. The areas of high particle density are generated on the left at a constant rate. This rate, the number of areas of high density that are generated every second, is called the wave's frequency. Frequencies can be very low, less than one ripple or one high-density area per second, or very high, thousands or millions or even billions of times per second. Frequencies are measured in hertz (Hz). A sound wave with a frequency of 200 Hz has 200 areas of high density generated per second at the sound's source.

There is a mathematical relation between a wave's wavelength, its frequency, and its speed. The relation is true for *all* waves:

$$v = \lambda \cdot f$$

Here v stands for the wave's speed in [m/s], λ stands for the wave's wavelength in meters, and f stands for the wave's frequency in hertz. The relation between the wavelength and frequency of electromagnetic waves is the same as for all other waves.

AMPLITUDE

Every wave has an amplitude. The amplitude is the magnitude of the disturbance relative to the situation where there is no disturbance. In the case of the water waves, the amplitude is typically given as the maximum height the water reaches above the height of the water in the pond when there is no wave. In Figure 5.4, the original pond level is the horizontal line through the center of the graph, so the amplitude is the height of the tallest part of the wave where it touches the dotted line above the center line For a sound wave, the amplitude is the maximum change in the density of the particles, so it is the density of the particles at areas of maximum density minus the density of the particles when there is no sound wave. The square of the amplitude (A^2) is a measure of the intensity of a wave; the greater the amplitude, the stronger the wave. Thus, a loud sound wave will have a larger amplitude and a soft sound wave will have a smaller amplitude.

SUPERPOSITION

When waves of the same kind (for example, two water waves) meet each other, they add up,

FIGURE 5.4

Amplitude and Wavelength

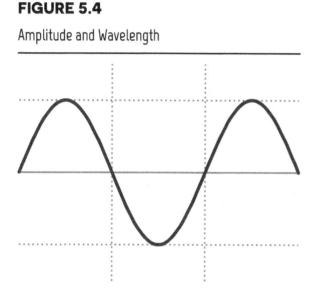

FIGURE 5.5

Superposition of Two Waves

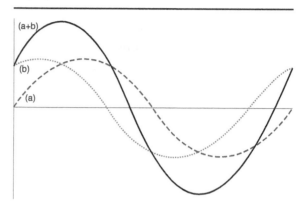

meaning that the height of the surface at any point in the pond will be equal to the height that point would have been if only one of the waves was in the pond *plus* the height of that point if only the second of the waves had been in the pond. Thus, *new height = height*(1) + *height*(2). In Figure 5.5, the height of the solid line at the crest of the wave and at the trough of the wave results from the summation of (a) plus (b). This summation of waves is called superposition. Notice, however, that the height of any point on a wave on the surface of the pond goes up and down, so that sometimes it is above the level of the surface of a quiet pond (positive height) and sometimes it is below this level (negative height). So, during the superposition of two waves the height of any point on the pond's surface may be higher or lower than it would have been if there had been only one wave.

Superposition is important because it helps predict what happens when two or more waves meet in various ways. For example, consider two waves with the same height that interact out of phase—that is, when one wave is increasing

while the other is decreasing. If these two identical waves are exactly out of phase, their sum will be zero and they will cancel out. An example of this being applied in real life is noise-canceling headphones. Noise-canceling headphones generate sound waves that are identical to those coming from the outside (the ambient noise) but opposite in phase. Because they are opposite in phase, the incoming noise is canceled out. DVD players provide another everyday example of superposition. Light is reflected from the DVD so that it is at the same phase or at the opposite phase as the wave that reached it. These two waves superimpose, making either a stronger wave (= 1) or canceling each other out (= 0). Because digital information is encoded as 1s and 0s, this superposition effect enables the digital storage and transfer of information in DVD and CD players. Superposition also allows us to deconstruct complex waves into the sum of many simple waves.

AMPLITUDE DECAY

As was described before in the Wave Dimensionality section (p. 78), the intensity of 2-D and 3-D

waves declines as the waves get farther away from their source. Since the square of a wave's amplitude is related to the wave's intensity, this mean that the wave's amplitude gets smaller as the wave gets farther away from its source. If you look at a water wave, you can see that it slowly dies out, so that after a certain distance from the spot where the stone entered the pond, the wave is no longer visible. When someone is far away from you, they need to shout to be heard because the amplitude (and the intensity) of the sound waves they create decrease as they get farther from the person, so by the time sound waves reach you, they are already much weaker than they were to begin with and are therefore harder to hear.

RESONANCE

Every object, or system, has natural frequencies, which are the frequencies at which waves naturally propagate, or spread, through the system. For example, when the stone was thrown into the pond, the waves that were generated had a frequency. Every time you throw another stone, whether it is bigger or smaller, into the same pond, the waves generated will have the same frequency. Thus, this frequency is a natural characteristic of the pond and has little to do with nature of the perturbation, or disturbance, that causes the waves (the stone entering the water). When you strike a tuning fork or pluck a guitar string, regardless of the force used, the sound wave generated always has the same frequency (in music, frequency is also called "pitch"). So, we say that the tuning fork or the guitar string have a natural frequency. However, systems can be forced to oscillate and generate waves at frequencies that are different from the natural frequency of their materials. For example, the membrane

of a speaker in a stereo system has a natural frequency, but the amplifier can force it to vibrate at many different frequencies, generating a range of sound waves with different frequencies. When a system is forced to generate waves at a certain frequency, this is called the forced frequency. Sometimes, intentionally or unintentionally, the forced frequency is identical to the system's natural frequency. When this happens, the waves generated can get larger and larger, even though the magnitude of the perturbation remains small. This situation is called resonance. It can be very useful, but it can also be catastrophic. It is the principle by which radios and musical wind instruments work. It can also cause a bridge to collapse, as happened to the Tacoma Narrows Bridge in 1940 as shown at *http://en.wikipedia.org/wiki/Tacoma_Narrows_Bridge_(1940)*.

INTERACTIONS WITH OBJECTS

All waves, when they reach a boundary between two objects or materials, behave in a combination of ways: They are reflected, transmitted, and absorbed. For example, how do we hear anything? Sound waves are absorbed by the eardrums, which transfers energy to them and makes them vibrate, generating a signal that is transmitted to the brain. How is an echo created? A sound wave is reflected off a large object, such as a cliff, which is far enough away that we hear the reflected echo noticeably later than we hear our original shout. How do we see? Light reflects off materials and onto our retinas, which transmit a message to the brain. Because different materials absorb different frequencies of light, we see light reflected back in different colors. We see a red sweater because the sweater reflects light with red frequencies and absorbs other frequencies. How does an ultrasound imager work? Ultrasound waves generated in a transducer are transmitted through our bodies and reflected at the interfaces between different tissues.

Allow students to experience simple light phenomena and provide them with relevant data. Next, have students construct models to explain the phenomena. Such experiences provide opportunities for students to make sense of phenomena using the important science practice of modeling and building knowledge of the DCI. This simple model can be expanded as students experience more phenomena and collect additional data.

PS4.B: Electromagnetic (EM) Radiation

PS4.B: Electromagnetic (EM) Radiation explores the question, "What are EM waves?" All electrons create an electromagnetic field in the space around them. When these electrons are forced to move, the electromagnetic field they create changes, first near the electron, then farther away as the change to the electromagnetic field spreads out through space, making an electromagnetic wave. This can occur, for example, when an electric circuit forces electrons to move inside an antenna. If the circuit makes the electrons move at a certain forced frequency, the electromagnetic wave generated can be a radio wave or a microwave, or any other wave in the electromagnetic spectrum. Just as we could see the waves on the surface of a pond or feel or hear the waves in a table, we can detect the electromagnetic waves generated by the electric current. Various instruments such as cell phones or radio receivers can detect and react to certain electromagnetic waves. The water molecules in a piece of food in a microwave can absorb electromagnetic waves created by a microwave. Our eyes, working with our nervous systems, can detect and react to electromagnetic waves in the visible region. Electromagnetic waves have properties like all waves, such as frequency and wavelength.

THE DIMENSIONALITY OF EM WAVES

When you turn on a light bulb, it shines in all directions, so the wave that is being generated is a 3-D wave. But what if light is shined into an optical fiber? The light can move through the fiber just as sound can move through a pipe. In this case, light propagates like a 1-D wave. Depending on the circumstances, EM waves can be 1-D, 2-D, or 3-D.

WAVELENGTH OF EM WAVES

EM waves are propagating perturbations—moving or spreading disturbances—of the EM field. If the EM field were "still" (it never is), the strength and direction of the EM field at any point in space would never change. However, because there are waves, the strength and direction of this field changes with time, getting stronger, then weaker, then stronger, then weaker again, and so on, just as any point on the surface of a pond gets higher and lower repeatedly when there is a water wave. EM waves spread out from sources just like water waves, except they typically expand in 3-D, so they expand as ever-increasing spheres rather than as circles. Just as in water waves, where water doesn't really move from its position but just bobs up and down in a coordinated way, in EM waves, nothing moves; the field just gets stronger and weaker in a coordinated way. Just as in water waves, where there is a constant distance between consecutive circles of the wave (areas where the water surface is high), there is a constant distance between

FIGURE 5.6

The Electromagnetic Spectrum

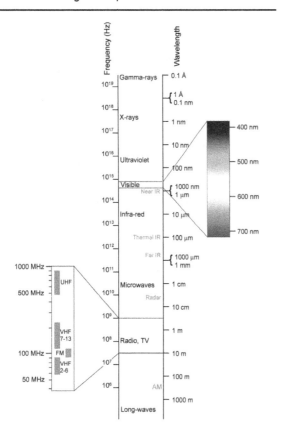

consecutive spheres of the EM wave (areas of maximum EM field strength). Again, this distance is called the wave's wavelength.

SPEED

EM waves are the only type of wave that does not need a medium to propagate. Their speed in a vacuum, regardless of their wavelength, is the speed of light, which is about 300,000 km/s. When EM waves enter a medium, they move slower than they do in a vacuum, but not by much. Their actual speed in a medium depends on the type of medium.

FREQUENCY

The Greek letter ν is used instead of f to represent the frequency, and the letter c is used instead of v to stand for the speed, so the relation between an EM wave's speed, wavelength, and frequency is shown in the following equation:

$$c = \lambda \cdot \nu$$

EM waves are grouped into categories according to their wavelengths and frequencies (Figure 5.6). Radio waves have the longest wavelengths and lowest frequencies; gamma rays have the shortest wavelengths and the highest frequencies.

AMPLITUDE

The amplitude of an EM wave is the difference between the maximum strength of the EM field due to the wave and the strength of the field if there were no wave, just as the amplitude of a water wave is the difference between the maximum height of the water's surface due to the wave and the height of the water's surface if there had been no wave. The greater the amplitude of an EM wave, the stronger its intensity.

RESONANCE OF EM WAVES

As described above, every object has natural frequencies, which are the frequencies at which waves naturally propagate through the system. A laser is an example of the resonance of EM waves. The term *laser* is an acronym that stands for "light amplification by stimulated emission of radiation." Lasers basically amplify light. EM waves are generated at a frequency identical to the natural frequency of an apparatus called a laser cavity, in which the waves combine and get stronger and stronger until they are released outside as a strong EM wave with a single frequency, called a laser beam. In "The Laser at 50," Scientific American (2010) provides an overview of the past, present, and potential future of lasers.

INTERACTION WITH MATTER

As with other waves, when EM waves reach a boundary, they can be reflected, transmitted, or absorbed. Light can be reflected in a single direction by a mirror or in many directions (scattered) by any object, which is how we see objects. Light is transmitted through glass, air, and many other substances. Many EM waves are transmitted through concrete, which is how we can use our cell phones inside buildings. Finally, EM waves are often absorbed by substances, which is why cars get hot in the Sun and food gets warm in a microwave oven. Whenever any type of wave is absorbed, some of its energy is transferred to the object absorbing it, and this energy enables something to happen in that object.

PS4.C: Information Technologies and Instrumentation

PS4.C: Information Technologies and Instrumentation explores the question, "How are instruments that transmit and detect waves used to extend human senses?"

How do you hear things? Your ears detect sound waves. The waves are absorbed by the eardrum, making it vibrate, which in turn generates a signal which is transmitted to the brain. How

FIGURE 5.7

How a Microphone Works

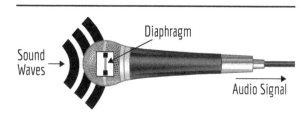

does a microphone detect sound waves? By the same principle: A membrane with a coil attached to it absorbs sound waves, causing it to vibrate, which generates an electric signal (Figure 5.7). For any kind of wave to be detected, it must be absorbed. The absorption of the wave transfers energy from the wave to the object absorbing the wave, and this energy enables something to happen (see Chapter 4, p. 55, on PS3: Energy).

Let's look more closely at how a microphone works. Microphones are devices that convert energy from one form to another. A microphone converts sound waves into electric impulses. All microphones have one aspect in common: They all have diaphragms. A diaphragm is a thin piece of material (such as paper or aluminum) that can vibrate when struck by a sound wave. When the diaphragm vibrates, it causes others parts of the microphone to vibrate as well. These vibrations are converted into electric signals that become the audio signal. A speaker converts the electric signal back into a sound wave. The eardrum is also a diaphragm, that is, a piece of tissue that can vibrate. This idea of a wave being absorbed by a material is fundamental to how materials can detect and transfer information. So hearing is really the detection and conversion of sound waves into some other form of vibrations.

5

HOW DO YOU SEE THINGS?

How we see works on the same principle as how we hear. It is vibrations of waves—EM waves—being absorbed and then converted into another signal. EM waves (in the form of light) from objects are transmitted to and through your eyes until they reach the retina at the back of the eyes where they are absorbed, generating a signal that is transmitted to the brain. How does a camera detect light waves? Either the light is absorbed by a special chip called a charge-coupled device, which generates an electric signal, or the light is absorbed by a special film, causing a chemical reaction that creates bright and dark areas on the film. Smartphones, like cell phones, detect microwaves (a type of EM wave). An antenna absorbs these waves, making electrons in the antenna vibrate back and forth, thus creating an electric current that can be decoded or converted in audio and visual signals. GPS systems do the same. Similarly, when you put your hand near a heat lamp, your hand absorbs infrared light (a type of EM wave), causing your skin become warm. All information transfer occurs by the absorption and conversion of waves.

GENERATION OF WAVES

As described earlier, any perturbation or disturbance that propagates is a wave, so almost anything has the capacity to generate waves. My tapping on the keyboard of my laptop generates sound waves that travel throughout the laptop and the air (that's how I hear the tapping).

EM waves are generated by two primary mechanisms: (1) Any accelerating electric charge creates an EM wave. A charge that oscillates back and forth (as in an antenna) will generate an EM wave that has the same frequency as that of the charge's oscillations. Atoms and molecules in all substances are always vibrating randomly. These particles have electric charges, so they emit EM radiation. At room temperature, this EM radiation lies in the infrared range. If it gets hot enough, the radiation will move to the visible range (which is why hot things glow). (2) In the quantum world, every object has possible energy levels. When an object transitions from a high energy level to a lower one, an EM wave is generated. This is how fluorescent lamps work, how solid-state lasers (such as the type in a CD player) work, and how gamma rays are generated; this is the principle underlying the operation of almost all apparatuses that use a single EM frequency.

TRANSMISSION OF INFORMATION USING WAVES

For information to be transmitted by a wave, it needs to be encoded. Information can be encoded in analog or digital form. In analog encoding, a wave is generated that is similar in "shape" (analogous) to the information being encoded. For example, when I say the word *wave*, my body forces the vocal cords in my throat to vibrate in a certain manner. These vibrations of my vocal cords change the density of the air next to them. This change is a perturbation that then propagates away from my vocal cords as a sound wave until ears or microphones or some other object absorbs part of the wave. This continues until it has insufficient energy to continue the perturbation to any measurable extent, or until other objects absorb the energy. If a graph were made of the change in air density over time due to this sound wave, it would look identical to the displacement of my vocal cords over time: They would have the same frequencies.

If you hold two paper cups with a thread stretched tightly between them and speak into one end, your voice can be heard at the other end. How? The sound waves generated by your vocal cords are absorbed by the base of the paper cup, making it vibrate. The vibrations of the bottom of the paper cup are analogous to those of the sound waves (and therefore analogous to the vibrations of your vocal cords). The vibrations of the paper cup pull and push on the thread, generating a sound wave (again, analogous to the prior vibrations and waves) which propagates along the thread to the other paper cup, and so on. The first paper cup acts like a microphone while the second is similar to a speaker.

Information can also be encoded digitally. In digital encoding, the information is "translated" into a code using on-and-off signals, which are then transmitted analogously. For example, in Morse code, a message is converted into a sequence of short signals, called dots, and long signals, called dashes, separated by short silences. Letters are encoded as unique combinations of dots and dashes. In digital media such as audio CDs, a sound or EM wave can be encoded in a similar way, where bits of information are represented by combinations of zeros and ones.

How Does Student Understanding of This Disciplinary Core Idea Develop Over Time?

One of the key features of DCIs is that they can be taught and learned over multiple grades at increasing levels of depth and sophistication. Let's see how this progression plays out for waves and what kind of simple experiences that require no special equipment can support them.

In the discussion below, what students should know related to a subcomponent of the core idea is shown in italics. This is followed by various potential learning tasks that could support students as they develop this understanding. Learning tasks are described only until the end of middle school because most of the ideas that are appropriate for high school require the use of special equipment.

By the End of Grade 2
PS4.A: WAVE PROPERTIES

- *Waves in water spread out in circles.*

Possible tasks: Students should make repeated observations by dropping objects into a tub of water and throwing stones into ponds. Have students look for patterns. Do the sizes of the waves change with the sizes of the rocks? What happens if the same rock is dropped from different heights? Have students make claims based on the patterns they observe. *Safety note:* Make sure students wear eye protection (safety glasses or goggles) for this task. Use caution when dropping objects so as not to injure feet. Immediately wipe up any water spilled or splashed on the floor to prevent a slip or fall hazard.

- *The surface of the water moves up and down while a wave spreads outward.*

Possible tasks: Students can observe this idea by first filling a large pot or tub with water, then tapping at the water near the center of the tub, and finally peering at the water waves with their eyes just a bit above the level of the water. Ask students to describe what pattern they see. They will clearly see the water move up and down. If a little boat is placed on the water, they will see it bob up and down but not move away with the wave. Have students make claims about the movement of the boat based on their observations. Students are not expected at this stage to understand that the water does not move away with the wave. *Safety note:* Make sure students wear eye protection (safety glasses or goggles) for this task. Immediately wipe up any water spilled or splashed on the floor to prevent a slip or fall hazard.

- *Vibrating solids can make sounds.*

Possible tasks: A plucked guitar string makes a sound. Have students feel the string and describe what they feel. Students will feel it vibrate if they touch it lightly. If they look closely at the string, they will also see it vibrating. What happens if the string is plucked harder? What do they feel then? The same can be done with a tapped tuning fork, music triangle, or cymbal. Students can also use a rubber band (this type of activity does not necessarily require special equipment). Have students stretch the rubber band to different lengths and then pluck it. How does this change the vibrations? What happens if they pluck it hard? Have students describe the patterns they observe.

PS4.B: ELECTROMAGNETIC (EM) RADIATION

- *Light is needed to see an object.*

Possible tasks: Take a shoe box and cut a hole the size of an eye in one end using a utility knife (many shoe boxes already have a round hole in one end). Glue an object inside the box at the far end (away from the hole). With the cover securely fixed on the box, have students peek through the hole and try to see the object inside. Then, open a window on the side of the box near the end where the object is glued so that light can get inside and have the students look into the box again. (You will need to cut this window using a utility knife. Make sure you only cut on the sides and the bottom so that the window is a flap.) Can they see the object now? What is the difference between the two conditions? You can also shine a light through the hole to provide more light. Have students make claims about what is needed to see. Have them support their claims with evidence. *Safety note:* Make sure students wear eye protection (safety glasses or goggles) for this task. Use extreme caution when working with utility knives. Sharps can puncture or cut skin!

- *Mirrors can redirect light.*

Possible tasks: Darken a room, then turn on a flashlight and aim it at the wall so that students understand that light is coming from the flashlight and traveling to the wall. Next, place a mirror in the path of the beam and move the mirror around so that it reflects the flashlight's beam in different directions. Have students construct a model to explain their observations. *Safety note:* Make sure to move all fragile or sharp items out of the students' path to prevent injury when working in a dark room.

- *Objects that are very hot give off light.*

Possible tasks: Light a burner and hold a wire in the flame until it begins to glow. Take it out of the flame so that the students see that it still glows a bit. Burn a stick of wood under a fume hood and blow out the flame so students can see that the embers still glow. Show the students a video clip of molten metal, molten glass, and lava in a volcano. Have students describe the patterns they see. Have students make claims based on their observations. *Safety note:* Make sure students wear eye protection (safety glasses or goggles) for this task. Use caution when working with active flames or hot objects. They can seriously burn skin!

- *Some materials let light bounce off them, others let light shine through them fully or partially, and others don't let any light get through them, creating shadows behind them.*

Possible tasks: Obtain a flashlight, a mirror, a sheet of white paper, a piece of clear glass, a clear CD case, and a key. Darken the room and shine a light on a mirror. Have students describe what they see. Students should observe that the light from the flashlight bounces off the mirror. Hold the piece of paper perpendicular to a wall and shine the flashlight on it at a 45° angle. Have students describe what they see now. An illuminated area on the wall will be seen, even though the flashlight is not pointing there, so the light must be bouncing off the sheet of paper. Now shine the flashlight at the glass and the CD case. Have students describe their observations. Students will see that the light goes through the glass and the CD case. Now shine the flashlight at the key. Have students describe what they see. The flashlight cannot be seen from behind the key, so it must be blocking the light; a key-shaped shadow is made. Have students make claims about the behavior of light and support their claims with evidence from their observations. *Safety note:* Make sure to move all fragile or sharp items out of the students' path to prevent injury when working in a dark room.

PS4.C: INFORMATION TECHNOLOGIES AND INSTRUMENTATION

- *People can detect light with their eyes, sound with their ears, and vibrations with their fingertips.*

Possible tasks: Blindfold students using a good sleep mask that blocks the light, and then turn a flashlight on and off while its beam is aimed at the wall. Ask the students if they can tell when the flashlight is on and when it is off. Have student explain why they can't see anything. Have students cover their ears tightly and turn around so that they're facing the back of the class. Do a few things that make sounds, such as tapping on a table, hitting a tuning fork, and whistling. After the students remove their hands from their ears, have them write down which sounds they heard you make. For feeling vibrations see the former activity on a vibrating string.

- *Many different devices are used to communicate over a distance.*

Possible tasks: Have students discuss in groups and build evidence statements showing that devices such as telephones, cell phones, and walkie-talkies communicate over a distance, without delving into how the devices work. Have students build a string telephone by attaching a 10 ft. string to two paper cups. First, cut a small hole in the bottom of one cup and thread the string through it. Then, secure the string by making a small knot. Next, make a small hole in the other paper cup and thread the string through it. Secure it by tying a knot. Now have students stretch the string. Have one student quietly talk into one of the cups and have the other listen by holding the other cup to his or her ear. Have students make models of how

5

they can hear each other talking using this method. Have them explore with different types of strings and cups. Have them also see how long a string can be before they can no longer hear each other. *Safety note:* Make sure students wear eye protection (safety glasses or goggles) for this task.

By the End of Grade 5
PS4.A: WAVE PROPERTIES

- *Waves can have different amplitudes or wavelengths and can constructively or destructively interfere with one another.*

Possible tasks: To help students understand that waves have these properties, use a stretched Slinky on the floor. Have one student hold one end fixed and another student move the other end of the Slinky back and forth sideways at a constant frequency. Waves will travel along the toy. Have students describe the pattern they see. The wavelength between consecutive peaks will be clearly visible. Next have the student moving the free end of the Slinky continue to do so at the same frequency but with smaller or larger movements. Ask students to describe the changes they see. The change in the amplitude of the waves will be apparent. Then, have the student shaking the Slinky move the free end back and forth at a higher or lower frequency. What pattern do the students observe now? The faster the free end moves back and forth (i.e., the higher the frequency), the smaller the wavelength will be, meaning that the consecutive peaks will be closer to each other, and vice versa, the slower the free end moves back and forth (i.e., the lower the frequency), the larger the wavelength will be. Have students make claims about the types of waves they observe and have them support their claims with evidence.

Next, have both students move their ends of the Slinky, not back and forth, but only once, creating a single peak that travels along the Slinky (actually two peaks, one from each end, traveling in the opposite direction). The students should create the pulse at the same time, moving their hands in the same direction so that both peaks are on the same side of the Slinky. Ask students to describe what they observe now. When the two peaks meet each other, they pass through each other, but when they are one on top of the other, they combine "constructively" so that the peak generated is the sum of both peaks. This is called constructive interference and is an example of wave superposition. Have the students repeat this exercise, but this time have them move their hands in opposite directions so that the peaks are on different sides of the Slinky. What pattern do students observe this time? When the peaks pass through each other, they combine "destructively" so that the new peak generated is smaller than each individual peak. There will be moments when there is no peak. This is called destructive interference and is another example of wave superposition. *Safety note:* Make sure students wear eye protection (safety glasses or goggles) for this task. Make sure there is a cleared path for Slinky movement on the floor or table top to prevent accidental damage.

PS4.B: ELECTROMAGNETIC (EM) RADIATION

- *Light from an object needs to enter the eye to be seen.*

Possible tasks: Glue a small object in a shoe box so that it is at the opposite end from the finger/eye hole that most shoe boxes have (if the shoe box doesn't have a hole, cut one into the box using a utility knife, being sure to keep the knife away from students). Hold the cover tightly on the box so that no light can enter it. Now peer at the object through the hole (see a description of this exercise in the By the End of Grade 2 section for PS4.B, p. 88). Have students describe what they see. Students should not be able to see the object because no light is reaching it, so no light can be scattered by it to their eyes. Now lift the cover of the box just a bit so that a crack of light can enter at the side near the object (or cut a flap in the shoe box near the object). Once again, peer through the hole. This time students should be able to see the object because light is reaching it and being scattered by it to their eyes. Have students construct a model that explains why they can see the object when the flap is open but not when the flap is closed. This model can be extended to explain why we can see through glass and why light reflects off a shiny surface such as that of a mirror. *Safety note:* Make sure students wear eye protection (safety glasses or goggles) for this task. Use caution when using a utility knife. Sharps can puncture or cut skin!

- *The color of an object depends on the color of the light illuminating it and the properties of the object.*

Possible tasks: Take a flashlight, a red apple, a green leaf, and two pieces of clear wrapping paper, one blue and one red. Go into a completely dark room. Place the apple and the leaf side by side. Illuminate them with the flashlight, holding the blue transparent paper between the flashlight and the objects so that both objects are illuminated with blue light. What do you see? What colors do the objects appear to be? Now replace the blue transparent paper with the red paper and repeat. What colors do the objects appear to be now? Have

students make claims and support their claims with evidence. *Safety note:* Make sure students wear eye protection (safety glasses or goggles) for this task. Make sure there is a cleared path where students are moving in the dark to prevent injury.

- *Lenses bend light and can be used to magnify images of objects.*

Possible tasks: In a dark room, using a laser pointer, direct a beam of light at a table at an angle. Now place a lens between the laser pointer and the table so that the beam passes through it. Change the angle of the lens so that the laser reaches it at different inclinations. Have students describe their observations. The spot on the table illuminated by the beam should move around as you tilt the lens, showing that the lens is bending and redirecting the beam. Also, if the lens is thick enough, you should be able to see the beam going through the lens itself and changing directions as it enters and leaves the lens. *Safety note:* Caution students to never look directly at the laser light beam. Never intentionally direct a laser beam toward your eyes or the eyes of others. Direct eye contact can cause serious eye tissue damage! Do not point a laser pointer at a shiny or mirror-like surfaces such as polished metal or glass. The reflected beam can hit you or someone else in the eye. *Some states and school districts do not allow the use of a laser pointer for classroom activities. Check state regulations and school board policies before using a laser pointer.*

PS4.C: INFORMATION TECHNOLOGIES AND INSTRUMENTATION

- *Information can be digitized and transmitted.*

Possible tasks: Show your students Morse code. Have them translate the sentence "Be my friend" into Morse, and then, using a flashlight, flash this message to other students. Have students invent other simple three-word sentences, encode them into Morse, and send them to others with a flashlight for decoding. This is an example of sending information digitally.

- *Technologies can be used to detect digitized signals.*

Possible tasks: Have students use their cell phones to make videos of their friends sending them Morse-based messages with a flashlight (as described in the former activity). Or, have students call each other on their cell phones, and then have them tap out a Morse-based message on their cell phones. Discuss how the video and wireless technologies in their cell phones have detected digitized signals.

By the End of Grade 8
PS4.A: WAVE PROPERTIES

- *A wave is defined by its amplitude, wavelength, frequency, and medium.*

Possible tasks: Repeat the first set of activities described above about wave properties for the end of grade 5 (p. 90) but use two or three different Slinkys, for example, a metal and a plastic one or two metal ones of different diameters. Have students make claims about the behavior of the Slinky and then support their claims. Different Slinkys can serve as different mediums, leading to different wave velocities. Have students measure the wavelength and the frequency of the waves generated at different frequencies, and from them calculate the wave velocity for each Slinky. They should be different but almost independent of the wave frequency. *Safety note:* Make sure students wear eye protection (safety glasses or goggles) for this task. Make sure there is a cleared path for Slinky movement on the floor or table top to prevent accidental damage.

- *Waves can be used to probe the Earth's structure.*

Possible tasks: Bring photos of an embryo made with an ultrasound imager and explain how the ultrasound imager uses high-frequency sound waves that are transmitted through the body and reflected at the surfaces of the different organs. The reflected waves are detected and then decoded to generate a picture of organs or an embryo. Likewise, seismic waves (sound waves traveling through the Earth) can be reflected from different parts and layers in the Earth and then detected by us at the surface. Decoding these waves allows us to learn about the structure of the Earth.

If you have a motion detector, you can use it to determine how far above the ground various objects are. A motion detector uses sonar waves and software to detect the distance of an object. You can use this feature to map the profile of a landscape you create in your classroom. Place boxes and other objects on the floor of the classroom and use the motion detector to trace the profile. Have students draw representations of the observations from the data of the motion detector. *Safety note:* Use caution when working around boxes on the floor. They are potential trip or fall hazards.

PS4.B: ELECTROMAGNETIC (EM) RADIATION

- *When light shines on an object, it is reflected, absorbed, or transmitted through the object, depending on the object's material and the frequency (color) of the light.*

Possible tasks: Repeat the activities about wave properties and color for the end of grade 5 (pp. 90–92). Explain how the colored plastic wrap "colors" the white light from the flashlight by selectively allowing certain colors (wavelengths) to be transmitted and reflected while others are absorbed. Now explain how the apple and leaf selectively reflect certain colors of light and absorb others, and describe how this makes them appear different colors. Now take an object with a different color and have students explain why it has that color. Look though a prism at the edge of an object that is bright (preferably white) on one side and dark (preferably black) on the other side, such as a sheet of paper that is white on one half and black on the other half. Ask students to describe what they see. The visible spectrum should appear. Explain how all the different colors of light, although they reach the prism in the same direction from the edge of the border, leave the prism in different directions because they are diffracted differently by the prism, which allows us to distinguish among them. *Safety note:* Make sure students wear eye protection (safety glasses or goggles) for this task.

PS4.C: INFORMATION TECHNOLOGIES AND INSTRUMENTATION

- *Technologies allow us to detect and interpret waves and signals in waves that cannot be detected directly.*

We are immersed in a sea of EM waves but are totally unaware of them. A cell phone can allow us to detect and interpret some of them, as can other appliances that have or act as antennas, such as ultraviolet beads or an ultraviolet intensity meter.

By the End of Grade 12

As mentioned earlier, learning tasks that can be used to support these understandings are not described here because all the ideas that are appropriate for high school require the use of special equipment. The Acoustics and Vibration Animations website (*www.acs.psu.edu/drussell/demos.html*) from the University of Pennsylvania acoustics program contains a number of appropriate animations illustrating acoustics, vibration, waves, and oscillation phenomena. The PhET simulations (*phet.colorado.edu/en/simulations/category/physics/light-and-radiation*) from the University of Colorado also have a number of interactives to illustrate light phenomena. A number of commercial companies also sell light probes that will allow students to explore various wave properties.

PS4.A: WAVE PROPERTIES

- *Waves of different frequencies can be combined to encode and transmit information.*

- *During resonance, waves in phase add up, growing in amplitude. Most objects have specific frequencies at which they resonate. This is the basis for the design of all musical instruments.*

PS4.B: ELECTROMAGNETIC (EM) RADIATION

- *EM radiation can be described as either waves of EM fields or as particles called photons.*

- *We can only identify an object with waves that have a wavelength that is similar to that of the object's size because waves are not much*

5

disturbed by objects that are small compared with their wavelengths.

- *All EM waves travel through a vacuum at the speed of light. The speed of an EM wave in any medium depends on its wavelength and the properties of the medium.*

- *When EM radiation with a wavelength equal to or longer than that of visible light is absorbed by matter, its energy is generally converted into thermal energy within the matter. EM radiation with shorter wavelengths can ionize atoms and cause damage to living cells. Photovoltaic materials emit electrons when they absorb EM radiation of a high enough frequency.*

- *The atoms of each element and the nuclei of each isotope emit and absorb characteristic wavelengths of EM radiation.*

PS4.C: INFORMATION TECHNOLOGIES AND INSTRUMENTATION

- *Many modern technologies are based on an understanding of waves and their interactions with matter.*

- *Knowledge of quantum physics has enabled the development of semiconductors, computer chips, and lasers, all of which are now essential components of modern imaging, communication, and information technologies.*

Conclusion

It is important for all students to construct a deep understanding of waves because waves are central to almost all 21st-century technologies and many older technologies. Wave phenomena allow scientists to examine the very small world of atoms or explore galaxies that are very far away. Waves also allow us to communicate large amounts of information quickly and reliably over long distances. Waves are ubiquitous and play a role in many phenomena. Many of the central issues facing society today cannot be fully appreciated without an understanding of waves. For example, a cell phone company wants to place cell phone antennas at the end of the street near your home. Should you be concerned? Do these antennas pose a health hazard? One cannot understand many aspects of this issue without having a deep understanding of waves. Without this understanding, it is difficult to answer important questions such as these: How does the radiation from the antennae travel to my home? How does this radiation get through the walls in my home? How strong is this radiation when it reaches my family and me? What happens to my body when this radiation reaches it? A person cannot be scientifically literate in this century without a basic understanding of waves. Waves are a big idea of science.

REFERENCES

American Association for the Advancement of Science (AAAS). 1993. *Benchmarks for science literacy.* New York: Oxford University Press.

Linder, C. J., and G. L. Erickson. 1989. A study of tertiary physics students' conceptualizations of sound. *International Journal of Science Education* 11 (5): 491–501.

National Research Council (NRC). 1996. *National science education standards.* Washington, DC: National Academies Press.

National Research Council (NRC). 2012. *A framework for K–12 science education: Practices, crosscutting concepts, and core ideas.* Washington, DC: National Academies Press.

Scientific American. 2010. The laser at 50: Advancing science through beams of coherent light. *www. scientificamerican.com/report/50-years-of-the-laser.*

LIFE
SCIENCES

LIFE SCIENCES

There are four life science disciplinary core ideas (DCIs) that explain the biological world within and around us. These core ideas highlight central explanatory models in biology, including natural selection and inheritance of traits and the impact that we, as humans, have on other organisms and their habitats. Understanding these ideas will allow students to answer relevant questions such as, "Why do siblings look similar to—but not exactly like—each other or their parents?" "Why have certain species gone extinct, and why are others currently endangered?" "How does human activity affect ecosystems and the services these systems provide?" and "How do we, and other organisms, respond to stimuli and learn?"

These core ideas explore and explain the amazing complexity and diversity of the living world, past and present. They highlight the web of interactions between living organisms and the environment—interactions that generate the ecosystems we depend on. As humans, we are an integral part of these ecosystems, and our behaviors affect them. Understanding the factors that govern the dynamics of ecosystems, including their ability to withstand changes to the environment, is critical to ensure that we are conscientious stewards of our local and global environments. Figure LS.1 highlights the core ideas and their components.

In Chapter 6, Aaron Rogat, Barbara Hug, and Ravit Golan Duncan discuss the first core idea in life science, LS1: From Molecules to Organisms: Structures and Processes. This DCI explains how the basic molecular building blocks of life generate the immense complexity we observe in the structure and function of living things. The authors explore the fundamental properties of living things: growth, development, reproduction,

FIGURE LS.1

Life Sciences Disciplinary Core Ideas and Component Ideas

LS1: From molecules to organisms: Structures and processes

   LS1.A: Structure and function

   LS1.B: Growth and development of organisms

   LS1.C: Organization for matter and energy flow in organisms

   LS1.D: Information processing

LS2: Ecosystems: Interactions, energy, and dynamics

   LS2.A: Interdependent relationships in ecosystems

   LS2.B: Cycles of matter and energy transfer in ecosystems

   LS2.C: Ecosystem dynamics, functioning, and resilience

   LS2.D: Social interactions and group behavior

LS3: Heredity: Inheritance and variation of traits

   LS3.A: Inheritance of traits

   LS3.B: Variation of traits

LS4: Biological evolution: Unity and diversity

   LS4.A: Evidence of common ancestry and diversity

   LS4.B: Natural selection

   LS4.C: Adaptation

   LS4.D: Biodiversity and humans

and the ability to sense and respond to the environment. The idea addresses how the many different structures within organisms enable them to engage in these life functions. The chapter also discusses the various ways in which organisms obtain and use matter and energy to support growth, development, and reproduction.

This core idea is connected to multiple other core ideas, and in many ways serves as the foundation for understanding life and living organisms in the most general sense.

In Chapter 7, Charles (Andy) Anderson and Jennifer H. Doherty explore LS2: Ecosystems: Interactions, Energy, and Dynamics. Humans benefit from and depend on services provided by ecosystems from physical materials (e.g., wood) to less tangible aspects such as protection from floods. Understanding the complex dynamics of ecosystems and, in particular, the impact of environmental and human changes (e.g., climate change) on these systems is the focus of exploration for this chapter. The authors discuss ecosystems from two perspectives: (1) the tracing of matter and energy through ecosystems and (2) the dynamic process of changes in populations of organisms in ecosystems.

In Chapter 8, Nicole A. Shea and Ravit Golan Duncan address LS3: Heredity: Inheritance and Variation of Traits. This idea explores the questions of how genetic traits are passed on from one generation to the next and how individuals of the same species (even siblings in the same family) can have different traits. The chapter looks at two related mechanisms: The first is how our genes and the information they carry bring about physical traits such as dimples or a genetic disorder such as albinism. The second is the patterns of inheritance, that is, how the genes you get from your parents result in the specific traits and trait combinations you have. In both cases, there is an emphasis on the sources of genetic variation, including random assortment of genes in sex cells (egg and sperm) and the impact of the environment on the genetic instructions (mutations), and

the differential use of the genetic instructions by cells (gene expression).

In Chapter 9, Cynthia Passmore, Julia Svoboda Gouvea, Candice Guy, and Chris Griesemer address the related ideas of the unity and diversity of life on Earth in LS4: Biological Evolution: Unity and Diversity. Their chapter explores how organisms are adapted to their environment and what happens when the environmental conditions change either naturally or through human intervention. The authors explain the core mechanisms of natural selection and descent with modification and how these processes can explain both similarities in organisms (life functions discussed in LS1) and differences between them in terms of the multitude of shapes, size, colors, and behaviors that organisms exhibit, from the invisible bacteria to the enormous dinosaurs of the past and the large mammals of today.

In conclusion, the four DCIs in the life sciences strand tackle familiar phenomena that students have experienced, including the need to breathe air, the amazing camouflage of insects, and those little differences between identical twins. They also help students understand strange and novel phenomena they have yet to experience, such as the swapping of sections between homologous chromosomes during meiosis, the similarities in DNA sequences and embryological development of many different-looking organisms (e.g., lions and dolphins), and the potential consequences of global changes to the carbon cycle. These big ideas are powerful and generative models in biology that will allow students to make sense of the phenomena they will encounter now, in their schooling, and later in life as they engage with science as literate citizens.

CHAPTER 6

CORE IDEA LS1

FROM MOLECULES TO ORGANISMS: STRUCTURES AND PROCESSES

Aaron Rogat, Barbara Hug, and Ravit Golan Duncan

What Is This Disciplinary Core Idea, and Why Is It Important?

Imagine sitting in your doctor's office trying to make sense of the news that you have the early stages of a neurodegenerative disease. You wonder how a disease that directly affects neurons could cause all the symptoms you are experiencing. Your doctor tells you about two new experimental treatments, one involving implanting stem cells to replace the dead nerve cells, the second involving chemical substances to reduce nerve degeneration. Which would you choose?

It would be difficult to decide if you did not know about the nervous system, nerve cells and their role in the nervous system, and what happens inside nerve cells that allows them to function. To make sense of the treatment options, you would need to know that cells have a multitude of proteins that allow them to function and that medications often target these proteins and alter their function. Likewise, understanding how cells take on specific functions in the body and

how they multiply can help you make sense of the stem-cell treatment option. This example and other phenomena such as how a cut heals, how we see and hear, and how a baby develops from a single fertilized egg, are all explained through the ideas captured in disciplinary core idea (DCI) LS1. Fundamentally, this core idea is about the main properties of living things, that is, how specialized structures are organized to carry out essential functions (e.g., growing and reproducing, using matter and energy to carry out life functions, and detecting and responding to the environment). Even the simplest of organisms, a single cell, has structures and processes that allow it to engage in these life activities of growth, reproduction, obtaining energy, and responding to the surroundings.

These properties of living things are embodied in the four component ideas of this DCI:

- LS1.A: Structure and function

- LS1.B: Growth and development of organisms

6

- LS1.C: Organization for matter and energy flow in organisms

- LS1.D: Information processing

Across the K–12 grades, this DCI shifts from the macroscopic descriptions to more mechanistic explanations of structures and functions at the cellular and molecular level that highlight the role of cells in complex systems. The crosscutting concepts of complex systems and structure-function are centrally relevant to this DCI.

LS1.A: Structure and Function

The central focus of LS1.A: Structure and Function, is the structure-function connections within and between the various levels of organization of an organism (cells, tissues, organs, etc.). Critical to reasoning about the hierarchical organization of complex organisms is understanding that cells are the basic units that "enable life's functions" (NRC 2012, p. 143). Cells are the fundamental building blocks of higher levels of organization (tissues and organs); they obtain energy, grow, divide, and carry out a multitude of functions within the body. The functions of cells subsequently bring about the functions of tissues and organs. For example, muscle cells working together allow our muscles to contract. The phenomenon of the heartbeat is due to the simultaneous and synchronized contraction of muscle cells in the heart causing the entire organ to contract, thus pushing the blood out.

Cells themselves can be viewed as hierarchical entities to which the structure-function correlation can also be applied. They are made up of many smaller structures including organelles and molecules such as proteins and DNA. These substructures work together to carry out life's functions within the cell, including capturing the energy in sugar molecules (e.g., the functional role of the mitochondria). Much like at the macro level, the specific structures of molecules afford and constrain their interactions with other molecules and therefore their function. For example, the specificity of antibodies is due to their three-dimensional structures, which allows them to interact with only specific foreign molecules (e.g., like a lock and key model).

Molecular structures within cells allow them to carry out both general life functions (e.g., obtaining energy, growing) as well as specialized functions such as carrying oxygen (red blood cells), movement (muscle cells), and sensing light (specific cells in the eye). Red blood cells are loaded with hemoglobin, a protein that can bind to oxygen; muscle cells are packed with contractile proteins that work together to move the entire muscle cell, and nerve cells in the retina in our eye have protein receptors that change their shape and convey a signal when exposed to light. These specialized structures are restricted to the cells that carry out the relevant function: Nerve cells do not have hemoglobin proteins and red blood cells do not have light receptors.

To understand how LS1.A can help us explain a wide range of biological phenomena related to disease, let's consider the example of diabetes, an often debilitating and unfortunately, all too common disorder. Individuals with untreated diabetes have high levels of sugar in their blood and urine, suffer from fatigue, and have trouble gaining weight. The root cause of this diverse array of symptoms is a problem at the cellular level. However, there are several different causes for this disorder. In type 1 diabetes, glucose in the blood is not taken up by the body's cells (e.g., muscle cells and skin cells). This results in elevated blood sugar levels and energy-starved cells. The blood sugar levels are high due to a defect in pancreatic cells. These specific cells do not produce the insulin protein hormone needed to signal the rest of the body's cells to take up glucose. Without the proper uptake signal, the body's cells do not take up the available glucose and instead become starved for energy, with the diabetic symptoms being the end result. Patients with type 1 diabetes can be treated with insulin, the missing hormone. In a related disease, type 2 diabetes, the problem lies with the body's cells themselves. In this case, the cells have a dysfunctional protein receptor or sensor for insulin. In healthy individuals, this protein sensor detects insulin and transmits the signal into the cell. In most instances of type 2 diabetes, the cells make a structurally deformed or altered receptor that cannot properly bind to insulin (Figure 6.1) and therefore do not transmit a signal into the cell. Providing insulin to type 2 diabetic patients usually does not help; their insulin sensor is "broken" and will not sense the presence of insulin in the body. This example illustrates how events and changes at one level of organization (protein structures and functions) can cause changes in subsequent levels (cells, tissues, and organs). It also highlights how critical structures, such as protein structure, are to functions.

LSI.B: Growth and Development of Organisms

In LS1.B: Growth and Development of Organisms, the emphasis is on understanding another key feature of living things: growth and reproduction. All organisms, from the smallest single-celled

FIGURE 6.1.

Function in Healthy and Type 1 and Type 2 Diabetic Cells

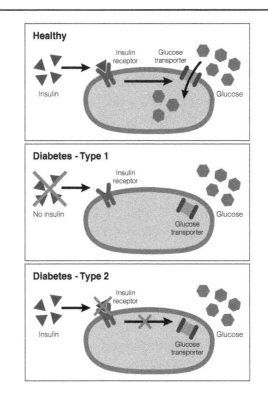

An understanding of structure and function as articulated in LSI.A can allow students to understand phenomena such as the development of diabetes symptoms. In a cell from a normal, healthy person (top), insulin binds the insulin receptor found at the surface of the cell. This action leads to a signal that causes glucose transporters to localize to the surface of the cell, which allows glucose to flow into the cell. In type 1 diabetes (middle), insulin is not present, and therefore the insulin receptor cannot initiate the downstream signals and the glucose transporter does not localize to the surface of the cell to allow glucose to enter the cell. In type 2 diabetes (bottom), there are either defects in the insulin receptor or in the downstream signaling events that prevent the glucose transporter from localizing to the cell surface so that glucose does not flow into the cell. In both types of diabetes, body cells do not properly take in glucose because of defects to subcellular structures and processes, so glucose accumulates outside the cells in the bloodstream.

amoeba to a human, grow in predictable ways. In many cases, there are identifiable life stages during which an organism may look and behave very differently from its adult form. For example, butterflies progress through a number of well-characterized life stages. As caterpillars, they have no wings, and it is only through the process of metamorphosis that they change into the recognizable winged insects. Even for animals in which the juvenile resembles the adult (such as dogs, lions, and fish), the young animal may exhibit different kinds of behaviors, and these behavioral patterns change as they mature. The notion that organisms do not simply get bigger over their lifetime but that they can also change internally and externally over the course of development, is important when we consider how changes to an environment might affect the various organisms that live in it. For example, in the 1960s, scientists suspected that a common pesticide, DDT, was harming wild birds. However, when studies showed that the pesticide did not have a significant negative effect on adult birds, scientists were stymied as to what was going on. Further exploration revealed that DDT causes the thinning of the shells of the eggs of birds (including the endangered falcons and condors), resulting in fewer eggs hatching and a decline in the population. This phenomenon illustrates how the negative effects of a chemical may only be evident at a particular stage in the life cycle.

The changes that occur in an organism as it develops are driven by alterations in the structure and function of its organs, tissues, and fundamentally, its cells. As the basic unit of life, cells grow, develop, and divide to produce more cells. Cell division (a process called mitosis) is the central mechanism by which organisms can increase their size and replace dead or damaged cells.

FIGURE 6.2.

Uncontrolled Cell Division Leads to Cancer.

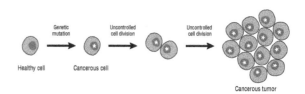

An understanding of growth through cell division as articulated in LSI.B can allow one to understand phenomena such as cancer formation. A normal, healthy cell does not divide frequently or rapidly (*far left*). If this cell develops a mutation that alters the regulatory mechanisms governing cell division, it can become cancerous and divide uncontrollably (*middle*) until it leads to the production of a tumor composed of a large number of cells (*far right*).

Cell division is a highly regulated process that first ensures the proper duplication of the genetic instructions and then its equal distribution to both daughter cells. When division of body cells, such as those of the skin, liver, lungs, or stomach, occurs uncontrollably, it can result in cancer—one of the quintessential phenomena that requires an understanding of cell division and growth. The initiation of a cancer, such as the skin cancer melanoma, can result from mutations at the gene level, which in turn affect the function of proteins that regulate cell division, causing the cells to replicate uncontrollably. This excessive cell division and growth at a macroscopic level looks like an abnormal lump or mass within the affected tissue as a result of the overgrowth of cells (Figure 6.2).

Almost all cells can divide to produce more cells; however, the rate at which this occurs differs dramatically depending on the cell's function. Skin cells and intestinal cells reproduce rapidly to replace old cells, whereas kidney or liver cells reproduce much more slowly. Differences in rates of division can, among other reasons, relate to how often existing cells are damaged and in need of replacement. Skin and intestinal organs are damaged and worn down daily due to the harsh environments they are in and therefore need replacement frequently so that these organs can continue to function normally. In contrast, liver and kidney cells are damaged, and in need of repair, much less often.

There is also a specific subset of cells that reproduce to generate sex cells (sperm or eggs) that carry only half the complement of the genetic instructions. These sex cells divide through a process called meiosis that is similar to mitosis but includes two sequential divisions resulting in four cells that each have half the genetic material. When sex cells unite (a sperm and an egg) through sexual reproduction, a new cell is formed with a full complement of genetic material. If sex cells did not reduce their genetic content by half, the fusion of sperm and egg would double the amount of genetic material and result in a nonviable embryo. The new cell that is formed from fertilization of an egg by a sperm cell can give rise to a whole new organism through numerous cell divisions that produce billions of new cells to carry out the numerous functions needed to sustain the organism.

How is it that so many different kinds of cells (e.g., nerve, muscle, skin, etc.) can arise from one original progenitor? First, it is important to realize that the vast majority of our cells all have the same full complement, or set, of genetic information. Within one individual, there is no difference in the genetic content of a muscle cell versus a skin cell. The cells differ in their shape, makeup, and function because each one is programmed to use only a subset of its genetic instructions, a process called

differential gene expression. Genes can be viewed as the primary recipes for proteins, and proteins have specific functions in the cell and body (as discussed above in LS1.A). For example, the brain cells and muscle cells of a particular organism all have the same set of genes, yet as a result of differential gene expression, they each use a different subset of all the genes. Therefore, they only make proteins that are needed for that type of cell's specific roles. There exists in the body a particular group of cells that retain their ability to use more of the genetic instructions—that is, to make the many different kinds of proteins encoded by the basic genetic instructions. These cells are referred to as stem cells, and they are particularly useful in basic science research and medicine because of their ability to express many more genes than more specialized cell types. In recent decades, scientists have identified ways of triggering stem cells to differentiate into particular kinds of cells. The ability to program stem cells to create specific types of cells underlies potential treatments for injuries or disorders that involve the damage or death of cells (e.g., neurodegenerative disease). The phenomenon of stem cells is a useful one to explore when trying to teach differential gene expression.

LS1.C: Organization for Matter and Energy Flow in Organisms

The component idea LS1.C: Organization for Matter and Energy Flow in Organisms can help explain an array of phenomena such as (1) how cows that eat only grass can build the meat we eat as steak; (2) why we need oxygen to survive; and (3) how plants are able to grow with just air, water, and some nutrients. At its core, LS1.C is about the reliance of organisms on energy and matter to build needed structures and carry out life functions. This idea explains how the food we and other animals eat is transformed and incorporated into our own body structures and how we obtain energy from food. A key point here is that we transform and change the compounds we consume as food and use the resulting new compounds to build structures in our bodies. This process begins at the basic level of the cell and its effects propagate through the hierarchical system (tissues, organs, and organ systems). For example, while eating meat helps us build muscle, our muscles are not actually made up of animal muscle proteins. Rather, we break down the proteins in the meat to their core components and then use those building blocks to create new proteins that are found in our own muscle cells. These transformations of matter are central to an organism's ability to grow, develop, and reproduce, and they occur in all organisms, no matter how small.

When our bodies, or the bodies of other animals such as cows, transform matter, they also transfer energy. We, and all other organisms, need energy for all life functions. Animals obtain their energy from the food they consume; through chemical processes this energy is transferred, stored, and used. These chemical transformations occur through a process called cellular respiration, which begins—as its name implies—at the cellular level. Cells break apart sugar molecules (glucose) and then reassemble the carbons into new molecules. As a result of these rearrangements, energy is transferred and stored in new molecules (Figure 6.3) that can be used for a number of important cellular functions, such as building cellular components to support growth or repair. Cellular respiration requires oxygen for the breaking and reassembling of carbon molecules, and the process results in carbon dioxide

FIGURE 6.3

The Chemical Processes of Digestion in a Cow

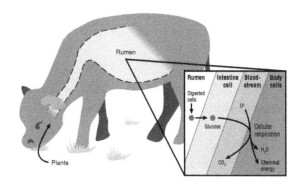

Cow growth through digestion of food can be explained by concept in LS1.C. A cow eats grass, which is broken down into glucose through a series of chemical reactions in the rumen (specialized stomach) of the cow. The glucose is then absorbed into intestinal cells and subsequently flows to the blood stream and, ultimately, to all the body cells. There, glucose is taken up and combined with oxygen in a series of chemical reactions that lead to the production of chemical energy, carbon dioxide, and water (*far right of the box*). The chemical energy can be used to drive reactions required to build cellular components to support growth.

gas molecules (see Figure 6.3). Breathing, therefore, is the body's mechanism of internalizing oxygen from the air to be used in cellular respiration and releasing the carbon dioxide products of this process. We breathe so that our cells can "respire." There are a few exceptions to this rule. Some single-celled organisms (e.g., bacteria), and to a limited extent our own cells, can engage in an altered process of breaking and reassembling glucose without using oxygen. This alternative path, called anaerobic respiration, is less efficient. The familiar phenomenon of acute pain that we feel in our muscles following some types of exercise is due to anaerobic respiration. Working muscle cells require a lot of energy (to contract), and if these cells do not get enough oxygen to keep up their respiration process, they will switch to anaerobic respiration. A by-product of this process is lactic acid, which causes the painful burning sensation we feel.

Another important focus in LS1.C is that energy for life is derived from the Sun. Plants capture light energy from the Sun and use carbon dioxide (from the air) to transform it into chemical energy, which is stored in the glucose that plants produce in a process called photosynthesis. The importance of plants for life on Earth is therefore evident: They are the ultimate producers of the matter and energy we, and other organisms, consume and depend on. For the photosynthetic process, plants need sunlight, carbon dioxide, and water. The by-product is oxygen, which plants release into the air. Plants then use the glucose they create to fuel their own cellular respiration process, and they use the resulting energy, just as animals do, to grow, develop, and reproduce. The phenomenon of hydroponic gardens illustrates these necessary and sufficient requirements for plant growth. These types of gardens provide light, water, some minerals, and access to air so that crop plants such as tomatoes and cucumbers can grow healthily without the need of soil (Figure 6.4).

LS1.C deals with the processes that living things use to obtain energy and matter for their life functions. Ultimately, the matter and energy (in all its various forms) are conserved in the ecosystem as a whole. Thus, the materials and energy generated by photosynthesis support the life of plants and the animals that eat them. Those animals in turn die and decompose, returning the matter back into the system. The glucose built by plants from carbon dioxide and water, using

FIGURE 6.4

Hydroponic Plant Growth

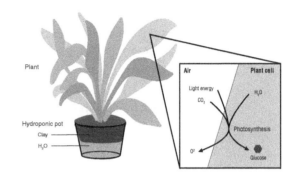

Plant growth through photosynthesis (not requiring soil) is a phenomenon explained by LS1.C concepts. Figure 6.4 shows a macroscopic image of growing plant and the molecular events (chemical reactions) occurring within leaf cells that lead to the production of glucose and oxygen as result of intake of carbon dioxide and water and absorption of light (box).

light energy, is broken down in cellular respiration to "retrieve" that energy, and the resulting products are carbon dioxide and water. The cycling of matter and energy in the larger system are focus concepts in core idea LS2: Ecosystems; therefore, there are many connections between this LS1 component idea and component ideas found in LS2.

LS1.D: Information Processing

The last component idea, LS1.D: Information Processing, emphasizes an understanding of how organisms sense and respond to the environment at the cellular level and at the system level (i.e., the nervous system). To obtain food, avoid bodily damage, and find mates, organisms need to be able to make sense of and react

6

to their environments. Even single-celled organisms are capable of sensing and responding to some environmental stimuli. For example, bacteria can detect food or toxins in their environment and move toward or away from the source—a phenomenon called chemotaxis. In more complex animals, there is an entire system devoted to sensing and mediating responses: the nervous system, at the center of which is the brain.

The functions of sensing and responding to the environment are afforded by various structures at the cellular, tissue, and organ level. As noted earlier, there are specialized sensory cells all over our body that essentially mediate our ability to see, hear, taste, smell, and feel. These cells send signals through other connecting nerve cells to the central nervous system—the spinal cord and brain. The central nervous system interprets these sensory inputs and sends out signals to mediate responses. Responses can be reflexes (e.g., moving away from a heat source), intentional actions (e.g., walking), and emotional states (e.g., feeling satisfied).

Cells are able to sense because of specific receptor proteins that react to specific stimuli and convey a signal to the cell. Thus, cells in our taste buds have receptor proteins that can react to substances that are sweet, sour, umami, or bitter. The receptors have specific shapes that allow them to exclusively interact with only a subset of molecules that trigger their signaling capacity. Altering these receptors or the cells that house them can alter our ability to taste. Interestingly, the phenomenon of "flavor" is a sensation we get when combining input of taste (taste receptors on tongue) and smell (olfactory receptors in nose). This is why we cannot fully taste food when we have a cold. While the smell and taste subsystems are distinct, their inputs are integrated in the brain to give us a more nuanced sense of flavor. The phenomenon of flavor illustrates the integrative nature of the brain. There are many parts in the brain that have specific functions; for example, the hippocampus is predominantly associated with creating memories, the occipital cortex is involved in visual processing, and the motor cortex is critical for mediating movement. However, there is also extensive collaboration and cross talk between the various areas of the brain.

There are complex circuits (e.g., neural networks in the brain) that control other more complex behaviors, such as seeking rewards, developing fears, and forming relationships with kin. These circuits and others are involved in the formation of memories and learning. For example, repeated exposure to an unpleasant stimulus can result in fear of it and, subsequently, of any stimulus that precedes it (e.g., a bell ringing before an unpleasant event occurs). The repeated exposures result in changes to the inside of nerve cells and to their connections to other nerve cells in ways that mediate this learned fear response. Learning is therefore—and fundamentally—about changing the strength of interactions between nerve cells in the brain (establishing or altering circuits). The amazing brain, and its complex circuitry, allows us to learn sophisticated ideas, execute complex actions, and ultimately, increase the chances of survival for us, our offspring, and our other kin.

In summary, it is important to remember that these four component ideas are part of the larger core idea that is really about understanding the properties of living things and how the structures and functions at various organization levels within organisms allow them to carry out life's key functions of growth, development, and reproduction.

Why Is This Core Idea Central to the Discipline of Biology?

This DCI is foundational to the discipline in that it allows one to explain a variety of phenomena that unite all living things. LS1 is organized around the key characteristics of living things, and it sets out to explain how the complex system that is a living organism is able to grow, develop, and reproduce and what the structures and functions are that allow us and every other living thing to live and prosper. This is a central idea that touches on and relates to many other life science core ideas (LS2: Ecosystems: Interactions, Energy, and Dynamics; LS3: Heredity: Inheritance and Variation of Traits; and LS4: Biological Evolution: Unity and Diversity). It identifies and explains the commonalities between a simple amoeba and a complex mammal. It allows us to understand how structures and functions at one level (e.g., muscle cell contraction) affect and generate structures and functions at higher organization levels (e.g., a working heart). Critically, this core idea explains why changes to structures and functions at one level (e.g., change to the structure of a protein receptor) can result in malfunction and disease at many different levels. Many important biological phenomena and advances in medicine and research relate to and depend on understanding the ideas embodied in this DCI. For example, medical treatments for diseases often focus on targeting interactions with the affected cells and / or systems (LS1.A: Structure and Function). The search for new ways to create stem cells from adult differentiated cells has added to our understanding of how development works (LS1.B: Growth and Development of Organisms). Our understanding of how plants survive in higher carbon dioxide levels is helping scientists predict the effect of global climate change on food production (LS1.C: Organization for Matter and Energy Flow in Organisms). A recent momentous government-funded research effort combines both science and engineering to map every connection of cells in the brain to develop a better picture and understanding of how the brain works (LS1.D: Information Processing). These diverse phenomena all draw on the idea that organisms are complex and have many structures specifically suited to perform the many functions that keep the living alive.

Not only is this DCI foundational to biologists, it is also central to those learning biology. Understanding how organisms are structured and how they function to address the needs of every living thing supports the learning of several other core ideas. Understanding reproduction as a core feature of living things and cell division as a basic mechanism for achieving growth and repair will help students better understand the cellular process involved in generating sex cells and passing genetic material to the next generation (a focus of LS3). Similarly, understanding the process of photosynthesis and cellular respiration will help students better grasp how matter cycles through ecosystems and how energy is converted from one form to another as it is used by organisms in the system (a focus of LS2). Lastly, the focus on structure function relationships in LS1 helps students develop an understanding of one *NGSS* crosscutting concept (structure and function) and one component of another *NGSS* life science DCI (LS4), specifically that organisms have traits, such as unique structural adaptations, that allow them to survive in Earth's diverse habitats. Thus, LS1, with its focus on properties of living things, can support the learning of all the other core ideas in life science.

6

Comparison to Prior Standards

If one compares prior standards with *A Framework for K–12 Science Education* (NRC 2012) in terms of the ideas captured in LS1, one finds many levels of overlap and some critical differences. While the ideas in LS1 are often the same as those found in previous standards (the *National Science Education Standards* and the *Benchmarks for Science Literacy*), there is a substantial change in focus with the intent of highlighting the complexity and interconnectedness of structures and functions across levels of organization within the organism. Concepts about the organ systems, cells, and photosynthesis, for example, are not presented as discrete ideas; rather, the goal in LS1 is to build a coherent and integrated understanding of how these ideas together contribute to an in-depth understanding of the life functions of living things. No longer is it sufficient to teach each system in isolation. In fact, the *Framework* does not call for teaching any system in detail other than the nervous system (as a focus system). Instead, instruction needs to emphasize the connections and interactions across all levels of organization and the ways in which structure-function correlations help us understand how organisms grow, develop, and reproduce.

There is also the increased emphasis on the nervous system and the brain in particular. Some of the ideas in LS1.D are new and reflect the importance of understanding the brain as a central organ and the nervous system as an elaborated example of how a system operates given its components and how it interfaces with other systems. Here again, the goal is not a detailed understanding of each part of the system, but an understanding of how it functions together as a system.

How Does Student Understanding of This Disciplinary Core Idea Develop Over Time?

In this section, we first discuss two major trends that describe students' progression in understandings across all four component ideas of LS1. We then turn to a more detailed description of how the four ideas progress through each grade band. Note that the progression we describe is based on a limited research base. This progression serves as a starting point for understanding student development and can inform instructional planning (see Appendix E of the *Next Generation Science Standards* [NGSS Lead States 2013]). However, we anticipate that with time, as more research is conducted, our understanding of student learning across the grades will improve.

There are two trends that broadly characterize the progression in LS1: (1) Phenomena are initially described at the macroscopic level, and descriptions gradually gain depth to include lower organization levels of cells and ultimately molecules. (2) There is also a concurrent shift from macroscopic descriptions to mechanistic explanations that identify cause-and-effect relationships within and across organization levels.

Within biological systems, there are often multiple levels of organization with the most visible being the macroscopic objects—such as beaks, legs, skeleton, lungs, and so on. In the early grades, students are expected to focus primarily on macroscopic structures, and we know young students can be quite adept at describing and characterizing what they can see. However, at later grades (middle school and high school), there is increased attention to unfamiliar and invisible entities at lower organization levels, with a focus on the cell level in middle school and the molecular level in high school.

A parallel expectation is that, as they become familiar with more levels, students will develop some facility with reasoning across these levels. The goal is for students to progressively develop explanations that causally link structures and functions at lower levels with their effects at higher organization levels. At lower grades, students are mostly engaged in observation and description. As they get older, they can begin using mechanisms at the cellular level to explain the observable phenomena they described in earlier grades. High school students can construct mechanistic explanations that span multiple organization levels, delineating how the functions of proteins (e.g., changes in protein shape) give rise to the behaviors and functions of cells (e.g., contraction) and subsequently tissues and organs (e.g., the beating heart). In essence, as students progress, they continually open up mechanisms at lower organization levels, which were black-boxed in earlier grades.

However, we would like to point out that even students in high school are not expected to provide detailed descriptions of cellular and molecular mechanisms; for example, it is not necessary for students to memorize and articulate the molecular mechanisms of the electron transport chain of photosynthesis, the steps of mitosis, or the Krebs cycle. Rather, the focus is on explaining how entities at one organization level cause effects at higher organization levels, developing causal mechanistic explanations that span organization levels. For example, regarding photosynthesis, teachers should focus on the larger picture of how the molecular and cellular events in the leaf promote plant growth. The goal here is to help students understand that a series of chemical reactions (no detail needed about these) in the leaf cells transforms light energy to chemical energy by "capturing" it in glucose molecules generated from the uptake and reaction of carbon dioxide and water. Students need to be able to connect and trace the flow of energy and matter in the plant: the glucose is turned to starch that is stored in the plant (which is why fruit and roots can be sweet). Students should develop models of how these cellular events in the leaf support visible plant growth. This focus on big picture mechanisms and multiple levels of organization may require the selective use of appropriate representations that are different from traditional representations in textbooks, which tend to include too much detail and separate molecular events from organ-, tissue-, and organismal-level events such as stem and root growth. The extensive details included in traditional textbook representations, however, do not lead to deeper or more meaningful understandings. One tends to lose the forest for the trees, and students often end up with a fragmented and incoherent view of key transformations of matter and energy across organization levels. Instead, to adequately connect the actions and behaviors at each level in the plant system, students need to have access to representations in which multiple organizational levels are represented simultaneously.

How Does Student Understanding of This Disciplinary Core Idea Develop Over Time?

Expectations for Grades K–2
LS1.A: STRUCTURE AND FUNCTION

In the early grades, the goal is to introduce students to key structures and functions of living things and help them understand that animals engage in behaviors that help them grow and reproduce and that help their offspring survive as well. At this stage, students engage predominantly in observations of structures they can see and with which they are mostly familiar. Students can observe how different organisms, both animals and plants, use their structures to carry out necessary functions such as finding food, creating shelters, caring for their young, and evading predators. An entry to the topic can be a discussion of human structures and functions; for example, what kinds of things we can do with our hands and our legs? Introducing structures that we do not have but that other organisms do, such as wings, tail, or pincers, can provide fodder for additional discussion of structure-function correlations.

LS1.B: GROWTH AND DEVELOPMENT OF ORGANISMS

While most ideas about reproduction are too complex for young students to understand, it is important that they recognize growth and reproduction as a core feature of living things. All living organisms (that young students are somewhat familiar with) have offspring, and many organisms, but not all, take care of their young. For example, some fish carry their young in their mouths, scorpions carry them on their backs (as do many monkeys);

parents also teach their young important behaviors such as hunting and hiding.

LS1.C: ORGANIZATION FOR MATTER AND ENERGY FLOW IN ORGANISMS

For many organisms, much of their time is spent looking for food. All organisms, including plants, need food to survive. Some animals eat plants; others eat animals (meat). Organisms have unique features that allow them to consume the food they like: Birds have beaks, whales have brush-like structures that capture shrimp they suck in with ocean water, tigers have canine teeth that are sharp and can dig into their prey, and sheep have flat teeth used to grind and mash grass. Plants also have structures they need to obtain food: They have roots to absorb water and leaves to absorb light.

LS1.D: INFORMATION PROCESSING

A key point to emphasize here is that animals also have structures that allow us to sense the world around us and to communicate with others of our kind. All animals depend on their senses to find food and avoid becoming food. In organisms that live in groups, communication is also central to survival, and many animals warn each other of danger. For example, deer raise their tail to show the white fur underneath, monkeys call out to each other, and buffalo form a circle around their young like a protective fence.

Expectations for Grades 3–5
LS1.A: STRUCTURE AND FUNCTION

In late elementary school, we can introduce students to biological structures and functions that may be less familiar or not visible. In other words, there is an elaboration or refinement of the macroscopic structures and behaviors that students should characterize. Students can explore the structures and functions of some internal organs. For example, the lungs look like balloons and fill up with air when we breathe, the muscles in our abdomen push the air out (students can try contracting their abs to feel the air being pushed out); the stomach and intestines also contract and expand, thereby squashing food as it is broken down into the nutrients we need to help our bodies grow and develop.

LS1.B: GROWTH AND DEVELOPMENT OF ORGANISMS

In terms of reproduction, students in late elementary grades are expected to understand the idea that organisms develop in stages and that some stages look very different from the adult form. Students can explore the life cycle of a variety of familiar organisms, including plants. Comparisons across organisms can help students generalize the universality of growth and development as a core feature of living things. The need to reproduce is also universal but can take many forms. Some organisms reproduce sexually (i.e., a male with a female such as in birds and mammals), whereas others reproduce asexually with one parent giving rise to offspring in the absence of a second parent (e.g. bacteria and fungi). However, all organisms have offspring to continue the chain of life from one generation to the next.

LS1.C: ORGANIZATION FOR MATTER AND ENERGY FLOW IN ORGANISMS

To carry out life's functions, organisms need materials and energy. This universal need has several solutions. Materials are needed to build and repair the body and are obtained from food. Energy is needed when building body structures during growth and repair, and it is also needed for movement and to keep the organism warm. Most organisms get energy from the food they consume, either other animals or plants. Plants, however, use sunlight as their source of energy. Plants, like animals, also need other materials such as water and minerals to develop and grow (LS1.C). Note that in late elementary school, students are expected to understand that food provides organisms with both matter and energy, whereas in earlier grades we do not distinguish these two contributions of food.

LS1.D: INFORMATION PROCESSING

The deepening of students' understanding of information processing at the late elementary level is mostly in terms of understanding the specificity of sensing and the role of both memory and perception in guiding behaviors. At this stage, students are expected to understand that we can specifically sense different kinds of inputs, including taste (the different locations of taste buds on the tongue is a good example), smell, colors, and sounds. These inputs are processed in the brain, and the organism can respond to them. Memory also plays a key role in the process; an organism's memory of the smell of an object can guide it in deciding whether to eat or avoid the item. Animals exposed to scary input, such as being chased by a predator in a particular location, will also exhibit avoidance behaviors. Thus, animals can learn what is good for them and what can harm them by combining sensory input with memories of past consequences from that input. Scientists can even train animals to have irrational behaviors, such as Pavlov's famous experiment with dogs salivating at the sound of a bell.

Expectations for Grades 6–8
LS1.A: STRUCTURE AND FUNCTION

A key expectation in the middle grades across all the components of LS1 is reasoning at the cellular level, shifting toward the invisible (microscopic), and using entities at the cellular level and invisible processes to explain some of the observable phenomena studied in prior grades. In LS1.A, the understanding that organisms are made up of cells, which are the basic unit that can carry out life's functions of growth, development, and reproduction (cell theory) is an achievement of the middle grades. Students can learn about and explore cells in terms of their roles and the structures within them that allow cells to live and function. A few important organelles such as the cell membrane, nucleus, and mitochondria can be discussed.

However, the goal is not to teach all the organelles featured in textbooks for the sake of knowing their definitions. Rather, the focus here is on the relationship between structure and function, with emphasis on a few select structures that are central to the cell's survival—allowing needed materials in and out of the cell (membrane), obtaining energy (mitochondria), and providing instructions for the cell's growth, development and role in the body (nucleus). Learning these structure-function relationships requires more than drawing a cell and labeling its functional parts; it requires exploring the role of key organelles in promoting life

functions through evidence such as microscope observations, simulations, and adapted primary literature. Along with understanding cells as the basic unit of life, this grade band also emphasizes the relationships between cell functions and the structure and functions at higher organization levels (tissues, organs, and organ systems). The evolution of multicellular organisms such as mammals was afforded by the ability of groups of cells to carry out specific functions and to cooperate such that the entire organism is better able to survive. The ability of groups of cells to specialize and have a particular function, as opposed to being jacks-of-all-trades, allowed for greater efficiency in carrying out those functions and gave multicellular organisms an advantage. Thus, the two related focuses for LS1.A for the middle grades are (1) understanding cells as a basic unit of life capable of surviving on their own, and (2) understanding the differentiation of cell function in multicellular organisms.

LS1.B: GROWTH AND DEVELOPMENT OF ORGANISMS

In terms of LS1.B, the focus on the cellular level allows for the introduction of asexual reproduction, since most unicellular organisms reproduce asexually (albeit many, like yeast, also have a form of sexual reproduction). The core feature of living things, their ability to reproduce, is applied to the cell level. Cells can reproduce by division, creating two identical daughter cells. However, cell division is not discussed in any detail (i.e., mitosis and all its steps) beyond this general understanding. Students also continue to deepen their understanding of sexual reproductions of plants and animals. They can explore some of the behaviors of animals that are aimed at increasing opportunities to reproduce (such as courtship dances of some fish and bird species), and the common dependence of plants on other organisms to help them reproduce (e.g., insects as pollinators). The dependence on the environment and other organisms is also evident in the ability of organisms to grow and develop through the life cycle. For example, the pink color in flamingos is due to the red pigments in the food they eat, Thus, their diet affects their color and ultimately their chance at reproducing, since brighter individuals are considered more attractive by mates. Thus, invisible factors, such as diet, affect growth and development, and one can explain an observable phenomenon, such as feather color, by postulating a hypothesis about less visible (or entirely unseen) mechanisms that can be investigated and tested.

LS1.C: ORGANIZATION FOR MATTER AND ENERGY FLOW IN ORGANISMS

Students delve deeper into the mechanisms involved in obtaining materials and energy from food, or sunlight, in the middle grades. The processes of photosynthesis and cellular respiration (focus on the cell is evident here, too) are introduced at a foundational level, in the form of inputs and outputs, without details of specific formulas or enzymatic reactions. The goal is for students to understand that organisms obtain their energy and materials to build themselves from food. This food is broken down into building blocks, and these are used to create new materials that the organism needs, and in the process, energy is also captured and stored. However, by the end of middle school, students must realize that the process of breaking down and reassembling material for the

purpose of energy storage involves chemical reactions inside cells and/or organs. Students are expected to view such chemical processes at a basic level and should know that atoms are rearranged to form new molecules; they are not required to know specific molecules, structures, or elements at this grade band—only substances like sugar (glucose), oxygen, and carbon dioxide. Again, there is emphasis on the interactions in and across organization levels: The digestive system and its organs break down the food so that cells can use the smaller components. There is also the emergence of some cellular and molecular explanations for these processes at a basic level. Cells in turn make up structures that allow them to function and contribute to the viability of the whole organism. In terms of photosynthesis, the emphasis is on understanding the general idea that plants capture energy from the Sun in sugar molecules, which they use themselves and which are subsequently used by organisms that eat the plants. Understanding the importance of plants in capturing the initial—and main—source of energy on our planet is a major achievement for students at this grade level. Like previously mentioned for breaking down and using food, students in middle school are required to understand that photosynthesis is a chemical reaction—but only at a basic level, with atoms rearranging to form new molecules—and should attend to substances such as carbon dioxide, water, glucose (sugar), and oxygen. Again, we wish to emphasize that the focus is on the big picture—inputs and outputs and the "purpose" of these central biological processes—not on the details often included in common texts. There is also the emergence of some cellular and molecular explanations for these processes involving photosynthesis in plants at a basic level.

6

LS1.D: INFORMATION PROCESSING

For information processing, students are expected to deepen their understanding of the specificity of our sense receptors. Different nerve cells can detect specific stimuli (chemical, mechanical [pressure], temperature) and convey these signals to the brain. Various inputs are processed in the brain and result in immediate responses and/or the formation of memories. The brain's ability to process stimuli, respond, and learn depends on large networks of interacting nerve cells. Establishing these networks and changing them is at the core of creating memories and learning.

Expectations for Grades 9–12

The high school expectations across all four component ideas of LS1 can be characterized as the further elaboration of the mechanisms and the opening of additional black boxes that allow students to broaden the range of phenomena they can explain. There is also a concurrent delving into the molecular level and the increased ability to reason about the organism as a complex system with interacting parts and feedback loops that maintain a range of conditions necessary for cell function (temperature, pH, available energy, etc.).

LS1.A: STRUCTURE AND FUNCTION

In the middle grades, students learned about the various functions that cells have and the idea of specialized cells for specialized functions. At the high school level, students explore the underlying mechanisms at the molecular level that allow for this differential functioning; while all cells carry the entire set of genetic instructions, individual cells are programmed to use only a subset of those instructions; deviations from this mandate have

dire consequences (e.g., cancer cells do not adhere to the programmed restrictions on the genetic instructions). On the other hand, phenomena such as cloning and stem-cell therapy are possible due to a cell's ability to reprogram itself.

LS1.B: GROWTH AND DEVELOPMENT OF ORGANISMS

Students are expected to understand that an organism's ability to grow, develop, and reproduce depends on chemical reactions that are mediated by proteins and that occur inside and outside of cells. While the idea that proteins carry out the work of the cell is introduced in the middle grades (under LS3: Heredity), at the high school level, students expand their knowledge of the roles that proteins have in carrying out and maintaining cellular and bodily functions. Moving beyond the input–output focus of the middle grades, students in high school also learn about the process of cell division, not as detailed steps, but as a highly regulated stage-based process that results in two identical daughter cells that both carry the full set of genetic instructions. The special case of sex cells that end up with half the set of genetic instructions, and why this is necessary, is also explored to broaden students' ability to explain genetic phenomena (although there is much overlap with the ideas captured in LS3).

LS1.C: ORGANIZATION FOR MATTER AND ENERGY FLOW IN ORGANISMS

The deepening and broadening of students' understandings of matter and energy in organisms is predominantly in terms of the chemistry involved and the idea that matter and energy are conserved throughout the chemical reactions that break apart and recombine molecules. In the middle and lower grades, food and matter were treated as singular entities, each a thing unto itself, but at the high school level, the black box of what these materials contain is opened, which allows students to understand the multitude of molecules that make up living things. Life on Earth is carbon based, and there are almost endless ways in which carbon, hydrogen, and oxygen (along with other elements) can be used to create a wide variety of substances with different structures and properties, such as DNA, proteins, sugars, and lipids. Students also broaden their understanding of cellular respiration by opening the black box of alternatives to oxygen-based respiration, namely the process of anaerobic respiration. Anaerobic respiration allows us to explain how some organisms can obtain energy even in low-oxygen environments and how our muscles are still able to function even when our body cannot supply them with enough oxygen (e.g., during strenuous exercise).

Concurrent with zooming in on the molecular level is a zooming out of sorts to understand key feedback mechanisms. For example, cellular respiration generates heat that, along with muscle contraction (movement) elevates our temperature. In turn, processes such as sweating and dilation of blood vessels near the surface allow heat to escape when the body overheats (e.g., during exercise). Overall, the body is maintained at a fairly constant temperature within a restricted range through feedback mechanisms that change the relative rates of the processes that generate and dissipate heat.

LS1.D: INFORMATION PROCESSING

The focus at the high school level is on the functional division of the brain, the complexity of the networks involved, and the brain's relationship to critical complex behaviors. In the middle grades, students learned about simple detection of inputs and transmission of the signal in the nervous system. In high school, the black box of the brain itself is opened, and students learn that there are structural domains of the brain that have important roles in carrying out critical functions such as odor recognition, auditory recognition, control of limbs, emotion, language, and higher cognition. While knowledge of specific brain anatomy is not expected, students should realize the more general principle that a system of functional domains in the brain and its connecting circuits allows animals to behave in characteristic ways (i.e., sense, respond, and interact with other organisms and their environment).

To help understand some of the shifting levels of thinking in the progressions for LS1, we illustrate how student ideas can become progressively sophisticated in Figure 6.5 (p. 116). While specific to LS1.D, the themes of increasingly greater focus on microscopic structures and the inclusion of more hidden mechanism, with greater complexity and interconnectivity within the biological system, apply to LS1.A, LS1.B, and LS1.C as well.

Students' Commonly Held Ideas

Students bring with them a plethora of both productive and unproductive ideas that often embody alternatives to canonical science. Many students' ideas can serve as a good starting place for deepening their understanding of LS1. However, some commonly held ideas might pose challenges to building deeper understanding of this core idea. In this section, we highlight some commonly held ideas relevant to LS.1 that curriculum designers and teachers should be aware of

FIGURE 6.5

The Shifting Sophistication of Student Models Related to LSI.D to Illustrate the Progression of Ideas

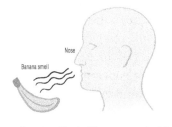

Grades K–2: Macroscopic Model
Includes easily observable external structures

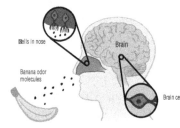

Grades 6–8: Microscopic Model
Includes some cellular & molecular structures

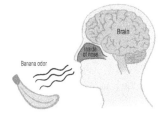

Grades 3–5: Elaborated Macroscopic Model
Includes some less obvious, internal macro structures

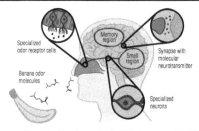

Grades 9–12: Elaborated Microscopic Model
Includes elaborated cellular & molecular
structures & systems

The modeled phenomenon is how we can identify the banana odor, highlighting the macro to micro shifts and the inclusion of increased mechanisms and system complexity. Though we note the *Framework* does not go into details about the molecular steps at synapses, we include synapses here to help illustrate the general expectation for more molecular mechanisms for LSI in high school, but we stop without emphasizing the molecular detail about what happens inside neurons.

to better craft instruction. We wish to emphasize again that a particular commonly held idea that may be incorrect is not necessarily a dead end but is rather a starting point from which we need to navigate toward more coherent and accurate understandings over time.

A key challenge, particularly in the early grades, is helping students move away from thinking of life functions in terms of what organisms "want" rather than what organisms need to survive (Carey 1985). Students' teleological views are not unexpected, as the language we—and they—use

emphasizes wants (we want to eat, sleep, grow, etc.). Issues arise when we discuss less familiar organisms such as plants, worms, and jellyfish. Students do not assume that these creatures "want" to grow or reproduce and thus may assume that they do not grow or reproduce.

Students also have difficulty in accurately conceptualizing which parts of living organisms are made of cells. Despite instruction, some students fail to recognize that plants are made of cells (Flores, Tovar, and Gallegos 2003), or that all tissues are made of cells. In fact, some students tend to think of only a small set of tissues, such as the blood and brain, as being made of cells. A related problem is that even older students (in middle school and high school) fail to think of living things as being composed of molecules. One reason for this problem may be that the difficulties students have in comprehending scale leads to confusion about the relationships between atoms, molecules, and cells (Driver et al. 1994).

Research has also extensively documented the difficulties students have in reasoning across multiple levels of biological organization (Hmelo-Silver, Marathe, and Liu 2007; Buckley 2000; Mintzes 1984). This is partly due to a lack of familiarity with structures that are invisible to students (e.g., internal organs or cells and their components). Students might also inappropriately ascribe behaviors and functions of macroscopic entities to cellular and molecular entities (Dreyfus and Jungwirth 1988). For example, they might view the nucleus as a miniature brain that can command the cell rather than as a cellular compartment for storing the genetic information (i.e., more like a library than a command center). Reasoning across organization levels may also be counterintuitive as structures and functions at one organization level may look entirely different from the structures and functions they produce at higher organization levels. For instance, muscle cells look and behave much like rubber bands, whereas the heart organ they make up looks like a balloon and also expands and shrinks like one. The related understanding that small changes at one organization level, say a change to a protein's structure, can result in very large changes at the organism level (disorder) may also be counterintuitive. These understandings need to be developed over time with substantial support (we discuss some useful strategies and resources in the next section).

One common difficulty in understanding reproduction stems from confusion about the functional differences and purposes of mitosis versus meiosis and where these two forms of cell division occur (Flores, Tovar, and Gallegos 2003; Lewis and Wood-Robinson 2000). Students also find the idea that an entire organism, with its variety of different cells, can be formed from one cell through numerous divisions to be counterintuitive and therefore fail to recognize the critical role of cell division in growth and reproduction (Hackling and Treagust 1982). These two related difficulties are not remediated by the extensive focus on the intricate details of mitosis and meiosis. The focus on detail detracts from the overall understanding about why cells undergo division in the first place and in what context they do so. In addition, some students have difficulty in differentiating between the process of fertilization (i.e., the fusion of egg and sperm) and the mechanism that brings this about (i.e., copulation in animals and pollination in plants) (Lewis, Leach, and Wood-Robinson 2000). Therefore, some students believe that sexual contact is necessary for sexual reproduction (Flores, Tovar, and Gallegos 2003). The confusion of sexual reproduction and copulation likely stems from the everyday uses of terms such as sex and sexual, which contrast with the scientific definitions. As a result, some students may not view plants as being capable of sexual reproduction.

The notions students hold about plants can also be a source of difficulty in reasoning about photosynthesis. Students tend to think of food as something that organisms take in from their environment and not as something that can be synthesized by plants; often, they believe that plants get their food from the soil through their roots (Leach et al. 1996). In turn, even when students understand that plants can create their own food, they frequently do not realize that plants also respire. Plant cells engage in cellular respiration just as animal cells do.

Understanding the relationship between breathing, energy, and food is also challenging for students. Students may fail to recognize that the digestion of food is a chemical transformation and that food consumed by animals is chemically transformed into smaller compounds that are incorporated into the growing parts of organisms (Leach et al. 1996). Relating breathing to the process of obtaining energy from food is also challenging. Students know that animals must breathe, and even that oxygen is transported in the blood. However, the idea that there is a "burning" process in cells that uses oxygen to ultimately capture the energy in food and store it in molecules the body can use is often novel and somewhat counterintuitive (how can we burn food without fire?). The challenge here is in understanding transformations of matter and energy (also discussed extensively in Chapter 7, p. 123). The idea that substances containing a fairly limited set of building blocks that can be broken down and reconstructed to create new substances, and that energy is transformed in these processes, is not trivial to understand and is at the core of relating digestion and breathing to cellular respiration.

What Approaches Can We Use to Teach About This Disciplinary Core Idea?
Developing, Using, and Revising Models

The *Framework* emphasizes that students should learn the identified core ideas through participation in a range of science practices. Since the focus of this book is on the DCIs, we do not focus on those practices; however, we do believe it is important to highlight the value of developing, using, and revising models when students are learning LS1. Research has shown the benefits of engaging middle school students in developing and using models to help them understand the structures and functions of body systems such as the respiratory and circulatory systems (Buckley and Quellmalz 2013; Hmelo-Silver et al. 2007). Furthermore, Penner, Lehrer and Schauble (1998) have demonstrated learning benefits of engaging elementary school students in developing and revising functional models of macroscopic structures such as the elbow. In such cases, students construct and revise their own models (e.g., drawings or 3-D physical models), and/or use simulations and other interactive media. In our view, models serve as tools to think with, they can help students conceptualize the mechanisms involved (in particular structure-function correlations), and they highlight conceptual gaps in understanding. It is not particularly helpful for students to create a representation, such as an image of a cell made out of paper and other craft materials strictly with the goal of creating a "replica" of what a cell looks like. This does not offer many learning opportunities compared with models that focus on mechanism (but that may be less aesthetically pleasing). Modeling not only is a practice that can support sense-making, it is also a great assessment tool for teachers. In fact, educational researchers have successfully examined students' drawings of the human systems and obtained rich evidence of students' understandings of body systems (Reiss et al. 2002).

Using Simulations and Multiple Representations

Simulations and animations can help students visualize and explore mechanisms that involve complex structures and functions and complex cause-and-effect patterns. There are numerous animations and simulations available in biology education, and we cannot review all of them here. We have chosen to highlight a few (most of which are free to use) that are particularly relevant and powerful for teaching LS.1.

WestEd's SimScientists (*www.simscientists.org/sci_topics/index.php*) is a set of formative assessments using animations and simulations that students can use to learn about cells and body systems. With this application, students are able to explore the movement of glucose and starch in the body and how blood sugar levels vary over time (Figure 6.6).

An additional example of using multiple representations to explore a phenomenon in different

FIGURE 6.6

A Screenshot From a SimScientists Assessment on Movement of Foodstuffs

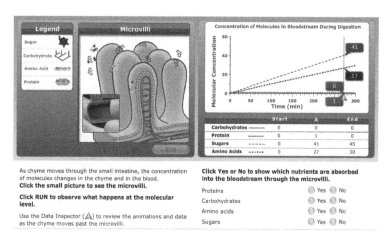

This image from a WestEd SimScientists assessment illustrates the movement of different food stuffs (i.e., carbohydrates, proteins, amino acids, and sugars) from the microvilli in the intestines to the blood stream, revealing that simple amino acids and sugars rapidly enter the blood stream through microvilli, whereas complex carbohydrates and proteins do not. Students can run a simulation to see what happens at the tissue level (*left*); simultaneously, students can see qualitative changes in graphs and tables (*right*). Students use this simulated data to make conclusions about what happens in the biological system.

Source: SimScientists Assesssment Systems: Life Science. Principle Investigator, Edys Quellmalz; Co-Principal Investigators, Barbara Buckley, Mark Loveland, Daniel Brenner, and Matt Silberglitt. IES R305A120390, simscientists.org.

ways is the *Leaf Photosynthesis* simulation developed by Concord Consortium (*http://concord.org/stem-resources/leaf-photosynthesis*). Using this simulation, students can alter the level of different inputs, including the amount of sunlight, water, and carbon dioxide, and then view both a visual representation of sugar in the leaf as well as graphs of sugar production (see Figure 6.7, p. 120). Such a simulation can help students create a conceptual model of photosynthesis in terms of the

6

FIGURE 6.7

A Screenshot From the *Leaf Photosynthesis* Simulation

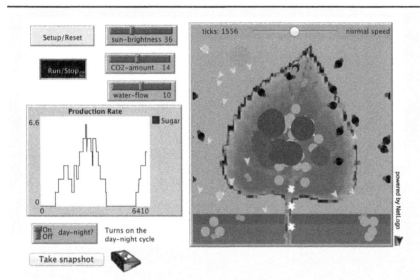

In Concord Consortium's *Leaf Photosynthesis* simulation, students can vary different environmental factors (e.g., sunlight, carbon dioxide, and water levels) and then run the simulation. They see a line graph of the amount of starch produced in the leaf over time (*left side*) as well as an animation of the starch produced in a leaf. Other components are represented as well, such as water and carbon dioxide.

relationships between various inputs and outputs at both the molecular and macroscopic levels.

A third example of using multiple representations to explore phenomena that span several organization levels is the Web-based Inquiry Science Environment's (WISE) curriculum units about mitosis, cellular respiration, and photosynthesis for the middle grades (*https://wise.berkeley.edu*). The WISE units begin with a problem scenario. For example, Mary (a seventh-grade student) wants to grow the most energy-rich plants as food for her pet rabbit (photosynthesis unit), and through a guided investigation, students develop a conceptual model of the relevant phenomena by building on their existing knowledge

and integrating it with new understandings.

In summary, given that students are likely to need help thinking about microscopic, complex, and dynamic events and will need to be able to make connections between multiple levels of organization to understand and use the ideas in LS1, we believe that engaging students in developing models that capture structures, functions, and mechanisms is a productive approach to understanding these complex ideas. In addition, the use of animations and simulations can help students reason about mechanisms that span time and space scales by helping them visualize relevant structures and functions and how events at one level affect subsequent levels. We hope that the few resources we have highlighted will prove a helpful starting point for developing instruction to support student learning of LS1.

Conclusion

The LS1 DCI is central to biology and also serves as the glue connecting all four DCIs in the life sciences strand. In essence, LS1 is about the properties of living things and explaining the complexity of life and the living by exploring their components and interactions across multiple biological organization levels. It addresses a plethora of familiar phenomena and questions such as, "How do cancer tumors form?" "How do plants get their food?" "How can you get an entire organism from one initial cell?" and "Why is it difficult to smell with a stuffed nose?" Teaching this DCI entails engaging students with many phenomena they "know" but may not understand the underlying mechanisms of (e.g., why we breathe) and providing them with powerful ideas to explain the biological world around them.

Acknowledgments

We want to thank the reviewers for their helpful comments and acknowledge Hillary Lauren for creating Figures 6.1–6.5. Funding for Hug and Lauren was provided through a Science Education Partnership Award (SEPA; award nos. R25RR024251 and R25OD011144) from the Office of the Director, National Institutes of Health (NIH). The content in this chapter is solely the responsibility of the authors and does not necessarily represent the official views of the National Institutes of Health, University of Illinois, Purdue University, or Rutgers University.

REFERENCES

Buckley, B. C. 2000. Interactive multimedia and model-based learning in biology. *International Journal of Science Education* 22 (9): 895–935.

Buckley, B. C., and E. S. Quellmalz. 2013. Supporting and assessing complex biology learning with computer-based simulations and representations. In *Multiple representations in biological education,* ed. D. F. Treagust and C.-Y. Tsui, 247–267. Netherlands: Springer.

Carey, S. 1985. *Conceptual change in childhood.* Cambridge, MA: MIT Press.

Chi, M. T., M.-H. Chiu, and N. deLeeuw. 1991. *Learning in a nonphysical science domain: The human circulatory system.* Pittsburgh, PA: Learning Research and Development Center.

Dreyfus, A., and E. Jungwirth. 1988. The cell concept of 10th graders: curricular expectations and reality. *International Journal of Science Education* 10 (2): 221–229.

Driver, R., A. Squires, P. Rushworth, and V. Wood-Robinson. 1994. M*aking sense of secondary science: Research into children's ideas.* New York: Routledge.

Flores, F., M. E. Tovar, and L. Gallegos. 2003. Representation of the cell and its processes in high school students: An integrated view. *International Journal of Science Education* 25 (2): 269–286.

Hackling, M., and D. F. Treagust. 1982. What lower secondary school students should understand about the mechanisms of inheritance and what they do understand following instruction. *Research in Science Education* 12: 78–88.

Hmelo-Silver, C. E., S. Marathe, and L. Liu. 2007. Fish swim, rocks sit, and lungs breathe: Expert-novice understanding of complex systems. *Journal of the Learning Sciences* 16 (3): 307–331.

Kanter, D. E., and M. Schreck. 2006. Learning content using complex data in project-based science: An example from high school biology in urban classrooms. *New Directions for Teaching and Learning* 2006 (108): 77–91.

Kesidou, S., and J. E. Roseman. 2003. Project 2061 analyses of middle-school science textbooks: A response to Holliday. *Journal of Research in Science Teaching* 40 (5): 535–543.

Leach, J., R. Driver, P. Scott, and C. Wood-Robinson. 1996. Children's ideas about ecology 2: Ideas found in children aged 5–16 about the cycling of matter.

6

International Journal of Science Education 18 (1): 19–34.

Lewis, J., and C. Wood-Robinson. 2000. Genes, chromosomes, cell division, and inheritance—Do students see any relationship? *International Journal of Science Education* 22 (2): 177–195.

Lewis, J., J. Leach, and C. Wood-Robinson. 2000. What's in a cell? Young people's understanding of the genetic relationship between cells, within an individual. *Journal of Biological Education* 34 (3): 129–132.

Mintzes, J. J. 1984. Naive theories in biology: Children's concepts of the human body. *School Science and Mathematics* 84 (7): 548–555.

National Research Council (NRC). 2012. *A framework for K–12 science education: Practices, crosscutting concepts, and core ideas.* Washington, DC: National Academies Press.

NGSS Lead States. 2013. *Next generation science standards: For states, by states.* Washington, DC: National Academies Press. *www.nextgenscience. org/next-generation-science-standards.*

Penner, D. E., R. Lehrer, and L. Schauble. 1998. From physical models to biomechanics: A design-based modeling approach. *Journal of the Learning Sciences* 7 (3–4): 429–449.

Reiss, M. J., S. D. Tunnicliffe, A. M. Andersen, A. Bartoszeck, G. S. Carvalho, S. Y. Chen, R. Jarman, S. Jónsson, V. Manokore, N. Marchenko, J. Mulemwa, T. Novikova, J. Otuka, S. Teppa, and W. Van Roy. 2002. An international study of young peoples' drawings of what is inside themselves. *Journal of Biological Education* 36 (2): 58–64.

CHAPTER 7

CORE IDEA LS2

ECOSYSTEMS: INTERACTIONS, ENERGY, AND DYNAMICS

Charles W. (Andy) Anderson and Jennifer H. Doherty

We are enthusiastic about both the reality and the idea of ecosystems. Real ecosystems can be a source of beauty and inspiration; the *idea* of them can help us appreciate the real thing more deeply and manage ecosystems at a time when they are gravely threatened all over the Earth (Hooper et al. 2012; Sayre et al. 2013; Vitousek et al. 1997). Charles Darwin conveyed both the wonder of ecosystems themselves and the wonder of ideas that we can use to understand them in the last paragraph of *On the Origin of Species:*

It is interesting to contemplate a tangled bank, clothed with many plants of many kinds, with birds singing on the bushes, with various insects flitting about, and with worms crawling through the damp Earth, and to reflect these elaborately constructed forms, so different from each other, and dependent on each other in so complex a manner, have all been produced by laws acting around us. … Thus, from the war of nature, from famine and death, the most exalted object which we are capable of conceiving, namely,

the production of higher animals, directly follows. There is a grandeur in this view of life, with its several powers, having been originally breathed by the Creator into a few forms or into one; and that whilst this planet has gone cycling on according to the fixed law of gravity, from so simple a beginning a endless forms most beautiful and most wonderful have been, and are being evolved. (Darwin 1869, p. 579)

Darwin was writing about another disciplinary core idea (DCI)—evolution—but as Darwin shows us, our concepts of evolution are entangled with our notions about ecosystems. We begin this chapter by asking why we should care. What do students need to understand as we seek to preserve the ecosystems that sustain us in a changing world? We then explore the core ideas about ecosystems in the National Research Council's *A Framework for K–12 Science Education (Framework;* NRC 2012), how we expect students to use them, and how they are connected with other DCIs, practices, and crosscutting concepts. We next look at what research on student learning tells us about the resources students bring and the barriers they must overcome to understand ecosystems better. Finally, we share a few ideas about teaching approaches that can help students deal with the pragmatic challenges of sustaining ecosystem services while coming to share some of Darwin's appreciation of the grandeur in the ecosystems around us.

What Is This Disciplinary Core Idea, and Why Is It Important?

What is it about ecosystems that makes them important enough to be a DCI? How can understanding ecosystems make all students' lives richer and our society more successful? We suggest that there are three important reasons for helping all students understand ecosystems.

Experience and appreciation of the natural world. All of our citizens deserve the opportunity to experience and understand the Earth's ecosystems. As Darwin suggests, we can learn to see grandeur in a tangled riverbank as well as in mountain vistas, and if we can do that, our lives will be richer.

Understanding ecosystem services. The Earth's ecosystems provide humans with all of our food, the oxygen we breathe, almost all of our clothing, shelter, and freshwater, and many other services great and small. We depend for our survival and well-being on these ecosystem services. Informed citizens need to understand how ecosystems produce these and how we exploit them.

Projecting how ecosystems will respond to disturbances. Ecosystems are dynamic, constantly changing in response to both natural events such as fire and drought and human disturbances such as land use and climate change.

We need to understand the nature and limits of ecosystems' responses to disturbances, and the difference between disturbances that cause minor changes and disturbances that profoundly affect how ecosystems function and the services that they provide.

Thus, an understanding of ecosystems can both make students' lives personally richer and prepare them to be citizens who make informed environmental decisions. They will be able to use science to guide their actions in both private roles (e.g., learner, consumer, worker) and public roles (e.g., voter, advocate) . A worldwide population of more than seven billion, unprecedented movement of people and goods around the planet, and increasing per capita resource use mean that all ecosystems are now deeply affected by humans.

The *Framework* and the *Next Generation Science Standards* (*NGSS*; NGSS Lead States 2013) recognize how important ecosystems are by making Ecosystems: Interactions, Energy, and Dynamics a DCI. In contrast, the previous *National Science Education Standards* (NRC 1996) did not emphasize the concept of ecosystems. The word *ecosystem* does not appear in the grade K–4 life sciences standards and appears only twice in the grade 9–12 standards—once in the life sciences standards and once in the section on Science in Personal and Social Perspectives. The interdependence of life and ways that humans can disrupt ecosystems are mentioned but with little elaboration.

Why such a contrast? Both our scientific understanding and the world have changed since 1996. Scientists have come to appreciate both the importance and the dynamism of ecosystems, which are the constantly changing systems in which life survives and evolves over time. And human effects on ecosystems—through land use changes, appropriation of water resources, pollution, and global climate change—now threaten ecosystem services essential for our survival. There has been a shift from understanding aspects of ecosystems such as food webs and succession (which is the focus of classrooms now) to understanding inter-relationships and the stability/instability of these complex systems. Thus, core ideas about ecosystems have moved from a peripheral to a central role in the science curriculum.

What Component Ideas Make Up the Ecosystems Disciplinary Core Idea?

In the previous section, we discussed why the Earth's ecosystems are important to us—how we depend on them and how we are changing them. But what are the key aspects of this concept that students need to understand? We have two kinds of answers to this question: First we consider the key that ecosystems play in the hierarchy of biological and Earth systems, making them essential to scientific ways of making sense of the world. Second we consider the importance of specific concepts that students should learn and use—the component ideas of the core idea of ecosystems.

ECOSYSTEMS AND ECOSYSTEM MODELS

Our understanding of ecosystems is built on system models that scientists have constructed, of ecosystems themselves, of their subsystems, and of the larger Earth system that ecosystems are a part of. Darwin emphasized the contrast between the complexity of an actual ecosystem and the simplicity of the laws that govern the lives of all the species in an ecosystem. This is a core challenge that we encounter when teaching about ecosystems: How can students learn to see and appreciate the simple principles that drive complex ecological processes?

We begin by explaining the location of ecosystems in a hierarchy of different scales. Ecosystems include many different individual organisms: plants, animals, fungi, and microorganisms. Yet, we cannot understand ecosystems simply by understanding the organisms they include. This is because ecosystems, like any other system, include many interacting parts, such that the whole is not simply an aggregate of the components but rather something new and complex. The patterns and behaviors of the system cannot be simply predicted based on the behavior and properties of its components. The system's behavior emerges from interactions of its components, and in many ways, these components can themselves be seen as systems at a smaller scale. Thus, the structure and functioning of an ecosystem cannot be predicted from the plants, animals, and decomposers that live in that ecosystem. How do we describe the emergent properties of ecosystems and the subsystems within them? Biologists' system models include a hierarchy of subsystems at different spatial and temporal scales:

Ecosystem scale: Ecosystems include both a living community and a nonliving environment. Matter and energy are constantly exchanged between the community and its environment.

Community and population scale: The living community is composed of populations of different organisms. The interactions within and among these populations are the focus of community ecology.

Individual organism scale: Every population is composed of individual organisms, both multicellular (plants, animals, fungi) and single-celled microorganisms.

7

Cellular and atomic–molecular scale: Organisms are made of cells, and cells are composed of atoms bonded together in molecules. All of the structures and functions of ecosystems ultimately involve atoms that are being rearranged into new molecules in the process of chemical change.

To understand ecosystems, students must *connect* system models at all of these different spatial and temporal scales. While LS1: From Molecules to Organisms deals primarily with the latter two scales (organism and cellular-molecular scales), LS2 deals mostly with the former (community and ecosystem). However, to truly understand ecosystems, one does need to understand at least some aspects of individual organisms and cellular-molecular interactions. For example, students need to understand how chemical processes, such as photosynthesis and cellular respiration, are responsible for large-scale movements of many tons of matter at the ecosystem scale. These connections are essential for students to be successful in understanding how we rely on ecosystem services and predicting changes in ecosystems in response to disturbances.

Component Ideas About Ecosystems

Understanding the functioning of ecosystems at multiple levels and the connections between these levels entails understanding the NRC *Framework*'s four component ideas about ecosystems, which we group into two broad themes. Most aspects of the first two components (LS2.A: Interdependent Relationships in Ecosystems; LS2.B: Cycles of Matter and Energy Transfer in Ecosystems) fall into the broad theme of *ecosystem science*, or studies of how organisms in ecosystems exchange the matter and energy essential for their survival. The other two components (LS2.C: Ecosystem

Dynamics, Functioning, and Resilience; LS2.D: Social Interactions and Group Behavior) and some of the first (LS2.A) fall into the broad theme of *community ecology*, or how populations change and interact within ecosystems.

ECOSYSTEM SCIENCE: TRACING MATTER AND ENERGY THROUGH ECOSYSTEMS

Ecosystem scientists analyze processes in ecosystems by using a key crosscutting concept—Energy and Matter: Flows, Cycles, and Conservation—to trace matter and energy through ecosystems by making connections among processes at different scales:

- Cellular metabolic processes such as photosynthesis, cellular respiration, and biosynthesis (LS2.B)

- Organismal-scale processes such as eating, breathing, growth, and digestion (LS2.A and LS2.B)

- Matter cycling and energy flow at the ecosystem scale (LS2.B)

Figure 7.1 shows in diagrammatic form many of the core ideas that students need to master about matter and energy in ecosystems: matter cycles and energy flows.

Matter cycles: The white arrows in Figure 7.1 show how all the atoms that make up the living community and the nonliving environment of an ecosystem cycle constantly between organic matter and inorganic materials. Carbon atoms move from carbon dioxide in the atmosphere into plants through the process of photosynthesis, are passed through food webs, and go back into the atmosphere. Other elements essential for life—such as nitrogen (note that nitrogen fixation and

FIGURE 7.1

Matter Cycles and Energy Flows

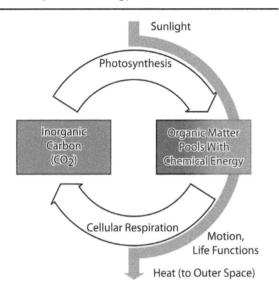

FIGURE 7.2

The Keeling Curve

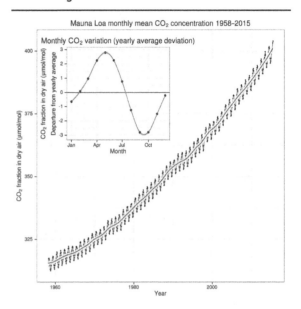

denitrification are not included in the NRC *Framework*), phosphorous, and calcium—also cycle, but through minerals in soil and water rather than through the atmosphere. So the carbon atoms (and other atoms) in our bodies have been in the bodies of thousands of other organisms—trees, insects, mushrooms, whales, and so on—since life began on Earth, cycling constantly between living organisms and the nonliving environment.

Energy flows: In contrast with matter, energy does *not* cycle. To keep functioning, ecosystems must have a continuous flow of energy that plants convert from sunlight to chemical energy in glucose and other forms of organic matter. All the organisms in ecosystems depend on this chemical energy for their life processes. So while the *matter* in the food we eat has been cycling on Earth for billions of years, the *energy* in the food we eat came to the Earth fairly recently in the form of sunlight. We will release it into the environment

as we lose body heat, and it will ultimately be radiated into space (for example, when the Earth cools down at night).

While Figure 7.1 shows some of the connections between the matter cycling and energy flow in ecosystems with processes in their subsystems, Figure 7.2 shows two phenomena involving ecological matter cycling and how these phenomena can affect a large-scale Earth system, such as the atmosphere. Figure 7.2 is a graph commonly known as the Keeling curve (for the scientist Charles David Keeling, who was initially responsible for the measurements). It shows data on atmospheric carbon dioxide concentration taken at the top of the Mauna Loa volcano in Hawaii—a remote location chosen because it generally reflects the concentration of gases throughout the Northern Hemisphere. There are two patterns (phenomena) depicted in the data: a regular annual cycle of carbon and an increasing long-term trend. We can explain the annual cycle phenomenon as an indicator of carbon cycling on a global scale. Every summer, plants grow rapidly, sequestering carbon from the atmosphere into their tissues and reducing carbon dioxide concentrations in the atmosphere. At the same time all organisms are putting carbon dioxide back into the atmosphere through cellular respiration. During the winter, rates of photosynthesis drop drastically, but cellular respiration continues and carbon dioxide concentrations rise again. So even on a remote mountain in Hawaii, atmospheric scientists can measure the collective carbon cycling of the ecosystems in the Northern Hemisphere. (For a fascinating video that compares results from carbon dioxide monitoring stations all over the world, showing the effects of local ecosystems and human technology, see *www.esrl.noaa.gov/gmd/ccgg/trends/history.html*.)

Figure 7.2 also reveals that the cycling of inorganic materials (carbon in carbon dioxide in this case) back into ecosystems is not always immediate or complete. Not all the carbon in living communities is released quickly back into the atmosphere. Sometimes that carbon is buried underground or underwater, where plant and animal materials are gradually transformed into fossil fuels—coal, petroleum, and natural gas. Today, we are digging those fossil fuels back out of the ground and releasing their carbon back into the atmosphere; this accounts for the phenomenon of the long-term trend of increasing carbon dioxide.

Changes to the carbon cycle over time, as displayed in Figure 7.2, are ecologically significant because the carbon dioxide in the atmosphere also affects energy flow; it absorbs heat that would otherwise be radiated into space, thereby causing global climate change. Climate change, in turn, is what ecologists call a press disturbance: a change in an ecosystem that continues and builds over time. Other examples of press disturbances include invasive species and human land use and infrastructure changes that alter water use and stream flow. The *Framework* advocates, appropriately we believe, that all students should learn about the causes and consequences of this global disturbance on ecosystems and ways that they function (note that climate change is also discussed in Chapter 12, ESS3: Earth and Human Activity, p. 225).

COMMUNITY ECOLOGY: DYNAMIC PROCESSES OF CHANGES IN POPULATIONS

Charles Darwin knew nothing of the cycles shown in Figure 7.1. Although he was familiar with the laws of conservation of matter and energy, the chemistry of his day was too crude to support attempts to trace matter and energy through ecosystems. So, the laws acting around us to which Darwin referred were laws of inheritance (which he mostly had wrong) and community ecology. Darwin recognized that *populations* of organisms with resources and relationships were essential to an understanding of biological communities (Mayr 1982). Thus, he was a founder of community ecology as well as evolutionary biology. Evolutionary biologists are especially interested in how the genetic composition of populations changes over time; community ecologists often focus on other attributes of populations, such as their size, range, and relationships with other populations.

Darwin and community ecologists since his time have recognized that the size of a population depends on the balance between the excess reproductive capacities of all organisms (parents produce more offspring than there are parents) and the many factors in their environments (limits to light or nutrients, harsh conditions, predators, parasites, etc.) that cause offspring to die before they can reproduce (LS2.A: Interdependent Relationships in Ecosystems).

Many ecologists once believed that there was an inherent balance of nature that kept communities and populations relatively stable unless they were disturbed. Today, though, most community ecologists see biological communities as inherently dynamic. Even the most robust populations can decline and become extinct if a resource or relationship that they depend on is altered. On the other hand, since every species has excess reproductive capacity, every species is potentially an invasive species, capable of growing exponentially. Thus, the stability of ecosystems can be maintained only if most of the organisms, in every generation of every species, die prematurely; otherwise, every population would grow out of control over time (LS2.C: Ecosystem Dynamics, Functioning, and Resilience).

Figure 7.3 shows a little creature that illustrates these ideas well. Mountain pine bark beetles (*Dendroctonus ponderosae* Hopkins) lived inconspicuously in western forests for thousands of years before humans arrived. Their populations usually remained small even though they had plenty of food and few successful predators or parasites. The limiting factor to their population growth was harsh winters that killed off most of the population every year. In the mid-1980s an ecologist named Jesse Logan began pointing out that without the harsh winters, beetle populations could grow exponentially until they hit some other limit (Logan and Powell 2001). And, in fact, this is the phenomenon happening now in the western forests. The new limit for pine bark beetle populations occurs when they run out of food, that is, when the pine trees in a section of forest are dead (Logan and Powell 2001). So, a small change in winter temperatures

FIGURE 7.3

Pine Bark Beetles and Their Effects

(a)

(b)

can transform mountain pine beetles from a little insect that was barely noticed to a native species invasive in its own habitats that is bringing down the mighty pines (LS2.A: Interdependent Relationships in Ecosystems; LS2.C: Ecosystem Dynamics, Functioning, and Resilience). (Although invasive species are generally introduced to a habitat, a native species can become invasive when it expands its range and changes community dynamics in response to a disturbance.)

Community ecologists organize their research and analysis around populations—such as populations of pine bark beetles and pine trees—because of the important differences in the relationships between populations (interspecific relationships) and within population (intraspecific relationships). In the *Framework*, LS2.A:

7

Interdependent Relationships in Ecosystems focuses on interspecific relationships (and to a lesser extent on intraspecific competition), while LS2.D: Social Interactions and Group Behavior focuses on intraspecific relationships.

The most important interspecific relationships concern *food or resources to make food*. Plants and other photosynthetic organisms are producers, and what they produce by consuming carbon dioxide and water is food—for themselves and for all the animals and decomposers in every ecosystem (and food is, of course, the source of matter and energy for all organisms). Sometimes one species (predators or parasites) simply uses another species as a food source. Other interspecific relationships almost always involve food or resources to make food. Competition, for example, occurs when individuals of one species restrict access to food by individuals of another species. Mutualisms occur when individuals of one species get food from another species while providing some other service in return. For example, flowering plants provide food to pollinators, and the pollinators in turn help the plants reproduce. Similarly, mycorrhizal fungi in the soil help plant roots acquire water and minerals while the plants provide sugar to the fungi.

Competition is one kind of interaction that occurs both within and between species. Many other important intraspecific relationships concern *reproduction*. Most directly, sexual reproduction requires organisms of the same species to get together. (We are fascinated by exceptions to these general rules, such as the phenomena of cannibalism and hybrid offspring produced by mating between closely related species. Learners need to understand, though, how rare those exceptions are and how strong the differences are between interspecific and intraspecific

relationships.) Other intraspecific relationships involve social interactions and group behaviors that can increase the survival of individuals and their kin, such as nurturing young, providing mutual protection, or sharing resources (LS2.D: Social Interactions and Group Behavior).

How Does Student Understanding of This Disciplinary Core Idea Develop Over Time?

Ecosystem science and community ecology can deepen our appreciation and understanding of ecosystems, but they rely on constructs that we cannot see. A visitor to an ecosystem can see individual plants, animals, and fungi but not the atoms and molecules of which they are made and which circulate among them. The core subsystems of community ecology—populations and communities—are in their own way as invisible as atoms and molecules. While atoms and molecules are too small to see, populations and communities are usually too large; they are dispersed across space and time. Furthermore, for most species we rarely see the connections between parents and offspring or members of a herd that tie a population together, or the connections among populations that tie a community together.

Scientific observations can provide evidence of these invisible entities and connections, but children entering school see primarily the visible plants and animals. Research on science learning is helping us explain the stages and processes of learning that elementary, middle, and high school students can go through to deepen their appreciation and understanding of ecosystems. In this section, we discuss some of that research and its implications for the K–12 curriculum.

Ecosystem Science: Learning to Connect Processes from Atomic–Molecular to Global Scales

Figure 7.1 (p. 127) provides a compact representation of the *Framework* ecosystem science–related goals for high school graduates. They should be able to explain processes that occur on ecosystem and global scales, such as carbon cycling, as consequences of processes that occur within cells on the atomic–molecular scale, such as photosynthesis and cellular respiration. Yet the world we perceive around us is "stuck in the middle": visible plants and animals rely on invisible cellular processes and contribute to invisible large-scale matter cycles and energy flows. Our research indicates that the understanding represented by Figure 7.1 is currently achieved by less than 10% of high school graduates (Jin and Anderson 2012; Mohan, Chen, and Anderson 2009), so there's a lot of work still to be done before most students achieve this goal. Next, we describe a possible progression from commonly held ideas of elementary school students to the goal represented by Figure 7.1.

ELEMENTARY SCHOOL LEARNING: CONNECTING ACTORS AND ENABLERS WITH MATTER AND ENERGY

It is not easy for students in elementary school to connect ideas about plants and animals with ideas about matter and energy. Figure 7.4 represents the stories elementary school students typically tell about living systems. They see plants and animals around them, and they are aware that the plants and animals have needs—"enablers" that allow them to live their lives successfully, including such things as food, water, air, and sunlight. It's not apparent at all, though, that those

FIGURE 7.4

Elementary Students' Ideas About Carbon-Transforming Processes

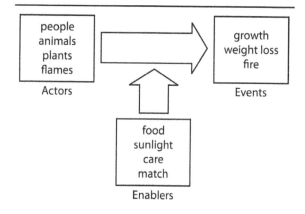

enablers are made of the same kind of "stuff" as plants and animals. So these students know that animals need food to grow but not that food actually *becomes* animal tissue.

Similarly, most elementary school students are aware that plants and animals need energy, and that they get energy from food. But the energy that elementary school students know about is very different from the energy in Figure 7.1. Elementary school students typically associate energy with life ("I got a good night's sleep, so I have a lot of energy today."), and connect energy sources with enablers that help them to feel lively or energetic.

So, before they can trace matter and energy though ecosystems, elementary school students have a lot to learn about scientific conceptions of matter and energy. The *Framework* and *NGSS* do not mention energy in their grades K–5 ecosystem goals, and our research supports this judgment (Jin and Anderson 2012); it is better to leave formal teaching about matter and energy transfers and transformations in living systems until middle school. But there are important things

7

about matter that students can experience and learn in elementary school:

- Distinguishing matter (solids, liquids, gases) from nonmatter (e.g., heat, light, and temperature)

- Measuring amounts of matter (weight/ mass, volume, and density)

- Recognizing that living organisms and nonliving materials are made of the same "stuff" (matter)

Although elementary school students generally are not prepared to trace matter or energy through their transformations in ecosystems, there is much that they can learn about food-based interspecific relationships. Children entering school already appreciate that food is essential for growth and life functions and that different kinds of living things need different kinds of food (NRC 2007, see Chapter 3). They can build on these understandings to start developing an idea of the roles of different organisms in food chains and food webs. For example, elementary school students can understand food chains as cause-and-effect sequences (each animal in the chain needs to eat the organisms below it in the chain to live), even if they do not see the food chain as a sequence of transformations of matter and energy. Similarly, students in elementary school can come to appreciate that plants, animals, and decomposer have different needs and grow in different ways.

- Upper elementary students can learn to recite that "plants make their own food using energy from the Sun," but we need to understand that saying this does not imply a functional understanding of the transformations of matter and energy

in photosynthesis. There are useful and important distinctions that elementary students can make between plants and other organisms: Plants need sunlight to produce food, while animals do not, and the nutrients that plants get from the soil are different from the foods that animals eat. In common and familiar food chains, plants are the only organisms capable of generating new food using light energy. Therefore all food chains start with plants.

- Elementary school students tend to focus on animals as the primary actors in ecosystems, with plants and nonliving organisms as mere enablers for their actions. During elementary school, they can begin to appreciate that their understanding of the relationship between plants and animals is "backward." We and other animals are dependent on plants for our survival, while plants could get along just fine without us. Elementary school students can learn, for example, how to trace even the highly processed and packaged foods in the grocery store back to animals and, ultimately, plants.

- Elementary school students are initially aware of decay as a process but not of decomposers as organisms. Even when they learn about decomposers, including microscopic bacteria and fungi, they are likely to see them as enablers of decay rather than as consumers of dead plants and animals (Jin and Anderson 2012). Thus, elementary school students can learn first that decomposers exist, then that they are like animals in that they use (dead) plants and animals as their food. Elementary school students can also learn to use food chains and food webs to reason about the effects of disturbances on ecosystems (Gotwals and Songer 2010). This involves developing an understanding of "what eats what" in an ecosystem, learning the conventions of representing food chains (e.g., that arrows go from prey to predator), and reasoning through food chains and webs about how a disturbance to one population can affect others. Reasoning both up the food chain (how a change in a prey population affects predators) and down the food chain (how a change in a predator population affects prey) can be challenging, especially if the organisms involved are unfamiliar to students.

MIDDLE AND HIGH SCHOOL LEARNING: MATTER CYCLES AND ENERGY FLOWS

We group middle and high school together because, unfortunately, our reading of the research on student learning doesn't show most students making a lot of progress in their abilities to trace matter and energy through ecosystems in their middle and high school years. Our research demonstrates that middle and high school students—and even college science majors—learn many details about the carbon-transforming processes in Figure 7.1 (p. 127). They can often reproduce chemical formulas for photosynthesis and cellular respiration. They can write about matter cycles. In physical science, they learn to recite the laws of conservation of matter and energy and write chemical formulas and equations.

And yet … for over 90% of middle and high school students, the ability to reproduce these facts and formulas masks fundamental misunderstandings of matter and energy in ecosystems. They are able to trace matter through physical changes that involve solids and liquids but not necessarily through chemical changes into or out of the gas phase (as happens in photosynthesis and cellular respiration). They inappropriately convert matter into energy and back again, explaining, for example, that people can lose weight by exercising because their fat is converted into energy. Their notions of energy in living systems continue to include the idea that "energy is anything that enables life," so many middle and high school students describe "matter and energy cycles" with energy and matter recycling through soil nutrients (Hartley et al. 2011; Jin and Anderson 2012; Mohan, Chen, and Anderson 2009; Rice, Doherty, and Anderson 2014).

Figure 7.5 is our representation of how all these ideas fit together for most middle and high school students. Rather than understanding that one carbon cycle moves carbon atoms into and out of the atmosphere (Figure 7.1, p. 127), they believe that there are two separate cycles, with gases—oxygen and carbon dioxide—cycling separately between solids and liquids. They typically do not ask where the carbon in carbon dioxide comes from. They recognize that sunlight is a source of energy for plants, but most students also believe that energy also recycles through soil nutrients.

All of this helps us to appreciate that understanding Figure 7.1 represents a significant intellectual accomplishment that requires four fundamental shifts in the ways that students perceive the world:

1. Students must learn to apply fundamental physical laws—conservation of matter and energy and processes of chemical

FIGURE 7.5

Middle and High School Students' Ideas About Carbon Cycling: Matter and Energy Cycles

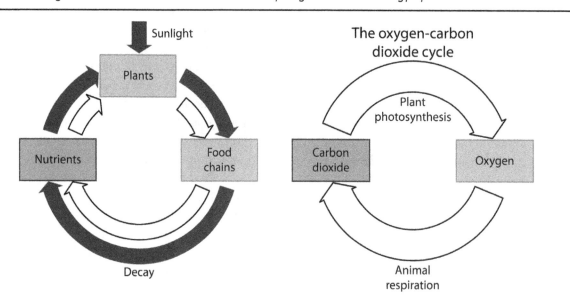

change—to living systems. If they recognize the relevance and importance of these laws, even students who know nothing about ecosystems should be able to see immediately that the "matter and energy cycles" in Figure 7.5 are impossible: Although energy in the absolute sense is conserved, energy within a local or global ecosystem process cannot be recycled, and there must be a source for the carbon in the carbon dioxide. This is difficult learning, though, because cycles in Figure 7.5 make intuitive sense to middle and high school students. Solid nutrients in the soil seem similar to solid plant matter, and gaseous oxygen seems similar to gaseous carbon dioxide. Students need to learn that gases can be massive, and that to understand chemical changes, we

must trace atoms, not observable materials such as soil, air, water, and wood.

2. Students must relate visible plants and animals (and invisible microorganisms) to large-scale matter pools. Ecosystems don't have a "shape," but scientists do represent their structure by organizing them into groups, or pools, of different kinds of matter. At the broadest scale, they distinguish between organic matter (in living organisms and detritus or soil carbon) and inorganic matter (including atmospheric gases, water, and soil minerals). So students must learn to group organisms according to their functional roles in ecosystems—plants, animals, and decomposers—and to focus on the matter and energy that those pools or groups contain.

3. Students must recognize flows or fluxes of matter and energy. Even ecosystems in a steady state maintain their stability through the constant exchange of matter and energy among their different pools. So students must be able to relate visible activities at the macroscopic scale—eating, drinking, breathing, and so on—to large-scale fluxes of matter and energy. They can do this only by learning to go down to the atomic–molecular scale (e.g., recognizing that cellular respiration moves carbon atoms from food into carbon dioxide, which organisms then breathe out into the atmosphere). Tracing matter and energy by making this series of connections across scales—from the ecosystem scale, to the macroscopic, to the atomic–molecular scale, and back up to the ecosystem scale—is immensely challenging for many students.

4. Students must distinguish between matter cycles and energy flows. Matter and energy "move together" through food webs, in the form of chemical energy stored in organic matter. Many middle and high school students conclude that they must move together all the time. And since they learn that energy (in the absolute sense) is conserved like matter, it must also be recycled like matter. They need to recognize that this is not a productive way to think about ecosystems. For example, photosynthesis combines light energy (which does not have matter) with matter (carbon dioxide and water) to produce organic matter with more stored chemical energy. (*Note:* Although all substances contain some chemical energy, carbon dioxide and water do not have energy that can be released by chemical processes in living systems.) The biochemical processes in food webs largely keep this stored chemical energy intact, but cellular respiration and its associated processes again separate the matter from the energy, producing heat, carbon dioxide, and water. Note that while energy is not exactly "stored" in molecules, this is a shorthand used to denote that when comparing the energy states of the reactants (carbon dioxide and water) with the energy state of the products (glucose and oxygen), the latter have higher energy states, and there is therefore a net increase in the energy of the system since the added energy from sunlight was transformed into chemical energy.

These are the specific learning goals that students must accomplish to use the insights of ecosystem science in the service of the three important reasons described above. Achieving these goals is a significant learning challenge for the students, and a significant teaching challenge for science teachers. However, with curricula and assessments that support the *NGSS*, we believe that students can make substantial progress in understanding the core idea of this chapter as described in the *Framework* and the associated progression (see Appendix E of the *NGSS*).

Community Ecology: Learning to Connect Individuals, Populations, Communities, and Ecosystems

We begin our discussion of learning about community ecology with a basic dilemma: While students can study ecosystem science inside the classroom, it is harder to see how they can study community ecology without going outdoors. To understand organisms and their relationships in nature (including highly altered nature such as yards and gardens), students need to *see* organisms in nature. And yet many American students spend little time outdoors (Louv 2008). When they try to understand relationships in ecosystems, they rely on the experiences they do have, including (1) their own experiences with other humans and with pets, and (2) depictions of biological communities in the media, including cartoons, such as *The Lion King*, and nature films, such as *March of the Penguins*. The nature of these experiences has important consequences for students' understanding of community ecology.

ELEMENTARY SCHOOL LEARNING: OBSERVING ORGANISMS IN THEIR ENVIRONMENTS

Although they are well aware that *The Lion King* does not depict the true nature of animals, many elementary students have an understanding of biological communities that is "*Lion King*–like" in important ways. This is not all bad. For example, most elementary school students are aware of many different types of plants and animals, mostly macroscopic organisms divided into broad groups, such as trees, grass, birds, and insects (Harris et al. 2013; Patrick and Tunnicliffe 2011). They are also aware of some important relationships among populations, especially predator-prey relationships. They can recognize the existence of food chains and describe how changes in one population in a food chain will affect others, especially if the populations are directly connected in a predator-prey relationship (Gallegos, Jerezano, and Flores 1994; Hogan 2000).

At the same time, elementary school students reason in ways that rely on inappropriate analogies to their own personal and media experiences. The main actors in their ecosystems are clearly the large animals, with plants and abiotic environments part of being the "scenery" and enablers for the large animals, rather than important parts of the ecosystems themselves. Microorganisms are largely invisible to elementary school students. They use human analogies to explain animal behavior: Animals want, like, or try to be comfortable, and animal families are like human families, with parents caring for their offspring and most offspring surviving to adulthood. A more subtle difference from ecological reasoning concerns what is "normal": Elementary students tend to see a natural order, with animals and plants playing the roles that they are meant to play, rather than dynamic systems that depend on the death of most offspring to remain stable.

As with teaching about energy, some of the key ideas of community ecology are best left for middle school and high school. The most important learning that elementary school students can do will come as a consequence of getting outdoors to observe and analyze actual plants, animals, and fungi, either in forests and fields or in more controlled settings such as school grounds, gardens, aquariums, and terrariums (Ero-Tolliver, Lucas, and Schauble 2013; Lehrer et al. 2000; Lehrer and Schauble 2012; Metz 2000). Key goals for them to achieve outdoors and in classrooms include the following:

• All ecosystems, even the yard outside the school or a city block, have many different types of organisms (e.g., many different kinds of insects, weeds, microbes, decomposers, and organisms that live in the soil). Students of all ages can go outside and observe these ecosystems and make collections of things such as insects, weeds, and decaying leaves. Using video microscopes or nature videos, young students can also observe the microscopic organisms that live in the soil and on decaying leaves.

- Different organisms have different life cycles, especially when contrasted with humans, and many organisms die young. Elementary students can learn about the life cycles of plants, insects, and fungi and how they are different from humans and each other. For example, students can learn that oak trees produce acorns throughout long lives whereas carrot plants only live for two years and only produce seeds in their second year. They can learn how coyotes have about six offspring per year and provide a lot of care, whereas sea stars make thousands of offspring and don't care for them at all, leading to high mortality among the sea star larvae.

- Young students often believe the biggest organism in a food web is the top predator and the smallest is the producer (Gallegos et al. 1994). Elementary students can expand their understanding of feeding relationships to include a diversity of predators and prey by learning about systems in which the top predator is a parasite, like the tiny deer tick, and the producer is a tree, like the towering balsam fir.

- All organisms depend on the materials in and the conditions of their habitats, and they all have relationships with other organisms of the same kind and different kinds. Elementary students can learn about examples of major types of relationships among species

(e.g., predation, mutualism, and competition) and the major types of relationships between species and their environment (e.g., all species have a range of temperature tolerance and water requirements, and all plant species have a range of sunlight and mineral requirements). Students should learn that every organism is helped and harmed by other organisms and by the environment. For example, having a drought can be beneficial to one species of plant but hurt another. All organisms have traits or adaptations that enable them to survive in the place where they live.

- Changes in one population in a food chain will affect others. Elementary students should learn that changes in a food chain will affect more than just the species one link away. For example, orcas have increased predation on sea otters off the coast of California. This has led to a decrease in the sea otter population over the last few decades. This has caused an increase in the populations of their preferred food, sea urchins. This increase in urchin populations has led to a decrease in their preferred food, kelp.

MIDDLE AND HIGH SCHOOL LEARNING: LEARNING TO REASON ABOUT POPULATIONS AND COMMUNITIES

March of the Penguins is a movie that, unlike *The Lion King*, is built around sustained scenes of real-life animal survival and reproduction. So it tells a true story, but not necessarily an ecological story. For example, here is what the narrator,

7

Morgan Freeman, has to say about the meaning of these scenes:

So in some ways, this is a story of survival. A tale of life over death. But it's more than that, really. This is a story about love. Like most love stories, it begins with an act of utter foolishness. The emperor penguin is technically a bird, although one that makes his home in the sea. So if you're wondering what he's doing up here on the ice—well, that's part of our story. Each year, at around the same time, he will leave the comfort of his ocean home and embark on a remarkable journey. He will travel a great distance, and though he is a bird, he won't fly. Though he lives in the sea, he won't swim. Mostly, he will walk. But he won't walk alone. (Jacquet 2005)

To this community ecologists would say, Well, maybe. But love is not our primary concern. This is a story about physical and behavioral adaptations that enable the penguin population to survive over time in its ecosystem. What advantages did emperor penguins gain by walking inland? Why is this not "an act of utter foolishness"? How do the penguins deal with the intense competition for nesting grounds? What changes in the ecosystem might affect penguins' continued survival (Barbraud et al. 2011)?

March of the Penguins was a popular movie in part because it failed to ask these questions. Instead, it organized footage of the penguins' behavior in their natural habitat around themes that humans resonate with: love, loyalty, parental care, and survival in the face of adversity. There is nothing wrong with this story; like all stories, it highlights some aspects of emperor penguins' lives while obscuring others. However, middle and high school students can also benefit from learning to ask and answer the questions of the community ecologists—by learning that the emperor penguin population depends on prey populations to survive (e.g., krill); that the penguins can be prey to other populations (e.g., walruses, predatory birds); that they are adapted to making the long walk to safer breeding grounds; and that their population is in decline as their cold environment becomes warmer.

Our research shows us that many middle and high school students are like elementary students in that they are (1) oriented toward visible, individual organisms and (2) believe there is a balance in nature that is normal and that will be restored after a disturbance (Doherty et al. 2014; Sander, Jelemenská, and Kattmann 2006). While middle school and high school students can reason about trophic cascades using food webs in a more sophisticated way than younger students, they often misunderstand ecosystem concepts due to a simplistic view of causality (Doherty et al. 2014). They often don't recognize cause-and-effect relationships when the effect is removed in space and time from the cause (Grotzer and Basca 2003). For example, suburban development provides opportunities for mice, which are hosts to deer ticks, to multiply, and this increase in the mouse population leads to larger tick populations and more cases of Lyme disease in humans. Therefore, here are some important goals for middle and high school learning:

- Students can learn to explain how changes in one population in a food web can affect other populations through multiple pathways of cause and effect, including indirect effects from changes in competitors. For example, students in middle and high school should be able to predict qualitatively the effects of humans hunting orcas or dumping cat litter containing microorganisms deadly to otters on the ocean on kelp forest growth.

- Students often struggle to relate interactions among individual organisms to consequences at larger scales. Students in middle and high school generally understand how individuals interact with other individuals or their environment (e.g., penguins eat krill, and weeds take up nitrogen from the soil), but they struggle to use that information to explain consequences at the population or ecosystem scale (e.g., penguins help regulate the number of krill in an area and too many weeds can decrease the amount of nitrogen available for corn to grow). Students need to consider how the collective actions of a group of individuals can influence populations or ecosystems.

- Students can expand their understanding of ecological relationships beyond food webs and learn to explain how all populations occupy niches that involve a wide variety of relationships and interactions with other populations (e.g., predation, mutualism, indirect competition through resources) and with the environment (e.g., shade or temperature requirements). Middle and high school students need to learn that there are many aspects of an ecosystem that a population interacts with and that each of these interactions affects the survival and growth of the population.

- Students can develop more sophisticated predictions of how a disturbance will affect the intricate web of relationships among populations and between populations and the environment.

In response to disturbance, populations may grow larger, smaller, migrate, or go extinct. Populations may also be able to survive and change through natural selection (see Chapter 9, "Core Idea LS4: Biological Evolution," p. 165). Middle and high school students should learn to use their understanding of a population's niche to predict what will happen in response to a disturbance. For example, how will pine tree populations in Colorado deal with increasing climate change? To answer this question, students will have to consider the positive effect increased CO_2 has on pine tree growth and the negative effect drought and increased numbers of pine bark beetles have on pine tree growth.

How much an ecosystem is altered by a disturbance may depend on functional redundancy, that is, whether species in relationships with a disturbed species have similar relationships with other species. Middle and high school students should understand that some species have commonalities (e.g., some species of birds eat fruits whereas others eat seeds) and that these commonalities can affect how an ecosystem may be changed or not by a disturbance (e.g., if only some fruit-eating birds are affected by a bird flu, the ecosystem might stay the same if the other fruit-eating bird populations grow).

- Students can refine their understanding of the different roles of interspecific and intraspecific relationships. While the points above relate primarily to relationships among organisms of different species, students can also learn to explain how all sexually reproducing populations must find one another and mate to reproduce. Some populations (such as mountain pine beetles) show little group behavior beyond sex; other populations (such as penguins) show much more elaborate forms of mutual protection and parental care. Students struggle to understand that it isn't just highly sophisticated mammals that engage in behaviors that benefit the group and that may look planned out or thoughtfully devised. So students need to learn that for some populations, such as social insects or schooling fish, group behavior that enables survival and reproduction can be explained by much simpler cognitive mechanisms, so "love" may not have anything to do with it!

With this learning, students can come to appreciate Darwin's "grandeur in this view of life." They can appreciate how, in Darwin's words, populations such as emperor penguins and mountain pine beetles, "these elaborately constructed forms, so different from each other, and dependent on each other in so complex a manner, have all been produced by laws acting around us." Furthermore, they can see how the same press disturbance—such as climate change—can have markedly different effects on different populations: The cold weather that kept the pine beetles in check was essential for the penguins' survival, so as the climate changes, the beetle populations explode and the penguin populations decline.

What Approaches Can We Use to Teach About This Disciplinary Core Idea?

We must help children extend the reach of their experiences, intellects, and imaginations to see the evidence of invisible processes and relationships in the world around them. In this section, we will describe teaching approaches we can use to help students achieve some of the goals described above. Since it is often appropriate to teach toward ecosystem science and community ecology goals together, we discuss both strands at each grade level.

Elementary School: Encountering Materials and Biodiversity

If your school has a yard or nearby outdoor space, there are some pretty interesting things happening out there. Exploring local biodiversity is a great way for students to not only engage in learning about ecosystems but to also experience and learn to appreciate the natural world. Students of all ages are interested and excited to find and collect organisms, learn their names, and learn about the relationships to other organisms and the environment and resources they need to live and reproduce.

We encourage activities to familiarize students with the local biodiversity of all groups: plants, vertebrates, invertebrates, fungi, and microorganisms. Beyond collection and identification of organisms in the school yard, carefully observing the organisms and where they are found provides opportunity for students to learn about the adaptations that enable them to live in a certain place.

Children readily associate organisms with particular locations and can come to see places as providing resources. This, however, is a very limited understanding of interaction. Differentiation of place represents a step toward a more nuanced view. An environment that is initially defined by a student's ability to see or walk around a place eventually becomes differentiated into a number of different microenvironments— the side of a rock that faces the current is now regarded as different from the downstream side because different organisms meet their needs there. The edge of the pond provides resources to cattails and similar plants that are not available elsewhere. The cattails, in turn, host a diverse range of insects, with differences in the resources provided above and below the water line. This early differentiation of place seems to co-occur with children's increasing fascination with a particular organism. We have repeatedly observed students "adopting" an organism like algae, damselfly larvae, or clams, and becoming the class expert on this particular organism. Seeing the place where it lives from that organism's perspective seems to help instigate the differentiation of place that we have described. (Lehrer and Schauble 2012, pp. 183–192)

It is also important to think about relationships among systems at different scales in working with elementary school children. Starting instruction from observations of organisms and building up to communities and ecosystems helps to maintain student interest and allows students to link what they learn about communities to what they see happening to individuals (Magntorn and Hellden 2007). As discussed above, we do not recommend activities that focus directly on transformations of matter and energy in living systems

for elementary school children. There are many fine activities focusing on matter and energy in nonliving systems (see Chapter 2, "Core Idea PS1: Matter and Its Interactions," p. 13). In the context of ecosystems, though, students in elementary school can begin to notice and discuss eating relationships and food chains—an important precursor to learning about matter cycling and energy flow at higher grade levels.

Middle School: Noticing Populations and Tracing Matter and Energy

Harris and colleagues (2013) describe interesting ways to help student become familiar with plant, invertebrate, and microbial diversity and provide links to resources you can use to help students collect and identify local organisms. For example, they describe an activity, "Outdoor Biology Instructional Strategies," in which students find as many samples of plants from their school yard as they can in 10 minutes. The activity concludes with students organizing the samples as a class, often becoming excited by the plant diversity that lives in a very small place.

Working with stream invertebrates is a great way for students to collect data on a local community. Students can make artificial leaf packs (bunches of dead leaves) and place them in a stream. In three or four weeks students collect and examine the packs for aquatic invertebrates in the classroom. The Leaf Pack Network (*www.stroudcenter.org/lpn*) is a network of students and teachers investigating their local stream ecosystems in this way, using freely available identification guides provided by the network. In addition to quantifying organisms, students can also measure the physical characteristics of the stream and locate their local watershed using a map. They can then use the physical habitat characteristics they measured and information land use they collected to draw conclusions about the relationships among habitat, land use, and macroinvertebrate diversity and density. The Pathways Project biodiversity curriculum (*www.pathwaysproject.kbs.msu.edu*) asks students to take the data analysis of their leaf pack further by exploring the functional and taxonomic diversity of the ecosystem, learning about food web relationships, and learning about the ways in which abiotic and biotic factors influence what organisms are present in a community.

Students at the middle school level can also begin tracing matter and energy through living systems. We feel strongly that connecting scales is important when they do this, starting with tracing matter and energy through individual organisms at the organismal and atomic–molecular scale (see Chapter 6, "Core Idea LS1: From Molecules to Organisms," p. 99), then moving on to connecting food chains and food webs with matter cycling and energy flow in ecosystems (Dauer, Miller, and Anderson 2013).

High School: Moving Toward Connected Reasoning and Quantitative Models

If all American high school students had the experiences and understanding described for middle school students above, we would be far ahead of where we are now. There are many additional experiences, however, that could help students advance beyond middle school understanding. Two areas in particular are quantitative modeling and working with large-scale data.

Using a computer simulation is a great way supplement outdoor activities and to have students explore spatial and temporal scales not possible to do in a school yard. EcoMUVE (*http://ecomuve.gse. harvard.edu*) is a curriculum that uses virtual environments to teach students about causal patterns in ecosystems. Students are tasked with finding the cause of a change in an ecosystem—the dying off of fish, for example—or figure out why the introduction of deer has different effects in different forests. In 3-D virtual worlds that have a look and feel similar to that of video games, students can "go back in time" to take measurements, observe organisms working at the atomic–molecular scale, and share their findings with their classmates. This can serve as an entrée into quantitative modeling of matter pools and fluxes in ecosystems.

Students can also participate in observing and monitoring trends associated with climate change and their effects on local ecosystems. For example, Project BudBurst (*www.budburst.org*) is a national network of people monitoring plants as the seasons change (phenology). Students as young as kindergarten age can use scientifically approved protocols to collect data on what day the leaves on a plant in their school yard first started to change color or when most of its flowers have fallen off. They can then contribute this information to the national phenology and climate change database that is freely available for use by scientists and educators. The project offers free, web-based mapping and data visualization tools (*www.budburst. org/fieldscope.php*) so students can analyze the effect of climate on Project BudBurst observations. For example, students can compare flowering time among species and across elevation or latitude gradients using data from all around the country and discover how the seasonal events that they are measuring are affected by climate. They can then predict what will happen as our climate is changing.

Conclusion

We began this chapter by suggesting three ways in which a deeper understanding of ecosystems could enrich students' lives and support their participation as informed citizens in a democratic society: They could develop a deeper appreciation of the natural world, appreciate how our lives and well-being depend on ecosystem services, and recognize how disturbances affect the functioning of ecosystems. The rewards of this kind of understanding are great, but its achievement is a significant intellectual accomplishment, requiring new experiences, important shifts in students' perspectives, and significant learning of science practices, crosscutting concepts, and ecosystems DCIs. In this chapter, we have tried to introduce some of the steps in students' journey toward that accomplishment and some of the ways that educators can help them in that journey.

REFERENCES

Barbraud, C., M. Gavrilo, Y. Mizin, and H. Weimerskirch. 2011. Comparison of emperor penguin declines between Pointe Géologie and Haswell Island over the past 50 years. *Antarctic Science* 23 (5): 461–468.

Darwin, C. R. 1859. *On the origin of species by means of natural selection, or the preservation of favoured races in the struggle for life.* 5th ed. London: John Murray. *http://darwin-online.org.uk.*

Dauer, J. M., H. K. Miller, and C. W. Anderson. 2013. Conservation of energy: An analytical tool for student accounts of carbon-transforming processes. In *Teaching and learning of energy in K–12 education,* ed. R. F. Chen, A. Eisenkraft, D. Fortus, J. Krajcik, K. Neumann, J. Nordine, and A. Scheff, 47–61. New York: Springer.

Doherty, J. H., L. M. Hartley, C. Harris, and C. W. Anderson. 2014. Developing understanding of evolution in complex contexts. Paper presented at the National Association for Research in Science Teaching Annual International Conference, Minneapolis, MN.

Ero-Tolliver, I., D. Lucas, and L. Schauble. 2013. Young children's thinking about decomposition: Early modeling entrees to complex ideas in science. *Research in Science Education* 43 (5): 2137–2152.

Gallegos, L., M. E. Jerezano, and F. Flores. 1994. Preconceptions and relations used by children in the construction of food chains. *Journal of Research in Science Teaching* 31 (3): 259–272.

Gotwals, A. W., and N. B. Songer. 2010. Reasoning up and down a food chain: Using an assessment framework to investigate students' middle knowledge. *Science Education* 94 (2): 259–281.

Grotzer, T. A., and B. B. Basca. 2003. How does grasping the underlying causal structures of ecosystems affect students' understanding? *Journal of Biological Education* 38 (1): 16–29.

Harris, C., A. Berkowitz, J. Doherty, and L. Hartley. 2013. Exploring biodiversity's big ideas in your school yard. *Science Scope* 36 (8): 20–27.

Hartley, L. M., B. J. Wilke, J. W. Schramm, C. D'Avanzo, and C. W. Anderson. 2011. College students' understanding of the carbon cycle: Contrasting principle-based and informal reasoning. *BioScience* 61 (1): 65–75.

Hogan, K. 2000. Assessing students' systems reasoning in ecology. *Journal of Biological Education* 35 (1): 22–28.

Hooper, D. U., E. C. Adair, B. J. Cardinale, J. E. K. Byrnes, B. A. Hungate, K. L. Matulich, A. Gonzalez, J. E. Duffy, L. Gamfeldt, and M. I. O'Connor. 2012. A global synthesis reveals biodiversity loss as a major

7

driver of ecosystem change. *Nature* 486 (7401): 105–108.

Jacquet, L. (Director). 2005. *March of the Penguins.* Burbank, CA: Warner Home Video.

Jin, H., and C. W. Anderson. 2012. A learning progression for energy in socio-ecological systems. *Journal of Research in Science Teaching* 49 (9): 1149–1180.

Lehrer, R., S. Carpenter, L. Schauble, and A. Putz. 2000. Designing classrooms that support inquiry. In *Inquiring into inquiry learning and teaching in science,* ed. J. Minstrell and E. H. van Zee, 80–99. Washington, DC: American Association for the Advancement of Science. *www.aaas.org/report/inquiring-inquiry-learning-and-teaching-science.*

Lehrer, R., and L. Schauble. 2012. Supporting inquiry about the foundations of evolutionary thinking in the elementary grades. In *The journey from child to scientist: Integrating cognitive development and the education sciences,* ed. J. Shrager and S. Carver, 171–205. Washington, DC: American Psychological Association.

Logan, J., and J. Powell. 2001. Ghost forests, global warming, and the mountain pine beetle (Coleoptera: Scolytidae). *American Entomologist* 47 (3): 160–173.

Louv, R. 2008. *Last child in the woods: Saving our children from nature-deficit disorder.* New York: Algonquin Books.

Magntorn, O., and G. Hellden. 2007. Reading nature from a "bottom-up" perspective. *Journal of Biological Education* 41 (2): 68–75.

Mayr, E. 1982. *The growth of biological thought: Diversity, evolution, and inheritance.* Cambridge, MA: Belknap Press.

Metz, K. E. 2000. Young children's inquiry in biology: Building the knowledge bases to empower independent inquiry. In *Inquiring into inquiry learning and teaching in science,* ed. J. Minstrell and E. H. van Zee, 371–404. Washington, DC:

American Association for the Advancement of Science. *www.aaas.org/report/inquiring-inquiry-learning-and-teaching-science.*

Mohan, L., J. Chen, and C. W. Anderson. 2009. Developing a multi-year learning progression for carbon cycling in socio-ecological systems. *Journal of Research in Science Teaching* 46 (6): 675–698.

National Research Council (NRC). 2007. *Taking science to school: Learning and teaching science in grades K–8.* Washington, DC: National Academies Press.

National Research Council (NRC). 2012. *A framework for K–12 science education: Practices, crosscutting concepts, and core ideas.* Washington, DC: National Academies Press.

Parker, J. M., E. X. de L. Santos, and C. W. Anderson. 2015. Learning progressions and climate change. *The American Biology Teacher* 77 (4): 232–238.

Patrick, P., and S. D. Tunnicliffe. 2011. What plants and animals do early childhood and primary students name? Where do they see them? *Journal of Science Education and Technology* 20 (5): 630–642.

Rice, J., J. H. Doherty, and C. W. Anderson. 2014. Principles, first and foremost: A tool for understanding biological processes. *Journal of College Science Teaching* 43 (3): 74–82.

Sander, E., P. Jelemenská, and U. Kattmann. 2006. Toward a better understanding of ecology. *Journal of Biological Education* 40 (3): 119–123.

Sayre, N. F., R. Kelty, M. Simmons, S. Clayton, K.-A. Kassam, S. T. Pickett, and F. S. Chapin. 2013. Invitation to Earth stewardship. *Frontiers in Ecology and the Environment* 11 (7): 339–339.

Vitousek, P. M., J. D. Aber, R. W. Howarth, G. E. Likens, P. A. Matson, D. W. Schindler, W. H. Schlesinger, and D. G. Tilman. 1997. Human alteration of the global nitrogen cycle: Sources and consequences. *Ecological Applications* 7 (3): 737–750.

CHAPTER 8

CORE IDEA LS3

HEREDITY: INHERITANCE AND VARIATION OF TRAITS

Nicole A. Shea and Ravit Golan Duncan

As aptly noted by John Stephen Jones, "genetics is to biology what atomic theory is to physics." Therefore, it is not surprising that heredity constitutes a core idea in *A Framework for K–12 Science Education* (*Framework*; NRC 2012) and the *Next Generation Science Standards* (*NGSS*; NGSS Lead States 2013). There are many, seemingly unrelated, phenomena that can be explained using knowledge of genetics: the rare resistance to human immunodeficiency virus (HIV), the amazing properties of stem cells, the appearance of a trait in a child that neither parent has, genetically engineered glow-in-the-dark cats, and suntanning causing skin cancer. Scientists have engaged in the study of inheritance for over a hundred years, with more ancient theories dating back to the Greek physician Hippocrates and the philosopher Aristotle. Our theories have evolved dramatically over the years and, along with advances in technology, there have been tremendous achievements in our understanding of genetics at the population, organism, cellular, and molecular levels.

Besides serving as a foundational idea in science, genetics also has many practical uses in the everyday lives of citizens. In this day and age,

the public is able to engage directly with genetic technologies, for example, by purchasing direct-to-consumer genetic profiles (e.g., 23andMe). Debates about genetics issues, such as the labeling of genetically modified organisms, also permeate public discussions (e.g., in 2015, members of Congress proposed a federal bill to establish rules for labeling foods as containing genetically modified or nongenetically modified ingredients). Genetic screens are routine in the care of pregnant women and newborns, and there are also a growing number of genetic tests for various cancer-causing genes (such as the gene *BRCA* for breast and ovarian cancer). Engaging in personal and public decisions about these issues entails understanding core genetics concepts, many of which are not trivial to learn. For instance, to properly ascertain the risk of developing cancer, one needs to understand that our traits are a result of complex interactions between genes and environmental factors.

Knowledge of heredity also supports the learning of another organizing theory in biology: evolution by natural selection. Natural selection operates on variation in traits, which is generated from variations in the genetic makeup. Changes to genes can result in detrimental, neutral, or (rarely) advantageous changes to a trait that can influence the individual's likelihood of survival and reproduction. Understanding the mechanisms that generate genetic variation is central to understanding heredity and evolution.

What Is This Disciplinary Core Idea, and Why Is It Important?

The heredity disciplinary core idea (DCI) addresses two core questions: How are genetic traits passed on from one generation to the next? And how can individuals of the same species (even siblings in the same family) have different traits? These are central questions in the field of genetics, and they are relevant to children's lives given the natural experience they have with noticing similarities and differences between themselves and their family members and other individuals. The *Framework* characterizes two component ideas for this DCI: LS3.A: Inheritance of Traits and LS3.B: Variation of Traits.

LS3.A: Inheritance of Traits

LS3.A deals primarily with the relationship between genes and traits within and across generations and explains how the invisible genes we get from our parents bring about our observable traits. In essence, this component idea provides an explanation of the mechanism that links the traits and genes parents have with the traits and genes of their offspring.

Central to LS3.A is the idea that genes are fundamentally instructions for proteins, and it is the proteins that carry out a multitude of functions that ultimately result in our observable traits. Proteins can transport substances (e.g., hemoglobin transports oxygen in blood), they can allow substances in and out of the cell (e.g., channels in the cell membrane), they are involved in signaling (many hormones are proteins), and they build parts of our cells and bodies (e.g., collagen gives skin its elasticity). A protein molecule is essentially a long chain of amino acids that folds onto itself to create a three-dimensional structure, much like a chain of beads can be scrunched into a ball structure or stretched to create a straight line. The type and order of the "beads" (amino acids) in the protein chain are determined directly by the genetic code. This code is universal, meaning that the genetic material of every organism is built from the same four chemical units, known as nitrogen bases. Phenomena involving the use of genes to cure disorders (gene therapy) and the genetic modification of organisms such as corn are possible because of the universality of the genetic code. For example, human genes can be inserted into a mouse such that a protein will be made by the mouse based on human genetic instructions; the reverse is also possible. A trait can therefore be transferred from one organism to another by providing the relevant genetic instructions. As an example, consider the somewhat sci-fi phenomenon of glow-in-the-dark cats. Scientists have taken a gene for a protein that glows in the dark found in jellyfish and have inserted it into cats, resulting in a new trait: cats that glow in the dark. The glow-in-the-dark trait has been transferred to many other organisms, including pigs and monkeys, using the same gene from jellyfish.

Note that the *Framework* and the *NGSS* limit the expectations for students in terms of the biochemical structures and processes involved in the "reading" of the genetic code. Students are not expected to know the specific steps in transcription and translation of genes to proteins or the structures of the entities involved in these processes (e.g., structure of amino acids, mRNA [messenger RNA], tRNA [transfer RNA], ribosomes). Rather, the focus is on the end-products of these processes and their biological roles, with the goal of understanding why proteins are important rather than what they are made of.

The relationships between proteins and traits can be rather complex. However, examples of genetically modified organisms (e.g., the glow-in-the-dark cat example) and genetic disorders offer a window into how proteins ultimately result in observable traits. Most genetic disorders are a result of one or more proteins that are either malfunctioning or entirely missing. For example, sickle cell anemia is caused by a misshaped hemoglobin protein that is "sticky" and tends to clump into long strands that deform the shape of the red blood cells in which these proteins are found (Figure 8.1). The sickle-shaped blood cells get stuck in blood vessels and can break, causing severe pain and potential clots. In patients with sickle cell anemia, the gene that has the instructions for making the hemoglobin protein contains an error that changes the shape of the resulting protein, making it sticky. It is important to point out here that the relationships between structure and function, as well as cause and effect, are two crosscutting concepts that are relevant to the exploration of a variety of phenomena including genetic disorders like sickle cell anemia.

Part of the answer to the driving question for LS3.A, "How are genetic traits passed on from one generation to the next?" is that we look like our parents (and other humans in general) because we share the same genetic instructions for making the same or similar proteins and therefore have the same or similar traits. The other part of the answer involves the generation of new combinations of

FIGURE 8.1

Comparing the Structure of Normal and Sickled Red Blood Cells

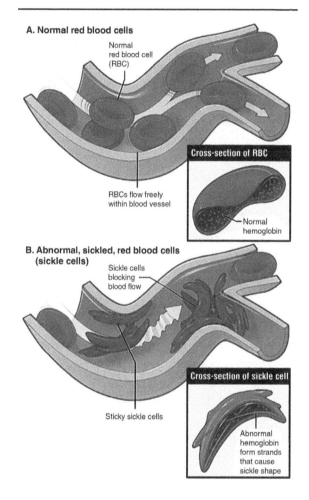

genetic instructions in the offspring by mixing genetic material from both the parents.

We get half of our genetic information from each of our parents. Humans have 23 pairs of chromosomes; each chromosome in each pair originates from either the mother or the father. A chromosome pair carries genes for the same traits (there are hundreds of genes on a chromosome). For example, the gene for hemoglobin is on the two chromosomes of pair number 11. The infamous *BRCA2* gene that is linked to breast cancer is on both chromosomes in the 13th pair. While each chromosome in the pair contains the same genes in the same order, the versions of the gene may differ between the chromosomes in the pair. A useful analogy here is ice cream flavors. If we think of a gene as a recipe for ice cream (the trait), then there would be a one version of the ice cream recipe for chocolate flavor and one for vanilla flavor. Both versions are recipes for ice cream (as opposed to some other food), but the resulting ice cream product (the trait) differs in significant ways. Note that this is a major simplification. Many traits involve multiple genes and exhibit very complex patterns of inheritance. We simplify the discussion here to focus on traits that are controlled by a single gene, and we first explain the simpler case of traits that are inherited as dominant or recessive.

As humans, we each have two variants for every gene. These variants are called alleles, and each originates from one of our parents. Together the two variants represent our genetic makeup for a particular trait. Scientists use capital or lower case letter (a or A) to denote the different allele versions. Traits also have variations, for example, we may have dimples or we may not, we may have attached or unattached earlobes, we may be able to roll our tongues or we many not, and so on. Which version of the trait we express depends on the specific combination of alleles we have in the pair: If there is one dominant allele in the pair denoted by a capital letter (either Aa or AA) we will express the dominant trait, if both alleles are recessive (denoted by lower case letters as aa) we will express the recessive trait. In the case of dimples, having dimples is dominant (AA or Aa), whereas the absence of dimples is recessive (aa).

The two alleles are essentially copies of the same gene but with slight differences in them, like two recipes of ice cream for different flavors.

It was the Austrian friar Gregor Mendel who figured out the necessary existence of two alleles per trait and the relationships (dominant, recessive) between pairs of alleles. The notion that we have two versions of each gene can help explain puzzling phenomena such as traits seemingly skipping generations (i.e., a trait is present in one of the grandparents and a grandchild but neither parent has the trait). Given that there are two alleles for each trait, individuals can carry an allele for the version of the trait they do not show. Therefore while the parents can carry the recessive allele (Aa) and show the dominant trait, their children may inherit two recessive alleles, one from each parent, and consequently show the recessive trait. This raises the question of why Aa individuals do not show the recessive trait—after all they do have the recessive allele. The answer lies in the instructions provided by each allele.

Let's consider the sickle cell anemia phenomenon again. Individuals with sickle cell anemia have an error—a mutation—in their instructions for the hemoglobin proteins. All the hemoglobin they make is misshaped. This is because, in these unfortunate cases, both alleles have an error in them. Sickle cell individuals are denoted as (ss) compared with healthy individuals who have (SS), or two correct copies of the gene for hemoglobin. What happens if you only have one correct copy (Ss)? Well, that depends on the disorder. In the case of sickle cell anemia, individuals with (Ss) are mostly healthy. They do suffer from slight anemia, yet for the most part they can function normally and are considered healthy. However, some traits and disorders are inherited as dominant, this means that individuals with two different alleles are sick, even though they have one normal copy of the gene. For example, some types of dwarfism are dominant. The gene in question provides instructions for making a protein growth factor needed for normal growth. If a person has only one correct copy of the instructions for the growth factor, they are still very short and considered a dwarf, because having one correct copy is simply not enough to make the necessary amount of growth factor. One needs two correct copies to make the requisite amount of this critical growth protein. Therefore, whether having one correct copy of the instructions is enough depends on the protein and the trait involved. Dominance and recessiveness is therefore not an issue of strength of one allele over the other but rather whether the resulting output of proteins from the two alleles can bring about one version of the trait or another (e.g., sickle cell or no sickle cell).

The dominant-recessive relationship that occurs between alleles is a central issue in genetics and is often the first one taught in school. However, there are several types of relationships between allelic combinations that give rise to different patterns of inheritance (correlation between genes and traits). For example, in incomplete dominance, another inheritance pattern, the dominant allele is not fully dominant over the recessive allele and therefore the Aa combination gives rise to a third, intermediate phenotype. The phenomenon of hair texture, curly versus wavy versus straight, is an example of incomplete dominance (wavy hair as an intermediate between curly and straight hair). The relationships between alleles and phenotypes can get rather complicated, and the *Framework* does not specify which of these additional inheritance patterns students are expected to know (beyond recessive and dominant). The high school curriculum often includes incomplete dominance, sex-linked, and codominance as additional relationships. However, these are not mandated in the *Framework* nor addressed by *NGSS* performance expectations.

So far we have explained how genes bring about our physical traits, and how combinations of alleles result in the expression of either the dominant or recessive version of the trait. One question remains: How do genes physically get from parents to offspring? The answer lies in our sex cells, egg and sperm, which are needed to make a new offspring. These specialized cells carry only half of the genetic information. That is, each sex cell has only 23 chromosomes, with one representative from each pair. When these sex cells combine through fertilization, the two half sets come together to form a new complete set in the resulting offspring.

Meiosis is the process by which sex cells are formed from ordinary cells that have the full complement of genetic information. A key aspect of meiosis is that it allows for random allocation of chromosomes from each pair into the sex cell, such that each sex cell has a unique combination of half pairs of chromosomes. This random allocation increases variation between sex cells and can explain why siblings, even though they come from the same set of parents, do not look exactly alike (more on this in the section on LS3.B later in this chapter). A key point to note here is that a representative from each of the 23 pairs must be present in these sex cells; deviations from this number have severe consequences because the offspring will end up with incomplete pairs or triplets instead of pairs. The phenomenon of Down syndrome, for example, is the result of having three copies of chromosome 21 instead of two (Figure 8.2, p. 150). Most other cases of missing or

FIGURE 8.2

Karyotype for Trisomy Down Syndrome

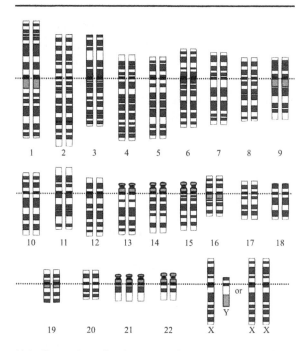

Note: Figure shows the chromosomal makeup of a male with Down syndrome. Note that there are three, rather than two, copies of chromosome 21.

extra chromosomes are not viable and the embryo does not develop.

The last aspect of LS3.A we would like to discuss relates to the puzzling phenomenon of the cloning of Dolly the sheep. Scientists at the Roslin Institute in Scotland created Dolly from a single cell that they took from the udder of an adult sheep (Figure 8.3). How is it possible that an udder cell can give rise to a whole sheep? Where did the genetic information for making the sheep's heart, lungs, eyes, brain, and everything else come from? It turns out, the information was in the udder (mammary) cell even though that cell did not use it. The udder cell only used

genes for making proteins that are necessary for the udder; genes for making blood, muscle, or brain proteins were not used. The idea that every cell carries the entire set of genes but uses only some of them might seem counterintuitive: Why would skin cell have genes for making muscle proteins? However, each cell does, in fact, have the entire complement of genetic information (all 23 pairs of chromosomes in humans) but makes proteins only from those genes it is programmed to use. Recent advances in genetic technology have allowed scientists to reprogram cells to use different sets of genes and thereby acquire new functions. In the case of Dolly, scientists took the nucleus (with the genetic information) from an all white Finnish Dorset ewe and combined it with a nucleus-free cell from a Scottish Blackface sheep. The newly combined cell developed into an early embryo (blastocyst) that was then implanted into a surrogate Blackface ewe. If the genetic information used to make the embryo came solely from the white sheep, the new lamb would be white; if, however, the procedure didn't work (i.e., the nucleus was not entirely removed from the cell of the Blackface sheep) then the lamb would be black-faced. Dolly turned out all white, which means that the genetic information to create her came from the reprogrammed mammary cell nucleus that came from her identical clone mother, the Finnish Dorset sheep.

Scientists can also use stem cells, which are essentially "unprogrammed," and induce them to use any subset of their genetic information and have them become any type of cell.

In summary, LS3.A deals with the mechanisms that explain why we look like our parents and other humans. Understanding these mechanisms entail understanding genes as instructions for specific proteins. Proteins in turn have a slew of functions, and our traits are a direct result of protein functions and interactions. When proteins malfunction, because of errors in the genetic instructions for making them, genetic disorders arise. The instructions for proteins come in pairs; there are two versions of the instructions for each protein that the body can make. Which traits we show depends on the combination of the gene variants we have for a particular trait. The combination in us may be different from what either of our parents have, and this explains traits seemingly skipping generations in a family. Thus, we are not identical to our parents or siblings because we may have allele combinations that are different from theirs. We discuss the basis for these differences in traits in more detail in the next section.

LS3.B: Variation of Traits

Many of the mechanisms discussed in LS3.A that generate the similarities between parents and offspring also play a role in generating differences between parents and offspring, which is the focus of LS3.B. For example, using the understanding that genes are instructions for proteins, we can think about variations to these instructions and their consequence for protein function and, ultimately, the trait. Similarly, the shuffling of chromosomes during meiosis to generate random assortments of alleles in the sex cells also contributes significantly to variations in the traits of sexually reproducing organisms. Organisms that do not reproduce sexually do not show such variation and suffer from the consequences of having a very homogenous population; a catastrophic event might wipe out the entire population because none of the individuals have potentially advantageous variations of traits. Another key source of variation is the influence of the environment on

FIGURE 8.3

The Cloning of Dolly

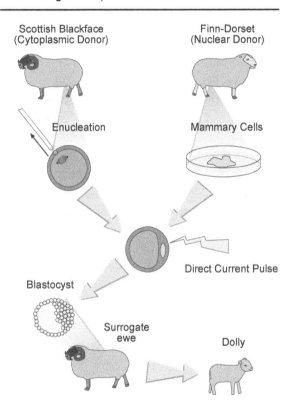

Dolly was cloned by removing the nucleus from the mammary cell of a Finn-Dorset sheep and inserting it into a nucleus-free cell from a Scottish Blackface sheep. The resulting sheep, Dolly, looked like the donor of the nucleus (nuclear donor) and not like the donor of the cell (cytoplasmic donor).

our traits. This influence is most obvious in cases of identical twins that show some differences in traits (height, skin color, hair color, etc.). Although genes determine our potential traits (e.g., how tall we could get), it is the interplay between genes and the environment (e.g., availability of food) that generates our actualized traits (e.g., how tall we do get). We discuss each of the central sources of variation below.

The first source of variation we address is mutations, that is, changes to the genetic code. Most commonly, mutations result from random errors that occur when chromosomes are replicated just prior to cell division. Although these errors are often corrected by specialized cellular machinery, some persist. These mutations can be silent (neutral) when they do not result in a change to the protein encoded by the gene. This is much like changing the spelling of the word color to colour, which would not make a difference to the meaning of the sentence since both are viable spellings of the word. More often, mutations do result in a change to the protein's shape and consequently its ability to function. Most mutations are therefore potentially harmful. A small percentage of mutations may result in beneficial outcomes. For example, the change in hemoglobin in sickle cell anemia has some benefits—it turns out that the malaria parasite has trouble infecting individuals with sickle-shaped red blood cells. Individuals with the Ss genotype are only slightly anemic but are also resistant to malaria; in their case, the mutation has a beneficial effect and results in an advantageous trait.

Another key source of variation stems from the random process that distributes chromosomes into sex cells, meiosis, which was discussed earlier. For example, in a mother with Aa alleles for a particular trait, probabilistically, half the egg cells will have the recessive allele (a) and the other half the dominant allele (A). Thus, her offspring have a 50% chance of inheriting either allele from her. If we consider two traits denoted by the genotypes Bb and Aa, then there are four possibilities for combinations in the egg cells: AB, Ab, aB, and ab. The segregation of alleles is independent as long as the genes for the A and B traits are on different chromosomes. That is, each combination of alleles for the two traits above is equally likely if the genes are on different chromosomes (i.e., A is on chromosome 1 and B is on chromosome 2). The randomness involved in the distribution of alleles in the parent sex cells, and the randomness of which two sex cells fertilize, give rise to new combinations of allele pairs in the offspring, which is why siblings do not look exactly alike.

There is yet another way in which alleles are further shuffled in meiosis, when chromosomes in the pair actually swap parts before the pair breaks into separate sex cells. As noted above, alleles for different traits (i.e., traits A and B) are segregated into sex cells randomly and independently as long as they are on different chromosomes. But what happens if the genes are on the same chromosome? Then, the specific alleles for each gene will be segregated into the egg or sperm cell together. In this case, if the mother has the variants Aa and Bb, with one chromosome in the pair carrying the alleles AB and the other carrying ab, the resulting eggs will have AB or ab, and none will have the combination Ab or aB. However, in some cases, the chromosomes swap sections during the beginning of the division process such that alleles are swapped, resulting in Ab and aB carrying chromosomes. This recombination step provides additional genetic variation because it results in four combinations: Ab, aB, AB, ab, rather than the original two options of AB and ab.

The third source of genetic variation discussed stems from interactions of genes and the environment. There are two main ways by which the environment can affect traits and genetic variation: (1) influencing gene expression and (2) physically altering the genetic instruction. A simple phenomenon illustrating the first point is suntanning. While our genes determine our "baseline" skin color, we can further darken our skin through exposure to ultraviolet rays. These rays induce the expression of genes that code for proteins involved in making melanin—the pigment that gives skin its brown color. It is the combined effect of our genetic makeup and the environment (Sun exposure) that results in the ultimate shade of our skin. Thus, environmental factors can alter which genetic instructions the cell uses and when they are used.

The second way in which the environment affects our traits is a change in gene instructions through mutation. Many chemicals and different forms of radiation (x-ray, ultraviolet, gamma) can physically change the genetic instructions by breaking the DNA molecule or causing other changes. As noted earlier, cells do have mechanisms to correct such errors, but when many errors occur at once, these mechanism are overwhelmed and fail to catch and correct all of them. The result can be changes to several genes and their protein products that are likely to affect the organism's traits. There are many known mutation-causing environmental factors (mutagens), such as benzo[a] pyrene found in cigarettes, ethidium bromide used in DNA electrophoresis gels, and benzene used as a precursor for nylon production. A phenomenon that clearly illustrates an event that overwhelms the mutation-correcting systems is radioactive poisoning. Large amounts of radiation cause so many errors that it often results in the death of cells and the individual.

Understanding these environmental effects is important because such influences underscore the nondeterministic nature of inheritance. While there are some examples of single gene mutations resulting in genetic disorders through relatively simple causal mechanisms (like sickle cell anemia), most genetic phenomena are far more complex and involve interactions of many genes and environmental effects such as changes in gene expression. In these more common cases, having a specific genetic mutation (i.e., allele) may or may not result in a particular trait depending on other factors such as lifestyle. Consider the phenomenon of genetic predisposition to breast cancer; having a mutation in the *BRCA* gene results in a predisposition to cancer but it in no way ensures the occurrence of cancer. Therefore, evaluating genetic risk and deciding on an appropriate course of action depends on an understanding of these pervasive interactions between genes and the environment.

In summary, the *Framework* highlights several mechanisms that generate variation, including mutation, random distribution of alleles in sex cells, and recombination. It also stresses the role of the environment in generating additional variation predominantly through changes in gene expression and mutations. While mutations can be deadly for the individual, genetic variations can be critical for the survival of populations of organisms, particularly when the going gets tough. In challenging times, when resources are scarce or after an environmental crisis (e.g., drought, hurricane), organisms that have variations that are better suited to the new situation can continue to survive and reproduce; thus, the survival of the entire population depends on the existence of individuals with beneficial variations. Populations that have little variation in their traits (across individuals) are less likely to withstand such environmental changes and may become extinct. For example, the Irish potato famine of the 1840s resulted from the use of a single type of potato—the Irish Lumper—in agriculture. Instead of generating new potato plants by reproduction, farmers planted pieces of parent plants that grew into new plants that were essentially clones. These potatoes turned out to be highly susceptible to a rotting disease that destroyed a vast portion of the crops, leaving one million people to starve. Genetic variation is the basis for evolution; without it, better-adapted organisms would not appear. We next discuss some of the main differences between the heredity DCI and the associated *NGSS* recommendations and the genetics concepts in the older *National Science Education Standards* (*NSES*; NRC 1996) and the American Association for Advancement of Science (AAAS) *Benchmarks for Science Literacy* (*Benchmarks*; AAAS 1993).

HEREDITY CONCEPTS IN THE NEW AND OLD STANDARDS

There are several ways in which heredity is addressed differently in the *Framework* compared with the preceding standards and benchmarks. First, there is substantially more focus, and at earlier grades, on elucidating the mechanisms that link genes to traits within an individual (the role of proteins). The old standards introduced genes as instructions for traits at the middle school level. The mechanisms of how these instructions bring about observable traits were not addressed at all. Presumably that is due to (unwarranted) assumptions about young students' abilities to reason about entities that are too small to see with the naked eye (such as proteins). The link between genes and proteins, as well as the biochemical processes of transcription and translation of DNA were relegated to the high school level. The *Framework* takes a somewhat different stance by embracing the idea that even middle school children can reason about abstract and invisible entities (NRC 2007; Smith, diSessa, and Roschelle 1994) and therefore are capable of understanding

aspects of the protein-based mechanism that link genes and traits.

The key difference here is that the *Framework* encourages students, and teachers, to open up the black box linking genes to traits and introduce the mechanisms in terms that young students can understand. For instance, students can reason about some protein functions that have analogues in the macroworld that are familiar to students, such as springlike proteins involved in absorbing the shock of muscle contraction, channel proteins that selectively let some substances into the cell, receptor proteins that can bind selectively to substances, and others. The *Framework* is not advocating for explanations of the genetic code or protein structure and function at the molecular level (nucleotide, amino acids, etc.). Rather, the focus is on conceptually accessible functions of proteins and genes as "recipes" for proteins. In dealing with structure-function correlations (a crosscutting concept) in proteins and genes, the emphasis is on shape and affordances of shape for function, without delving into molecular structures and interactions.

There are analogous differences between the *Framework* and the *NSES* in terms of their treatment of trait variation. The *NSES* relegated understanding the relationship between combinations of gene variants (alleles) and traits to the high school level. At the middle school level, the *NSES* were mostly about reproduction at the cellular (sex cells) and organismal levels; the take home message was that genes determine traits, but the mediating mechanisms are black-boxed. These mechanisms are discussed in the *NSES* but only at the high school level and with more emphasis on molecular structures and biochemical processes. The *Framework*, in contrast, introduces the idea of two alleles per trait at the middle school level. At the high school level, the explanation of what causes genetic variation is further deepened by adding the mechanism of chromosome recombination during meiosis to the existing stories of independent assortment and random segregation during sexual reproduction and the occurrence of random mutations.

Another key difference between the old and new standards is the emphasis on the interplay between genes and the environment in determining our traits. In particular, the *Framework* explicates the idea that environmental factors can contribute to heredity in two ways: (1) by altering gene expression and (2) by causing mutations. Emphasis is placed equally on both ideas with introduction starting in fifth grade. The AAAS *Benchmarks* and the *NSES* placed greater emphasis on environmental factors contributing to heritable mutations than influencing gene expression and reserved these ideas for high school.

While there are many complexities in inheritance that are not addressed by the standards (new or old), there is an important emphasis on the complex nature of genetics and the difficulty in predicting variation and appearance. Both the *Framework* and NGSS acknowledge the nondeterministic nature of the genetic information in relation to traits, starting in high school. The notions that not all DNA codes for protein and that some DNA serves regulatory and structural capacities (and that some DNA has no known function) are new concepts not acknowledged in previous standards. It is important to take note of what is new and different in the updated standards, both in terms of the emphases and sequencing to achieve a coherent and focused curriculum.

How Does Student Understanding of This Disciplinary Core Idea Develop Over Time?

Over the past 10 years, several research-based models have been developed to describe how student understanding of genetics develops over time from early elementary to late high school (e.g., Duncan, Rogat, and Yarden 2009; Roseman et al. 2006). This research base informed the development of the heredity DCI and its progression over grade bands. The main thrust of the progression is from a naturalistic theory of kinship (offspring look similar to but not exactly like their parents, but without an explanatory mechanism) to a more fully fledged theory of inheritance that involves mechanisms for generating both physical traits and genetic variation. As students progress through schooling, more of the "black boxes" of genetic phenomena are opened and investigated such that students progressively build a larger tool kit of mechanisms and understand these mechanisms in more depth. Depth in this case often involves understanding the mechanisms at lower organization levels, moving from the macro to the micro, and eventually studying molecular mechanisms. In this section, we will briefly discuss the progression in terms of the two component ideas of LS3.A and LS3.B (Table 8.1, p. 157).

Grades K–2

During the early grades, K–5, the two component DCIs are not differentiated. For the lower grades, K–2, the main focus is on recognizing similarities between parents and offspring. Children at this age develop a theory of kinship: We look like our kin. They also understand that kittens look like their cat parents and puppies like their dog parents. Thus, the relationship between parents and offspring extends beyond humans. Along with recognizing similarities between kin, there is also emphasis on noticing differences, that is, variations. Kittens and their parents may differ in their markings, and a mixed-breed puppy will share some traits with both parents. Students can come to see these similarities and differences as a consistent phenomenon across many organisms, both familiar (dogs and cats) and less familiar (fish, snakes, etc.).

Grades 3–5

At the upper elementary level (grades 3–5), students are expected to understand that offspring look similar to their parents because they share genetic information. This notion of genes-as-information is important and serves as the foundation for later understanding regarding what the genetic information actually specifies about our traits. At this grade band, students are also expected to notice, but not explain, the effects of environments on our traits; for example, an animal's diet can affect its traits (e.g., the flamingo's pink color is from the food it eats). Many behaviors of animals have a genetic component and a learned component. Burrow and nest building by many species are both genetic and learned behaviors. Rats instinctively build burrows in the ground; however, the efficiency of their burrowing is a learned behavior from observing other rats' burrows and through trial and error with their own constructions.

Thus, during the early grades the focus is on attending to and noticing important aspects of genetic phenomena such as kinship similarities and environmental effects. This noticing sets the stage for later investigations of the mechanisms that underlie these early observations. The two component ideas are combined at this grade band, but at the middle school level, they split into two separate but related progressions.

Middle School Grades

In terms of LS3.A, middle school students are introduced to the core mechanisms of inheritance: Each trait is determined by two alleles, one inherited from each parent, and the relationships between the alleles result in the expression of a particular version of the trait (e.g., dimples or no dimples). This mechanism explains many observed patterns of inheritance, such as traits skipping generations. The detailed mechanism of how organisms create sex cells is not discussed; rather, the process is presented in terms of its input (full set) and output (half set) and the generation of new combinations of alleles in the offspring.

At the middle school level, students also add a layer of mechanism to their understanding of gene function by learning that the instructions genes carry are for making proteins. At this stage, students are likely to view proteins as little machines that do the work of the cell, since their functions are similar to those of familiar objects and machines, such as those used for transport, stretching, passageways, and building blocks. Mutations are also introduced at this grade band as errors in the instructions that may result in altered protein function. Thus, the focus at this grade band is the understanding that proteins are a key mediator of genetic phenomena, and that problems in protein function have serious consequences to the organisms' traits.

TABLE 8.1

Progression of Disciplinary Core Idea LS3

Grade Band	LS3.A Inheritance of Traits	LS3.B Variation of Traits
K–2	Young organisms are very much, but not exactly, like their parents and also resemble other organisms of the same kind.	
3–5	Different organisms vary in how they look and function because they have different inherited information; the environment also affects the traits that an organism develops.	
6–8	• Genes chiefly regulate a specific protein, which affects an individual's traits.	• In sexual reproduction, each parent contributes half of the genes acquired by the offspring, resulting in variation between parent and offspring. Genetic information can be altered because of mutations, which may result in beneficial, negative, or no change to proteins in or traits of an organism.
9–12	• DNA carries instructions for forming species' characteristics. Each cell in an organism has the same genetic content, but genes expressed by cells can differ.	• The variation and distribution of traits in a population depend on genetic and environmental factors. Genetic variation can result from mutations caused by environmental factors or errors in DNA replication or from chromosomes swapping sections during meiosis.

Source: NGSS Lead States 2013.

In high school, the relationship between genetic information and traits is further deepened. Students learn about DNA as the molecule that carries the genetic code and that not all segments of DNA code for proteins—some are involved in regulation of gene expression and others have yet unknown functions. The idea that all cells carry the same information but use it differentially (i.e., differential gene expression) is also a focus for this grade band, and allows students to explain phenomena such as the use of stem cells to generate a wide variety of tissues types.

In terms of LS3.B, middle school students are introduced to the important role that randomness plays in generating variation. The treatment of meiosis is limited to inputs and outputs, but for this component idea, the emphasis is on how the process shuffles alleles and results in new combinations of alleles in the sex cells. Another source of variation introduced at this grade band is mutations and their role in generating variation in traits, mostly harmful but occasionally neutral or beneficial.

High School Grades

At the high school level, additional sources of variation are discussed. Recombination of chromosomes is introduced as a further source of variation stemming from meiosis. The role of environmental factors in generating variation is expanded in the two ways discussed earlier: environmentally induced mutations that alter the genetic instructions thereby generating genetic variation, and environmental factors altering which genes are expressed in the cell, thereby generating trait variation (without actually altering the genetic instructions per se).

Lastly, for complete progression (in both component ideas), the movement toward more mechanistic accounts is accompanied, naturally, by delving into events that occur at the cellular and microscopic organization levels. Thus, younger children explore traits at the organismal level, observing similarities and differences and exploring different kinds of traits and their expression in plants and animals. At the middle school level, the focus is on cellular mechanisms, in particular the role of proteins, in bringing about those physical and physiological traits observed in prior grades. High school students delve into the molecular level and explore the molecular mechanisms involved in generating genetic and trait variation.

Challenges to Students' Understandings

We know quite a bit about the conceptual obstacles that students encounter as they learn genetics. Genetics is plagued by confusing terminology, multiple representations, and abstract ideas that, taken together, can impede students' understandings. Many students not only struggle to define terms such as gene, protein, allele, DNA, and chromosome but are also challenged to specify the relationships among such entities and how they contribute to explanations of inheritance (Cisterna, Williams, and Merritt 2013; Lewis and Wood-Robinson 2000; Venville, Gribble, and Donovan 2005). The mechanisms of inheritance pose unique difficulties because they span multiple organization levels (e.g., organism, cellular, molecular), involve unfamiliar and invisible entities such as alleles and proteins, and can be counterintuitive. We discuss some of the commonly held ideas students have in genetics—and the more pervasive conceptual obstacles—in further detail in the following section.

Research has shown that students initially view genes not as informational units but as passive particles associated with traits (Venville and Treagust 1998). At this level of understanding, students do not really distinguish between genes and traits and may use the words synonymously. In essence, they do not really have an explanation of how genes bring about our traits at all. With targeted instruction, students' notions of genes undergo conceptual change, and they begin to view genes as having information about our traits. This is a move in the right direction. However, the genetic information is seen as specifying both structure and function of entities at many organization levels. Students may argue that genes control the rate at which our hearts beat and the shape of a cell, and that they are literally a blueprint for an entire human (Duncan and Reiser 2007). Such a view circumvents the need for proteins as a mediating mechanism between genes and traits because genes are seen as fully determining everything about us from top to bottom. As students' ideas develop they do come to view genes as instructions for proteins. This is the canonical view of genes targeted by the *Framework*.

In some ways, the idea that genes only code for proteins is rather counterintuitive: an entire blueprint just for proteins? How could mere proteins possibly give us all our traits? In a way, students' difficulties in limiting the content of the genetic information to "only proteins" is caused by their lack of knowledge about what proteins are and what functions they have in our body. This is not to say that students cannot reason about proteins—they certainly can—but few have had the opportunity to do so. Therefore, to help students build a more coherent and complete explanation of how genes bring about our traits, they need to learn about the many functions of proteins.

Another challenging idea for students is the nature of the genetic relationships across generations. Young students do not assume equal contribution from both parents and may think that the mother, or the same-sex parent, contributes more genes (Engel Clough and Wood-Robinson 1984). In some cases, these problematic views persist into adulthood. For example, in a study of adults (ages 18–50) on their understanding of the heritability of cancer, de Vries and colleagues (2005) found that 93% of participants believed that if a son looks like his father, he is more likely to inherit cancer if his father has cancer. In addition, students do not necessarily understand that genes are physical entities that must be passed down from parents to offspring. That is, they accept explanations in which genes mysteriously appear or disappear (literally skip generations) and will suggest that some genes come from relatives who are not parents or grandparents, such as aunts and uncles. In these cases, students do not seem to fully realize that to show a trait the individual must have the genes for it, and that

those genes must have come from the individual's parents directly (Freidenreich, Duncan, and Shea 2011).

Students also tend to have trouble reasoning about the genetic content of sex cells in relation to the genetic makeup of the parents. For example, a student may realize that an individual with a recessive genetic disorder has the genotype aa, but when asked what is in this individual's sex cell, she may say that some sex cells have an A allele. This is obviously not possible and indicates a problematic understanding of the input and output of the process by which sex cells are formed. Studies of seventh graders showed that these students had difficulty explaining the difference between the processes of mitosis and meiosis and also how these processes contributed to the passage of genetic information from parent to offspring (Williams et al. 2012). Students' ability to distinguish between the two processes depends on their notions of the purposes and products of each process. Instruction that stresses the details of these processes does not help students understand the big picture; it may even confuse students and impede understanding of the core ideas. Practice with Punnett squares, a common instructional strategy, is also not helpful, as students tend to use this algorithm without understanding the underlying biological processes (Stewart, Hafner, and Dale 1990). What is needed is a concerted effort to help students understand the purpose and outcomes of meiosis, and only then is practice with various algorithms useful. In the next section, we offer some insights about productive teaching strategies to address the heredity DCI that can help students build on their existing understandings toward more sophisticated explanations of inheritance.

What Approaches Can We Use to Teach About This Disciplinary Core Idea?

There are several important aspects to consider when designing instruction in genetics, including the science practices of genetic inquiry, accessible phenomena, and productive use of visual representation. Given that the main thrust of this core idea is the development of progressively more sophisticated mechanistic models of genetic inheritance and variation, engaging students with scientific modeling is a productive practice for learning this idea. To this end, instruction can engage students in the evidence-based development and evaluation of models of genetic phenomena.

For example, in our own work, we have developed an instructional module in genetics that presents students with an intriguing phenomenon: individuals who are genetically resistant to HIV (Rinehart, Duncan, and Chinn 2014). Students are presented with two competing models of the mechanism underlying this phenomenon and are asked to use a provided set of evidence to argue for the best model. Through this activity, students can learn about the role of proteins in mediating this particular phenomenon. Obviously, other examples should be provided for students to investigate with the end goal of developing a more abstracted model that links genes to traits via a protein-based mediating mechanism. The activity described above is mostly paper-and-pencil based, but students can also engage in hands-on experiments using Wisconsin Fast Plants (*fastplants.org*) to test models in genetics (Cisterna, Williams, and Merritt 2013). Using this system, students can rapidly breed plants to test ideas about the relationship between putative genetic factors (i.e., genes) and observable traits, much as Mendel himself did with pea plants. Models can then be revised in light of the experimental evidence, and the revised models can yield new predictions that can be tested through further breeding experiments.

As we discussed earlier, research shows that students, even young ones, can reason productively about unfamiliar cellular and molecular structures such as chromosomes, DNA, and proteins. The key, however, is to engage students in scientific investigations of accessible phenomena. The choice of phenomena is critical as not all exciting discoveries in genetics make for good instructional contexts. We suggest a the following heuristics for selecting phenomena for exploration: (1) the phenomenon should be well understood by science so that there is ample research about the underlying mechanism that can be used to craft evidence for students to use; and (2) the proteins involved should have functions that are accessible to students, functions that have analogues in the macroworld. Additionally, select multiple phenomena because exploration of one or two is insufficient to develop robust understandings of genetic mechanisms. Examples of interesting phenomena that can be used are the disorders of sickle cell anemia, Duchenne muscular dystrophy, albinism, diabetes, familial hypercholesterolemia, blood types, hair texture, and others. It is also important to use examples of normal traits rather than focusing solely on disorders (e.g., hair texture, blood types). Examples of beneficial mutations can help students develop a more nuanced understanding of mutation; resistance to HIV is such an example. Overall, the more examples the better, but it is equally critical to have students generalize from the many examples and build a more abstracted model that can account for a variety of genetic contexts.

Lastly, we want to underscore the importance and careful use of visual representations in genetics instruction. Visual representations are a double-edged sword: On the one hand, they can really help students "see" the interactions between entities that would otherwise be invisible; on the other, too many disconnected representations result in a muddled conceptual mess. As teachers and experts in the domain, we can recognize chromosomes even when they are represented in very different ways, but students have a more difficult time recognizing and relating different types of representations (Kindfield 1994). Providing representations that are linked across organization levels, like those provided by the Concord Consortium's genetic game Geniverse and the older BioLogica software (*http://concord. org*) is therefore important. These engaging games and simulations allow students to move fluently between representations of chromosomes in cells, to gene sections within those chromosomes, to DNA sequences within those genes. Students can see how entities such as chromosomes, alleles, and DNA are related to each other structurally.

There are several visualization tools that can be used to help students better understand proteins as well, such as Concord Consortium's Next-Generation Molecular Workbench (*http://mw.concord.org*). There are also physical models that can be used. A particularly useful one is a wool model of chromosomes developed by Venville and Donovan (2008) and illustrated in Figure 8.4.

This model shows the relationship between DNA (represented by wool), chromosomes (represented by the wool wrapped around a Popsicle stick), and alleles (represented as stretches of different colored wool), with dominant alleles being a darker shade than recessive alleles. Students

FIGURE 8.4

The Wool and Wood Stick Model of Chromosomes

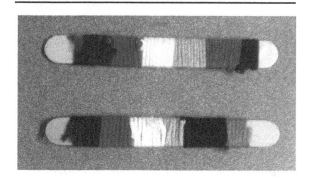

Different-colored wool sections represent genes on a DNA strand. The wool is wrapped around a wooden craft stick to represent a chromosome and its corresponding alleles (Venville and Donovan 2008).

can also use these models to represent meiosis and fertilization and figure out how genotypes of parents relate to the genotypes and phenotypes of offspring. Venville and Donovan (2008) provide a detailed description of how to make and use the wool model to support students' learning about meiosis and fertilization. Unfortunately, the physical structure of these models does not afford teaching recombination (the sticks would have to be physically broken), but one could pose the problem of how a chromosome with a new combination of alleles would arise. The only solution to such a conundrum is the potential breaking of chromosomes. If students were to reach this conclusion, the teacher could follow up with the explanation that chromosomes do, in fact, break and swap sections during meiosis.

Conclusion

The heredity DCI is about the biological mechanisms that underlie many familiar and less

8

familiar phenomena such as genetic disorders, genetically modified foods, gene therapy, and others. Explaining how and why we are similar and different is at the heart of this DCI, and these explanations unfold over time as students gain meaningful understandings of key entities and processes in genetics. An important point, which we have raised before, is that there a shift away from memorizations of structures and steps of processes toward conceptual understandings of mechanisms, inputs and outputs, and the overall "purposes" of relevant processes. If students can draw the structure of a tRNA (transfer RNA) molecule or a peptide bond but do not understand that proteins mediate all genetic traits, we have not achieved our goal. If students can repeat the stages of meiosis but fail to see that a genotype of AA can only yield sex cells with the A allele, we have not achieved our goal. We therefore need to be vigilant about how we carve out the scope and sequence of instruction in genetics such that students develop deep and generative understandings of this core idea. We have highlighted a few instructional strategies and tools that we believe can aid in this mission. Genetics is a fascinating domain that continues to make its way into our daily personal and civic lives. Providing students with an understanding of this core idea will undoubtedly serve them well in their future.

Acknowledgments

This material is based on work supported by the National Science Foundation (grant nos. 0529582 and 1008634). Any opinions, findings, and conclusions or recommendations expressed in this material are those of the author(s) and do not necessarily reflect the views of the National Science Foundation.

REFERENCES

American Association for the Advancement of Science (AAAS). 1993. *Benchmarks for science literacy.* New York: Oxford University Press.

Cisterna, D., M. Williams, and J. Merritt. 2013. Students' understanding of cells and heredity: Patterns of understanding in the context of a curriculum implementation in fifth and seventh grades. *The American Biology Teacher* 75 (3): 178–184.

Concord Consortium. 2014. Geniverse. *http://concord.org/projects/geniverse.*

de Vries, H., I. Mesters, H. van de Staag, and C. Honing. 2005. The general public's information needs and perceptions regarding hereditary cancer: An application of the integrated change model. *Patient Education and Counseling* 56 (2): 154–165.

Duncan, R. G., and B. J. Reiser. 2007. Reasoning across ontologically distinct levels: Students' understandings of molecular genetics. *Journal of Research in Science Teaching* 44 (7): 938–959.

Duncan, R. G., A. Rogat, and A. Yarden. 2009. A learning progression for deepening students' understanding of modern genetics across the 5th–12th grades. *Journal of Research in Science Teaching* 46 (6): 644–674.

Engel Clough, E., and C. Wood-Robinson. 1985. How secondary students interpret instances of biological adaptation. *Journal of Biological Education* 19:125–129.

Freidenreich, H. B., R. G. Duncan, and N. A. Shea. 2011. Exploring middle school students' understanding of three conceptual models in genetics. *International Journal of Science Education* 33 (17): 2323–2350.

Kindfield, A. C. H. 1994. Understanding a basic biological process: Expert and novice models of meiosis. *Science Education* 78 (3): 255–283.

Lewis, J., and C. Wood-Robinson. 2000. Genes, chromosomes, cell division and inheritance—Do students see any relationship? *International Journal of Science Education* 22 (2): 177–195.

National Research Council (NRC). 1996. *National science education standards.* Washington, DC: National Academies Press.

National Research Council (NRC). 2007. *Taking science to school: Learning and teaching science in grades K–8.* Washington, DC: National Academies Press.

National Research Council (NRC). 2012. *A framework for K–12 science education: Practices, crosscutting concepts, and core ideas.* Washington, DC: National Academies Press.

NGSS Lead States. 2013. *Next Generation Science Standards: For states, by states.* Washington, DC: National Academies Press. *www.nextgenscience. org/next-generation-science-standards.*

Rinehart, R., R. G. Duncan, and C. A. Chinn. 2014. A scaffolding suite to support evidence-based modeling and argumentation. *Science Scope* 38 (4): 70–77.

Roseman, J., A. Caldwell, A. Gogos, and L. A. Kurth. 2006. Mapping a coherent learning progression for the molecular basis of heredity. Paper presented at the annual meeting of the National Association of Research in Science Teaching, San Francisco, CA.

Smith, J. P., A. A. diSessa, and J. Roschelle. 1993. Misconceptions reconceived: A constructivist analysis of knowledge in transition. *Journal of the Learning Sciences* 3 (2): 115–163.

Stewart, J., B. Hafner, and M. Dale. 1990. Students' alternate views of meiosis. *The American Biology Teacher* 52 (4): 228–232.

Venville, G., and J. Donovan. 2008. How pupils use a model for abstract concepts in genetics. *Journal of Biological Education* 43 (1): 6–14.

Venville, G., S. J. Gribble, and J. Donovan. 2005. An exploration of young children's understandings of genetics concepts from ontological and epistemological perspectives. *Science Education* 89 (4): 614–633.

Venville, G. J., and D. F. Treagust. 1998. Exploring conceptual change in genetics using a multidimensional interpretive framework. *Journal of Research in Science Teaching* 35 (9): 1031–1055.

Williams, M., A. H. DeBarger, B. L. Montgomery, X. Zhou, and E. Tate. 2012. Exploring middle school students' conceptions of the relationship between genetic inheritance and cell division. *Science Education* 96 (1): 78–103.

CHAPTER 9

CORE IDEA LS4

BIOLOGICAL EVOLUTION: UNITY AND DIVERSITY

Cynthia Passmore, Julia Svoboda Gouvea, Candice Guy, and Chris Griesemer

In the biological sciences, we ask fundamental questions about how life on this planet has changed over time. By understanding this history and the mechanisms that drive it, we can explain both the amazing diversity of life on Earth and the important commonalities among every living thing. In this chapter, we describe the core and component ideas of disciplinary core idea (DCI) LS4: Evolution: Unity and Diversity and show how they connect to each other and to other core ideas in biology. In doing so, we hope to portray the content knowledge of biology as a set of deeply interconnected ideas that, together, help us make sense of a broad range of biological phenomena and lead to further questions and explorations. The ideas represented in LS4 are central to those interconnections.

We begin by examining what the core idea of Biological Evolution: Unity and Diversity is all about. We also describe some of the things that make it challenging for students to come to deep understandings of evolution and how competence with this idea, and its component ideas, can build over time. Woven throughout this exploration are recommendations and some potential ways to approach teaching these ideas in a manner that

supports *A Framework for K–12 Science Education* (*Framework*; NRC 2012) and the *Next Generation Science Standards* (*NGSS*; NGSS Lead States 2013).

What Is This Disciplinary Core Idea, and Why Is It Important?

As described in the *Framework*, the power of an evolutionary perspective is that it can help us make sense of both the *unity* and *diversity* of life and come to a deeper understanding of the interconnectedness of all living things. Evolution employs a *universal* set of tools in response to a wide variety of challenges such as extremely cold or hot environments, lack of water, and other challenging situations. Evolutionary processes have generated the diversity we observe in the fossil record and all around us today. Proficient understanding of the processes through which all life on Earth changes over time will also lend itself to advancing student thinking about the ways in which humans affect the environment and the living things within it and how biodiversity in turn affects us as humans.

Some common molecular and cellular machinery unifies all organisms. For example, they all have DNA, which carries the genetic instructions, and this DNA molecule is "read" by the cell in the same way across organisms. Similarly, the cellular proteins and organelles used to carry out life core functions (such as mitochondria) are almost identical. Many organisms also exhibit similar traits, behaviors, and body plans—even those that are not very closely related. Consider the presence of social behavior in organisms as diverse as humans, birds, ants, and fungi. Indeed, sometimes the closer we look at organisms, the more similarities we can see. Terrestrial vertebrates (such rabbits, horses, and snakes) look and move differently and yet have strikingly similar bone structures. Flowers come in a wide variety of shapes and colors but ultimately share many of the same component parts.

At the same time, living things exhibit an incredible diversity of forms, behaviors, and life history patterns. When we look at these differences, we often see specialized traits that allow organisms to thrive in varied environmental conditions, from those that seem hospitable to us to those that seem extreme: There are bacteria that live in geothermal vents, fish that live in the deep ocean, plants that live in salt water, and mammals who live their whole lives underground. We wonder where all of this diversity came from and how it is that organisms are so well-suited to the amazing array of environmental conditions found on Earth.

Evolutionary principles help us make sense of these two broad classes of phenomena: the *unifying characteristics of life* and the *patterns of biological diversity* we see across space and over time. In our biology classrooms we want to place wondering about these patterns as the key driver of our investigations and explorations.

Why Is Evolution: Unity and Diversity Considered a Disciplinary Core Idea in the Life Sciences?

Biologists have long collected, described, and classified living things, and this work continues today. Yet, prior to the publication of *On the Origin of Species* and the widespread adoption of Darwin's ideas, there was little cohesion to emerging patterns in biology. Take for example, two important 18th- and 19th-century biologists, Carolus (Carl) Linnaeus and Gregor Mendel. The Linnaean hierarchical organization and classification of organisms from species to kingdom was the result of a lifetime of collections and observations. Linnaeus noticed the similarities between broad classes of organisms and formalized a scheme for organizing and describing living things based on these similarities. This scheme gives us many of the scientific names of organisms to this day.

Mendel's descriptions of the variation and generational patterns in several traits of pea plants were the beginnings of understanding inheritance. Mendel studied patterns of similarity and difference over generations within a species but did not connect his findings to variation between species. Linnaeus described patterns of similarity and difference among species but did not account for population changes over time. It was not until Darwin proposed the mechanisms of evolution and the idea of common descent that a coherent explanation existed for these patterns of unity *and* diversity (Figure 9.1). For students to begin to understand the complexity of life, a foundational knowledge in the mechanisms of evolution is necessary. As Theodosius Dobzhansky (1973) famously stated, "Nothing in biology makes sense, except in the light of evolution."

The Four Component Ideas of LS4

As we just described, Darwin (Figure 9.1) made two important contributions to the field of biology: He identified the patterns of similarity and difference among organisms as the object of scientific study, and he provided the foundational evolutionary principles for explaining those patterns.

Here we separate the component ideas of the DCI of biological evolution in terms of the *broad patterns of unity and diversity* that we observe among living organisms and the *core evolutionary mechanisms* that help us explain those patterns. The aim of this section is to illustrate some of the ways in which a robust understanding of evolution can help students make sense of a variety of interesting natural phenomena and build up a more coherent understanding of biology as a whole.

PATTERNS OF UNITY AND DIVERSITY

The four component ideas of LS4 each draw attention to the patterns of unity and diversity in different ways. LS4.A: Evidence of Common Ancestry and Diversity invites students to explore the data patterns that help us see the unity and diversity of life in terms of measurable similarities and differences among DNA sequences, patterns of development, and morphological traits evident in both living organisms and in the fossil record. For example, humans and chimpanzees share over 90% of genes, whereas humans and mice share about 80%. Many of the shared genes are involved in basic functions of cells, organs, and embryonic development. Similarly, shared structures in bones of humans and whales also point to shared ancestry, despite the very different living environments whales and humans inhabit today.

FIGURE 9.1

Charles Darwin

Groups of organisms that are unified by common traits (e.g., all butterflies have wings) also exhibit variation within (those wings can display different colors and patterns). All organisms share certain fundamental machinery and must solve fundamental problems (e.g., replicating their DNA and acquiring energy) to be alive, but different species do so in different ways (e.g., producers photosynthesize and consumers eat other organisms). And these patterns of similarity and difference themselves vary over both space and time (e.g., there are many more species in the tropics than the arctic; species number increased dramatically during the Cambrian explosion but then plummeted during the Triassic extinction).

9

Together, DCIs LS4.B: Natural Selection and LS4.C: Adaptation draw attention to another pattern: Species tend to have traits that allow them to survive and reproduce, and these traits vary in different environments. One of the most easily observed patterns in biology is the incredible diversity of solutions organisms exhibit that allow them to survive and propagate. Many organisms appear to be well-suited to particular environmental conditions. In some cases, we can observe traits shifting over time as the environment changes in a process called adaptation. Some common phenomena that illustrate this process include shifts in the beak sizes of Darwin's finches in the Galápagos in response to drought and the availability of certain kinds of seeds, the shifting frequencies of color morphs in the peppered moth in response to pollution in Industrial Revolution England, the development of bacterial resistance in response to antibiotic use, or the acquisition of adult lactose tolerance in humans in response to the availability of cow's milk as a food source.

Finally, LS4.D: Biodiversity and Humans highlights global patterns of diversity and how humans can affect those patterns. Over the past hundred years, we have observed a marked increase in extinctions and an increasing number of species are considered endangered. Human activity that results in habitat loss, resource depletion, or the disruption of ecosystem relationships can dramatically reduce species abundance and diversity in ways that can ultimately negatively affect human populations.

Patterns of unity and diversity are a recurrent theme in the natural world that we see repeated everywhere on Earth and throughout history. Many of these patterns can be noticed just by careful observation and can be used as a rich source

FIGURE 9.2

Questions About Unity and Diversity

Why do all organisms appear to be well-suited to their environments?

How do populations shift over time to match changing environments?

Why do we see so many different species?

Why do we see more kinds of species in certain places?

How do new species form?

Why do species share so many traits?

What explains the disappearance of forms in the fossil record?

What explains the emergence of new forms in the fossil record?

How do species go extinct today?

How can we explain the existence of traits that do not seem advantageous?

Why do some species look so similar to other species?

Why do similar species exist in different biomes?

of questions about important phenomena in the natural world (Figure 9.2).

These questions inspire the need to develop and use models to generate explanations and to evaluate these models against empirical data. Engaging in biological practice involves developing and reasoning with the core explanatory mechanisms that can account for the patterns of unity and diversity seen in the natural world.

CORE EXPLANATORY MECHANISMS

In addition to highlighting the patterns of unity and diversity, the four component ideas of LS4 also contain the key to understanding the

FIGURE 9.3

Mayr's Model of Natural Selection

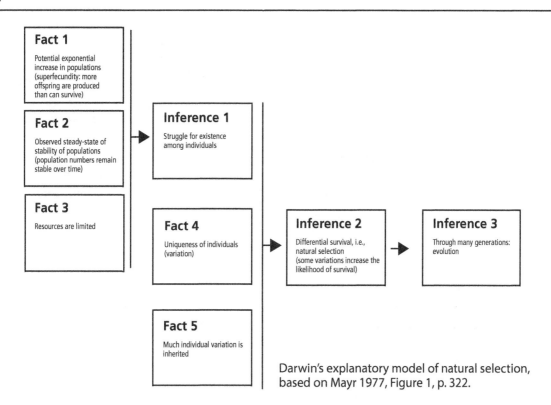

Fact 1

Potential exponential increase in populations (superfecundity: more offspring are produced than can survive)

Fact 2

Observed steady-state of stability of populations (population numbers remain stable over time)

Fact 3

Resources are limited

Inference 1

Struggle for existence among individuals

Fact 4

Uniqueness of individuals (variation)

Inference 2

Differential survival, i.e., natural selection (some variations increase the likelihood of survival)

Inference 3

Through many generations: evolution

Fact 5

Much individual variation is inherited

Darwin's explanatory model of natural selection, based on Mayr 1977, Figure 1, p. 322.

mechanisms behind those patterns we see in the natural world. At the heart of the evolutionary *Framework* is Darwin's model of natural selection, which describes the primary mechanism by which populations can shift to better match environmental conditions over time (LS4.B and LS4.C). The basic Darwinian model describes how natural selection exploits existing (genetic) variation within populations (LS4.B). In response to changes in the environment, certain existing variants may be more successful than others. That is, those variants will produce more offspring and ultimately the traits that allowed those individuals to survive and reproduce will increase

in frequency across the population (LS4.C). Any time the environment shifts there is the possibility for other variants to succeed and for the population to change over time as those variants gain an advantage in survival and reproduction. Natural selection is always happening within populations, but we don't always notice its effects. We tend to only see dramatic shifts in populations when the selection consistently favors a particular variant (or variants) over time, for example, consider the common example of peppered moths, in which the darker variant was favored during the Industrial Revolution due to the polluted environment.

9

The core evolutionary model of natural selection can be built up from a series of observations and inferences. One very useful depiction of the natural selection model was developed by Ernst Mayr in 1991 (Figure 9.3, p. 169).

The natural selection model can be used to develop explanations and can serve as a theoretical framework about which to argue from evidence. Consider the patterns of change that have been observed in the beaks of Darwin's finches. The research of evolutionary biologists Peter and Rosemary Grant (1999) documented how, in times of drought, the environment in the Galápagos shifted; small soft seeds became scarce compared with larger tougher seeds. The Grants observed how birds with larger beaks were more successful at cracking tough seeds. These birds tended to survive longer and have more offspring. Over a span of just a few generations, the surviving larger-beaked birds passed on the genes associated with larger beaks to the next generation, and the average beak size of the population increased. This phenomenon demonstrates how natural selection can account for patterns of match to the environment *within populations*.

To understand broader *patterns of species biodiversity* and *patterns of descent*, we need to expand our evolutionary framework beyond natural selection. LS4.D builds to the concept of speciation. Two important factors in driving speciation are diversity of habitats and natural barriers that separate populations. When populations become separated, natural selection can continue to shift each population in different ways. Over time, populations will look more and more different due to natural selection and changes in each population due to chance. When these differences become large enough to prevent interbreeding, we say that a new species is formed. For example, the

greenish warbler population originated in Nepal and spread across the two sides of the inhospitable Tibetan Plateau in the Himalayas, resulting in two populations that cannot interbreed and are thus two distinct species.

LS4.D also includes the process of extinction. This process can occur through catastrophic events in which populations are wiped out. But, more often, extinction happens when conditions change so rapidly that populations of organisms are suddenly mismatched to their environments. If there are not enough variants that can survive and reproduce under these new conditions, the species goes extinct. Thus, we see that variation within populations is critical to survival under changing conditions because natural selection can only act on existing and heritable variation. When populations get too small, the range of variation is often reduced, making the species even more vulnerable to extinction as the environment changes.

Loss of habitat is a big driver of extinction. In addition, because so many species have evolved relationships with one another, the loss or introduction of one species can have devastating effects on other species in the system. This is particularly noticeable in island habitats, where the loss of a resource can have immediate consequences. Patterns of change on the Channel Islands off the coast of California present a good example of how environmental changes driven both by climate change and by human interference (LS4.D) can change ecosystems. For example, habitat disturbance caused by feral pigs—originally brought to the islands as a food source for residents in the 1800s—has had a direct effect on several native species. The pigs root around, digging up native plant species, consequently creating abundant space for a nonnative weed, wild fennel, to flourish and grow. The wild fennel provides shelter for the pigs and is causing space, an already limited resource on an island, to become further diminished. The introduction of pigs to Santa Cruz Island has also affected endemic foxes. Given the substantial increase in the pig population, the golden eagles have an unlimited food source. Before the introduction of pigs to the island, the eagles were not in the habit of visiting the island. The eagles now nest there and also prey on the island fox, a species that is now critically endangered.

FIGURE 9.4

Cladogram of Primates

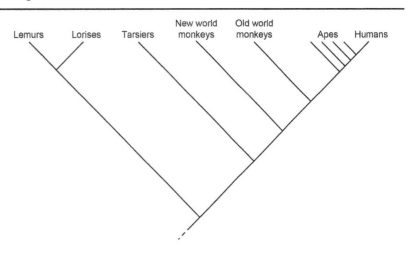

LS4.D builds on the foundation laid by LS4.B and LS4.C to establish a view of the biological world as a dynamic system. Ecosystems, and the tenuous balance between players in them, are the product of generations upon generations of natural selection. Everything in the system has the potential to affect everything else. This is true on both local and global scales.

Finally, LS4.A zooms out to describe how the processes of natural selection, speciation, and extinction allow us to organize our understanding of all organisms (both living and extinct) as connected through lines of common descent or a "tree of life." The process of speciation generates branches on the tree. Over time, each lineage will continue to change due to natural selection and random events and the species will become less and less similar in many respects, while maintaining a number common characteristics (e.g., the basic cell processes). Having a rich understanding of common descent is necessary to really make sense of the unity we see among living things.

The idea of common descent allows us to make inferences about evolutionary histories. If two species share many similarities we can often infer that they share a relatively recent common ancestor. Domestic dogs, wolves, and wild dogs all share a common ancestor. The differences we see among related species reflect different evolutionary trajectories. Domestic dogs, for example, have undergone a lot of change recently due to the effects of humans selecting for particular structural and behavioral traits.

Natural selection can only act on existing structures and variants, leading to a many-branched tree of life, where descendant species are connected to their common ancestor by branches. Split points in the tree represent population separation (through geographic or reproductive isolation) creating new species that will continue to evolve independently from one another. Some of these species will ultimately go extinct, but others persist over time and eventually split again, generating more new species.

Figure 9.4 (p. 171) depicts a cladogram (a branching diagram showing common ancestor and descendants) for living primates. Humans, apes, lemurs, and many other species are included because they all descended from a common ancestor in the past, depicted in the diagram by the first branching point near the base of the tree. As one moves up along the tree, the branching pattern represents processes of divergence and speciation. Importantly, the cladogram fundamentally illustrates the nested relationships among species. Lemurs and lorises, for example, are more closely related than lemurs and humans, as the former pair shares a more recent common ancestor. The nested groups or clades depicted in the tree are based on data (DNA sequences, described or measured traits) that describe the degree of similarity and divergence among species. As such, the branching patterns and our understanding of the relationships may change as new data become available, most especially in an era of increased interest in sequencing the genomes of a multitude of species.

Thus, tree diagrams like this one describe the complex history of evolutionary relationships we see among living organisms across the globe and in the fossil record in terms of common descent and modifications to particular lineages. Common traits, like those associated with molecular inheritance and cellular machinery, point to a shared history among all living things (LS4.A), whereas rare and specialized traits indicate the unique circumstances in which different populations have evolved (LS4.C).

In addition to common descent, populations may also resemble each other if they experience similar selection pressures. For example, unrelated species of cactuses across the Earth's desert ecosystems can share similar traits due to parallel evolutionary responses to arid environments rather than direct lines of descent. So, an interesting question one can ask about similarities among organisms is whether the resemblance comes from recent common descent or the unique emergence of particular variations in more distantly related species under similar selection pressures.

Integrating across the four component ideas of LS4 can lead to a deep understanding of and appreciation for the interactions between and among organisms and the environment. Populations of organisms change over time in response to physical features of the environment (like climate) and to other organisms (predators, competitors, or prey). Understanding how particular organisms might change over time will require understanding the biological system in which that organism lives and, ultimately, will allow students to grasp the consequence of human actions that affect the biotic and abiotic environment.

Connections to the Other Life Science Disciplinary Core Ideas

When viewed through an evolutionary framework, many of the details about the living world are brought into focus. For this reason, LS4 brings coherence to the rest of the DCIs in the life sciences.

LS1: From Molecules to Organisms fleshes out the details of survival and reproduction at the organism level. All organisms acquire resources, interface with the environment, grow, and reproduce. Natural selection acts on these traits and over time we see a wide variety of structures and functions among species.

LS2: Ecosystems expands the idea that populations of organisms evolve in interaction with their environments, which include both abiotic and biotic factors. Organisms survive and reproduce in these environmental contexts and interact with other organisms as they compete and cooperate to obtain the resources they need to survive. LS2 thus speaks to the selective pressures (including human activity) that drive populations to change and then to change again (and so on).

LS3: Heredity elaborates on the mechanisms that produce and maintain variation within populations that natural selection can act on. LS3 also describes how that variation gets passed through generations so that the influence of natural selection can be seen over time. Variation that is not heritable does not play a role in this process.

Comparisons to Prior Standards

Overall there are more similarities than differences among the *Framework*, the *NSES*, and the *Benchmarks*. All three documents have a strong focus on the evidence for evolution over time and they include attention to adaptation and biodiversity. However, there are three key ways that the concepts related to biological evolution are treated differently in the *Framework* compared with those earlier standards document. First, the core focus on unity *and* diversity was not present in *NSES* and the *Benchmarks*. The *Framework* begins the description of LS4 with two questions: "How can there be so many similarities among organisms yet so many different kinds of plants, animals, and microorganisms?" and "How does biodiversity affect humans?"

These questions then provide the basis for an integrated view of species diversity and the origins and changing patterns in that diversity over time. In the *Benchmarks*, the ideas of diversity and evolution are treated separately, and although there are many conceptual links between them, the resulting benchmarks portray a learning trajectory that may not have engaged students in thinking about the important connections between diversity *and* the unity that provides evidence for common ancestry. The *NSES* likewise treats them in two separate lines and the connections are not as robust.

The second key difference is in how biodiversity is treated. In the *Framework*, biodiversity is linked to human success and sustenance in more explicit ways than in the *NSES* or the *Benchmarks*. The focus of LS4.D on the benefits of biodiversity and the mechanisms and consequences for depletion of species diversity is new in the *Framework*. The previous documents established ideas related to biodiversity but did not have clear expectations that students would grapple with both the ways in which humans rely on the diversity of species in the natural world and the ways in which human activities are having adverse affects on that diversity.

The third key difference is that in the *Framework* there is greater focus in earlier grades on ideas related to natural selection and on the mechanism of natural selection itself. The *Framework* establishes a sound basis for these ideas, and students should have a solid understanding of the mechanism by the end of eighth grade that they go on to refine in high school. The *Benchmarks* and *NSES* left much of this work to the high school level. Connections to genetic mechanisms and their role in evolution are also more clearly delineated in the current *Framework*.

How Does Student Understanding of This Disciplinary Core Idea Develop Over Time?

Anyone who has tried to teach students about evolution, adaptation, and natural selection can attest to the fact that this can be a difficult set of ideas for students to understand. Why does it seem so hard? Both our experience and studies in science education point to a few key areas of difficulty for students. Below we explore the kinds of thinking around evolution that we want to foster in students. Our approach here is to consider some of the powerful, intuitive ideas that students often have related to evolution and how, as teachers, we might push students to use those ideas in productive ways that are consistent with how scientists think with and about ideas in this discipline. In addition, we will discuss how some of the commonly held ideas that students bring to class can be carefully considered and shaped for productive use in the science classroom. In the next section, we continue to explore the development of ideas about evolution over time (grades and grade bands) and offer some suggestions for productive instructional strategies and resources that can help move students' ideas forward toward deeper understanding and greater sophistication across the four component ideas of LS4.

Researchers have identified a number of core concepts that students will need to grapple with in building a coherent evolutionary framework. These include the following:

The range and importance of variation: Students have a productive and fairly deep understanding of variation as applied to humans but don't always notice that same capacity for variation in other organisms. In other words, with little prodding, even very young students can name and describe a wide range of ways that humans vary from one another, but they tend to describe zebras, corn plants, and snails as being of one type. They also have much less experience with variation of internal structures (lungs, muscles) compared with external and easily seen ones, making it more difficult for them to reason about selection acting on these less visible traits. One way to think about overcoming this difficulty is to help students expand their ideas about variation and notice variation as a universal feature of all populations and across all levels of biological organization.

When to think of individual versus population-level processes: Students often recognize that individual organisms can respond to their environment to some extent. However, they often need support in distinguishing this idea from changes in trait distributions that have a genetic basis. Within an organism's lifetime, change may occur in response to needs and drives, but across generations, change is not goal directed; rather, it is the outcome of differential survival and reproduction of certain variants over others within populations. The distinctions between the ways in which individuals respond to their environment and the way populations shift over time in response to the environment are important to draw out.

Making the leap from microlevel evolution to large-scale changes: Once students have grasped the basic idea of natural selection, they are often able to see how this process could play out from one generation to the next, but it can be challenging to play this process out over even longer periods of time and coordinate the various evolutionary forces at play that result in transformations in the type and abundance of species. The mechanisms that drive evolution do not allow for a linear path in which one species is driven to extinction and is replaced by a more well-matched one, such as that illustrated in Aristotle's great chain of being. Instead, gradual changes in the distribution of traits within populations played out over deep geologic time have resulted in the many-branched tree of life.

The paradox of teaching evolutionary ideas is that they can seem intuitive, but at the same time, the challenges described above are not trivial to overcome. Students have many intuitive ideas about the natural world they live in, but these intuitions may not be applied appropriately.

Consider the example of appropriately applying individual versus population-level thinking. Students may feel as if they already have sufficient explanations for evolutionary patterns such as why organisms seem matched to their environments. That species match their environments can be a taken for granted. If you ask students to explain why an organism has a particular trait, they are likely to respond that the reason is because the individual organism *needed* the trait to survive. These kinds of responses are often criticized as being incorrect because they are teleological, that is, they imply that the evolution of the traits was driven toward a purpose.

Another way to think about these responses is that they are a productive starting point but are technically incomplete. *Individual* organisms do indeed have a variety of needs. They need to acquire resources, avoid predators, find mates, and so on. And, ultimately, *populations* do evolve in response to those needs. But explanations like this are missing the details of how this actually happens over generations.

One of the central aims of teaching evolution is to help students refine and flesh out their initial ideas and get more precise in their language. Because it is so natural to talk in terms of needs and goals, it is important for teachers to be clear about what will count as a complete explanation and to provide appropriate scaffolding for students in building up explanations of this type. For example, changes in the way a pattern is presented to students could make a difference in the kinds of responses students provide. Asking, "Why does species A have X trait?" (e.g., Why do tigers have stripes? Why do giraffes have long necks? Why do turtles have shells?) may result in explanations about how species needed these traits to survive. Indeed, now they do. But being clear that the question really is, "How did species A come to have trait X when an ancestral species did not?" focuses the explanation on the process of change rather than the current state.

Teleological explanations can be useful. After all, even experts can be seen to use teleological explanations as shorthand for more detailed, more technically correct explanations. The difference between experts and novices is that the experts are able to elaborate on these shorthand explanations in ways that novices might not yet be able to. Students tend to focus on the goal-directed behavior of individuals rather than on the changing distribution of traits across populations as a result of differential survival. The important thing for teachers to do is leverage the useful intuitive ideas students have about survival and help them translate the actions and effects at the individual level to shifts in trait frequency in populations across generations.

What Approaches Can We Use to Teach About This Disciplinary Core Idea?
Building Competence Over Time

We have chosen the word *competence* for the header in this section for deliberate reasons. In the current reform context, it is no longer enough for students to simply "know" information and be able to repeat back what they have been told about something in the natural or designed world. Instead, we want to support in students the capacity to *reason* with the core ideas in the disciplines. They need to be able to use these ideas to make sense of the world. Thus, as we think about developing content knowledge over time, it is not about a slow accretion of facts building up on top of each other but about developing increasing sophistication with regard to what one notices about the world and how one deploys knowledge to explain and predict. Indeed, this is what is called for in the *Framework* and the *NGSS* around the practices, so in this new paradigm for science education we cannot consider only what ideas we need to teach but how we can engage students with those ideas through participation in science practice.

Scientific investigation of phenomena and the development of explanatory models is a process of refining ideas over time in the face of evidence. Similarly, successful engagement in *NGSS* practices requires repetition. As educators we must be willing to invest classroom time in moving toward student competency in higher-order sense-making.

Teaching Ideas

From our exploration of the various components of the DCIs, we can make some recommendations for teaching evolution. The sequence of the presentation of the core and component ideas in the *Framework* should *not* be considered prescriptive of a teaching sequence. We recommend taking a much more integrated approach to the core ideas presented here (and all of the DCIs, really). This means conceiving of evolution as a thread that weaves through and connects ideas, not as a stand-alone unit that is complete unto itself. Furthermore, as discussed above, one of the key innovations of the *Framework* and *NGSS* is the *coupling* of disciplinary content (DCIs and crosscutting concepts) with the science practices. So, as you begin to plan for teaching the core life science ideas, try not to think of them as a list of discrete facts for students to know, but instead think about how you can help students develop and use these ideas to make sense of the world (see Passmore et al. 2013 for a description of a high school natural selection unit focused on the practice of modeling).

In the case of the component ideas under the umbrella of Evolution: Unity and Diversity, the *Framework* identifies grade band endpoints that suggest that in early grades students should gain experience grappling with data patterns and phenomena in the world. The progression from early elementary to late elementary is about becoming more sophisticated in describing the relationships and patterns between and among organisms both within a single species and across ecosystems. When students reach middle and high school, they become concerned with explaining how these patterns have emerged and the reasoning becomes more about causes and predictions.

This progression is important because without a deep understanding of the patterns in the natural world and the evidence for change over time, work on the mechanisms is difficult.

Building From Student Ideas in Early Grades

Childhood development researchers out of Vanderbilt (Lehrer and Schauble 2012) emphasize building on the productive seeds of young children's knowledge. Elementary school children can begin to think about the following:

- **Traits of organisms:** Students can notice and measure organism traits (e.g., plant height) and think about the function of those traits. Researchers have realized that first-grade students can think deeply about the diversity of forms seeds can take and how different seed structures can function to help plants better survive and reproduce (e.g., Metz 2008).

- **Adaptation to the environment:** Students can notice how traits relate to and function in particular environments (e.g., polar bears have white fur).

- **Variability:** Students can observe, measure, and document (e.g., in drawings) variations among individuals within populations.

- **Population-level change:** Students can measure and track changes in populations over time (e.g., building simple frequency distributions).

- **Ecosystem interactions:** Students can generate narratives and diagrams that show how organisms are related to their environments and other organisms, and think and talk about how those relationships are connected to survival and reproduction. For example, in one study, third graders designed investigations to test the effect of variables such as Sun, water, and crowding on plant success as defined by the number of seedpods produced. They were able to develop ideas about evolutionary success in terms of numbers of offspring (Manz 2012).

Young students should look at and carefully examine the phenomena in the world, ask questions about those phenomena, and develop an ever more sophisticated view of the patterns of living things on this planet throughout its history and the deep interconnections between and among living things. Throughout these early years, they can begin to think about the complexity of the environment as being made up of the physical surroundings and weather patterns and the other living things surrounding any focal organism. It is not simply about knowing *that* environments and organisms have changed over time but also learning through specific examples and experiences about the important relationships between organisms and their environments. Even young children have productive, intuitive ideas about survival and how organisms are dependent on both the living and nonliving elements in the environments around them.

One can imagine a classroom of primary learners engaged in a group discussion about the variety of organisms found in their local environment, whether it is urban, suburban, or rural. For example, in a green space near an urban school, students can observe that there are different types of flowering plants: The colors, shapes, and sizes vary as do the leaves and plant height. While this is an observation that can easily be taken for granted, it can provide an avenue for developing conceptual understanding around LS4.C and LS4.D. That is, in any one area, plants can display a wide array of structures for solving common problems (e.g., attracting pollinators and dispersing seeds), and at the same time, the plants are adapted to their environments. Future lessons can focus on a flowering plant that is important to the local context, and then expand out to include similar plants in diverse habitats. At this basic level, elementary learners can begin to understand the complexity of life on Earth and begin to ask productive questions about why plants have similar structures (roots, stems, leaves) yet vary in their color or size.

Students should emerge from elementary school with a deep and fairly sophisticated understanding of observable patterns in the biological systems around them. They should have experience thinking about global patterns of biodiversity and the particulars of survival in different kinds of habitats. They should have a basic idea about the hereditary links between parents and offspring and how those connections result in offspring that are similar to their parents, but not exactly like them. Finally, they should have experience thinking about how different variations assist organisms with survival and reproduction. These basic ideas provide the fodder for model development at the middle and high school level.

Refining Intuitions in Middle and High School

In middle and high school, according to the progression laid out in the *Framework*, students begin to grapple with the *mechanisms* that underlie the phenomena related to unity and diversity and patterns of change over time and consider the consequences of these mechanisms in the natural world and in the world with vast human influences. One resource that will be useful to teachers is the Understanding Evolution website (*http:// evolution.berkeley.edu*). This is a comprehensive compilation of resources that can be used to teach these core ideas.

It is in middle school that students begin to explore the details of recreating the timeline of the history of life on Earth using the fossil record and careful examination of existing characteristics of living things that imply descent with modification. They begin to use ideas around variation and artificial selection to explain how populations are malleable and can change over time.

In grades 6–8, students will be asked to develop a model of natural selection that can help them make sense of how organisms have become so well-suited to their particular environment. Students in this grade band can also begin considering the effects of reproductive isolation and generating explanations for how new species form.

These students are prepared to wrestle with more subtle differences among organisms and have a basis in the other life science DCIs that can allow them to reason about advantage in more sophisticated ways. For example, in middle school, students are also developing an understanding of metabolic processes and should start putting together ideas about how organisms obtain and use energy in their bodies to support survival and reproduction. They can begin to appreciate that even seemingly minor differences between organisms can have profound effects in the context of intense competition for scarce resources. To return to the finch beak example, students can be given data about the difference in beak size across the population and asked to develop ideas about how even just a few millimeters difference in beak size can translate into better outcomes related to survival and, ultimately, reproduction when food availability shifts depending on environmental conditions (e.g., drought). The Biology Guided Inquiry Learning Environments Project (BGuILE) offers a free web-based software application that allows students to explore data and patterns in the information about the Galápagos finches in terms of their features, behaviors, and environment before and after a devastating drought event (*http://bguile.northwestern.edu*).

Students' understanding of genetic mechanisms is also becoming more detailed and nuanced at this grade band, and therefore the important connections between broad models in genetics and evolution should be made here. For example, students can be asked to work with data related to artificial selection experiments in plants or domesticated animals and to examine the difference between traits that are environmentally influenced versus those that have a tight genetic component. Simulations (such as those freely available from NetLogo [*https://ccl.northwestern.edu/netlogo*] and PhET Interactive Simulations [*https://phet.colorado.edu*]) can be very useful for students to explore the relative effects of different parameters such as the strength of the selection pressure or the degree of heritability.

At the high school level, the overall progression toward competence includes both continuing to help students notice and explore the patterns of unity and diversity at the individual, population, and ecosystem levels and developing and refining the core explanatory ideas and models that students can use to make sense of those patterns. Based on the foundations laid in earlier grades, students are ready to explore and use the natural

selection model to make sense of a wide range of phenomena from molecular evidence of common ancestry to the amazing array of specialized traits seen among living things that allow them to survive and thrive in every kind of environment on Earth. By the time they are finished with high school, students should be able to view the world through the lens of natural selection and apply that model across a wide range of contexts (LS4.B and LS4.C).

High school is when students are asked to take their understandings of the mechanisms for evolution and consider how these processes, acting on massive timescales and across the globe, can account for both current and past biodiversity. One consequence of running the natural selection model over time and space is the consideration of what happens when populations become isolated from one another. In grades 9–12, students can continue to develop understanding of how new species form and also think through the causes and consequences of extinction (LS4.D). All of this should be done by building on ideas established in middle school about descent with modification and the tree of life.

As their understanding of DNA increases, students' ability to coordinate DNA evidence with the fossil record and comparative anatomy increases (LS4.A). In other words, it is at this level that students need to take ideas that may have been presented separately up to this point and consider how they reinforce one another and collectively provide powerful tools for figuring out evolutionary relationships.

Furthermore, students at this level should be asked to examine human impacts on these systems (LS4.D). Because they have developed a deep understanding of both patterns and mechanisms at play in natural systems they can begin to use models in a predictive sense. Thinking with an evolutionary lens, students should be able to reason through the consequences of habitat destruction and fragmentation and of pollution and climate change on global patterns of biodiversity and consider how those changes affect all the other species, including humans, in the complex web of life on this planet. There are a number of compelling and complex examples of these factors interacting. One that comes with an incredible wealth of resources for teachers and students is the Isle Royale wolf-moose project (*www.isleroyalewolf.org*), which has data spanning 50 years tracking the wolf and moose populations on the island. Students can investigate, using data-rich resources, how habitat and population structure changes, inbreeding, and other factors have contributed to the decline and near-extinction of the wolf population in this ecosystem.

While student thinking is going to look different both over time and in different contexts, the objective across all learning environments is to get students noticing, describing, and wondering about the evolutionary patterns and sharing, articulating, and refining their reasoning about how and why these patterns have come to exist.

Conclusion

We hope that this chapter has given you a bit more insight into the DCI of Evolution: Unity and Diversity. Taking an evolutionary perspective on biology is one of the most powerful ways that scientists make sense of and reason about organisms in the natural world. The evolutionary perspective allows us to understand why living things are the way they are and, importantly, it allows

the scientific community to continue to wonder and ask questions about the natural world and our place within it. It is this last piece, humanity's place within the natural world and influence on it, that may hold the key to our continued survival.

REFERENCES

Dobzhansky, T. 1973. Nothing in biology makes sense except in the light of evolution. *The American Biology Teacher* 35 (3): 125–129.

Grant, P. R. 1999. *Ecology and evolution of Darwin's finches.* Princeton, NJ: Princeton University Press.

Lehrer, R., and L. Schauble. 2012. Seeding evolutionary thinking by engaging children in modeling its foundations. *Science Education* 96 (4): 701–724.

Manz, E. 2012. Understanding the codevelopment of modeling practice and ecological knowledge. *Science Education* 96 (6): 1071–1105.

Mayr, E. 1977. Darwin and natural selection: How Darwin may have discovered his highly unconventional theory. *American Scientist* 65 (3): 321–327.

Mayr, E. 1991. *One long argument: Charles Darwin and the genesis of modern evolutionary thought.* Cambridge, MA: Harvard University Press.

Metz, K. E. 2008. Narrowing the gulf between the practices of science and the elementary school science classroom. *The Elementary School Journal* 109 (2): 138–161.

Passmore, C., E. Coleman, J. Horton, and H. Parker. 2013. Making sense of natural selection: Developing and using the natural selection model as an anchor for practice and content. *The Science Teacher* 80 (6): 43.

EARTH
AND SPACE
SCIENCES

EARTH AND SPACE SCIENCES

Earth and space sciences consists of three disciplinary core ideas (DCIs) that help to explain a wide variety of Earth-related phenomena, including the motion of the planets, changes in climate, and the shape of Earth structures. These DCIs include ESS1: Earth's Place in the Universe, ESS2: Earth's Systems, and ESS3: Earth and Human Activity. Each of the core ideas comprises a set of component ideas. These understandings are developed by drawing from core ideas in the life and physical sciences, such as ecosystems, energy, and matter and its interactions, while also reflecting aspects of several crosscutting concepts including systems and change over time. Figure ESS.1 highlights the Earth and space sciences DCIs and their components.

In Chapter 10, Julia D. Plummer addresses a topic that has been a source of wonderment since the dawn of humankind, "What is the universe, and what is Earth's place in it?" Exploring the core idea of ESS1: Earth's Place in the Universe allows students to address questions related to our relationship with the universe and what is out there beyond our world. These are topics that many students find fascinating and which tap into their imaginations and adventurous spirits. In this chapter, Plummer addresses the development across grades of three component ideas of this DCI: the structure, composition, and history of the universe, the ways in which the solar system operates, and Earth's planetary history.

In Chapter 11, Ann E. Rivet tackles ESS2: Earth's Systems, which answers the question, "How and why is Earth constantly changing?"

FIGURE ESS.1

Earth and Space Sciences Disciplinary Core Ideas and Component Ideas

ESS1: Earth's place in the universe

    ESS1.A: The universe and its stars

    ESS1.B: Earth and the solar system

    ESS1.C: The history of planet Earth

ESS2: Earth's systems

    ESS2.A: Earth materials and systems

    ESS2.B: Plate tectonics and large-scale system interactions

    ESS2.C: The roles of water in Earth's surface processes

    ESS2.D: Weather and climate

    ESS2.E: Biogeology

ESS3: Earth and human activity

    ESS3.A: Natural resources

    ESS3.B: Natural hazards

    ESS3.C: Human impacts on Earth systems

    ESS3.D: Global climate change

The chapter focuses on the continual interactions between the Earth's key global systems and how they result in conditions and features on the Earth's surface that vary in complex yet predictable ways. Addressing this question allows learners to explain real-world phenomena that we experience every day, such as weather, erosion, and earthquakes, and examine them across a range of space and timescales. This DCI comprises the following component ideas: Earth's systems, plate tectonics, the role of water in Earth processes, weather and climate, and biogeology. Each of these has its own associated questions, addressed in the chapter, that develop throughout the grade levels.

In Chapter 12, Nancy Brickhouse and colleagues consider ESS3: Earth and Human Activity by addressing a key question that is both timely and relevant to today's society, "How do Earth's surface processes and human activities affect each other?" Through examining this question, learners are able to explore a range of reciprocal relationships between humans and the environments they live in, focusing on both the causes and the consequences of specific phenomena, such as hurricanes and consumption of fossil fuels, for both the planet and humankind. The

core idea consists of four components: Natural Resources, Natural Hazards, Human Impacts on Earth Systems, and Climate Change. Brickhouse and colleagues elaborate on how each component idea develops across grade levels and relates to other core ideas within Earth and space sciences and other disciplines.

As a whole, the DCIs in the Earth and space sciences emphasize the field's move away from a perspective of the planet as a static entity that can be easily described through observation. Rather, these ideas paint a picture of the Earth as a complex dynamic system with conditions that are constantly changing in response to both internal and external factors. Understanding Earth's history and the dynamic nature of Earth's processes is critical for developing sustainable solutions to many of society's challenges for future generations.

CHAPTER 10

CORE IDEA ESS1

EARTH'S PLACE IN THE UNIVERSE

Julia D. Plummer

What Is This Disciplinary Core Idea, and Why Is It Important?

The first disciplinary core idea (DCI) in the Earth and space sciences section of *A Framework for K–12 Science Education* (*Framework*; NRC 2012), ESS1: Earth's Place in the Universe, "describes the universe as a whole and addresses its grand scale in both space and time. This idea includes the overall structure, composition, and history of the universe, the forces and processes by which the solar system operates, and Earth's planetary history" (NRC 2012, p. 170). Studying this topic allows students to understand how our planet is part of the largest system imaginable: the universe. This DCI begins to answer some of the important questions that have long intrigued human kind: "What is out there, beyond our world?" "What is our relationship to the universe as a whole?" and "Where did our world come from, and what is its history?" This DCI helps students learn how to make sense of the changing skies above them and to interpret astronomical phenomena they read about in the news, because new discoveries in astronomy are part of the everyday world they live in. It also supports the kind of knowledge

students need to have to interpret evidence that tells us about the history of our planet, from the formation of familiar landscapes to long-term changes in climate.

ESS1 is organized around three major components. The first addresses the nature, structure, history, and composition of the universe, including how it was formed according to the big bang theory, our use of light to understand this and other processes in the universe, and the life cycle of stars. The second component examines the Earth's place in the solar system, concentrating on how motions of objects in the solar system explain our observations from the Earth's surface, the nature of those objects, and the use of physics to explain the patterns of motion of the objects. The third component focuses on the history of the planet Earth, with particular attention to our evidence for the sequences of events that occurred to create the Earth as we know it and the formation of the solar system itself. The ideas that make up Earth's Place in the Universe are not easy to define in a single underlying model, as is often the case for other DCIs. Instead, these ideas hold together as multiple ways of understanding and explaining phenomena that exist at the largest scales and

10

across the longest time spans. For example, students may initially learn explanations for how the Earth's rotation causes the Sun's daily apparent motion in the sky separately from explanations for how the relative movement of the Sun, Earth, and Moon cause the changing lunar phases, but as they develop more sophisticated understandings of these individual explanations, students also learn that the two are related and recognize how they are part of a larger explanatory system for the way the universe behaves.

The understandings included in the ESS1 portion of the *Framework* differ in notable ways from previous standards for astronomy and Earth history. Rather than focusing on a collection of facts and concepts, the DCI is organized to help students grasp the major explanatory models that govern our understanding of the world around us. This puts further emphasis on helping students understand not just the *what* of Earth and space sciences but also the *how do we know* of these big ideas, via the integration of science practices. The *Framework* also emphasizes the importance of crosscutting concepts that span all the DCIs, such as the role of patterns and energy in the ideas included in ESS1. For example, observing patterns in celestial phenomena such as the lunar phases or the change in seasons leads to questions about how these patterns arise and in turn to the development of explanations that use the patterns of motion of the Earth and Moon in the solar system. Similarly, global patterns of rock strata led scientists to develop explanations that account for the history of events that shaped the Earth.

In the following sections, I will discuss how the ESS1 DCI is organized around increasingly sophisticated explanations for the Earth's place in the universe, first by discussing progress toward the explanatory models of astronomy in the DCI

and then showing how this connects to understanding elements of Earth and space sciences included in this DCI.

Overview of Component Ideas

The *Framework* looks at the Earth's Place in the Universe concept from three perspectives: (1) how the Earth fits into the structure of the universe and the processes that formed the universe (ESS1.A), (2) developing explanations for our observations of the solar system using the Earth's motion (ESS1.B), and (3) understanding the evidence we have for how the planet was shaped and evolved over the course of its history (ESS1.C). These strands are woven together, with concepts developed at lower grades supporting increasingly sophisticated explanations across different spatial and temporal scales as students move through school.

ESS1.A: THE UNIVERSE AND ITS STARS

The *Framework* begins by posing a guiding question to organize how students should come to understand the universe: "What is the universe, and what is the Earth's place in it?" The first component idea of this DCI, ESS1.A: The Universe and Its Stars, begins the task of answering that question. The universe is everything … everything we can observe and beyond, including our planet, the stars, other planets, our galaxy, and other galaxies. The universe began in an event known as the big bang about 13.8 billion years ago, when the universe was extremely hot and dense. Immediately, the space between matter began to expand rapidly. During the early moments of the big bang, nearly all of the hydrogen and helium in the universe was formed, followed by the formation of the first stars and galaxies. The *Framework* has placed these elements of the DCI primarily at the middle and high school level because delving into these explanations requires an understanding of other fundamental aspects of chemistry and physics. For example, the evidence for the big bang and the history of the early universe relies on an interpretation of the cosmic microwave background radiation (CMBR); thus, knowledge of light and spectra (discussed in PS4.B: Electromagnetic (EM) Radiation; see Chapter 5, p. 75) is important to understanding how the CMBR was released in the early moments of the universe and how this evidence fits predictions that the universe began in a period of extreme temperature and density.

Across grade levels, students build toward understanding how our observations from the Earth only tell part of the story. Central to this is the awareness of how the *relative* size and distances of stars compares with the Earth and nearby celestial objects and the ways that this understanding allows students to develop more sophisticated explanations for phenomena they observe from the Earth. For example, in elementary school, children can begin this process by learning how stars only appear to be small points of light when they are actually large like our Sun and at great distances from us compared with the distance to the Sun and Moon. This understanding of size and distances takes a dramatic leap in middle school as students learn about our place in comparison to our own galaxy and other galaxies and as they begin to explore the history of the solar system and the universe through a study of the formation process of the solar system as well as how the big bang led to the formation of the universe. Finally, in high school, students develop even more sophisticated explanations

for the nature of the universe as they learn to use light spectra as evidence for the big bang theory and the nature of stars. Their understanding of stars and our own solar system is further extended through explanations of how stars form and their life cycles.

ESS1.B: THE EARTH AND THE SOLAR SYSTEM

While ESS1.A establishes the Earth's place with respect to the stars and galaxies, as well as the history of the formation of our solar system and universe, the second component idea, ESS1.B: The Earth and the Solar System, concentrates on supporting student understanding of observable patterns of motion in the solar system and explanations for those motions. The *Framework* poses a question to guide how students learn across grades: "What are the predictable patterns caused by Earth's movement in the solar system?" This question hints at the progress of science, as it is scientists' observations, predictions, and identifications of patterns that lead to the development of models that help scientists explain the universe. This progression of understanding begins with students learning the patterns of motion and change in celestial objects as observed from the Earth's surface. Such phenomena may include daily patterns in the Sun, Moon, and stars' apparent motion, seasonal patterns in the Sun's motion, seasonal changes in constellations, phases of the Moon, and the wandering pattern of the planets against the background of stars. It continues as students learn to explain these phenomena with the motion of the Earth, Moon, and planets in the solar system, and to recognize how these objects' relative positions, as well as our own position on the spherical Earth, can be used to explain those patterns of motion and change. These ideas are

10

explored further in ESS2.D: Weather and Climate when students build on their understanding of the causes of seasonal patterns in temperature change to begin to reason about long-term patterns in climate data. Eventually, students also develop explanations that include more sophisticated concepts of physics, such as gravity to explain orbital motion and energy to explain the seasons.

ESS1.C: THE HISTORY OF THE PLANET EARTH

In addition to considering explanations for phenomena by looking out beyond the Earth, the third component of this DCI, ESS1.C: The History of Planet Earth, delves into the evidence for how the Earth was shaped and has evolved. The *Framework* poses the question, "How do people reconstruct and date events in Earth's planetary history?" Because children's everyday experiences with the world around them may suggest that the Earth's surface is relatively static, studying the history of the Earth helps put current Earth surface phenomena in the context of how the planet changes over time. Developing this understanding allows children to see how seemingly divergent Earth phenomena, such as earthquakes and mountain chains, are part of a bigger system that is constantly changing. This idea is developed further in ESS2: Earth's Systems; students cannot understand our dynamic Earth without also understanding its history.

Students begin by examining evidence from observations of "the structure, sequence, and properties of rocks, sediments, and fossils, as well as the locations of current and past ocean basins, lakes, and rivers, to reconstruct events in Earth's planetary history" (NRC 2012, p. 177). In doing so, they begin to learn how the relative ages of

events in Earth's history are revealed by studying the layering of rocks and fossils; further complexity is introduced as students make sense of rock layers that have been rearranged as the result of plate tectonics (see ESS2.B: Plate Tectonics and Large-Scale System Interactions [pp. 207–210]). To fully explain this planetary history requires connecting to their understanding of the Earth's place in the solar system, because studying the Earth's formation process yields additional information about its history. For example, though dynamic processes have destroyed much of the evidence for events that occurred on the Earth's surface during its early formation, the density of craters on other objects in the solar system, such as the Moon and other rocky worlds, provides evidence for the age of the Earth and its early history of bombardment from asteroids.

How Does Student Understanding of This Disciplinary Core Idea Develop Over Time?

The answers to the three guiding questions for the component ideas of ESS1 develop together toward a coherent understanding of the Earth's place in the universe as students' understanding of astronomy improves across grades.

Lower Elementary

In grades K–2, the *Framework* recommends students learn that we can begin to understand celestial objects, such as stars, planets, and the Moon, by observing their light and that telescopes can help us see more stars than we can see with the naked eye and show additional details of the Moon and planets. In this manner, students should begin to understand the discipline of astronomy from their own Earth-based perspective. Children's early experiences using tools such as binoculars to distinguish new details will help them begin to understand how astronomers built our complex understanding of space using more sophisticated tools of astronomy, including telescopes.

Understanding celestial objects from their own perspective continues through the elementary grades as children learn to describe patterns observable from the Earth's surface, such as the daily pattern of the motions of the Sun, Moon, and stars and seasonal changes in the Sun's path. Children may already know that the Sun and Moon appear to move, but they may not understand that this pattern of motion is a regular, smooth path across the sky; further, they are unlikely to recognize that the stars also appear to move (Plummer 2009a). This is because children's everyday experiences are unlikely to lead to an understanding of these patterns of motion, including the change in the Sun's path over the seasons, given the complexity of making the observations needed to reveal the patterns across position and time. Though these patterns of rising and setting of celestial objects are the result of the Earth's rotation, that is not the way that students on the Earth's surface experience them. Thus, in early elementary grades it is important for students to begin building an understanding of these patterns from their own perspective, such as tracing the Sun's apparent motion relative to their home or their school, rather than starting by learning about the Earth's rotation. Beginning with children's own Earth-based observations of celestial phenomena is an important foundation for their understanding of astronomy; they must first develop an understanding of astronomical phenomena before later learning how to explain

those observations. This process mirrors the way scientists work by first recognizing and studying a phenomena and later trying to explain it using scientific principles and theories.

Also at this time, children should begin to learn about geologic events, including those that occur relatively quickly, such as earthquakes, and those that take much longer, such as the formation of the Grand Canyon. Developing an understanding of the relative temporal scales of Earth phenomena will help students begin to categorize these events and will provide a foundation as they work toward a deeper understanding of time in later grades. Phenomena can also be categorized in terms of whether they occur in cycles, such as day and night, or as distinct events with a beginning and end, such as volcanic eruptions (NRC 2012). Children are likely to have some ideas about these events prior to instruction; Ross and Shuell (1993) found that early elementary students are already aware of the earthquake phenomena before instruction but are likely to conflate it with other types of natural hazards, such as volcanoes and inclement weather. Children may be drawing on what they hear from the media to develop their understanding of these events (Ross and Shuell 1993).

Upper Elementary

In grades 3–5, students should build on their understanding of how tools help us understand celestial objects as they learn that the Sun is merely a very nearby star and that stars come in a wide variety of sizes and are different distances from the Earth and Sun. While children may be able to parrot the idea that "the Sun is a star," this is not sufficient for them to understand what it means that the Sun and other bright objects

in the nighttime sky are the same type of object (e.g., Agan 2004). Children often believe that the stars are smaller than the Moon and located in the solar system or around the Moon (Agan 2004; Plummer, Kocareli, and Slagle 2014). Even with instruction addressing the actual size of the stars with respect to the Sun and planets, children continue to believe that, in addition to very large stars located at great distances, there are also very small stars located in our solar system (Plummer et al. 2014). Thus, even by upper elementary, the *Framework* is asking students to engage in sophisticated reasoning about sizes and scales to progress in their understanding of astronomy.

Comprehending the relative sizes and distances between objects may also support their developing explanations for the observed patterns of motion. In upper elementary grades, children begin to use the Earth's own motion to explain observable patterns developed in early elementary, such as the day–night cycle, the changes in length and direction of shadows, and the daily, monthly, and yearly change of position of the Sun, Moon, and stars. They also learn about the change in the planets' positions in the sky as they orbit the Sun. These explanations use students' developing spatial reasoning abilities to visualize how movement observed from their own Earth-based observations can be explained by the Earth and other celestial objects' motions and relative positions (Plummer et al. 2014). For example, the Sun's apparent rising and setting across the sky can be visualized from an Earth-based perspective, but its explanation requires visualizing how the Earth's rotation would cause us to see the Sun appear to move when it is actually we who are moving. Beginning this process of visualizing the connections between their own observations and how objects actually move in

space will help them as they move toward more sophisticated explanations that rely on this same shifting of perspectives in middle and high school when they learn to explain lunar phases and the seasons (Plummer 2014).

Similarly, the temporal focus of early elementary continues in grades 3–5 as children develop increasingly complex notions of how the surface of the Earth changes over time. This can include understanding processes of weathering and erosion as well as how earthquakes change rock formations over time (see also Chapter 11, "Core Idea ESS2: Earth's Systems," p. 205). Children should also begin to understand the evidence available to interpret the history of rock layers, such as identifying the relative location of different fossils to determine the order in which layers of rock have been formed. Learning to use static records of rock layers to understand notions of time may be challenging for children because it relies on them grasping the principle involved in interpreting layers of sediment being laid down sequentially over time and relating this to notions of "deep time"—timescales that extend far beyond the child's own experiences (Dodick and Orion 2003).

Middle School

In grades 6–8, students should develop increasingly sophisticated explanations for celestial phenomena that explain patterns of Earth-based observations, with elements of the how objects move in space relative to our position on Earth along with an understanding of relative size and scale. For example, the *Framework* includes explanations for the lunar phases and seasonal changes in temperature across the globe at the middle grades. These require more complex reasoning than explanations for phenomena developed in elementary school, as children are asked to apply knowledge of light and energy to make sense of these phenomena. For example, explaining the seasons requires understanding the ways in which our observations of the Sun change due to our location on the spherical Earth and our position in its yearly orbit. But it also requires understanding how the changing position of the Sun in the sky changes the amount of energy our location receives, thus affecting the local temperature patterns. A significant body of literature points to the challenges students face in constructing these explanations due to the nature of the spatial reasoning involved (Kavanagh, Agan, and Sneider 2005). Students will need support during instruction on how to imagine the Moon as a sphere, illuminated by the Sun as it orbits the Earth (Plummer 2014) or how the Sun's altitude and path length changes seasonally as a result of the changing orientation of one's position on the Earth during its orbital cycle (Plummer and Maynard 2014). Supporting students over time in visualizing and using these changing perspectives is important for them to successfully engage with this DCI.

Students should also begin to develop a systematic understanding of the properties and motions of objects in the solar system. This builds on some of their initial understanding of the nature of celestial objects, such as the Sun, Earth, and Moon, as well as the motion of those objects (rotation and revolution), which they gained as they explained observable phenomena throughout elementary school. Rather than understanding that planets orbit the Sun in the same direction and roughly on a plane, students often enter middle school believing that the organization of the planets in the solar system is random, with some objects holding stationary or moving erratically

(Sharp and Keurbis 2005). While gravity as a force that pulls objects down is introduced to explain everyday observations in elementary school (see Chapter 3, "Core Idea PS2: Motion and Stability: Forces and Interactions," p. 33), this is extended to explaining how objects move in the solar system in middle grades. In particular, students should learn that planets and other solar system objects, such as comets and asteroids, maintain their orbits about the Sun, rather than flying off into space, due to the gravitational force of attraction between the object and the Sun. On the Earth, we observe the attractive force between objects and the Earth when objects fall as they are dropped or thrown. However, planets and other objects in stable orbits are traveling forward in their orbital trajectory at a velocity great enough to maintain a constant, roughly circular "fall" about the Sun. Many students are likely to have alternative ideas about the nature of gravity, such as the belief that there is no gravity in space or that gravity only extends as far as the Earth's atmosphere (Williamson and Willoughby 2012). Students also often believe that only certain objects exert a gravitational force rather than all objects with mass (Plummer et al. 2015). And even when students have learned that planets are held in orbit around the Sun due to the Sun's gravitational pull on them, students are often unsure why planets do not crash into the Sun because they are unable to articulate the role of the planets' tangential velocity in maintaining the orbital motion (Plummer et al. 2015). Exploring the explanation for planetary orbits at a conceptual level (considering both the role of gravity and the planet's tangential velocity) will provide a stronger foundation for more sophisticated quantitative reasoning about orbital phenomena in high school.

10

Students' systematic exploration of solar system phenomena should also include organizing and classifying objects in the solar system toward a better understanding of the common properties and patterns of the solar system's constituents (Rubin et al. 2014). While instruction often focuses on the individual properties of the different planets in the solar system, a constructive approach is to focus on grouping objects according to their properties. This allows students to see how planets and other solar system objects with similar compositions and sizes (such as asteroids, comets, or Kuiper belt objects) are found at similar distances from the Sun. The focus shifts from superficial details and facts to systematic properties that organize the solar system. This way, students can begin to engage with important questions, such as, "Why do objects in the solar system orbit the Sun in the same direction and on the same plane?" and "Why are objects with similar physical properties found at similar distances from the Sun?" These and other observable patterns can be explained by the solar system's formation process.

The solar system formed from a cloud of dust and gas, drawn together by gravity. By shifting the focus from learning about the solar system as a collection of disconnected facts toward a coherent system with important patterns, students have further opportunity to learn how science is a process of developing models that explain our observations of interesting phenomena. To learn how the formation model explains our current observations of the solar system, students will need to continue to develop an understanding of how gravitational forces and momentum can shape how the solar system came to be and how it continues in its present form. Explaining how the planets formed involves learning how

microscopic materials (gas, dust, and ices) can build up by "sticking together" (through electrostatic forces) until sufficient mass has accumulated such that gravitational forces can take over the building process at a macroscopic scale. Different types of planets and other objects formed initially because of the decrease in temperature with distance from the Sun; rocky and metallic objects, such as asteroids and the rock planets, formed closer to the Sun, whereas gas giant planets, comets, and Kuiper belt objects formed farther out where gases could condense into ice particles. One challenge that students have when first learning about this model is that they confuse the solar system's formation process with the big bang theory, an event that occurred billions of years before our solar system formed (Prather, Slater, and Offerdahl 2002).

In middle school, students should also have the opportunity to extend their understanding of sizes and scales of phenomena in the universe by learning how the Earth and the solar system are part of our Milky Way galaxy, one of billions of galaxies in the observable universe. Research suggests that students are likely to overestimate the distance to the Moon while underestimating, often by several orders of magnitude, the distances to the Sun, nearest stars, and other galaxies (Miller and Brewer 2010). Rather than just teaching children about the relative size and scale of objects in the universe, scales can be contextualized while teaching them to explain how the solar system formed from a large cloud of gas and dust that was itself part of a larger nebula in our Milky Way galaxy. This may help students place these objects on a scale and connect objects and relative size to important events and explanations in astronomy. Appreciation of the relative size of the cloud that formed the solar system may help students understand that the Sun and planets formed from an large cloud of gas that contracted due to gravity rather than from an explosion of material, a common idea held among students (Plummer et al. 2015). Student can build on this perspective of the relative size of the initial gas cloud and our own solar system to help appreciate how we fit into a larger collection of star systems, which formed from similar gas clouds, which make up the Milky Way galaxy.

With respect to Earth's own history, middle school students deepen their understanding of how we use evidence from rock layers and fossil records to understand the history of major events that have shaped the Earth and consider ways to organize our understanding of the long time periods of the Earth's history. Analysis of rock strata and the fossil record provide evidence for events such as volcanic eruptions, the formation of mountain chains, large-scale extinction events, and periods of mass glaciation. However, at this level, students' understanding of the evidence only leads to relative ordering of events and not an absolute timescale. Research on middle school students suggests that they may be aware of major geologic events, such as the movement of continents or ice ages, but their sense of the chronology is limited. Instead, they tend to focus on grouping events as "extremely ancient" and "less ancient" (Trend 1998). Several other studies with students from middle school to college also suggest that students do not have a grasp of deep time (e.g., Dodick and Orion 2003; Kortz and Murray 2009).

As with the study of astronomy, students' study of the Earth's history also engages them in particular elements of spatial reasoning that draw on the ability to understand geologic structures. Students will need support in this area as

research has found that some have difficulty with the type of visualization needed to interpret these problems (Kali and Orion 1996). The challenge in understanding the three-dimensional nature of rock strata may also make interpreting the temporal scales challenging, since students are using these structures to interpret timelines of events (Dodick and Orion 2003). Student understanding of how rock strata and the fossil record could provide evidence of the Earth's history may also be limited because many believe sedimentary rock is formed just beneath the Earth's surface or that these layers are the same as the larger-scale layers of the crust and mantle (Kortz and Murray 2009). These alternative ideas suggest different ways that students misunderstand the spatial scales involved, and perhaps the temporal scales of the formation process as well. While sedimentary rocks are initially formed from the deposition of materials at the Earth's surface or within water, to form this material into rock requires a long-term process of sediment deposition that compresses lower layers sufficiently to compact the material into rock. Thus, rather than sedimentary rocks being a shallow feature of the Earth's surface, they are actually formed at great depths in order for enough pressure to be exerted from the weight of the surface layers. Further, the deposition of those layers requires immense amounts of time. Students often confuse sedimentary layers with crust and mantle layers, indicating they do not appreciate the spatial scale of these different types of "layers"; sedimentary rock is only a thin overlay on the Earth's crust.

High School

In high school, students build on concepts learned in middle school by developing more quantitative

explanations for phenomena in the solar system while also expanding the range of phenomena they can explain to include those that occur on longer timescales than just days, months, and years. Students extend their understanding of orbital motion, developed at a descriptive level in elementary and middle school, to more quantitative explanations of these patterns using the mathematics of Kepler's laws and exploring how gravitational interactions can influence orbital motions. Students should also build from their explanations for seasonal temperature changes in middle school to learn about cycles of climate change on the Earth's surface that happen on much longer timescales (e.g., tens to hundreds of thousands of years). These changes occur due to long-term shifts in the shape of the Earth's orbit and the tilt in the Earth's rotational axis with respect to its orbital plane. Over time, these two factors alter the distance between the Earth and Sun at different times of the year and affect the intensity of sunlight, thus changing the patterns of energy absorption across the Earth's surface (see also ESS2.D: Weather and Climate [pp. 211–214]). Developing a sophisticated explanation for natural climate change provides a background for students to engage in understand human-induced climate change (Lombardi, Sinatra, and Nussbaum 2013), discussed in more detail in Chapter 12, "Core Idea ESS3: Earth and Human Activity" (p. 225).

Students deepen their understanding of our Sun and the billions of stars in the universe, as well as how the big bang began the processes that led to the formation of the universe, by further developing their explanations for astronomical phenomena in ways that extend their notions of both spatial and temporal scales. For example, students' observations of the Sun and stars from an Earth-based perspective and across their own life span may suggest that these objects are constant. However, stars, though long-lived, have life cycles that culminate in millions to billions of years. The Sun can be studied as an exemplar case of how stars form from clouds of gas and dust (first discussed in middle school), exist stably for most of their lives, and then die dramatically as their fuel source (hydrogen, initially) runs out. Our own Sun will end as an expanding red giant star after exhausting its source of hydrogen for nuclear fusion (see PS1.C: Nuclear Processes [p. 27], which discusses the process of nuclear fusion in middle and high school) and then become a planetary nebula, leaving behind its core as a white dwarf star. Understanding the stellar evolution of more massive stars will help students understand where many of the building blocks of life and all that we know on Earth originated. A sufficiently massive star will eventually go supernova, spewing out a multitude of elements heavier than those formed during the big bang (hydrogen and helium). These elements are then seeded into new clouds forming new stars and planets, continuing the cycle of star birth, life, and death.

While in middle school, students learned about how the solar system formed only 4.6 billion years ago, in high school students more deeply explore how the universe itself began around 13.8 billion years ago with the rapid expansion of space between matter, as described by the big bang theory. The development of our model of how the universe began is an elegant story that can engage students with a series of phenomena that are consistent with the predictions of the big bang theory. The first phenomenon that led astronomers to the development of the big bang theory was the apparent motion of distant galaxies away from our own position in space. Just as the Sun *appears* to move across the sky during the day due to the Earth's own rotation, the galaxies are not actually moving away from us; it only *appears* this way from our Earth-based perspective. Instead, the apparent motion is due to the expansion of the space between clusters of galaxies. If one imagines this process running in reverse, the conclusion drawn is that the universe began with everything packed together in a hot, dense state (see Figure 10.1). This concept of the early universe leads to the next piece of observable evidence for the big bang: the ratio of low-mass elements in the universe. Astronomers predicted that during those first moments, when the universe was extremely hot and dense, it behaved similarly to the core of a star. Particles collided to fuse, forming the first atoms: hydrogen, helium, and a small amount of lithium. Current observations of the ratios of these elements match what was predicted by the big bang theory. The final strong piece of observational evidence for the big bang is the CMBR. An object that is extremely hot and dense will emit a characteristic spectrum of light that corresponds to its temperature; the very early universe itself was hot and dense, which produced this characteristic spectrum of light based on its temperature. A few minutes after the universe began to expand, that light became free to stream through space. We are still able to observe this leftover light from the early moments of the universe. Its spectrum matches what astronomers predicted we would observe if the universe began in that hot, dense state.

For students to understand how astronomers develop complex explanations for stellar, galactic, and extragalactic phenomena, they will need to develop increasingly sophisticated understandings of how astronomers interpret the light received from these objects. For example, as

FIGURE 10.1

The Expanding Universe

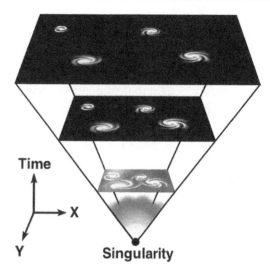

Time moves forward from the bottom to the top of the figure. While the size of the galaxies (shown as spirals) stays the same, the space between them expands. At the time of the big bang, the universe was an infinitely dense singularity.

mentioned above, one piece of evidence for how the universe began is drawn from our observations of the motion of galaxies. When we view the spectrum of light emitted by the stars that make up a galaxy, we observe a pattern of bright bands and dark lines. The dark lines are where light emitted by stars has been absorbed by elements in the stars' atmospheres. Each element has a characteristic pattern of these dark absorption lines that can be used like a fingerprint to identify that element, because they always appear in the same pattern and at the same wavelengths of light. However, if the objects that contain the atoms that are absorbing the light are in motion—in this case, the stars in a distant galaxy—those lines will be shifted proportionally to the speed of

10

the object's motion. Therefore, when we observe that a galaxy's spectrum with its characteristic pattern of absorption lines appears to be shifted toward the red end of the spectra, we interpret this as the galaxy itself moving away from us (relatively speaking) due to the expansion of the universe. This aspect of the DCI connects to the understanding of light that students are developing in PS4.B: Electromagnetic Radiation, which examines the nature of light across the electromagnetic spectrum, how it travels, and how it interacts with matter.

Similarly, across elementary and middle school grades, students develop increasingly sophisticated notions of how we establish evidence for long-scale change over time on the Earth. This serves as the foundation for developing more sophisticated explanations in high school. Students should begin using knowledge of radioactive decay lifetimes and isotopic content as the method to date rock layers and develop an absolute scale for the history of events on Earth. In doing so, students will need an initial understanding of nuclear physics (See PS1.C: Nuclear Processes [p. 27]). Students may have alternative ideas about radioactive decay that will make using this concept to explain our understanding of Earth's history challenging. For example, students may have more colloquial ideas about the word *decay*, such as suggesting that the atoms are losing pieces or disintegrating, that electrons are simply change states, or that radioactive decay involves an interaction between the nucleus and valence electrons (Prather 2005). Their understanding of half-life may be similarly problematic; students often believe that half of the radioactive material will be gone after a half-life rather than having become a different element (Prather 2005). Addressing the full history of the Earth and its formation may need to include a

focus on the relationship between when life arose on the planet Earth; many college students believe life already existed on Earth when it formed (Libarkin et al. 2005).

Radiodating only provides an age for the oldest rock on Earth; however, given the Earth's state of constant change due to plate tectonics and erosion (see Chapter 11, "Core Idea ESS2: Earth's Systems," p. 205), students should learn how looking out into the solar system can provide evidence for the age of the Earth and its early history. Rocky objects in the solar system, such as the Moon and asteroids, have gone through much less change during the course of the solar system's history compared to the Earth. Planetary scientists use radiodating on meteorites to determine the age of the Earth and solar system. As they connect the age of the Earth's formation in the solar system to other events in the universe's history, students will need support in understanding that the big bang occurred well before the Sun formed (13.8 billion vs. 4.6 billion years ago) as students often conflate these two events (e.g., Trend 2000). The earliest epoch of the Earth's existence was a time of heavy bombardment of asteroids and comets throughout the solar system. Though little evidence of this past bombardment is evident on the Earth itself, the record of this period in the Earth's history can be inferred from observations of the Moon, Mercury, and other rocky objects in the solar system. We can still observe evidence of their past bombardment through the numerous craters on their surfaces. Thus, students will need to understand that the solar system's formation process must have produced far more asteroids and comets than we currently observe to account for the impacts seen on the rocky planets and moons.

What Approaches Can We Use to Teach About This Disciplinary Core Idea?

Progress in the Earth's Place in the Universe requires integrating key science practices with instruction that moves students toward more sophisticated explanations for the nature and origins of the solar system, the stars, and the universe. In elementary school, instruction should support students in developing representations for the observable patterns of change and motion. This is a good opportunity to begin engaging students in making claims based on patterns they uncover in observations of celestial objects. Data could include their own observations of the Sun's location throughout the day or the visibility of stars at night but not during the day. And while it is important for students to have the opportunity to make their own firsthand observations in astronomy, time and weather can limit the extent to which this can happen in the classroom. Students can also make and record observations using computer simulations of the day and night sky, such as *Stellarium* (*www.stellarium.org*) or *Starry Night* (*astronomy.starrynight.com*) which show realistic views of the sky as seen from the Earth's surface (e.g., Hobson, Trundle, and Saçkes 2010; Plummer, Wasko, and Slagle 2011). Looking for patterns in their observations, such as the apparent path of the Sun and Moon or the changing appearance of the Moon's phases, engages students in the science practice of analyzing and interpreting data.

In upper elementary and middle school, these initial evidence-based claims about the patterns in celestial motion become the impetus to construct more complex model-based explanations that lead to an understanding of the relative motions of objects in the solar system. Students can engage in scientific argumentation as they collaborate with peers and are guided by their teacher to construct models of the Sun, Earth, and Moon to explain the observed patterns. Though the phenomena differ, this trend of developing evidence-based claims about the patterns of celestial events and then engaging in argumentation with models to make sense of the patterns continues from the simplest phenomena, such as the daily apparent motion of the Sun, through the most complex, such as the seasonal change in temperatures (Plummer, Kocareli, and Slagle 2014; Plummer and Maynard 2014; Plummer 2014). The use of models in the classroom should do more than simply show students motions and relationships; students need to engage in using models to explain their observations. For example, after developing a representation of the Sun's apparent path across the sky (from observations of changes in their shadows over the course of the day or by recording the Sun's position while watching a computer simulation, like *Stellarium*), students can use models to explain their observations. Using a ball or lamp to represent the Sun and a globe to represent the Earth, small groups of students can then work together to determine which direction the globe should rotate for the Sun to appear to move from east to west as they observed in their data.

Engaging students with physical models offers several advantages in supporting student learning. Physical models may be key to improving students' spatial thinking in astronomy (Parker and Heywood 1998; Plummer 2014). Engagement with physical models may help reduce the amount of information students need to keep in mind at one time, because elements are kept in

the models and available for use when needed (Wilson 2002). Engagement with physical models may also provide teachers with access to their students thinking during instruction, because teachers can observe the ways in which students manipulate those models to solve problems. For example, if students are trying to make their Earth globe orbit the Sun when modeling the reason the Sun appears to rise and set, the teacher can visually assess that the students have an alternative idea about the reason for the day/ night cycle. Finally, these types of experiences will allow students to learn how models and modeling is central to the authentic practices of scientists (Rivet and Kastens 2012).

Students' own kinesthetic and embodied experiences (physical movements), as they attempt to construct explanations in astronomy, can also support the complex spatial reasoning in this domain (Plummer 2014). Gesture use may help facilitate problem solving (e.g., Liben, Christensen, and Kastens 2010; Parnafes 2012) and has been found to help students solve tasks that require visualization and mental transformations, such as those required to explain how our Earth-based observations are explained by relative motions in space (Chu and Kita 2011). Gestures and whole-body interaction can be designed to be a purposeful part of instruction and to support student learning (e.g., Padalkar and Ramadas 2011; Plummer 2009b; Plummer et al. 2014). For example, students can physically trace out the apparent path of the Sun as it appears to move across the sky and then model the explanation by pretending to be the Earth as they rotate and observe a model Sun appearing to move from their location (Plummer, Wasco, and Slagle 2011; Plummer, Kocareli, and Slagle 2014). These experiences offer both visual

and kinesthetic support for students learning to explain astronomical phenomena.

Students' investigations of the solar system in middle school can also be an opportunity to engage in scientific argumentation to promote a systems-based understanding of our place in the solar system. Students can learn to organize the objects in the solar system according to their properties, such as composition, distance from the Sun, and size (Rubin et al. 2014). Students should be encouraged to gather and record data about multiple properties (e.g., mass, size, distance from the Sun, density) for solar system objects from reliable websites (such as those created by NASA). They should then use these data to make claims about how to group objects and back up their claims with evidence from the data they collected from websites. Though students may want to use existing classification schemes, they should be encouraged to focus on using the evidence they have gathered to develop groups for themselves. In doing so, they move toward an understanding of the solar system that focuses on the underlying features needed to be explained by its formation process (Rubin et al. 2014), in particular patterns in objects' composition, distance, and size.

Once students appreciate the different properties of objects in the solar system and how they are distributed, they can learn to explain solar system formation by participating in a whole-class modeling activity called *Active Accretion* (Ristvey, Bogner, and Cobb, n.d.). During this model, each student represents a particle from the initial cloud of gas and dust that collapsed to form the Sun, planets, and other objects. During the course of simulating collisions between particles, students "stick" to the same particle type (such as metals or ices) through electrostatic forces until a particle of sufficient mass has built up (enough students) so that gravity can take over the process of pulling in more material to build up a planet. This simulation helps middle school students understand the microscopic process of small particles sticking together to begin building up to form planets; but students may still need more support in understanding gravity's role in how planets build from small planetesimals to full-sized planets (based on research by Julia Plummer, Christopher Palma, KeriAnn Rubin, Alice Flarend, and Yann Shiou Ong).

Computer simulations can also support students as they learn to explain how and why objects orbit in the solar system. For example, students can engage with a computer simulation (such as those from PhET at *http://phet.colorado.edu*) that models the solar system to test how varying mass, distance, and initial velocity influence the nature of planetary orbits. Student groups can share data they have collected from such a computer simulation to look for trends across data sets (Flarend and Palma 2013). This allows them to begin developing claims that relate the balance of velocity to the magnitude of the gravitational pull in maintaining a stable orbit. Another useful simulation is *Newton's Cannon* (*http://waowen.screaming.net/revision/force&motion/ncananim.htm*), which can also be used as a thought experiment in class. Imagine a large cannon is placed on top of the tallest mountain on Earth. Cannonballs are then shot out horizontally with different amounts of force and therefore different initial velocities. Those with small initial velocities will fly small distances and eventually crash to the surface of the Earth because of the pull of gravity. Those with very high velocities will move fast enough to escape. But a cannonball fired with just the right initial velocity will be pulled down by gravity in a path that matches the curvature of the Earth's

FIGURE 10.2

Cannonball Trajectories for the Newton's Cannon Thought Experiment

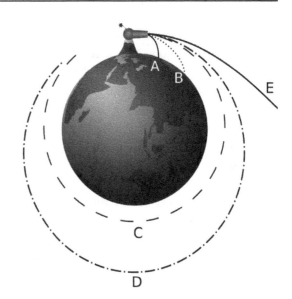

Newton's Cannon is a thought experiment describing a large cannon placed on top of a tall mountain on Earth. The cannonballs fired for trajectories A and B were fired with small initial velocities, and therefore gravity pulled them down to the Earth's surface. The cannonball fired for trajectory E was fired at the highest initial velocity and escaped Earth's gravity. Cannonballs fired for trajectories C and D were fired with velocities that sufficiently balanced the gravitational pull on the cannonballs as they fell toward the Earth, producing an orbital path.

surface, forming an orbit around the Earth (see path C in the Figure 10.2).

In high school, students can continue to develop model-based explanations for observed phenomena as they study the relative size and distances of stars, the evolution of stars, and the formation of the universe. Instruction should engage students in constructing explanations

10

that support the big bang theory using available evidence. This will require students to apply knowledge of light spectra to interpret evidence from the apparent recession of distant galaxies and the nature of the CMBR, and to use atomic physics to understand how the proportions of light elements found in the current universe can be explained by the process in which they were formed 13.8 billion years ago. Thus, instruction should shift toward helping students construct their own explanations for how all the disparate pieces of evidence support an explanation for the formation of the universe.

Instruction that supports students in developing a deep and rich understanding of Earth's history integrates experiences with science practices as the students work toward explanations for the history of events on the Earth. This can begin with early elementary students' investigations of the timescales of natural events on Earth. Such investigations could engage students in obtaining and evaluating information about the length of events such as volcanic eruptions, earthquakes, and erosion to determine that some happen quickly and others very slowly. This can lead to more sophisticated opportunities to construct explanations based on evidence from rock formations and fossils in rock layers observed during classroom investigations. As students engage with gathering data by making observations of rock strata to learn how geologists sequence events in geologic history, it will be important for them to make contextualized observations. Specifically, the science practice of observing is discipline specific, relying on the students developing understanding of the theoretical constructs of geology (Ford 2005).

Students should continue to learn about the history of the Earth by constructing explanations based on evidence from rock strata in

middle school. However, the level of sophistication increases as they work toward understanding the geologic timescale of the Earth's history, rather than a more localized approach to understanding changes in landscape over time in elementary school. In middle school, teachers should support students in using their developing understanding of scientific principles in geology to support their process of explaining evidence of the geologic timescale. This may build on their understanding of how fossils can be used to establish relative ages of major events, the processes that led to the formation of mountain chains and ocean basins, and the theory of evolution (NGSS Lead States 2013). Constructing explanations will also require students to interpret spatially complex geologic structures. Instruction should be designed with this in mind so teachers can help students envision cross sections of structures and improve their perception of spatial configuration of layers in complex structures (Kali and Orion 1996). Students may be more likely to use gesture as they are learning new concepts (Liben, Kastens, and Christensen 2010) and should be encouraged to do so; teachers can promote gesture use by engaging students with 2-D representations, physical models, or other artifacts (Kastens, Agrawal, and Liben 2008). For example, when interpreting events in Earth's history from maps or representations showing different layers of rock strata, students should be encouraged to gesture both to each other and to their teacher in ways that help them identify key elements and relationships, such as how one layer relates to another layer, and to manipulate these representations in ways that help them make sense of how to interpret change over time. Research has found a link between children's knowledge of geology and their spontaneous gesture use (Matlen et al.

2012). Teachers can also use gestures to help convey spatially complex issues (Kastens et al. 2008).

Conclusion

The Earth's Place in the Universe DCI engages students in increasingly large spatial and temporal scales as they move from elementary to middle to high school. Supporting student learning across the grades begins with supporting their connections to what they can observe and experience but then quickly moves out to scales that require models, simulations, and representations within which to interact and make sense of the phenomena. Students will need support in engaging in the types of spatial reasoning required to construct scientific explanations in this DCI. They will also need to begin integrating other DCIs as they move up the grades, including those about gravitational forces, nuclear processes, and energy.

Acknowledgments

The author would like to thank her colleagues in the Earth and Space Science Partnership of Pennsylvania (ESSP) for stimulating discussions on student thinking in this domain. This work was partially supported through the ESSP (National Science Foundation award no. DUE-0962792).

REFERENCES

Agan, L. 2004. Stellar ideas: Exploring students' understanding of stars. *Astronomy Education Review* 3 (1): 77–97.

Chu, M., and S. Kita. 2011. The nature of gestures' beneficial role in spatial problem solving. *Journal of Experimental Psychology: General* 140 (1): 102–116.

Dodick, J., and N. Orion. 2003. Measuring student understanding of geological time. *Science Education* 87 (5): 708–731.

Flarend, A., and C. Palma. 2013. The role of gravity in planetary orbits. *The Earth Scientist* 29 (2): 323–6.

Ford, D. J. 2005. The challenges of observing geologically: Third graders' descriptions of rock and mineral properties. *Science Education* 89 (2): 276–295.

Hobson, S. M., K. C. Trundle, and M. Saçkes. 2010. Using a planetarium software program to promote conceptual change with young children. *Journal of Science Education and Technology* 19 (2): 165–176.

Kali, Y., and N. Orion. 1996. Spatial abilities of high school students in the perception of geological structures. *Journal of Research in Science Teaching* 33 (4): 369–391.

Kastens, K. A., S. Agrawal, and L. S. Liben. 2009. How students and field geologists reason in integrating spatial observations from outcrops to visualize a three-D geological structure. *International Journal of Science Education* 31 (3): 365–393.

Kavanagh, C., L. Agan, and C. Sneider. 2005. Learning about phases of the Moon and eclipses: A guide for teachers and curriculum developers. *Astronomy Education Review* 4 (1) 19–52.

Kortz, K., and D. P. Murray. 2009. Barriers to college students learning how rocks form. *Journal of Geoscience Education* 57 (4): 300–315.

Libarkin, J. C., S. W. Anderson, J. Dahl, M. Beilfuss, W. Boone, and J. P. Kurdziel. 2005. Qualitative analysis of college students' ideas about the Earth: interviews and open-ended questionnaires. *Journal of Geoscience Education* 53 (1): 17–26.

Liben, L. S., K. A. Kastens, and A. E. Christensen. 2011. Spatial foundations of science education: The illustrative case of instruction on introductory

10

geological concepts. *Cognition and Instruction* 29 (1): 45–87.

Lombardi, D., G. M. Sinatra, and E. M. Nussbaum. 2013. Plausibility reappraisals and shifts in middle school students' climate change conceptions. *Learning and Instruction* 27 (October): 50–62.

Matlen, B. J., K. Atit, T. Göksun, M. A. Rau, and M. Ptouchkina. 2012. Representing space: Exploring the relationship between gesturing and geoscience understanding in children. In *Spatial Cognition VIII*, ed. C. Stachniss, K. Schill, and D. Uttal, 405–415. Berlin, Germany: Springer-Verlag Berlin Heidelberg.

Miller, B. W., and W. F. Brewer. 2010. Misconceptions of astronomical distances. *International Journal of Science Education* 32 (12): 1549–1560.

National Research Council (NRC). 2007. *Taking science to school: Learning and teaching science in grades K–8*. Washington, DC: National Academies Press.

National Research Council (NRC). 2012. *A framework for K–12 science education: Practices, crosscutting concepts, and core ideas*. Washington, DC: National Academies Press.

Padalkar, S., and J. Ramadas. 2011. Designed and spontaneous gestures in elementary astronomy education. *International Journal of Science Education* 33 (12): 1703–1739.

Parker, J., and D. Heywood. 1998. The Earth and beyond: Developing primary teachers' understanding of basic astronomical events. *International Journal of Science Education* 20 (5): 503–520.

Parnafes, O. 2012. Developing explanations and developing understanding: Students explain the phases of the Moon using visual representations. *Cognition and Instruction* 30 (4): 359–403.

Plummer, J. D. 2009a. A cross-age study of children's knowledge of apparent celestial motion. *International Journal of Science Education* 31 (12): 1571–1605.

Plummer, J. D. 2009b. Early elementary students' development of astronomy concepts in the planetarium. *Journal of Research in Science Teaching* 46 (2): 192–209.

Plummer, J. D. 2014. Spatial thinking as the dimension of progress in an astronomy learning progression. *Studies in Science Education* 50 (1): 1–45.

Plummer, J. D., A. Kocareli, and C. Slagle. 2014. Learning to explain astronomy across moving frames of reference: Exploring the role of classroom and planetarium-based instructional contexts. *International Journal of Science Education* 36 (7): 1083–1106.

Plummer, J. D., and L. Maynard. 2014. Building a learning progression for celestial motion: An exploration of students' reasoning about the seasons. *Journal of Research in Science Teaching* 51 (7): 902–929.

Plummer, J. D., C. Palma, A. Flarend, K. Rubin, Y. S. Ong, B. Botzer, S. McDonald, and T. Furman. 2015. Development of a learning progression for the formation of the solar system. *International Journal of Science Education* 37 (9): 1381–1401.

Plummer, J. D., K. D. Wasko, and C. Slagle. 2011. Children learning to explain daily celestial motion: Understanding astronomy across moving frames of reference. *International Journal of Science Education* 33 (14): 1963–1992.

Prather, E. 2005. Students' beliefs about the role of atoms in radioactive decay and half-life. *Journal of Geoscience Education* 53 (4): 345.

Prather, E. E., T. F. Slater, and E. G. Offerdahl. 2002. Hints of a fundamental misconception in cosmology. *Astronomy Education Review* 1 (2): 28–34.

Ristvey, J., D. Bogner, and W. Cobb. (n.d.) *Active accretion: An interactive learning game on solar system origins.* Denver, CO: Mid-Continent Research for Education and Learning. *http://dawn.jpl.nasa.gov/DawnClassrooms/PDFs/ActiveAccretion_Dawn.PDF.*

Rivet, A. E., and K. A. Kastens. 2012. Developing a construct-based assessment to examine students' analogical reasoning around physical models in Earth Science. *Journal of Research in Science Teaching* 49 (6): 713–743.

Ross, K. E. K., and T. J. Shuell. 1993. Children's beliefs about earthquakes. *Science Education* 77 (2): 1912–05.

Rubin, K., J. Plummer, C. Palma, H. Spotts, and A. Flarend. 2014. Planetary properties: A systems perspective. *Science Scope* 37 (Summer): 68–72.

Sharp, J. G., and P. Kuerbis. 2006. Children's ideas about the solar system and the chaos in learning science. *Science Education* 90 (1): 124–147.

Trend, R. 1998. An investigation into understanding of geological time among 10- and 11-year-old children. *International Journal of Science Education* 20 (8): 973–988.

Trend, R. 2000. Conceptions of geological time among primary teacher trainees, with reference to their engagement with geoscience, history, and science. *International Journal of Science Education* 22 (5): 539–555.

Williamson, K. E., and S. Willoughby. 2012. Student understanding of gravity in introductory college astronomy. *Astronomy Education Review* 11 (1): 1–26.

Wilson, M. 2002. Six views of embodied cognition. *Psychonomic Bulletin and Review* 9 (4): 625–636.

CHAPTER 11

CORE IDEA ESS2

EARTH'S SYSTEMS

Ann E. Rivet

What Is This Disciplinary Core Idea, and Why Is It Important?

Planet Earth is a complex, dynamic, and fascinating place. There is a huge variety of different phenomena that can be explored across time and space, including landforms such as mountains and canyons; biomes such as deserts and forests; and weather events such as hurricanes and droughts. What causes these things to happen on Earth? The second disciplinary core idea (DCI) in the Earth and space sciences section of *A Framework for K–12 Science Education* (*Framework*; NRC 2012), ESS2: Earth's Systems, explores this key question. This DCI focuses on developing explanations for the array of phenomena that result from Earth's interacting systems. The Earth's Systems DCI is centrally about understanding how the surface of the Earth "works" to create the world we see around us, specifically in terms of how matter and energy interact between the geosphere (land), atmosphere, hydrosphere (water), and biosphere (living things) at a range of spatial and temporal scales. ESS2 includes many fundamental explanations for Earth phenomena, including the planet's

large-scale structure and composition; interrelationships between global systems, including the rock cycle, the water cycle, and the surface processes of weathering, erosion, and deposition; mechanisms that drive Earth's internal motions; causes of weather and climate; and the pivotal role that water plays across all of these global systems and surface processes.

Overall, the Earth's Systems DCI aims for students to develop two important perspectives about the world. The first is that *the Earth is constantly changing*. Systems are dynamic; there is no such thing as a static system. The movement, change, breaking down, and building up of Earth materials is constantly happening, all the time. For example, land is perpetually being eroded from one location and deposited in another; heat energy is continuously transported around the globe by large-scale oceanic and atmospheric currents. Though it may seem to students as if the world around us does not change very much, this DCI aims to foster in them a sense that as a whole, the full-scale Earth system is constantly and continually shaping and reshaping itself. The second perspective developed through the DCI is that *different aspects of the Earth are interconnected and influence each other.* Earth's systems interact in complex yet predictable ways across a wide range of space and timescales, creating phenomena that we experience on Earth every day. For example, the atmosphere and hydrosphere interact to create weather, climate, and biomes that vary based on the topography of the land. Similarly, the geosphere and hydrosphere interact to create landforms such canyons and plains that allow biomes and habitats for different organisms to exist; concurrently, changes to the biosphere also have an effect on the locations and rates of erosion and deposition that change the shape of the geosphere. These two perspectives are crucial for students to develop a robust and usable understanding of how the surface of the Earth functions.

There are several significant differences in how students are expected to understand Earth's systems as outlined in the *Framework* compared with previous versions of national and state science standards. Importantly, previous standards and curriculum tended to focus on individual parts of Earth systems in isolation and lacked an overarching view of how the parts interact on local and global scales to create the phenomena we experience in our world every day. The study of Earth systems as presented in the *Framework* addresses this gap by placing more emphasis on interactions between key global systems, the role of energy and water across systems, and the effect of these interactions on the environments that we live in (both physical and biological). It does this by developing and using several of the key science crosscutting concepts (i.e., systems, energy, patterns, scale, and cause and effect) to explore and explain Earth phenomena. Multiple connections to the physical and life sciences are also emphasized across this DCI, as these ideas are necessary for understanding how the Earth

works. In particular, the crosscutting concept of *change* is also foregrounded with this DCI much more than in previous standards, as both a concept in and of itself and a lens through which to view the consequential outcomes of Earth processes.

Overview of Component Ideas

The Earth's Systems DCI is guided by the core question, "How and why is the Earth constantly changing?" This question is continually revisited across the K–12 learning trajectory as students explore and describe a variety of surface Earth phenomena and processes. Through this study, they develop more sophisticated explanations for the ways that energy flows and matter cycles within and among the Earth's atmosphere, hydrosphere, geosphere and biosphere. To support students in describing these phenomena and developing related explanations, the *Framework* organizes the DCI into five components with associated subquestions, discussed in more detail below. Research exists regarding students' commonly held ideas for many of these components; however, descriptions of students' thinking is currently lacking for others. When available, a synopsis of our current understanding of students' commonly held conceptions is provided.

ESS2.A: EARTH MATERIALS AND SYSTEMS

The first component idea of this DCI is guided by the subquestion, "How do the major Earth systems interact?" This subquestion encompasses the descriptions of the four global Earth systems (atmosphere, hydrosphere, geosphere, and biosphere) and their parts and distinguishing processes. But more than just learning about these observable features of the Earth, the focus is on explaining how all processes within these systems are the result of energy flowing and matter cycling within and among them. It is the transfer of energy and movement of matter that causes the chemical and physical changes among the Earth's materials and living organisms, which then result in observable phenomena on the Earth's surface.

For example, the *Framework* expects students to do more than identify *that* the water cycle is related to weather and climate patterns and consequently to biomes and ecosystems. Students must also explain *how* the water cycle involves the interaction of the atmosphere, hydrosphere, and biosphere, specifically describing how water and energy move within and across these systems to create the weather and climate patterns that result in differing biomes and ecosystems. Similarly, more than simply identifying the water and rock cycles as related phenomena, the DCI aims to develop models of how the water cycle interacts with the geosphere via the rock cycle, leading to the creation, destruction, and movement of different kinds of rocks and minerals and to the formation of different landforms.

Describing the rate at which systems change is also an important aspect of explaining processes because aspects of the Earth's systems may at times appear not to change at all, to change slowly over long periods of time, or to change abruptly. When weather conditions change rapidly, this indicates that a large amount of energy is being transferred across systems. In comparison, the fact that it can take thousands of years for a canyon to form demonstrates that even small movements of matter and energy across systems can have large impact on the surrounding environment. Importantly, a key emphasis of this subquestion is understanding how and why changes

in one part of a system can cause further changes to that system or other interconnected systems, often in complex and unanticipated ways.

Research has demonstrated that students often have difficulty understanding and explaining systems. They often perceive a system as unrelated parts or pieces of information and fail to recognize the dynamic, cyclic, and systemic aspects (Assarf and Orion 2005). For example, students have difficulty articulating the connection between the atmospheric components of the water cycle and the geospheric components, particularly those underground. Most students tend to view groundwater as a static subsurface lake, disconnected from the water cycle overall with no connections to the surrounding rocks (Assarf and Orion 2005). A study by Kali, Orion, and Eylon (2003) describes how middle school students were able to identify both granite and sandstone at different points along a single riverbank but were unable to connect various components of the water and rock cycle together into a coherent explanation for why both kinds of rock would exist there. Since the concept of systems and their interactions is central to this DCI, it is particularly important to support students' understanding of this idea across the learning trajectory.

ESS2.B: PLATE TECTONICS AND LARGE-SCALE SYSTEM INTERACTIONS

The second subquestion for the DCI outlined in the Framework, "Why do continents move, and what causes earthquakes and volcanoes?" focuses on the structure and dynamic nature of the interior of the Earth. This component of the DCI is about descriptions of three Earth surface phenomena that are of particular interest to students: earthquakes, volcanoes, and movement of continents over long periods of time. The DCI presents how the Earth's surface is made up of large pieces of crust called tectonic plates and describes how the tectonic plates move in relationship to each other to create the shape of the Earth's surface as we know it today. Tectonic plates move very slowly, usually only a couple of centimeters a year, in small start-and-stop spurts. However, this slow movement over long periods of time has created significant large-scale landforms on the surface of the Earth. In some places the tectonic plates move apart, creating rift valleys like the East African Rift area that extends between Ethiopia and Mozambique, and large trenches that characterize the Mid-Atlantic Ridge that runs through the middle of the Atlantic Ocean. The tectonic plates also move toward each other in some places, pushing the land up and creating mountain ranges. This is the current process that is occurring as the Eurasian plate and the Indian plate collide, creating the Himalayan Mountains in Asia, which are still (slowly) increasing in height today. The movement of plates can also create phenomena that occur very quickly. In some locations, there are faults where the tectonic plates are sliding past each other in spurts that occur occasionally over time, such as the San Andreas Fault in California. Earthquakes are common in these areas. There are also places where one tectonic plate slowly slides underneath an adjacent plate. As the top plate pushes down on the moving plate below it, the pressure melts the crust to form magma and causes the magma to be pushed upward through fissures in the overlying rocks, resulting in volcanoes. Many of the volcanoes along the western edge of the South American continent and the islands of Japan are created through such processes.

Important to this component idea, however, is not only a description of what these Earth surface phenomena are but also *what causes them to happen*. The explanation for why the tectonic plates move and create large-scale landforms, earthquakes, and volcanoes is provided by the theory of plate tectonics. Scientists worked for decades to develop the theory of plate tectonics by synthesizing across several different kinds of data, including mapping the spatial distribution of different types of rock, measurements of the relative rate of seismic waves as they move across and through the Earth, and using processes such as radioactive decay to determine the ages of various rock layers and fossils at different locations. In brief, plate tectonics outlines how the tectonic plates on the surface of the Earth (the crust) are supported by a layer underneath (the mantle), which is not solid but viscous. The movement of the mantle is driven by the core of the Earth, where the radioactive decay of elements releases energy in the form of heat. The heat from the core warms the mantle above it, but does so unevenly, with areas of more intense heat in different locations. This uneven heating creates convection currents of the mantle's viscous rocks (see Figure 11.1), where warmer pockets of mantle rock rise toward the Earth's crust and push cooler rock back toward the core. The circular motion of the mantle drags the crustal tectonic plates at the surface very slowly in different directions, causing them to push together, pull apart, and slide next to and underneath each other. Plate tectonics is a theory that not only helps us explain the way the Earth's surface has changed in the past and is changing now but also how natural resources such as oil, coal, and natural gas were created over long periods of time and why they are found where they are on Earth. Scientists use

FIGURE 11.1

Motion of Tectonic Plates

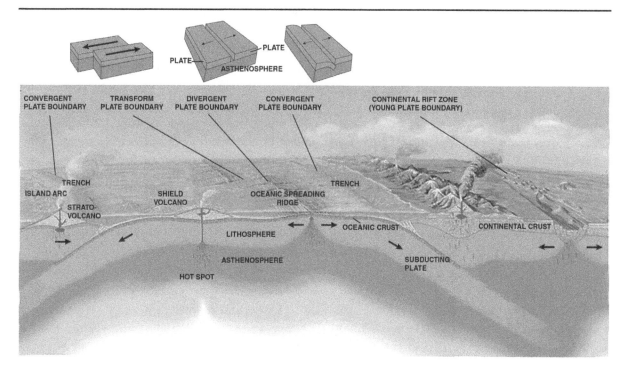

plate tectonics to predict how the shape of continents may change in the future.

Students have been shown to demonstrate an array of different ideas regarding the structure of the Earth, plate tectonics, and related phenomena as they develop understandings across grades K–12. For example, some students believe that the surface of the Earth is not directly on top of the tectonic plates but that the plates are inside the Earth and that the motion of the plates is separate from the Earth's surface (Ford and Taylor 2008; Libarkin et al. 2005). Other students describe large gaps or spaces between the plates that are filled with ocean or magma. Students also tend to view the continents and plates as the same thing and think that the continents move by floating across the oceans on water or molten rocks. However, other students believe that the continents do not move at all, or at least they have not moved position since the breakup of Pangaea (Ford and Taylor 2008). Students give a wide variety of explanations for the causes of earthquakes, including heat, temperature, climate, weather, animals, gas pressure, gravity, the rotation of the Earth, processes at the Earth's core, or volcanoes (Libarkin et al. 2005). Similarly, students tend to believe that volcanoes only occur on islands, that they are associated with warm climates, that they only occur along the equator, and that they are caused by earthquakes. They often do not connect the existence and location of volcanoes with plate tectonics (Libarkin et al. 2005). Importantly, students tend to view all Earth processes as occurring at the same rate or on the same timescale, with all changes on Earth occurring so slowly that they cannot be detected during a human lifetime (Ford and Taylor 2008).

ESS2.C: THE ROLES OF WATER IN EARTH'S SURFACE PROCESSES

Water is the central idea in the third subquestion of the DCI, "How do the properties of water shape the Earth's surface and affect its systems?" Similar to the other component ideas in the Earth's Systems DCI, this concept encompasses both the observable phenomena related to water on the Earth's surface and explanations of the unique characteristics of water that allow for such phenomena to occur.

The *Framework* highlights the important role water plays in Earth processes. Water is found just about everywhere on Earth, including all over the surface, in the atmosphere, and below the surface in the crust and mantle layers of the geosphere. Water also behaves differently from other substances (in fact, unlike any other natural substance), and those unique behaviors result in interactions that change Earth's surface over time. For example, when water runs over rocks or soil, it can dissolve them into smaller particles (chemical weathering) and carry these pieces to new locations (erosion and deposition). In the atmosphere, water not only creates clouds and precipitation but also allows heat energy to move around the globe, and more locally, it causes the air to feel warm and heavy when it is about to rain. The unique properties of water are the root cause for these (and many other) vastly different phenomena that exist across Earth systems.

The *Framework* has identified four of water's unique properties that students use to explain some of Earth's complex processes. The first key feature of water is that it has exceptional capacity to absorb, store, and release large amounts of energy as it changes state or goes between gas (vapor), liquid, and solid (ice) forms. When water moves from a solid to a liquid, or from a liquid to a gas, it absorbs energy from the surrounding environment as the molecules of water move farther apart. So when water evaporates from a lake, for example, it absorbs some of the energy from the surrounding air and transports it higher up in the atmosphere. The familiar phenomena of the air feeling cooler by the shore than inland on hot summer days is due to there being less energy in the surrounding air because it has been absorbed by the evaporating water.

The second characteristic is that water expands upon freezing. As liquid water becomes ice, the water molecules become organized in a ridged lattice structure and no longer slide past each other as they do in liquid form. Thus, frozen water is less dense than liquid water because the molecules are farther apart, which explains why ice cubes float in a glass of lemonade and icebergs float in the ocean. The act of freezing also means that water, as it expands into and becomes ice, exerts a force on the materials surrounding it. This process is called mechanical weathering. So when water is caught in cracks in rocks, as it freezes it pushes the rock apart. It might seem that water wouldn't be able to exert a big enough force to break rocks, but it can. In particular, if the water in crack of rock freezes, then melts, then freezes again, each additional time it expands it pushes on the rock and weakens it, making it more likely to fall apart. This is the precise reason that sidewalks and roads in the northeast crack during the spring: The fluctuating temperatures melt and freeze the remaining snowpack that has seeped its way into the cracks, resulting in potholes.

The third key characteristic of water is that it can dissolve and transport many different materials, including both chemical substances and physical items such as sediment, debris, and organisms. Water molecules are highly polar, which means that one end of the molecule tends to have a more positive charge and the other a more negative charge. This polarity is the main reason that water can dissolve many materials, including the minerals that make up rocks. It is also the reason that small particles of soil and debris can float around in water: The polarity of water molecules creates temporary but strong bonds with many different kinds of substances and therefore can "hold" these materials as they are transported to new locations. This polarity property of water is also developed in PS3 (in terms of molecular interactions), while understanding how this property of water at the molecular level applies to large-scale phenomena at the macro and global levels is the focus of the ESS2 DCI.

Lastly, water also has the ability to lower the viscosity and freezing points of material it is mixed with. Because water absorbs and holds energy differently than any other substance due to its unique molecular composition and structure, it can make other materials move in fluid-like ways and freeze at much lower temperatures than it would without the presence of water. This is particularly observed in the rocks in the interior of the Earth. The rocks that make up the mantle also contain water. The energy released from the Earth's core causes these water-containing mantle rocks to flow in convective patterns, which then in turn drives plate tectonics at the surface of the Earth. Similarly, a key reason that magma flows within volcanoes is that not only is there a huge amount of energy, but also the melted magma contains water which allows it to flow and erupt.

As can be seen by these descriptions of its unique characteristics, water is centrally responsible for how rocks, soil, and other Earth materials move within and between Earth's systems. This continuous, complex interplay of water and Earth materials leads to the changing shape of the land that we observe.

ESS2.D: WEATHER AND CLIMATE

One of the most multifaceted concepts addressed in ESS2 centers around the subquestion, "What regulates weather and climate?" To address this question, it is first necessary to distinguish between the phenomena of weather and climate and to describe the relationship between them. Congruent with the crosscutting concepts of patterns and scale, *weather* is defined as the conditions of the atmosphere at any given place and time, whereas *climate* is the range of a region's weather over one year or many years, which can vary from place to place within that region because of latitude and other geographic features. Although not explicit in these definitions of weather and climate, *change* is a central component of each of these phenomena. At different timescales, changes in weather and climate are described in different ways. Weather can change within an hour or over the course of a day, while typical weather patterns are described in terms of several days, weeks, or months. A region's climate is considered a relatively stable description on scales of years and decades, but when viewed across decades and centuries, climate descriptions also evolve over time. Other key phenomena addressed through this component idea include

11

the greenhouse effect and climate change, which are described in more detail below.

Explanations for why weather and climate vary in the ways that they do are rooted in the understanding that both heat and light energy from the Sun interact with oceans, ice, landforms and living things on the surface. Specifically, the Sun's energy heats the surface of the Earth, which then heats the atmosphere above it. This leads to the development of a dynamic mix of water and gases at various temperatures and densities in the atmosphere that move around constantly, creating weather phenomena that are constantly changing yet relatively predictable. The predictability of weather phenomena results from the fact that the planet Earth is spherical in shape, with it is axis tilted with respect to the Sun as it moves in its orbit. This means that all locations on the Earth's surface do not receive equal amounts of solar energy; amounts vary by both location and time of year. Additionally, different types of surfaces (such as forests, deserts, ice caps, and human-developed areas) warm the atmosphere above them to different extents, resulting in further variations in atmospheric temperature patterns. The rotation of the Earth, combined with the location of continents and oceans, influences and controls the large-scale atmospheric circulation patterns (such as the jet stream and prevailing westerlies). It is through the continuous movement of both the atmosphere and the ocean that energy is redistributed across the surface from the equator toward the polar regions, resulting in more moderate and stable climates around the globe.

So why doesn't all of the energy we receive from the Sun just bounce off and go directly back into space? The reason is the greenhouse effect, which is another important factor in the moderation of global climate. The greenhouse effect refers to the complex process by which a mixture of gases in the atmosphere (including water vapor, carbon dioxide, methane, and nitrous oxides) trap a portion of the heat energy that is released from the Earth's surface and reradiates it back in the atmosphere toward the surface (see Figure 11.2). This allows a balance to be maintained between the energy coming into the Earth system and the energy going out, and keeps the Earth's surface much warmer than it would be without these atmospheric gases. This process is crucial for maintaining life on this planet, for without it the Earth would be much too cold for life to exist. However, changes to the concentrations of these greenhouse gases, such as increases to the amount of carbon dioxide in the atmosphere, can cause areas of the Earth's surface to become too hot to support many different kinds of organisms. For example, the atmosphere on the planet Venus has very high concentrations of carbon dioxide, and the surface temperature is 864°F. This is even hotter than the planet Mercury, which orbits closer to the Sun!

A key facet of this component idea is examining and understanding the nature and causes of climate changes. This is an important topic frequently in the news, but what does it really mean? Climate change refers to a significant and persistent change in an area's weather conditions. Such changes often include increased droughts or intense precipitation (rain or snow), or an increase in the number and intensity of severe storms in an area. Scientific explanations for these changes to an area's weather patterns involve examining how one or more of the Earth's global systems may have changed over time. For example, increases in the release of carbon dioxide from the burning of fossil fuels may

FIGURE 11.2

The Greenhouse Effect

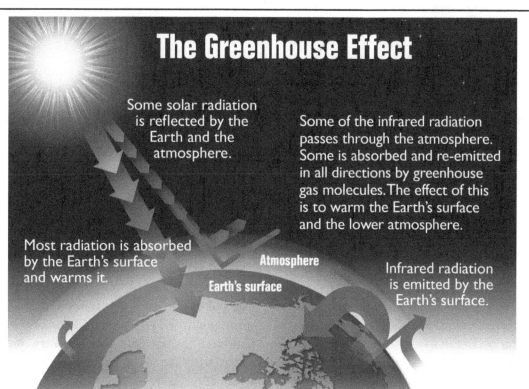

change the composition of the atmosphere, which in turn affects the way it absorbs and transports energy over large distances, along with altering the rate of the processes of evaporation, condensation, and precipitation in the water cycle at both local and global scales. Similarly, as the polar ice sheets melt and become smaller, this may cause the overall reflectivity of the Earth to decrease and thus change the balance between the amount of the Sun's energy that is absorbed by the surface versus that reflected back to the atmosphere. Changes to any one of these large-scale global systems have rippling effects across the other systems and the weather and climate processes and

phenomena that occur as the systems interact. The Earth has existed through many climate changes. Geological evidence shows that some of these changes were rapid, perhaps caused by events such as meteor impacts or large-scale volcanic eruptions. Other climate changes have been more gradual, for example, those caused by variations to the angle of the Earth's tilt, or by the increase of plant life that changed the atmosphere due to photosynthesis. It is important to note, however, that changes to Earth's systems, whether from human or natural causes, result in changes to the amount of energy from the Sun that enters and is maintained in Earth's systems and affects the

11

weather and climate processes and phenomena that we experience every day.

One challenge that students have in developing understandings of weather and climate is in making the connection between the energy that the Earth receives from the Sun and the types of weather that they experience. For example, Polito, Tanner, and Monteverdi (2008) found that a majority of middle school students did not view any connection between the Sun and wind. They found that although students could state that the Sun provides heat and energy to the Earth, they did not connect that energy with events that happen on the surface. Rather, they viewed the Moon, clouds, and oceans as the primary causes for wind and other weather phenomena. Another key challenge relates to misinterpretations of the greenhouse effect, the ozone layer, and their relationships to climate change. Commonly held ideas about climate include that the seasons are caused by the Earth's distance from the Sun (Schneps and Sadler 1985; see also ESS1: Earth's Place in the Universe); climate is simply long-term weather, so it cannot be predicted (McCaffrey and Buhr 2008); global warming and the greenhouse effect are the same thing; the greenhouse effect is bad and will cause all living things to die; and the ozone hole is a hole in the sky (Henriques 2000). Some students view the increase in global temperature as caused by increased solar energy coming to Earth through the hole in the ozone layer (Gautier, Deutsch, and Rebich 2006). Many students have difficulty with the concept of the greenhouse effect, believing that it is either purely reflected solar energy or greenhouse gases themselves that are trapped in the atmosphere, rather than being due to reradiated energy from the warmed Earth's surface. They often do not view the greenhouse effect as a natural process that allows Earth's environment to

remain habitable and do not connect an enhanced greenhouse effect to issues of human-induced climate change (Gautier, Deutsch, and Rebich 2006; Henriques 2000).

ESS2.E: BIOGEOLOGY

The fifth component idea in the Earth's Systems DCI highlights the links between the physical and living worlds by addressing the subquestion, "How do living organisms alter Earth's processes and structures?" The aim of this component idea is to further develop an understanding of how the physical environment allows for and influences the development and evolution of living organisms, while concurrently examining how living organisms influence the properties and characteristics of the physical environment. As described previously, Earth's interacting systems continuously alter the conditions of the Earth's surface. As these conditions change, organisms respond through adaptation and increasing variation. Likewise, as new and evolved species develop, they become integral components in Earth processes. For example, different kinds of plants have evolved to live in specific environmental conditions (e.g., varying temperatures, amounts of rainfall, and types of soil). Thus, a cactus is adapted to the hot, dry conditions of the desert, while pine trees need a cooler, wetter environment to survive. However, those same plants affect not only the surrounding animal and plant life but also influence the soil and rocks, the amount of available water, and even the weather conditions in local areas. As the roots of pine trees slowly grow, they break apart compacted soil and add nutrients, which allows other types of plants to grow as well. Plants also absorb and store both energy and carbon dioxide through photosynthesis, which is why the air above forests is cooler than, say, a parking lot. The global carbon cycle is another excellent illustration of the interdependence of physical and biological aspects of the Earth. Carbon plays a key role in both physical and biological processes, including the greenhouse effect and biological growth, as it continually cycles through the various global systems.

Little research exists on young students' views of the interconnections between organisms and their physical environment. A few studies show that students tend not to believe that the oxygen we breathe comes from plants (Henriques 2000) and think that respiration affects only organisms rather than acting as an interaction between organisms and the surrounding atmosphere (Hartley et al. 2011; see also LS2: Ecosystems: Interactions, Energy, and Dynamics). Additionally, studies have found that adaptation is a difficult process for learners to grasp, even college students. Most importantly, students often do not recognize that adaptation of organisms to an ecosystem occurs over many generations as a result of continuous emergence of genetic variations and natural selection processes. Research has found that most students tend to believe that animals and plants "want" or "need" to live in particular places, so they intentionally cause physical changes that meet new environmental conditions, and that this process of adapting to an environment occurs rapidly over short periods of time, typically within a single life span (Gregory 2009). These ideas about the interconnections between organisms and the environment are also discussed at length in LS4: Biological Evolution: Unity and Diversity.

How Does Student Understanding of This Disciplinary Core Idea Develop Over Time?

The five component ideas to the Earth's Systems DCI described above combine across K–12 to support students in developing a coherent and robust view of how the Earth works. The progressive development of these component ideas occurs concurrently across the grades, described in more detail below at the various grade bands.

Lower Elementary

In grades K–2, the Earth's Systems DCI is focused on helping students observe, connect, and explain the physical characteristics of specific places. Where is water found? What does it look like? What about different rocks? Soil? Animals? What is the weather like? They are asked to represent those locations on a map and describe the patterns they see. These initial observations and representations are important because they begin to help students recognize characteristics of the four major Earth systems (atmosphere, hydrosphere, geosphere, and biosphere) in their own local place. This also sets the foundation for the understanding that all of these Earth systems can exist in the same location on Earth, and in fact, they operate and interact at all locations on Earth simultaneously.

A second key idea in early elementary school is how the shape of the land can change, and initial explanations are developed for what can cause it to change. Students describe the effects of moving water and blowing air (wind) on the shape of land and other materials, perhaps by experimenting with sand tables or going outside to look

11

for the effects of moving water or wind in their local environment. They record weather variables each day and identify patterns in how the variables are related, such as the relationship between clouds and precipitation, and describe how the weather changes over time. They investigate how animals and people have changed the land over time by, for example, building structures, carving out roads, removing vegetation, and constructing dams. They then use this evidence to make preliminary predictions about ways that the environment may change in the future. Although primarily descriptive at this stage, these experiences with recording, analyzing, and interpreting observational data provide the initial stepping stone understandings of how Earth's systems interact and how we can see them interacting based on the phenomena around us.

Upper Elementary

In grades 3–5, student understanding of the Earth's Systems DCI progresses from descriptions of phenomena from a single local perspective (what is this place like?) to descriptions that emphasize comparison and patterns across locations and time (how are these places similar and different?). Descriptions of the four major Earth systems and the ways that they interact are further developed in this grade range. For example, students are expected to understand not only the ways in which the water and rock cycle operate, but also how rain and the movement of water downhill toward the oceans created distinct and identifiable shapes on the land and how the processes of weathering and erosion result in different environments that can support different kinds of organisms and ecosystems.

The analysis and interpretation of maps and other spatial representations of data to identify and describe patterns in Earth phenomena continues to be developed in upper elementary school. Three key areas in which spatial patterns are emphasized include the locations of water, landforms that result from tectonic processes, and patterns of weather that form distinct climate zones and biomes.

For example, students coordinate simulations, numerical data, and maps of the locations of water both locally and around the globe to develop understanding that water exists almost everywhere on Earth but in different amounts and different forms depending on its location. They then use this information to explain how the vast majority of the water is in the oceans, but most of the freshwater exists underground as groundwater or at high altitudes and polar regions in the form of glaciers.

Similarly, students use maps to explore the locations of earthquakes and volcanoes and large-scale landforms such as mountain ranges and mid-ocean ridges. Through comparing the similarities and differences between locations, they identify the common patterns that exist among these surface features that were all created through processes related to plate tectonics.

Finally, students explore current and archival weather data including maps and charts at local, regional, and global scales to identify and describe patterns in climate. They use the data to compare similarities in climate between geographic locations and at a single location over time. Across all of these topics, students are deepening their understanding of the interconnections between and among the global systems, the relationship between their local place and other places around the world, and the use of maps and other spatial tools to help them identify and understand these connections and relationships.

Middle School

In middle school, the Earth's Systems DCI moves from describing what the Earth is like to explaining the mechanisms that drive the Earth's changing systems. The crosscutting concepts of *energy flow* and *constant change* play important roles as students explore questions about why the Earth behaves the way that it does and how we can both explain and predict that behavior. A central concept developed in the middle grades with respect to ESS2 is that energy flows and matter cycles within and among Earth's interconnected systems. This important concept can be considered in three parts: (1) Where does the energy come from and where does it go? (2) What effect does the flow of energy have on how the system(s) work? (3) What evidence can we see that energy and matter are moving in and among systems? By addressing these three questions together, students develop productive explanations for not only how specific Earth processes and phenomena operate but also a broader perspective on energy movement and conservation, and connecting Earth processes to core understandings in the physical and biological sciences.

Two key processes are emphasized in the middle grades as students develop understandings of the role of energy and matter in how the Earth changes. The first key process is plate tectonics and its relationship to the rock cycle. Building from spatial patterns of the physical features that result from tectonic processes developed in upper elementary, in middle school the emphasis turns to how plate tectonic processes function to create those landforms. Students use maps, models, and other representations to explore how the energy from the interior of the Earth continuously drives convection in the mantle, resulting in the constant movement of tectonic plates on the surface, and creates earthquakes, volcanoes, mountain ranges, and trenches, and drives key aspects of the rock cycle. By tracing the movement of energy from the interior to the surface of the Earth and the consequential effect of this energy movement on the shape and composition of rocks and landforms, students develop an understanding for how and why the surface of the Earth has changed, and continues to change, over long periods of time. This explanation, combined with local and global geologic evidence, including stratigraphy, index fossils, and geologic mapping, helps us reconstruct and better understand Earth's geologic history (see also ESS1.C: The History of the Planet Earth).

The second key process emphasized in middle school related to understanding how energy flows and matter cycles within and across Earth systems is the relationship between the water cycle and large-scale weather and climate phenomena. Building on explanations of phase change (PS1.A: Structure and Properties of Matter) and energy movement (PS3.B: Conservation of Energy and Energy Transfer) developed in the physical sciences, descriptions of evaporation, condensation, precipitation, transpiration, and downhill flow of surface and groundwater are explained in terms of the constant movement of matter (water molecules) driven by energy from the Sun and by gravity. The continual, nonlinear cycle occurs across multiple spatial scales, from small-scale local processes that can be personally observed to the large-scale movement of vast amounts of water across the globe, all driven by the same energy flow processes. Weather and climate are

11

also strongly influenced by the ways that the different Earth systems interact. The shape of the land, ocean temperature variations and currents, winds, and density of plant life and other organisms, all cause complex changes in the movement of water vapor in the atmosphere, resulting in differential weather patterns in various locations. At the same time, different weather phenomena, combined with the movement of water both on the surface and underground, cause weathering and erosion of Earth materials to occur and result in different kinds of land features and underground formations such as caves. An important perspective to understanding these interacting processes is that the movement of water between and across the geosphere and atmosphere is complex and not consistent across space and time. Large-scale patterns of water movement are relatively predictable (which we describe as climate) and can be represented on maps. However, because these patterns are so complex and are influenced by a wide array of factors, weather events for a given location can only be predicted probabilistically.

In middle school students also explore the role of the oceans as an influencing force on weather and climate. The oceans serve as a key component of the hydrosphere and play a significant role in the creation and stability of Earth's current climate conditions. The oceans continually absorb a massive amount of energy from the Sun and transport and release it around the globe via large-scale ocean currents. These interconnected ocean currents are driven not only by temperature but also by salinity differences in the water, which cause masses of water to have different densities and flow differently due to convection. This constant global distribution of energy from the equator to the poles is a key regulating influence on the Earth's weather and global climate, and prevents extremes in the distribution of temperature. Without these global-scale ocean currents, the poles would freeze solid and the equator region would be so hot as to be uninhabitable.

High School

At the high school level, the component ideas in the Earth Systems DCI become more formalized, with an emphasis on explaining the global, interconnected, and dynamic character of the Earth as a whole. In particular, students in high school are expected to be able to articulate and model the complex interactions between Earth's systems and question and explore the effects of perturbations to one or more of these systems. Through such investigations, students develop explanations that describe the ways in which the dynamic and interacting characteristics of the Earth's systems can cause feedback effects when changes are introduced in a system, which can either amplify or minimize the original change. For example, an increase in the amount of reradiated energy held in the atmosphere by greenhouse gases may result in increasing rates of water evaporation from the surface. This would increase the amount of water vapor in the air and lead to more reradiated energy from the surface being trapped in the atmosphere, which in turn would continue to amplify the evaporation process. This is an example of a positive feedback effect. Conversely, an increase in the amount of cloud cover in the atmosphere may cause more sunlight to be reflected back to space rather than traveling to the Earth's surface, resulting in less energy being absorbed and thus cooler surface temperatures. This is a related but negative feedback effect that would act to moderate the influence on the global system. Many of these delicate and dynamic feedbacks involve interactions between the biosphere and other Earth systems, which influence both the physical environment and organisms themselves, resulting in the continual coevolution of Earth's surface and the life that inhabits it. Importantly, students come to understand that changes or perturbations to the system often have both positive and negative feedbacks that interact in complex ways and are difficult to predict. Scientists have made progress in their efforts to understand and explain the causes and effects of these feedbacks, but there is also much that is not currently understood about the complexities in how, and how quickly, Earth's systems respond to changes over time. These unknowns limit our ability to predict changes in Earth systems' behaviors, and the effects of those changes on local environments. Current social debates around investments in a community's severe storm preparations or proposed changes to building codes to account for rising sea levels reflect the challenges we have in predicting the local impacts of changes to global systems.

A second area that is explored in more detail at the high school level is the nature of the interior of the Earth and how processes inside the planet affect past and current changes on the surface. Students should understand that we cannot explore the Earth's interior directly, but scientists have developed a rich understanding of its composition and dynamic nature based on an array of evidence from different sources. For example, by measuring the speed at which earthquake waves travel through Earth's interior, scientists have been able to ascertain the layered structure of the Earth and obtain information about the thickness, density, and composition of the different layers. Building on explanations developed in middle school for how the convection of the mantle drives the movement of tectonic plates that result in phenomena such as earthquakes and volcanoes, high school students explore the source of energy in the interior of the Earth and how that energy moves through the planet to the surface. Students make connections to physical science by exploring the energy generated by the radioactive decay of unstable isotopes in the Earth's interior, which travels through the planet via the processes of conduction and convection (PS3.B: Conservation of Energy and Energy Transfer). The convective motion of the mantle causes the crustal plates to move slowly over time, creating landforms such as mountain ranges and volcanoes. These surface features, along with phenomena like earthquakes, provide evidence of this internal energy generation and flow that can be observed on the Earth's surface.

A third area of focus in high school is centered on further exploration of water's unique physical and chemical properties, and the effects of those particular properties on the dynamics of how Earth's systems behave. Students investigate water's exceptional ability to absorb, store, and release large amounts of energy and how that is central to explaining atmospheric and oceanic circulation. Water's ability to transmit sunlight not only allows energy from the Sun to reach and warm the Earth's surface, but also allows for a wide diversity of organisms to exist and evolve in the oceans and other water bodies, including everything from tiny plankton to the enormous blue whale. Students explore how the fact that water expands upon freezing operates as a central mechanism in the process of mechanical weathering, whereas its ability to dissolve and transport materials plays a crucial role in both physical weathering and the processes of erosion and deposition. Additionally, both its ability to expand upon freezing and to dissolve and transport materials are key factors that affect the chemistry of natural water bodies, including their salinity and pH. Finally, water's ability to lower the viscosities and melting points of rocks is a means to explain the viscous properties of the mantle that allow it to transfer energy via convection, and why magma and lava have the ability to flow.

Finally, in high school students extend their views of climate from general descriptions of weather patterns in a region to an understanding of global climate as related to the movement of energy into, out of, and around the Earth's surface. Global climate is explained as a dynamic balance between the amounts of energy that fall on the Earth's surface, that same energy's reflection, absorption, storage and redistribution by Earth's atmospheric, oceanic, and terrestrial systems, and the amount of that energy reradiated back into space on various timescales. Importantly, *climate change* will occur if any part of the Earth's systems becomes altered, affecting this dynamic global energy balance. Climate change essentially refers to the Earth's systems changing from their currently recognized stable, interconnected state toward a new (and potentially notably different) stable interconnected state that accommodates the alteration of one or more of the component systems. Students can investigate how geologic evidence demonstrates that the Earth's climate used to be very different from what it is today, and the ways in which the climate has changed. Evidence shows that some changes to the global climate were sudden, resulting from events that had significant effects on processes in the atmosphere, like a possible meteor impact. Other changes to climate have occurred over longer periods of time, such as ice ages that happened over thousands of years that were caused by variations in

solar output, Earth's orbit, or the tilt of the axis over time. And other climate changes were more gradual still, over millions of years, such as the slow change in atmospheric composition due to the evolution and distribution of plants and other organisms that consumed carbon dioxide and respired oxygen. More recently, human activity has increased the concentration of carbon dioxide in the atmosphere and affected the climate. (More information regarding human-induced climate change is included in discussion of the DCI ESS3.D: Global Climate Change [pp. 229–230].) Scientists use global climate models to predict future changes, including those influenced by both natural factors and human actions. Students can work with global climate models themselves to explore how they are developed using known relationships between factors from past climate data (such as greenhouse gas concentrations and global temperature), predictions for future levels of human-generated greenhouse gas outputs, and our most current understanding of the complex feedback relationships among Earth's systems that influence the overall global climate.

What Approaches Can We Use to Teach About This Disciplinary Core Idea?

With respect to science instruction, there are several teaching strategies that are particularly supportive of students developing the new kinds of understandings called for in the Earth's Systems DCI. The first is for both teachers and students to consistently make connections between phenomena and their explanations across local, regional, and global spatial scales. Quality instruction should continuously help students contextualize and relate the new scientific explanations and arguments that they develop to phenomena in the world directly outside of their home and school. For example, as students are learning about the factors that affect rates of erosion and deposition, they should use these ideas to begin explaining local landforms, such as the shape of a stream or coastline. At the same time, students should regularly engage in the process of comparing locations, in particular their own local place, to others around the globe. The aim of this constant comparative approach is to not only identify similarities and differences between places but also develop understandings for how broad Earth science explanations are manifested differently in distinct locations, with diverse implications for the composition and character of the environment in those places. Concurrently, students will also develop the practices and awareness of how scientists use spatial comparisons to understand and explain regional and global processes.

A second key instructional strategy critical to supporting this DCI is the extensive use of maps and other spatial representations of data. The learning goals heavily emphasize the interconnection between spaces and places through Earth's systems. Thus, maps of all different types and scales become necessary tools to develop these robust understandings. Digital geographic mapping tools such as geographic information systems or Google Earth provide opportunities for students to visually examine relationships between factors and phenomena at a range of different scales. Students at every grade should have multiple opportunities to work directly with maps, globes, and other geographic tools (both existing tools and ones they create on their own) as part of daily instruction to address developmentally appropriate questions related to the goals outlined in the DCI. Examples

of such tools include ArcGIS Online (*www.arcgis.com/home*), the MapMaker Interactive tool from the National Geographic Society (*mapmaker.education.nationalgeographic.com*), and Google Earth (*earth.google.com*).

A key challenge with learning about Earth's systems is that these are global phenomena, which for the most part are larger than what can be experienced directly by students and which cannot be brought into the classroom. Thus, instruction around Earth's systems relies heavily on the use of models, including three-dimensional models, diagrams, simulations, and other representations to help students visualize and conceptualize the phenomena and relationships between components. Models have many affordances, such as being manipulable, testable, and able to facilitate spatial and temporal understandings. However, models themselves also have limitations that should be addressed during instruction. All models are inherently simplifications of the real world, developed in a way to reduce complexity and more clearly explain the target process or phenomena. Care should be given to helping students see those simplifications and limitations, to avoid developing a perspective that the model *is* the science to be understood. This can be accomplished by providing opportunities for students to reflect and critique the models that they work with, identifying which aspects are intended to accurately reflect the real Earth system and which ones are simplifications or omissions that allow for reducing complexity. Iterative experiences across K–12 with critical and reflective engagement of models helps students develop an appreciation of them as tools for understanding large-scale phenomena, along with the knowledge and skills to develop and critique their own increasingly sophisticated models over time.

11

Another key emphasis in ESS2 is a focus on complex and dynamic systems. Systems are challenging to represent and explain. One approach to assist students with learning about specific systems and their interactions is to engage them in multiple rounds of development and revision of systems concept maps. When used in conjunction with other models and visualizations, concept maps can help students identify and express relationships among and between system components, which are oftentimes complex and multifaceted. Effective use of concept maps is a strategy that develops over time with practice. In the younger grades, effort should be made to help students learn how to represent objects and relationships, along with how to share, critique, and collaborate with their classmates around their concept maps. As students progress to the upper levels, digital system modeling tools can be introduced, which allow students to explore more complex and dynamic factors within systems and investigate perturbations to systems in terms of their feedback effects. Many digital modeling tools, such as global climate models, use actual historical data to develop and refine their projections. Using these tools with a range of existing large-scale data sets, students can explore and develop sophisticated explanations for a variety of complicated relationships across time and space.

Conclusion

The Earth exists as one large system, consisting of an array of interconnected subsystems. Often, scientists focus their efforts on exploring and explaining smaller, individual subsystems or even smaller relationships within these subsystems. However, within this work, scientists maintain an awareness of the context of their investigations as nested within broader, interacting systems, and how that context influences and is affected by the particular aspects and functions under study. Unfortunately, this nested relational context has often been simplified or overlooked in traditional Earth sciences instruction, resulting in the perception that aspects of the Earth are isolated and static, which is far from the truth.

The Earth's Systems DCI learning goals outlined in the *Framework* address this erroneous view. The new goals promote students' development of robust and applicable understandings of how the Earth actually works from multiple systemic perspectives. These expectations ask students to be able to reason about spatial relationships and interconnections at a young age. As students progress in their understanding, the goals evolve to focus on complex system interactions, including feedback loops, and on the application of core principles of chemistry and physics to explain mechanisms that drive observable phenomena. Although this work is challenging, students who are armed with this knowledge and these skills and perspectives about the Earth will be ready to address many of the challenges facing society as engaged and productive citizens in the 21st century.

REFERENCES

Assarf, O. B. Z., and N. Orion. 2005. A study of junior high students' perceptions of the water cycle. *Journal of Geoscience Education* 53 (4): 366–373.

Ford, B., and M. Taylor. 2008. Investigating students' ideas about plate tectonics. In *Readings in Science Methods, K–8*, ed. E. Brunsell, 81–88. Arlington, VA: NSTA Press.

Ford, D. J. 2005. The challenges of observing geologically: Third graders' descriptions of rock and mineral properties. *Science Education* 89 (2): 276–295.

Gautier, C., K. Deutsch, and S. Rebich. 2006. Misconceptions about the greenhouse effect. *Journal of Geoscience Education* 54 (3): 386–395.

Gregory, T. R. 2009. Understanding natural selection: Essential concepts and common misconceptions. *Evolution: Education and Outreach* 2 (2): 156–175.

Hartley, L., B. Wilke, J. Schramm, C. D'Avanzo, and C. Anderson. 2011. College students' understanding of the carbon cycle: Contrasting principle-based and informal reasoning. *BioScience* 61 (1): 65–75.

Henriques, L. 2000. Children's misconceptions about weather: A review of the literature. Paper presented at the annual meeting of the National Association of Research in Science Teaching, New Orleans, LA.

Kali, Y., N. Orion, and B.-S. Eylon. 2003. Effect of knowledge integration activities on students' perception of the Earth's crust as a cyclic system. *Journal of Research in Science Teaching* 40 (6): 545–565.

Libarkin, J., and S. Anderson. 2005. Assessment of learning in entry-level geoscience courses: Results from the geoscience concept inventory. *Journal of Geoscience Education* 53 (4): 394–401.

Libarkin, J., S. Anderson, J. Dahl, M. Beilfuss, and W. Boone. 2005. Qualitative analysis of college students' ideas about the Earth: Interviews and open-ended questionnaires. *Journal of Geoscience Education* 53 (1): 17–26.

McCaffrey, M., and S. Buhr. 2008. Clarifying climate confusion: Addressing systemic holes, cognitive gaps, and misconceptions through climate literacy. *Physical Geography* 29 (6): 512–528.

Polito, E., K. D. Tanner, and J. P. Monteverdi. 2008. Assessing middle school and college students' conceptions about tornadoes and other weather phenomena. Paper presented at the 24th Conference on Severe Local Storms, Savannah, GA.

Schneps, P. and P. Sadler. 1985. *A private universe.* Cambridge, MA: Harvard-Smithsonian Center for Astrophysics, Science Education Department.

CHAPTER 12

CORE IDEA ESS3
EARTH AND HUMAN ACTIVITY

Nancy Brickhouse, J. Randy McGinnis, Nicole A. Shea, Andrea Drewes,
Emily Hestness, and Wayne Breslyn

What Is This Disciplinary Core Idea, and Why Is It Important?

This chapter focuses on the disciplinary core idea (DCI) ESS3: Earth and Human Activity. As stated in *A Framework for K–12 Science Education* (*Framework*; NRC 2012), ESS3 asserts that by

connecting the [Earth and space sciences] to the intimate scale of human life, this idea explains how Earth's processes affect people through natural resources and natural hazards, and it describes as well some of the ways in which humanity in turn affects Earth's processes. (NRC 2012, p. 170)

ESS3 explains how the Earth's natural resources, natural hazards, and changing climate affect humans as individuals, communities, and activity systems; concurrently, it also describes ways in which humanity affects Earth's processes.

Human activity has become one of the most significant agents of change to Earth systems, with both positive and negative effects. Humans are dependent on the Earth's resources. Throughout history, civilizations have flourished or withered relative to the extent to which the local environment was able to provide the resources needed to sustain the population. At times, humans have been excellent stewards of the Earth's resources, developing cultivation techniques to enhance the production of needed resources and protecting the environment from undesirable hazards. However, the Earth is a planet of finite resources, and its growing density of inhabitants currently consumes those resources at a rate that cannot be sustained. The quality and quantity of water is of serious concern in many parts of the world. Naturally, water quality and many other environmental issues are closely related to questions of human health. For us to develop practical solutions to these serious challenges, we must have both a scientifically literate workforce and a citizenry that is capable of formulating and vetting policy solutions and practical actions to ensure that our natural environment is able to sustain the demands of an ever-increasing human population. The existence of natural threats such as

 12

tsunamis, earthquakes, drought, and volcanic eruptions has also shaped communities and culture throughout human history. Understanding the causes of natural hazards as well as the extent to which scientific models are able to predict their frequency and severity is essential to building understandings of ways to mitigate their effects on human populations in the future.

Humans have also had a profound impact on the Earth's climate. Global climate change is a distinguished component of this DCI, as both the scientific community and society increasingly recognize it as a key driver of powerful environmental changes on the planet. Climate change has been identified by numerous scientific agencies as one of the grand challenges of our time. As documented in reports published by the Intergovernmental Panel on Climate Change (IPCC), at least since the time of the Industrial Revolution human activities have vastly increased the concentration of greenhouse gases in the atmosphere to levels unprecedented in the past 800,000 years, and it is extremely likely that human influences have been the dominant cause of the observed warming at the surface of Earth since the mid-20th century (IPCC 2013). In addition, projected reductions in surface ice caps, sea-level rise, more extreme weather events, and ocean acidification due to carbon dioxide emissions are all anticipated to have significant consequences for ecosystems and human economic and cultural systems that cannot be fully predicted. Addressing this challenge will require a human response—one that is informed by scientific understandings and active debate about economics, policy, politics, and ethics. Understanding climate change requires a rigorous understanding of the nature of matter and energy, the chemical changes involved in combustion, the effect of climate on habitats and

the diversity of life they support, and other key concepts in the life and physical sciences. Like many of the other grand challenges we face today, sophisticated understandings draw from multiple disciplines, not only in the natural sciences but also in social sciences and humanities.

The DCI ESS3: Earth and Human Activity is strongly related to other DCIs, such as ESS2: Earth Systems. Understanding how humans interact with the Earth requires a fundamental understanding of the Earth's systems and how energy and matter are cycled through the hydrosphere, geosphere, and atmosphere over scales that range from the global to the microscopic and over time periods from billions of years to fractions of a second. Similarly, LS2: Ecosystems: Interactions, Energy and Dynamics is also highly relevant to this DCI, since understanding the interaction between living and nonliving components of an ecosystem is necessary to explain how ecosystems are affected by human-induced physical changes such as ocean acidification or the salination of soil due to sea-level rise.

Previous science standards such as the *National Science Education Standards* (*NSES*; NRC 1996) include expectations for learning about human use of natural resources; however, those standards have few expectations articulated for student learning about anthropogenic climate change. This DCI is consistent with established science since the publication of the *NSES*.

Overview of Component Ideas

Component ideas of this DCI identified by the *Framework* include ESS3.A: Natural Resources, ESS3.B: Natural Hazards, ESS3.C: Human Impacts on Earth Systems, and ESS3.D: Global Climate Change. These four ideas overlap significantly. For example, our use of natural resources that produce greenhouse gases influences climate change, and climate change influences natural hazards such as extreme weather events and sea-level rise.

ESS3.A: NATURAL RESOURCES

The first component idea, Natural Resources, focuses student understanding on the ways in which humans depend on a variety of natural resources, including air, water, soil, minerals, metals, energy, plants, and animals. Students should recognize that some kinds of resources are replaceable or renewable in the time frame of human lifetimes; others are renewable on the time frame of many generations; and others are essentially nonreplaceable. Understanding the nature of renewable and nonrenewable resources leads to important considerations for the responsible short- and long-term management of them. Students should recognize that many of the natural materials necessary for industry are not distributed evenly over the planet, and where present, often require processing to be used. Human populations have been drawn to live in areas that offer ample natural resources; consequently, over time, as the population has increased in both specific areas and overall, natural resources have become more scarce.

One major challenge for students' understanding of Earth and environmental sciences is conceptualization of large spans of time and space. Students often have difficulties understanding the vastness of Earth's and the universe's history (e.g., Dodick and Orion 2003; Libarkin and Anderson 2005; see also ESS1: Earth's Place in the Universe). Deep time refers to the knowledge that the universe has existed for an extraordinarily long time and also that life, especially humans, have existed for a brief period of that history. Countless millennia or even thousands of years are conceptually challenging notions for students to grasp in relation to their comparatively short personal life history of only a decade or two. Robust understanding of the notion of deep time, however, is particularly relevant as students consider the use and formation of natural resources. Many students have difficulty understanding the span of time required to generate fossil fuels and the rate at which humans consume this resource relative to its formation. Students also struggle to understand why natural resources are concentrated in some geologic areas and not others (see also ESS2.B: Plate Tectonics and Large-Scale System Interactions), making the notion of resource reliance hard for students to grasp. The idea of deep time is one that is needed for understanding Earth and space sciences, as well as life sciences like evolutionary biology (see LS3: Heredity: Inheritance and Variation of Traits).

ESS3.B: NATURAL HAZARDS

The second component idea of this DCI focuses on natural hazards. Students focus on how humans and local ecosystems are affected by natural hazards such as severe weather events (floods, blizzards, droughts, and hurricanes), earthquakes, volcanic eruptions, wildfires, landslides, and coastal erosion. These events have the ability to disrupt populations and activities and cause significant changes to the physical environment. Students should explore how a combination of historical and current observations, along with understanding the ways in which global Earth systems interact to create such events, allows humans to have a good understanding of where such natural hazards commonly occur

and the conditions that create them. Importantly, although these events cannot be prevented, humans are able to use their understanding of where and how such events typically take place to design systems that can protect and mitigate against the severe effects and develop increasingly more accurate prediction systems.

Similar to the concept of deep time, the understanding of geographic scale is another important discipline-wide challenge that students encounter (e.g., Dickerson et al. 2005; Jones et al. 2007; Tretter, Jones, and Minogue 2006), and becomes particularly relevant as students come to understand both the characteristics and causes of natural resources. The scale of the Earth is so grand that students frequently have conceptual difficulties understanding the relative effect of local, regional, or global phenomena. For example, exploring scale with respect to natural hazards can prove challenging for many students who consider events such as hurricanes as only relevant to Florida, think that earthquakes only happen in California, or believe that some tornadoes are large enough to cause damage across an entire state, such as Kansas.

ESS3.C: HUMAN IMPACTS ON EARTH SYSTEMS

The third component idea, Human Impacts on Earth Systems, focuses students' attention on the effect of human activities on the environment, particularly those related to meeting the needs of a growing and industrialized human population. Students explore how collectively we have modified the shapes of rivers, created lakes, and removed water from underground. We have transformed large areas of forests, grasslands, and wetlands into agricultural areas or human settlements.

Consequently, over time, humans have become one of the most significant agents of change to the Earth's interconnected systems, with rippling effects that cause both anticipated and unexpected changes across systems. Multiple examples of these effects can be explored, such as how human actions have altered or eliminated many natural habitats and led to the extinction of numerous species, or how pollution caused by human activities has affected the condition of the atmosphere, rivers, and lakes, which has harmed organisms and affected human health. Students develop understandings of the interconnections between activities and Earth systems and processes through exploring how human activity has affected the environment in ways that resulted in changes in the number and frequency of natural hazards such as storms and droughts. However, students also consider that, with sustained effort and responsible management, some of the negative impacts of human activities on Earth systems can be reduced or even reversed. Examples include the regulation of the amount of contaminants that are released into the atmosphere and water systems, which has reduced acid rain and stream pollution over time. Similarly, the development of new alternative energy sources combined with greater efforts to reuse and recycle existing materials can reduce the environmental effects that otherwise would have resulted from the use of fossil fuels.

The *Framework* also acknowledges the social implications of the DCIs relevant for ESS3. Influenced by alternative views, students frequently have difficulty understanding how social, economic, and political factors shape human influence on Earth systems and vice versa (Roth and Lee 2004; Zeidler, Sadler, Simmons, and Howes 2005). Many students believe events such as global climate change (ESS3.D: Global and Climate

Change) affect only natural systems (e.g., water, carbon, and energy cycles). In many instances, students do not consider how a changing climate can also affect humans, especially in terms of the relevant social, economic, and political implications that influence actions such as global climate change mitigation efforts. Many students believe that reducing greenhouse gas output is a straightforward charge. However, many other factors that do not contribute directly to a changing climate act as obstacles for reducing the use of fossil fuels and increasing use of renewable energy sources.

Understanding how their personal contributions can affect the environment has been shown to be a challenge for students (Andersson and Wallin 2000; Boyes and Stanisstreet 1993, 2001; Lester et al. 2006; Pruneau et al. 2003; Skamp, Boyes, and Stanisstreet 2013). Often, students feel compelled to contribute to environmental issues in meaningful ways but have difficulty identifying productive strategies or methods that have lasting effects. For example, students have reported that participating in beach clean-ups, reducing aerosol spray usage, and recycling plastic materials were all actions that could be taken to directly mitigate global climate change (e.g., Pruneau et al. 2003). In many cases, these actions contribute to the sustainability of ecosystems, reduce the effect of natural hazards, and improve the longevity of natural resources, but have little or no effect on reducing human-induced climate change.

ESS3.D: GLOBAL CLIMATE CHANGE

The final component idea of this DCI, Global Climate Change, focuses students on the notion of climate change as a driver of change to the Earth's surface processes. It exemplifies the interaction of humans' activities and natural effects, which in the case of climate is predicted to have major environmental and societal consequences if humans do not engage in informed personal and societal action. A major focus of this component idea is for students to understand how, through using scientific evidence of past climate conditions to develop predictive models, we have the capability to anticipate the ways that the climate will likely change over the long term and how other Earth systems may respond to these changes. Many of these changes and responses will be uneven and will affect various regions of the globe differently. Because such phenomena are incredibly complex with numerous natural, economic, political, and behavioral factors affecting the long-term outcomes, there are inevitable uncertainties in these model forecasts. However, climate change models provide data that can be used to make informed decisions and plan for ways to address and adapt to the anticipated future environmental conditions.

Understanding the mechanisms underlying geologic and climatic events is a key challenge for many students. Too often, students reflect on superficial aspects of events, such as identifying only the inputs and outputs of systems, without knowing how or why events take place. Without a mechanistic understanding of events, students may have difficulty predicting future events based on data or interpreting graphic representations of data that illustrate future scenarios. This is particularly relevant for notions of global climate change. For example, to explain global climate change, students can often identify that an increase in carbon dioxide (an input) will cause temperatures to rise, causing glacial ice melt and sea-level rise (an output) (Breslyn, McGinnis, McDonald, and Hestness, Forthcoming), but they

12

often fail to grasp the mechanism by which those two events are related (e.g., the enhanced greenhouse effect) or how rises in global temperature can be mitigated (e.g., Boyes and Stanisstreet 1993, 1994, 1997, 1998, 2001; Choi et al. 2010; see also ESS2: Earth's Systems). Without an understanding of the mechanism, students lack the capacity to consider ways that they as individuals or as a part of society can contribute to reducing human-induced climate change and the relative contributions specific actions provide to changes in climate (Jin and Anderson 2012; Osterlind 2005; Smith et al. 2006).

How Does Student Understanding of This Disciplinary Core Idea Develop Over Time?

Throughout their K–12 science education, learners are expected to develop an understanding of how now, unlike any other time in the Earth's and human history, the planet's surface processes and human activities are interacting in ways that are resulting in significant changes to the environment (Earth Science Literacy Initiative 2010; National Geographic Society 2013). The progression of ideas through this DCI supports students in developing this critical perspective on the interactions between the Earth and human activity. We recognize that accounts of how many of these important ideas develop over time are limited, and further research in this area is needed. Thus, we present a general description of the ways in which the component ideas in this DCI develop across the grade bands as informed by the *Framework*. We then share a specific, more detailed account of the development of component idea ESS3.D: Global Climate

Change that has been informed by our current research and development efforts in this area.

Lower Elementary

In lower elementary grades, the Earth and Human Activity DCI expects students to understand that humans, like all other living organisms, such as plants and animals, need things to survive, including water, air, soil, minerals, and materials for food, protection, and shelter. These are called resources, and they are referred to as *natural resources* because they come from the natural world. People use natural resources everyday for just about everything they do: to grow food, to build shelter and warm living environments, and to create objects and tools for everyday use. Importantly, students in early elementary school should also begin to recognize that natural resources do not exist everywhere on Earth in the same amounts, and so we humans tend to live in places that have the things we need. This is the reason people usually live in places where water is plentiful, such as near rivers, lakes, and oceans, and in climates where food can be easily grown rather than in harsh climates such as deserts, high mountains, or the polar regions.

The fact that people live in different kinds of environments around the globe means that they need to pay attention the different kinds of weather events that occur in those areas, because they vary from place to place. Specifically, some kinds of severe weather such as hurricanes or droughts are more common in some areas than others. Our ability to forecast these weather events, prepare for them, and respond to them when they occur has allowed us to settle successfully in a wide variety of environments. Yet, as we humans work to meet our needs in different areas, we must identify and process a range of local natural resources. Students should recognize that people can make choices about their use of natural resources that can reduce the effects on the local environment, for example, by conserving water or recycling to reduce the amount of trash created.

Upper Elementary

In upper elementary school (grades 3–5), learners progress in their understanding that natural and human actions are related to environmental challenges. They consider ways to prepare for natural disasters, such as developing warning systems for earthquakes, volcanic eruptions, and tsunamis, or forecasting severe weather. They also further consider ways to reduce the human impact on the environment. At this level, learners should be able to use their growing understanding of Earth systems (i.e., the hydrosphere, atmosphere, geosphere, and biosphere) and ways that they interact (see ESS2.A: Earth Materials and Systems), and their developing notions of energy transformations (see PS3: Energy) to consider means for protecting Earth's resources and reducing natural hazards and human effects on Earth's processes. For example, students can explore renewable and nonrenewable energy sources, where they come from, and the ways they affect the local environment. Similarly, students can also conduct research to understand different kinds of pollution, their sources and potential impacts, and possible strategies to mitigate their damaging effects.

Middle School

In middle school, the Earth and Human Activities DCI progresses by introducing more sophisticated

concepts related to human use of natural resources and to monitoring (with the goal of predicting) and mitigating environmental hazards. While most environmental hazards cannot be eliminated, their effects can be reduced (e.g., by locating and avoiding hazardous danger zones). At this level, students will investigate more deeply the geologic phenomena that cause natural hazards, such as plate tectonic processes that cause earthquakes and volcanoes (see ESS2.B: Plate Tectonics and Large-Scale System Interactions) and large-scale weather processes that cause hurricanes and blizzards (see ESS2.D: Weather and Climate). These processes also result in the varied distribution of natural resources such as coal, oil, and minerals across different areas of the Earth. Students study the effects of resource consumption on Earth systems, and engage in designing methods for monitoring and minimizing human impacts on the environment.

The specific effects of global climate change are first introduced in the middle grades, including global atmospheric warming. Students explore the factors that have caused the rise in global temperatures over the past centuries. At this level, humans are identified as the most significant agent of change to Earth's systems. For example, human activities have significantly altered the biosphere by changing or destroying natural habitats, resulting in the extinction of many living species.

High School

In grades 9–12, the Earth and Human Activities DCI expects students to engage in developing sophisticated understandings of the complex and dynamic relationship between humans and the Earth system not only in solely scientific terms but in how they relate to and interact with

12

economic, social, environmental, and geopolitical dimensions of human society. Students should come to recognize how the availability of resources has guided the development of human society and how benefits as well as risks (e.g., economic, social, environmental, and geopolitical) are associated with resource extraction. Students investigate how natural hazards have been a driving force throughout human history, including how they have affected population changes and migration. Similarly, some natural hazards (e.g., flooding, forest fires) are increasing in frequency and intensity due to increases in human population densities in areas prone to environmental changes. They explore how international agreements regulating human activities may mitigate the extent of these global effects (e.g., case studies on acid rain and the ozone hole).

As part of the Human Impacts on Earth Systems component idea, they also consider the role of scientists and engineers in developing technologies that produce less pollution and waste, and how these developments may aid in maintaining the biodiversity necessary for a sustainable future. How the ocean, atmosphere, and biosphere interact and are modified in response to human activities is under active investigation. Thus, scientists use climate modeling to understand these complex processes related to global climate change. For example, understanding the current health of the coral reefs (the biosphere) necessitates consideration of how a human activity—releasing increased amounts of carbon dioxide in the environment (the atmosphere)—has resulted in the acidification of the coral reefs' environment (hydrosphere).

A Case in Point
HOW LEARNERS DEVELOP AN UNDERSTANDING OF GLOBAL CLIMATE CHANGE

Woven throughout the Earth and Human Activities DCI are concepts relevant to understanding the topic of global climate change (USGCRP 2009) in progressively more sophisticated ways. Due to increased attention to human-produced (anthropogenic) climate change as a significant driver of ongoing changes in the environment that must be monitored carefully (Moran 2010), and because it exemplifies a key aspect of the interactions between natural and human systems that is a focus of the Earth and Human Activities DCI, we present the development of this particular component idea in additional detail. (Climate change education is the focus in our National Science Foundation–funded project MADE CLEAR [Maryland and Delaware Climate Literacy Education, Assessment, and Research], *www.madeclear. org*; *www.ClimateEdResearch.org*.)

ELEMENTARY SCHOOL: FOUNDATIONS FOR UNDERSTANDING GLOBAL CLIMATE CHANGE

Beginning in the early elementary grades, the ESS3 DCI emphasizes that learners need to understand that human activities both use and affect the resources available in the local environment, land, water, air, and other living things. This idea is foundational for later explorations of global climate change. In developing an early understanding that human activities can and do affect the natural environment, learners will be better equipped to understand how human activities have made specific contributions to global climate change.

In upper elementary school, the ESS3 DCI elaborates on the idea that human actions are related to both environmental problems and solutions. One focus is on learning about renewable and nonrenewable energies and how their use affects the natural environment. In learning about the ways in which various forms of energy are generated, learners develop foundational understandings of the connections between energy, natural resources, and sustainability. Building on standards from earlier grades, learners might consider specific effects of energy choices (see also PS3: Energy).

At the elementary school level, an early understanding that humans can incite positive environmental change, which may have important affective implications for later introductions to global climate change, empowering learners to consider ways they can contribute to productive solutions as scientifically literate citizens, and potentially, as future practicing scientists or engineers. A performance that is posited to be particularly effective in learning this DCI is for learners to communicate solutions for reducing the human influence on the local environment. Initially, the expectation is for solutions that are accessible to young learners (e.g., reusing paper, recycling cans and bottles), and that pertain to the local environment (i.e., familiar to and experienced by the learner) to make concrete the concept of solutions that reduce human effect on the environment. By fifth grade, learners should be investigating and synthesizing information about ways individual communities use science ideas to protect the Earth's resources and environment. At the upper elementary level, learners could meaningfully develop this DCI through student engagement in research of their own community's climate

change mitigation practices or case studies across local or global communities.

MIDDLE SCHOOL: AN EXPLICIT FOCUS ON LEARNING THE DRIVERS OF GLOBAL CLIMATE CHANGE

At the middle school level, the component idea of Global Climate Change (ESS3.D) takes a step forward in sophistication by focusing more student attention explicitly on the phenomena of climate change itself. In this grade band, more direct emphasis is placed on learning about factors that have resulted in the rise in global temperatures over the past century. Students examine both human activity factors, such as fossil fuel combustion, and natural processes, such as volcanic activity. Related to understanding this idea are investigations that include examining issues concerning population growth and per capita consumption of natural resources and constructing arguments about how such factors affect Earth's systems, particularly in the ways that nature responds to changes in the system (see also ESS2.A: Earth Materials and Systems). These topics have clear connections to further understanding the drivers and mechanisms of human activity affecting global climate change, especially as learners examine consumption of energy resources or, perhaps, consumption of food products whose production may contribute to changes to Earth's terrestrial, aquatic, or atmospheric systems.

Middle school students are also posited to benefit from learning about climate change by investigating solutions to environmental issues as well as developing their own. They could design methods for monitoring and minimizing human impact on the environment, such as by protecting

12

and restoring wetlands, which is a critical concern for coastal communities needing to buffer the effects of climate change due to sea-level rise and storm surge. Middle school learners are thought to be able to engage productively in using data to forecast future catastrophic events to inform the development of technologies, such as technologies for forecasting hurricanes and floods, which could be used by community members to mitigate and adapt to severe weather.

HIGH SCHOOL: DEEPENING AND BROADENING AN UNDERSTANDING OF GLOBAL CLIMATE CHANGE

In high school, students build on their learning about forecasting catastrophic events and mitigating human effects on the natural environment with an increasingly direct emphasis on global climate change. Examining the nuances of the dynamic relationship between humans and the Earth system, especially through the lens of global climate change, aims to develop the kinds of science and engineering literacy that will prepare high school graduates to address major global environmental challenges. For example, high school learners should be able to analyze geoscience data and climate models (e.g., precipitation or temperature data) to forecast and plan informed actions based on rates of climate change and associated future effects such as changes in sea level and glacial ice volumes. Importantly, at this grade level, students begin to recognize the effects of climate change as both regional changes and global ones. This emphasizes the idea that climate change has differential effects across different places on Earth, depending on various geophysical factors. By the end of high school, learners should have analyzed at least

one example of a climate change and forecasted its associated affects. Building on their thinking around design solutions from middle school, high school learners should also evaluate or refine technological solutions for reducing effects of associated activities on natural systems. One example would be for them to critically evaluate the use of large-scale geoengineering solutions (like radically changing the atmosphere or oceans) for altering global temperatures.

At the high school level, students examine global climate change from a variety of perspectives. They illustrate the ways in which human activities are modifying the relationships among Earth systems (see ESS2.A: Earth Materials and Systems) and the ways in which issues associated with natural resource use (e.g., fossil fuel consumption) and natural hazards (e.g., severe weather potentially associated with climate change) have influenced human activity. As human activities lead to changes on Earth, changes on Earth lead to changes in human activities. For example, an examination of changes in sea level reveals that new patterns of temperature and precipitation and consequently changes to the types of agriculture that are possible and impossible in new climatic conditions, can have significant affects for human populations—potentially even driving mass human migrations that could place stress on the world's current social systems.

What Approaches Can We Use to Teach About This Disciplinary Core Idea?

Encouragingly, Earth and space science offer many opportunities for students to learn about current environmental issues, consider ways in which they can contribute to engineering design solutions, and understand how Earth's systems interact with one another to support global, regional, and local ecosystems. Learning the DCIs to support understanding in this topic area is not trivial and requires specific supports that teachers can provide.

First, from the perspective of challenges to students' understandings of a disciplinary nature, it is critical that students be able to distinguish between and also make connections across local and global phenomena (e.g., Clark et al. 2009; King 2008). It is important to address how large-scale environmental and climatic events can also manifest themselves on a regional or local scale. When teaching this idea, it is important that students understand that natural processes can take millions or billions of years to drive environmental and climatic changes. Only recently have humans generated changes that occur more rapidly than ever seen before in Earth's history. Students may benefit from interactive models that represent such changes over time. To demonstrate more recent changes, one example is National Oceanic and Atmospheric Administration's Global Climate Dashboard, which provides an interactive mapping of climate change factors, climate variability, and climate predictions from 1880–2090 (NOAA 2014). Other resources demonstrate changes over much longer spans of time. For example, NASA provides teaching materials that use real-world data to track carbon dioxide levels in the atmosphere up to 400,000 years ago (NASA 2013). Importantly, the resource also describes how scientists collect and interpret the data that support the finding that carbon dioxide levels are on the rise.

Not only are these core ideas complex in terms of the science knowledge needed to think deeply about environmental issues, they are often associated with sensitive topics such as food and water scarcity, land use, economic and policy issues, and many others. This complexity can often excite students when learning about environmental science but may also overwhelm those who wish to contribute to the mitigation or adaptation of environmental issues both locally and globally. Although environmental issues are often a combination of both scientific and social factors, it is important to support students' learning of the science behind such issues using real-world data and evidence first before turning to discussions of the economic, political, and social implications. Often students wonder about their personal stake in environmental issues, that is, what can they do to help? Teaching science first, followed by other social factors, sets the stage for preparing learners to engage with environmental science in ways that are based on scientific understandings.

Incorporating current socioscientific topics—such as air and water pollution, chemical food additives, and mining of natural resources—is included under the guidance of the *Framework*. In doing so, teachers may introduce how varied factors—including social, political, and economic factors—are relevant for addressing such issues (Kolstø 2001; Stern 2007; Nielson 2012; Zeidler et al. 2002). One means to demonstrate multiple perspectives is through stakeholder analysis—not only human stakeholders but environmental stakeholders such as animals, plants, and geologic deposits. It is important that students be given opportunities to acknowledge and explore multiple perspectives to gain an understanding of the complexity of issues such as the use of natural resources, the prevalence of natural hazards, and global climate change. Engaging in "democratic dialogues" (e.g., Brookfield and Preskill 2012;

Crocco and Grolnick 2008) is one form of effectively engaging in stakeholder discussions.

Educators can support students' understanding of the nature of scientific arguments and how evidence is used to support scientific arguments (e.g., Nussbaum, Sinatra, and Owens 2012; Osbourne, Erduran, and Simon 2004). Scientific, and especially environmental, issues can have multiple points of view from which to approach the problem, each with its own corresponding evidence. Encouraging students to investigate these various perspectives for validity encourages them to analyze and interpret data and develop arguments based on evidence. One way to engage students in this way is to assign them stakeholder roles about an issue and ask them to investigate, support, and refute their positions. In this case, it is important to incorporate the primary scientific knowledge needed to understand the issue but also to emphasize the diversity of drivers behind each position, whether they are political, economic, or social in nature. For example, students can participate in the *Great Energy Debate* (NGE 2014). This lesson, designed by National Geographic, encourages students to research types of energy used in the United States and their communities, describe how energy consumption can affect land use, and take stakeholder positions in a mock debate format to argue from evidence different perspectives on energy generation, sustainability, and land use. The National Science Teachers Association (NSTA) also offers similar resources to help teachers and students examine environmental issues using this case study approach to investigate various perspectives. For climate case studies see *Climate Change from Pole to Pole*, and for energy-related content see *Fuel for Thought* for additional resources for middle and high school teachers. For an even greater variety

of science content case studies and lesson ideas, the National Center for Case Study Teaching in Science provides numerous plans and teaching ideas that are readily available online. Through a case study approach, students can develop their conceptual understanding about topics such as natural resources (ESS3.A) along with their capacity to analyze and interpret data and ask questions from critical perspectives. Activities such as the *Great Energy Debate* can also link to the other DCIs, such as ESS3.D: Global Climate Change. For example, students may also debate over the effect a changing climate will have in their local area on energy source access and how to sustain future development (ESS3.C: Human Impacts on Earth Systems) in light of the increase of future natural hazards (ESS3.B: Natural Hazards).

Finally, educators should strive to provide students with realistic and meaningful ways to contribute to the issues (e.g., Anderman, Sinatra, and Gray 2012). Students often feel compelled to take responsibility for their actions in ways that improve environmental issues, and too often messages about environmental issues take on doom-and-gloom perspectives that can paralyze learners. Helping students identify ways they can make a personal difference at home and in their school, community, and society improves students' engagement with science. A positive strategy is to accompany lessons on environmental science topics with clear action statements that can provide students with a means for engaging in the topics. These positive experiences need to be integrated into the learning experience to encourage students to act on an individual, family, school, or community level to address the problem. Incorporating students' families and communities participation through events like science nights or green carnivals offers ways for students to demonstrate their science knowledge while also engaging others in learning about appropriate civic action for these environmental issues (Birmingham and Calabrese Barton 2014).

Another strategy for initiating discussions about meaningful environmental actions is to help students understand how they personally use natural resources. For example, using a carbon footprint calculator is one way students can determine their energy use and carbon outputs in their home, school, and community. From this information students can begin to explore specific methods to become efficient energy users. Interactives, such as the climate change mitigation simulator featured by the National Academy of Sciences, offer students a portal for engaging in salient mitigation and adaptation strategies (NAS 2014). The American Association for the Advancement of Science (AAAS) offers lessons such as *Energy for You* that help students identify energy sources in their communities using real-world data and provides examples of how to maintain and preserve energy resources for future generations (AAAS 2014). Additionally, project InTeGrate (Interdisciplinary Teaching about Earth for a Sustainable Future) offers teaching resources adaptable for high school classrooms that encourage students' awareness of and participation in mediation strategies (InTeGrate 2014). It is important that lessons addressing the DCI of Earth and Human Activities end with a hopeful message for change and offer students specific methods for becoming environmentally savvy in their daily lives.

Conclusion

Of all the fields of scientific study, the Earth sciences are one of the most interdisciplinary. This is particularly true for the DCI of ESS3: Earth and Human Activity, which focuses on society's interactions with the planet's complex systems. Duschl, Bismark, Greeno, and Gitomer (2013) note that there has been very significant change in the nature of Earth science research with advances in technology. Historically, the Earth sciences have been oriented toward solving very practical problems of commerce and industry. For example, mapping the Earth's terrain was key to establishing the transportation pathways to facilitate trade. Mining and energy exploration required a thorough understanding of geological formations. Today, Earth sciences research is motivated by a different set of concerns and uses different methodologies. Changes in technology have enabled the development of sophisticated visualizations and quantitative models for exploring, explaining, and predicting Earth's complex systems. In particular, understanding the Earth requires reasoning across multiple systems, such as the biosphere, the hydrosphere, the geosphere, and the atmosphere. This research is driven by the desire to create predictive quantitative models that can provide the detailed knowledge to explain and explore an ever-changing biosphere. The component ideas of ESS3 reflect this contemporary view of the Earth sciences.

The biggest takeaway from this overview of ESS3 is the central understanding that natural processes and human activities are intimately linked in clearly identified ways. This realization is strategically advanced across K–12 schooling and offers opportunity for humans to take informed and responsible actions (individually and collectively) to produce and maintain a sustainable planetary environment into the future.

12

Acknowledgments

This material is based on work supported by the National Science Foundation (grant no. 1043262). Any opinions, findings, and conclusions or recommendations expressed in this material are those of the author(s) and do not necessarily reflect the views of the National Science Foundation.

REFERENCES

American Association for the Advancement of Science (AAAS). 1993. *Benchmarks for science literacy.* New York: Oxford University Press.

American Association for the Advancement of Science (AAAS). 2014. Energy for you. *http://sciencenetlinks.com/lessons/energy-for-you.*

Anderman, E. M., G. M. Sinatra, and D. L. Gray, D. L. 2012. The challenges of teaching and learning about science in the twenty-first century: Exploring the abilities and constraints of adolescent learners. *Studies in Science Education* 48 (1): 89–117.

Andersson, B., and A. Wallin. 2000. Students' understanding of the greenhouse effect, the societal consequences of reducing CO_2 emissions and the problem of ozone layer depletion. *Journal of Research in Science Teaching* 37(10): 1096–1111.

Birmingham, D., and A. Calabrese Barton. 2014. Putting on a green carnival: Youth taking educated action on socioscientific issues. *Journal of Research in Science Teaching* 51 (3): 286–314.

Boyes, E., and M. Stanisstreet. 1993. The 'greenhouse effect': children's perceptions of causes, consequences and cures. *International Journal of Science Education* 15 (5): 531–552.

Boyes, E., and M. Stanisstreet. 1994. The ideas of secondary school children concerning ozone layer damage. *Global Environmental Change* 4 (4): 311–324.

Boyes, E., and M. Stanisstreet. 1997. The environmental impact of cars: Children's ideas and reasoning. *Environmental Education Research* 3 (3): 269–282.

Boyes, E., and M. Stanisstreet. 1998. High school students' perceptions of how major global environmental effects might cause skin cancer. *The Journal of Environmental Education* 29 (2): 31–36.

Boyes, E., and M. Stanisstreet. 2001. School students' ideas about the 'greenhouse effect' a decade on. *Canadian Journal of Environmental Education* 6 (1): 77–101.

Breslyn, W., J. R. McGinnis, C. McDonald, and E. Hestness. Forthcoming. Developing a learning progression for sea level rise, a major impact of climate change. *Journal of Research in Science Teaching.*

Brookfield, S. D., and S. Preskill. 2012. *Discussion as a way of teaching: Tools and techniques for democratic classrooms.* Hoboken, NJ: John Wiley and Sons.

Choi, S., D. Niyogi, D. P. Shepardson, and U. Charumsombat. 2010. Do Earth and environmental science textbooks promote middle and high school students' conceptual development about climate change? *Bulletin of the American Meteorological Society* 91 (7): 889–898.

Clark, S. K., D. F. Sibley, J. C. Libarkin, and M. Heidemann. 2009. A novel approach to teaching and understanding transformations of matter in dynamic Earth systems. *Journal of Geoscience Education* 57 (4): 233–241.

Crocco, M. S., and M. Grolnick. 2008. Teaching the levees: An exercise in democratic dialogues. *Journal of Educational Controversy* 3 (1): 16.

Dickerson, D., T. J. Callahan, M. Van Sickle, and G. Hay. 2005. Students' conceptions of scale regarding groundwater. *Journal of Geoscience Education* 53 (4): 374–380.

Dodick, J., and N. Orion. 2003. Measuring student understanding of geological time. *Science Education* 87 (5): 708–731.

Duschl, R., A. Bismark, J. Greeno, and D. Gitomer. 2013. Standards for science education: Quantitative reasoning and modeling concepts. Paper presented at the Waterbury Summit, Pennsylvania State University, University Park, PA.

Earth Science Literacy Initiative. 2010. *Earth science literacy principles: The big ideas and supporting concepts of Earth science.* Arlington, VA: National Science Foundation. *www.Earthscienceliteracy.org/es_literacy_20june14may_.PDF.*

Intergovernmental Panel on Climate Change (IPCC). 2013. Summary for policymakers. In *Climate change 2013: The physical science basis. Contribution of working group I to the fifth assessment report of the Intergovernmental Panel on Climate Change*, ed. T. F. Stocker, D. Qin, G.-K. Plattner, M. Tignor, S. K. Allen, J. Boschung, A. Nauels, Y. Xia, V. Bex, and P. M. Midgley. New York: Cambridge University Press.

InTeGrate. 2014. Interdisciplinary teaching about Earth for a sustainable future. *http://serc.carleton.edu/integrate/index.html.*

Jakobsson, A., A. Makitalo, and R. Saljo. 2009. Conceptions of knowledge in research on students' understanding of the greenhouse effect: Methodological positions and their consequences for representations of knowing. *Science Education* 93 (6): 978–995.

Jin, H., and C. W. Anderson. 2012. A learning progression for energy in socio-ecological systems. *Journal of Research in Science Teaching* 49 (9): 1149–1180.

Jones, M. G., T. Tretter, A. Taylor, and T. Oppewal. 2008. Experienced and novice teachers' concepts of spatial scale. *International Journal of Science Education* 30 (3): 409–429.

King, C. 2008. Geoscience education: An overview. *Studies in Science Education* 44 (2): 187–222.

Kolstø, S. 2001. Scientific literacy for citizenship: Tools for dealing with the science dimension of controversial socioscientific issues. *Science Education* 85 (3): 291–310.

Lester, B. T., L. Ma, O. Lee, and J. Lambert. 2006. Social activism in elementary science education: A science, technology, and society approach to teach global warming. *International Journal of Science Education* 28 (4): 315–339.

Libarkin, J. C., and S. W. Anderson. 2005. Assessment of learning in entry-level geoscience courses: Results from the geoscience concept inventory. *Journal of Geoscience Education* 53 (4): 394–401.

Moran, J. M. 2010. *Climate studies: Introduction to climate science.* Boston, MA: American Meteorological Society.

National Academy of Sciences (NAS). 2014. Climate change mitigation simulator. *https://koshland-science-museum.org/explore-the-science/Earth-lab/responses#.U6RVBBauoao.*

National Aeronautics and Space Administration (NASA). 2013. Climate change: How do we know? *http://climate.nasa.gov/evidence.*

National Geographic Education (NGE). 2014. The great energy debate. National Geographic. *http://education.nationalgeographic.com/archive/xpeditions/lessons/16/g912/energydebate.html?ar_a=one.*

National Geographic Society (NGS). 2013. Ocean literacy: The essential principles and fundamental concepts of ocean science learners of all ages (version 2). Washington, DC: National

12

Geographic Society. *http://www.coexploration.org/ oceanliteracy/documents/OceanLitChart.PDF.*

National Oceanic and Atmospheric Association (NOAA). 2013. Carbon tracker CT2013. *www.esrl. noaa.gov/gmd/ccgg/carbontracker.*

National Oceanic and Atmospheric Association (NOAA). 2014. Global climate dashboard. *www. climate.gov/#understandingClimate.*

National Research Council (NRC). 1996. *National science education standards.* Washington, DC: National Academies Press.

National Research Council (NRC). 2012. *A framework for K–12 science education: Practices, crosscutting concepts, and core ideas.* Washington, DC: National Academies Press.

Nielson, J. A. 2012. Science in discussions: An analysis of the use of science content in socioscientific discussions. *Science Education* 96 (3): 428–456.

Nussbaum, E. M., G. M. Sinatra, and M. C. Owens. 2012. The two faces of scientific argumentation: Applications to global climate change. In *Perspectives on scientific argumentation: Theory, practice, and research*, ed. M. S. Khine, 17–37. Dordrecht, the Netherlands: Springer.

Osborne, J., S. Erduran, and S. Simon. 2004. Enhancing the quality of argumentation in school science. *Journal of Research in Science Teaching* 41 (10): 994–1020.

Osterlind, K. 2005. Concept formation in environmental education: 14-year olds' work on the intensified greenhouse effect and the depletion of the ozone layer. *International Journal of Science Education* 27 (8): 891–908.

Pruneau, D., H. Gravel, W. Borque, and J. Langis. 2003. Experimentation with a socio-constructivist

process for climate change education. *Environmental Education Research* 9 (4): 429–446.

Roth, W-M., and S. Lee. 2004. Science education as/for participation in the community. *Science Education* 88 (2): 263–291.

Skamp, K., E. Boyes, and M. Stanisstreet. 2013. Beliefs and willingness to act about global warming: Where to focus science pedagogy. *Science Education* 97 (2): 191–217.

Smith, C. L., M. Wiser, C. W. Anderson, and J. Kracjik. 2006. Implications of children's learning for standards and assessment: A proposed learning progression for matter and the atomic-molecular theory. *Measurement* 4 (1–2): 1–98.

Stern, N. N. H., ed. 2007. *Stern review: The economics of climate change.* Cambridge, UK: Cambridge University Press.

Tretter, T. R., M. G. Jones, and J. Minogue. 2006. Accuracy of scale conceptions in science: Mental maneuverings across many orders of spatial magnitude. *Journal of Research in Science Teaching* 43 (10): 1061–1085.

United States Global Change Research Program (USGCRP). 2009. *Climate literacy: The essential principles of climate science.* Washington, DC: USGCRP. *http://cpo.noaa.gov/sites/cpo/ Documents/PDF/ClimateLiteracyPoster-8_5x11_ Final4–11LR.PDF.*

Zeidler, D. L., T. D. Sadler, M. L. Simmons, and E. V. Howes. 2005. Beyond STS: A research-based framework for socioscientific issues education. *Science Education* 89 (3): 357–377.

Zeidler, D. L., K. A. Walker, W. A. Ackett, and M. L. Simmons. 2002. Tangled up in views: Beliefs in the nature of science and responses to socioscientific dilemmas. *Science Education* 86 (3): 343–367.

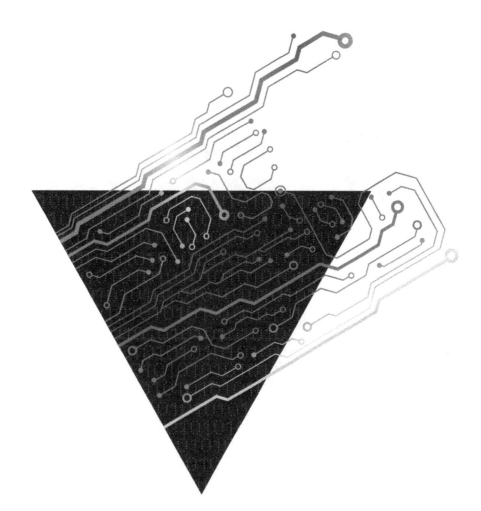

ENGINEERING, TECHNOLOGY, AND APPLICATIONS OF SCIENCE

ENGINEERING, TECHNOLOGY, AND APPLICATIONS OF SCIENCE

While three of the four sets of disciplinary core ideas (DCIs) focus on specific disciplines, the fourth concentrates on the tight relationships between science and engineering and their effects on the natural and designed world. Humans have engineered much of the environment around them: The homes we live in, the cars we drive, and the food we consume are all products of human ingenuity and technological capacity. Through scientific, engineering, and technological progress, we are able to harness nature's bounty to enhance our quality of life. Scientific inquiry and the resulting knowledge play a key role in enabling this progress, yet they are not the sole component of it. Engineers use scientific knowledge to develop technologies that address the problems and needs of the human populations. In return, these technologies and engineered solutions can contribute to the furthering of scientific inquiry.

The Engineering, Technology, and Applications of Science (ETS) DCIs address questions about the ways in which engineers use science to develop solutions, the process of design, and the effects of our designed world on nature and, ultimately, on our own fate. It is important that students understand that sometimes our solutions to existing problems can create new problems. For example, our progress in one dimension, developing

FIGURE ETS.1

Engineering, Technology, and Applications of Science Disciplinary Core Ideas and Component Ideas

ETSI: Engineering Design

    ETSI.A: Defining and delimiting an engineering problem

    ETSI.B: Developing possible solutions

    ETSI.C: Optimizing the design solution

ETS2: Links Among Engineering, Technology, Science, and Society

    ETS2.A: Interdependence of science, engineering, and technology

    ETS2.B: Influence of engineering, technology, and science on society and the natural world

refrigerants, has contributed to a new problem: the depletion of the ozone layer. Thus, the interactions between science, engineering, and technology include complex trade-offs between costs and benefits that we need to consider as a modern society.

ETS includes two core ideas: ETS1: Engineering Design and ETS2: Links Among Engineering, Technology, Science, and Society. These ideas and their components are illustrated in Figure ETS.1. Each chapter in this section addresses one of the DCIs and its component ideas.

In Chapter 13, David Kanter and David Crismond discuss ETS1: Engineering Design. This DCI explores how engineers go about identifying or setting problems, finding the best viable solution from a pool of potential solutions, and then modifying this solution to obtain an optimized solution. This process involves characterizing the problem in terms of goals and constraints of the required design and then going through an iterative process to develop and refine the design. The resulting optimized solution is not an ideal in the absolute sense, but rather represents the best-fitting solution given a set of goals and constraints and the resulting trade-offs. The authors discuss the interrelated stages of the design process and the potential difficulties students encounter in thinking about engineering design, then offer some strategies for engaging students in the imaginative and productive use of science to solve engineering problems.

In Chapter 14, Cary Sneider explores the core idea of ETS2: Links Among Engineering, Technology, Science, and Society. This chapter builds on and expands the prior DCI by highlighting the roles that science, engineering, and technology play in our everyday lives. The author discusses our capacity to change the natural world around us and the effects of this basic human tendency. As humans, we have modified, often beyond recognition, the environment in which we live so that it better suits our needs and desires. These changes have had both positive and negative impacts on the environment, and in many cases, we are just beginning to understand the effects of the changes we have made.

In conclusion, the two core ideas under Engineering, Technology, and Applications of Science can help students see the utility of science beyond developing explanatory models. The focus on engineering and technology highlights the important ways in which science is ever-present in our daily lives. This focus also underscores the ways new scientific discoveries are afforded by technological advances and our own engineered solutions.

CHAPTER 13

CORE IDEA ETS1
ENGINEERING DESIGN

David E. Kanter and David P. Crismond

What Is This Disciplinary Core Idea, and Why Is It Important?
What Is Engineering Design, and Why Is It a Disciplinary Core Idea?

This is not the first time that a new science standards document intended for a national audience has included ideas about engineering design as a central component of teaching science. The American Association for the Advancement of Science (AAAS) did something similar in 1991 with its *Benchmarks for Science Literacy* (*Benchmarks*) and the National Research Council's *National Science Education Standards* (*NSES*) did so as well in 1996. However, with the *Next Generation Science Standards* (*NGSS*; NGSS Lead States 2013), engineering design has been included as a disciplinary core idea (DCI). What does this mean for science teachers?

First of all, what is engineering design? Of all the DCIs in the *NGSS*, this one may be the most foreign to science teachers, given that they are trained in science but only rarely in engineering or design. How do engineers go about solving problems in the built world, and what disposition and skills are required?

Second, understanding that engineering design in the *NGSS* is both a verb and a noun, what does it mean to learn about engineering design as a DCI where ideas are necessarily nouns? Engineering design is explicit in the *NGSS*'s engineering practices, but learning to do engineering design as a practice or verb is very different from learning about engineering design as a noun or DCI (Cunningham 2014).

Finally, why should students learn about engineering design in the science classroom? Isn't engineering just building and construction? Where does learning science come in? These are the essential questions we aim to address by the end of this chapter.

We will begin by discussing what the engineering design DCI encompasses. Engineering design is a form of problem solving that creates products, systems, and technologies—things not found in nature. Engineering design challenges have been called ill-defined problems (Jonassen 2003) because the very problem that the designer is trying to address typically changes as the designer learns more about the problem and what is needed becomes clearer; sometimes the problem even changes entirely.

Our readers are likely to be familiar with one or more of the following engineering design challenges commonly posed in science classrooms, and which are provided here simply as a common starting point for discussing the engineering design DCI. By the end of this chapter, the reader will understand how the authors recommend improving on classic design challenges such as the following:

- **Model bridge challenge:** Create a scale model of a bridge with cardboard (or even pasta!) that can span a given distance and hold a specified load.

- **Egg drop challenge:** Design and build a system that protects an egg from cracking when dropped a distance of 3–5 m.

- **Paper tower challenge:** Design the tallest freestanding tower possible with a single sheet of paper and a foot of masking tape.

When trying to solve such engineering design challenges, the work will typically take place in three phases. First, engineers must read over a problem or challenge statement, called a brief, and be able to describe the problem context in their own words and how an acceptable solution must function within given constraints. Next is the creative phase of work, in which engineers propose a number of different ways to solve the problem, investigate some of those ideas, and then choose one to pursue more fully as a prototype. Finally, engineers build their prototype, and improve it through a process of repeated testing and adjusting, called iterative design, to optimize its performance.

Engineers move fluidly among these three phases (see Figure 13.1), which are reflected in the

FIGURE 13.1

The Three Component Ideas of the Engineering Design DCI Capture the Three Phases of Doing Engineering Design.

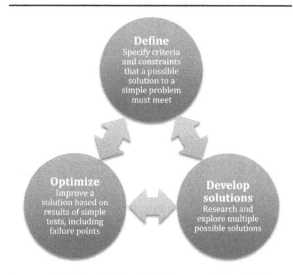

Source: NGSS Lead States 2013, Appendix 1, p. 105, grades 3–5.

three component ideas of the engineering design DCI: (1) ETS1.A: Defining and Delimiting an Engineering Problem, (2) ETS1.B: Developing Possible Solutions, and (3) ETS1.C: Optimizing the Design Solution. These are described in more detail in the section "What Are the Component Ideas of ETS1?"(p. 248).

Engineering design is also a motivating context for learning and using science concepts, as we will explore in the next part of this paper.

Why Is Engineering Design Important for the Science Classroom?

Students need to learn about the engineering design DCI for four reasons: (1) to deepen their understanding of the usefulness of core science ideas, (2) to deepen their understanding of the science practices in the *NGSS*, (3) to build their understanding of how science and engineering practices are often used together to solve real-world problems, and finally, (4) to develop a "can do" attitude with projects that engage them.

Understanding this DCI means that students can come to see the utility of using core science ideas. For example, asking students to build a bridge to span a given distance and hold a given load can require students to apply core science ideas such as net forces and stability. Students can also realize connections among different science disciplines by seeing how core science ideas from different disciplines are often used together to complete design challenges.

It is also important for students to learn this DCI because doing so reinforces and extends students' understanding of the science practices in the *NGSS* and, relatedly, the scientific mode of investigation. Science practices and engineering design practices both cover the same three spheres of activity: investigation, construction of explanations or designs using models and reasoning, and analysis and evaluation of explanations or designs (NRC 2012, p. 44). Students can come to understand the strong parallelism (along with the key differences) between scientific investigation and engineering design. For example, a model that a scientist uses of a natural system is like a designed artifact, which can be evaluated as a product would be, based on its strengths and weaknesses.

In addition, students can come to understand that engineering design and scientific investigation modes go back and forth in a dance with the one informing the other, as shown in Figure 13.2.

FIGURE 13.2

Engineering Design and Science Practices Support Interrelated Investigation Modes That Inform One Another.

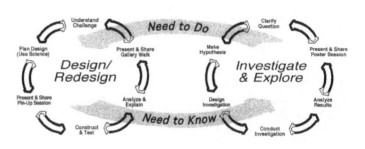

Source: Kolodner 2002.

Reinforcing and extending students' understanding of the *NGSS* science practices by comparing them with the *NGSS* practices of engineering design is one way we can build in students a broader and more flexible understanding of the scientific mode of investigation.

Lastly, engineering design is inherently motivating for students because we inhabit a world in which we are surrounded by engineered products. In the classroom, students can experience the creativity inherent in designing such products. The resultant understanding of how creative the application of science can be, as well as how much of an impact the application of science can have on their lives and on society, can motivate students to stay interested in science and pursue STEM-related careers.

What Is New About Engineering Design in the *NGSS*?

As mentioned briefly in the introduction, teaching about engineering design has been part of several recent national science education standards

13

initiatives. The AAAS Project 2061 *Benchmarks* came out in 1994, and they placed significant emphasis on engineering design. The *Benchmarks* included sophisticated ideas about engineering design: understanding constraints, trade-offs, and optimization.

In 1996, the NRC's *NSES* included an even greater emphasis on engineering design. This showed up in three different ways. First, the document used the term *technological design* synonymously with engineering design, and it established design as the technological parallel to inquiry in science. Second, each grade band in the *NSES* also included a science and technology content component, in which ideas about engineering design were just as important as science ideas. Third, the Understanding About Science and Technology standard in the *NSES* covered the nature of the engineering design cycle itself and is very similar to the Engineering Design DCI in the *NGSS*. Overall, the instructional goals around engineering design are fairly similar among all three national science standards documents. However, more so than the preceding standards documents, the *NGSS* have elevated engineering design to a DCI that is at the same level of organization in the document as the DCIs for science.

In a recent report, the National Academy of Engineering (2010) decided not to recommend the creation of separate standards for K–12 engineering education. Instead, one sees engineering folded into the *NGSS* so that teaching engineering can reinforce science education. A few states where there is a tradition of teaching engineering design as a topic unto itself have implemented separate standards in their technology education programs, but this is not what the *NGSS* advocate. Instead, the *NGSS* recommend that engineering design be folded into science teaching

and its standards. The *NGSS* aim for students to experience how science ideas can help them understand the built world and solve practical problems in it. Prior to the *NGSS*, few states other than Massachusetts and Minnesota integrated an engineering design component into their science standards (Carr, Bennett, and Strobel 2012). This may have been due to entrenched beliefs that classroom science instruction should emphasize only investigations into our natural world, even though investigations of the built world have long been part of science instruction.

What Are the Component Ideas of ETS1?

In this section, we gain a deeper understanding of ETS1: Engineering Design by elaborating on its three component ideas: (1) ETS1.A: Defining and Delimiting an Engineering Problem, (2) ETS1.B: Developing Possible Solutions, and (3) ETS1.C: Optimizing the Design Solution. As briefly mentioned in the introduction, these component ideas fit together in a very natural way to describe the engineering design cycle. They form the backbone of most published process models of engineering design, which contain three or more phases in linear, spiraling, or iterative configurations (Figure 13.3).

ETS1.A: DEFINING AND DELIMITING AN ENGINEERING PROBLEM

In almost all published engineering design cycles, design thinking starts with an engineer attempting to understand the problem at hand. Experienced engineers are aware that how they go about defining the design challenge will influence and potentially limit the potential range of solutions

FIGURE 13.3

Models of Engineering Design Contain Three or More Phases.

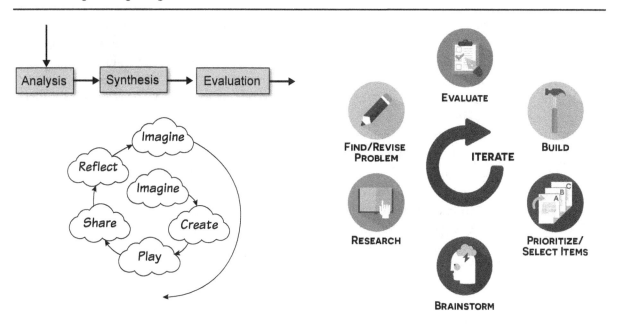

Note: Models of engineering design vary greatly in the sequence and number of activities included. Some models depict design as a linear process (upper left [Lawson 1990]), a spiraling process (lower left [Resnick 2007]), or an iterative process (adapted from GTRC 2004).

they might come up with. However, a preliminary understanding of the problem is necessary to proceed. This typically includes grasping how the design solution is supposed to function, while adhering to given constraints such as cost or time. A teacher's first mission in helping students encounter a design challenge should be comprehension. This includes helping students understand the problem context, clarifying the performance requirements, and establishing the limits of what can be counted as a viable solution.

This first component idea is revisited after students have done preliminary investigations and brainstorming, when students are ready to do what is called problem framing (Adams, Turns, and Atman 2003). Problem framing entails

problem comprehension–based reading and grasping the brief and articulating an approach that will be taken in solving the design problem.

ETS1.B: DEVELOPING POSSIBLE SOLUTIONS

The second component idea emphasizes students doing a creative part of engineering design, that is, generating multiple possible solutions to meet the criteria and constraints of the design challenge. Brainstorming and a host of like-minded strategies are used here as ways for students to consider the challenge and its many possible solutions. Brainstorming also helps students avoid a pitfall that beginning designers are often prone to: getting fixated on their first design solutions

(Gero 2011). They avoid this pitfall by producing as many ideas as possible.

Another facet of this component idea involves testing possible solutions so that one solution can be chosen for prototyping. This testing can involve gathering data using many different types of models: drawings, physical models, mathematical models, and simulations. Adding a drawing step to the traditional egg drop design challenge would involve students sketching different approaches to see which looks most viable. For example, a student might draw a cushioning system inspired by a car's air bag. Such a drawing is already a model: a simplified version of a more complex system that is being envisioned.

Science teachers worry (and rightly so) that design challenges in the science classroom can sometimes be solved by students solely using craft knowledge to build prototypes and solely using trial and error to find solutions. It is in this phase of developing possible solutions during the engineering design cycle that students can use relevant science DCIs to make big strides toward solving the design challenge. A mini-lesson on the impulse-momentum formula (see below) can prompt students to focus their solutions on particular parts of the formula. This formula states that in order to stop something that is moving, one needs to apply an impulse, a force that is applied over a finite period of time.

FΔt	=	Δmv
Impulse	=	*Change in Momentum*
[force times duration of impact]		[mass times velocity just before impact]

Students can immediately use this science formula to improve their egg drop systems. Some students design cushioning systems to extend the duration of impact, which for a given impulse results in a proportional decrease in the force on the egg during impact. Other students use a parachute to slow the egg down during descent so that it hits the pavement at a slower speed, with less momentum, thus reducing the impulse that brings the egg to a stop. Some students simply try to keep the total mass of their egg drop systems low to keep the total momentum of the system to a minimum. Ultimately, students learn and use the science DCI related to Newton's second law—from which the impulse-momentum equation is derived—to design solutions.

The above example aims to show how a "classic" engineering design challenge can be improved by careful scaffolding designed to motivate students to learn and use science DCIs in the context of engineering design. Overall, students are required to go beyond trial and error to articulate the science behind suggested modifications that should improve their designs. Insuring that our design challenges do motivate students to learn and use science DCIs is essential if we are to justify spending science instructional time on engineering design. This important issue is discussed further in the "Which Strategies Work for Teaching Engineering Design?" section (pp. 258–259).

Students can also investigate possible solutions by designing and conducting investigations in which they control all but one design variable to better understand how the device they are creating works. Insights from these experiments can help students choose from among competing approaches and later suggest ways to modify the final prototype they will develop. Improving on the traditional egg drop design challenge, students might conduct fair-test investigations with a proposed parachute approach, systematically varying the size of a vent hole in the canopy while controlling all other features of the design. Another team might experiment with systematically varying the canopy's surface area. The outcome variable in both cases would be the length of time it takes the falling egg to reach the ground intact. As discussed in the "How Does Scientific Investigation Help Teach Engineering Design?"section (p. 259), these types of investigations are critical opportunities for students to experience how the *NGSS* engineering and science practices support one another.

ETS1.C: OPTIMIZING THE DESIGN SOLUTION

The third component idea emphasizes students understanding the last part of the engineering design cycle, which focuses on iteratively building and testing prototypes. Note that the prototype testing done here is to compare performances of earlier and later prototypes, in contrast with the experimental testing described as part of ETS1.B. Learning from failure is a much-touted mantra for engineers, and with good reason. Engineers with any experience doing design work have seen repeatedly, and almost without exception, that the first prototype they build is rarely the best solution. Some aspects of the prototype will undoubtedly fail. These failures need to be noticed and then understood in order for the prototype to be improved. With a model bridge challenge, students may first think that a simple beam bridge design would be sufficient, but after using a bridge simulation program (e.g., Engineering Encounters' Bridge Designer 2015 software), they determine that supporting structural members are needed.

After building their first actual bridge with support trusses, they might notice that one truss was bending more than others or that two trusses keep coming apart. Such prototype testing will lead students to figure out ways to strengthen the bridge where the prototype testing reveals a weakness in the design.

Students come to understand that engineering design requires this kind of cycling that yields improvements, often in small steps. Through this process of iteration, of making changes to address earlier failures large and small and then conducting subsequent tests and learning from any new failures, a design solution can be optimized.

It bears repeating that just as was the case during ETS1.B, ETS1.C is helped by students learning and using science DCIs. A knowledge of relevant science concepts can help students identify ways to optimize their designs that may not have otherwise been intuitive or readily discovered. In the bridge example, a knowledge of the balance of forces (statics) and the use of free-body diagrams can lead to less trial-and-error designing and even to creative new choices regarding the location and placement of a bridge's supporting structures. Additionally, the science practices continue to be helpful in optimizing the design solution and are useful for designing and conducting fair-test investigations on one design variable at a time.

Ultimately, students who deeply understand all three of these engineering design DCI component ideas will also understand that they work together and that engineers move fluidly and iteratively among the phases of the engineering design process (see Figure 13.1, p. 246).

How Does Student Understanding of This Disciplinary Core Idea Develop Over Time?

Students' knowledge of engineering design and its component ideas builds and develops over time. We briefly present ideas about engineering design "learning progressions" across grade bands, synthesizing information found in the *NGSS* Appendix I on Engineering Design, in *A Framework for K–12 Science Education* (NRC 2012), and in the research literature. That said, the existing research about the development of students' ideas about engineering design is rather sparse, and this is our best effort to provide a progression and a rationale based on current knowledge in the field.

Elementary School

In grades K–2, students can understand that engineers are able to address design problems that they think up or that are provided to them. Students learn that this is done by making observations, asking questions, and gathering information. Students in this grade band can come to know that one typically proposes more than one design solution to the same challenge and that these can take the form of sketches, drawings, or physical models. When thinking of solutions, students can also understand that these solutions typically are not wholly original—that is the job of an inventor, not an engineer—and can come to realize that they can find and adjust or combine solutions to best meet the goals of the design. These students can also understand that one can compare different design solutions to the same design challenge. Engineering design curricula developed for this grade band emphasize simple troubleshooting

and iteratively improving a design (e.g., *Now You're Cooking: Designing Solar Ovens* [EiE 2008] or *Invent a Wheel* [City Technology 2013]). For example, in *Invent a Wheel*, students in grades K–2 can learn about iteration when they create and redesign different ways to move an object across a table with the least amount of force by using marbles as bearings, pencils as rollers, or wheel-and-axle systems. They are able to observe and identify sources of friction in the prototypes and suggest ways to improve their performance. By the end of this grade band, students move beyond the idea that solutions should be selected in a near-random fashion.

In grades 3–5, students can begin to understand engineering design as a more formalized and differentiated type of problem solving. Learning from failures in prototype performances leads not only to improvements in the product itself but to further improvements in ideas about how devices work. In this grade band, students can learn that design problem definitions include the criteria and constraints that the solutions must address. These students can use fair-test experiments in which a single variable of the design is investigated. They can also look at the evidence they gather from their experiments for patterns in data regarding how key design variables influence product performances. Students can build connections between these experiments and their growing understanding of scientific experimentation.

Middle School

In grades 6–8, students come to know that one must specify the criteria and constraints associated with engineering design problems with more precision, often using numbers. These criteria and

FIGURE 13.4

The Fastenings Chooser Chart

	Ease of use	Ease of fitting	Variety of types	Strength	Ease of care	Cost
Buttons 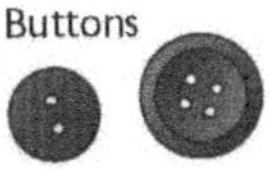	● ●	● ● ● ● holes ●	● ● ● ●	● ●	● ●	▲ ▲
Toggles 	● ● ●	● ● ●	●	● ●	● ●	▲ ▲
Zips 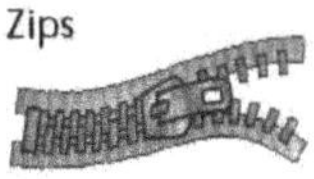	● ● ●	●	● ●	● ● ● ●	● ●	▲ ▲ ▲
Velcro 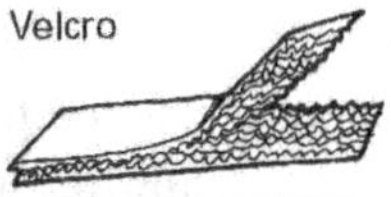	● ● ● ●	● ● ● ●	●	● ● ● ●	● ● ●	▲ ▲
Clips/buckles 	● ●	● ● ●	● ●	● ● ●	● ● ●	▲ ▲ ▲

● = few blobs for worse, ● ● ● ● = more blobs for better
▲ = cheap, ▲ ▲ ▲ = most expensive

The chooser chart makes visible various fastener options and their competing attributes, including costs to be weighed when making design decisions.

constraints may include ones related to aesthetics and how solutions look and behave. In this grade band, students can understand for the first time the need to optimize design solutions. Such thinking requires students to learn to reason with ratios of costs and benefits. This is directly related to the *NGSS* practice of Using Mathematics and Computational Thinking. The cognitive demands of optimizing a final design solution are not trivial. Doing so requires coordinating two or more competing concerns (e.g., keeping costs lower, which typically lessens product quality, while still improving performance). This is often expressed as a cost–benefit ratio. While such ratios can be understood by younger learners (Purzer et al. 2013) and used to *maximize* performance along a single dimension of a design, it is only in grades 6–8 that students come to understand the need to balance multiple competing concerns and thus optimize their product's performance using numerical weighting systems and trade-off matrixes, which we discuss next.

Developmental theories such as Fischer's skill theory (Fischer 1980, p. 490; Fischer and Bidell 1998) suggest that K–2 designers would tend to

focus only on the strengths of a design idea they preferred or the drawbacks of an idea they did not like. They would be able to coordinate and balance fewer pros and cons than older students when making design decisions (Crismond and Adams 2012, pp. 761–762). For example, students can be asked to design a rain jacket that is comfortable to play in and can be easily opened and shut. One of the decisions that the student designers will need to make involves which type of fastener they will use: buttons, zippers, Velcro, and so on. Five different types of fasteners are shown in the chooser chart (Figure 13.4, p. 253; Barlex and Givens 1995, p. 50) to make visual the competing concerns that designers weigh when selecting from among a number of viable options.

Each fastener option can be assessed according to certain beneficial behaviors that are important to consider when selecting a jacket's fasteners: ease of use, ease of fitting, strength, and ease of care. Designers are continually faced with a counter issue, such as cost, which forces them to balance competing concerns. The best fasteners might be too expensive. Grade 6–8 students can hold all these issues in mind, whereas younger learners might not be able to hold as many ideas about multiple competing concerns in mind. These older students can also develop an awareness that design problems have no single right answers and that the original problem framing, the solution approach, and its assumptions will often need to be revisited at some point during the design process. In contrast, in grades 3–5, students can only weigh one beneficial behavior at a time against cost and only in more qualitative terms, without the kind of numerical weighting system shown in the chooser chart. In grades K–2, students can consider only a few of the fastener options most familiar to them and can work to

systematically and iteratively improve each one, but they will act without any notion of balancing pros against cons.

High School

In grades 9–12, students can come to know engineering design as an approach with the potential to solve problems of broad social and global concern. Such problems involve more and more varied users, whose needs often clash. Students are also able to approach problems that require consideration of additional constraints set by society. (For more on this theme, please see Chapter 14, "Core Idea ETS2: Links Among Engineering, Technology, Science, and Society," p. 263). In this grade band, students can also continue to deepen their knowledge of the importance of using numerical data derived from investigations and quantitative analytic methods to make and justify design choices. This is another way to reinforce the *NGSS* practice of using mathematics and computational thinking.

While this section focuses on the development of students' understanding of just the engineering design DCI across grade bands, as we began to discuss above and continue in the "Which Strategies Work for Teaching Engineering Design?" section (pp. 258–259), a well-chosen engineering design challenge provides students with the motivation and opportunity to learn various science DCIs and subsequently use that science in instrumental ways to *optimize* a design. However, as seen in the other chapters in this volume, students' understandings of the science DCIs are changing across grade bands at the same time. As such, an effort must be made to identify design challenges for a particular grade band that use not just an appropriate depth of understanding of engineering design but also adequately address science ideas at the depth of understanding that is anticipated for students of that age. It is an important goal to in this way interweave the engineering design DCI with the science DCIs, in addition to interweaving these DCIs with the engineering and science practices (as well as the crosscutting concepts) as emphasized by the *NGSS*.

What Do Students Find Challenging About Engineering Design?

There are a number of patterns in some beginning designers' thinking that engineering design educators and researchers have identified as commonly held ideas that teachers should be on the lookout for, just as they would be for commonly held ideas that students have about other science DCIs.

Students think that *design is the same as invention* and therefore believe that what they are being requested to come up with in solving a design challenge must be something completely new and original. With this commonly held idea in mind, students tend to view looking at "prior art" (things previously made by other designers) or the work of another design team as cheating. They do not understand that the synthesis of two or more existing ideas is typical in engineering design and that engineers do this all the time.

Students believe that the problem described in the design brief is well defined, just like end-of-chapter questions in a textbook. Therefore, they think it is *okay to commit to a single solution pathway*, which they do too early and proceed immediately to follow, but which quite typically does not address aspects of the problem that will only become apparent later on (Cross 2000).

Students mistakenly believe that they need to *define and frame the problem and check assumptions only once*—at the outset of the engineering design process—rather than at regular intervals (Adams, Turns, and Atman 2003). Once their first prototype is built, students need to know that they will have to reflect back and question the assumptions that they began with and their initial understanding of the design challenge. Not doing so can result in students working too long on a solution that has fatal flaws, addresses suboptimal goals, or violates key constraints.

Beginning designers also mistakenly think that *solutions that do not work should be thrown in the trash*. Films depicting the frustrated engineer working at a desk with dozens of crumpled sheets of paper destined for the garbage suggest that bad ideas should be trashed rather than archived and reviewed. One of the enduring challenges of teaching engineering design is finding ways to preserve students' interim ideas so that they can reflect on the evolution of their ideas and see how their framing of the challenge has changed over time.

Another beginner's idea is that there can be a *final solution and right answer to any design challenge*. All experienced engineering designers recognize that there will always be another version of the design on the horizon that might be an even better solution (Crismond and Adams 2012, p. 750). Designers know that they must set a point in time when they will "freeze" their design (Wedman and Tessmer 1991), after which no fundamental changes can be made. They do this for sake of good time management, while still acknowledging that a "final solution" will never be reached.

Beginning designers *see no need to repeat steps they have already done*. This can be driven by the mistaken view that the steps of the design process are linear as opposed to design being an iterative

13

process (see Figure 13.3, p. 249). They think design practices are done in an invariant order, once and only once, and that the design work is concluded when the last step is finished (Newstetter and McCracken 2001, p. 68). Beginning designers find iteration frustrating and a poor use of time (Adams and Fralick 2010). It is pretty straightforward to demonstrate to students through example the value of iterating upon a solution that represents a "good start" but is not yet a finished idea, and then students can come to understand that design involves learning from failure.

Finally, students can be quite surprised that *science ideas have utility in engineering design* (Kanter 2010; Crismond 1997). They may have previously only ever learned science ideas outside of the context of a real-world question or challenge and thus have never successfully used science ideas to solve a real-world problem as opposed to an end-of-chapter assessment. As a result, when working on an engineering design challenge, students may expect to complete the challenge relying solely on craft knowledge or trial-and-error approaches or systematic approaches but not ones informed by any previously learned science ideas. Students seem to be expressing their impression that science ideas have no practical utility for engineering design when they state in science class, "I won't ever need to use this."

What Approaches Can We Use to Teach About This Disciplinary Core Idea?
Which Engineering Design Challenges Work for the Science Classroom?

While the focus of this chapter has been on the engineering design DCI itself and not on the engineering practices that students will be asked to perform, it is almost always the case that the best way to motivate someone to learn *about* engineering design is to involve them in *doing* engineering design and have them reflect on the process along the way. From an early age, children naturally engage in engineering design thinking—even though they do it tacitly or unconsciously—as they aim to contribute to their own built world. They can therefore be very motivated when encountering engineering design challenges in the science classroom. We next discuss ideas for teaching the engineering design DCI by involving students in doing engineering design.

The use of engineering design projects in the science classroom may already be familiar to some science teachers. Tasks found in science curricula that started to be developed post-Sputnik like the Elementary Science Studies (e.g., clay boats [EDC 1976], simple electric circuits, or electromagnets) were at the time called "scientific investigations." We might call these "engineering design challenges" today. Compared to those of the past, today's engineering design challenges are not very different: designing a toy car that uses different propulsion systems (EDC 2002; GTRC 2009), designing more personally relevant objects (e.g., a shopping bag; (Benenson and Neujahr 2002), redesigning items from nature (e.g., whirligigs that work like maple tree seeds; Crismond, Soobyian, and Cain 2013), or doing nature-inspired design (e.g., biomimicry, drawing on the microscopic structure of burdock burrs to design Velcro; Grillo 1960, p. 47).

In addition to these kinds of challenges that emphasize the building of mechanisms to perform a particular task, doing a "conceptual design" of just a plan or an approach can be just as motivating and fruitful an engineering design learning opportunity (while oftentimes less materials intensive). For instance, in *Amazon Mission* (Museum of Science, Wong, and Brizuela 2007), students must prevent the outbreak of influenza in a remote village in the Amazon. They must devise a 30-day plan that will use one or more of four interventions, each of which have different levels of effectiveness and costs, to insure that the percentage of villagers who get infected is never above 25%, all within a given budget.

Those interested in curricula that focus on the use of engineering design challenges in the classroom can find some great resources in a review of K–12 engineering education curricula by Ken Welty (NAE and NRC 2009) and Cary Sneider's *The Go-To Guide for Engineering Curricula* series (2014).

In sum, there is a wide range of engineering design challenges available to use with students. However, there is a problem: Students can pursue engineering design challenges but skirt the science and instead use craft knowledge to arrive at a designed solution. They can rely solely on craft knowledge to build a prototype and use trial and error to get to viable solutions without ever needing to learn or use any science ideas. Engineering design challenges only belong in the science classroom if they can create students' demand to learn new science ideas and science practices and also provide students with the opportunity to use the new science ideas and practices to make progress on the design challenge.

Let us look next at an example of how to solve this essential problem using curriculum design and pedagogical approaches. The *I, Bio* curriculum asks middle grades students to redesign their school lunch menus. To do so, they must design ways to measure the energy in food and the energy their bodies use up. Kanter (2010) describes the difficulty of developing the *I, Bio* design challenge to motivate students to learn new science content. The teacher ultimately knows that the new content will be helpful to students to do the design challenge, but that it is necessarily unfamiliar to students at the outset. Kanter describes curriculum design approaches called Unpack the Task, Highlight an Incongruity, and Try to Apply to address this problem. He then discusses a second problem of insuring that the design challenge allows students to use all the new content they have learned to improve their designs. He explains how to Analyze and Refocus the design challenge or Identify an Alternative to it to make sure that all the new content is used. Lastly, he describes the need for students to have the chance to use the new content close in time to when it was first learned, and how to Piece Apart the design challenge to do this (Kanter 2010).

Middle grades students who did the *I, Bio* design challenge improved in their knowledge of human biology content 3.7 times more than what would otherwise have been anticipated. They also improved 2.2 times more than would have been anticipated in their ability to apply the content in a new context. These outcomes suggest that it is possible to craft engineering design challenges with a good chance of helping students learn science content; however, we have to recognize that

13

this is in no way guaranteed for every engineering design challenge as we might first conceive of it. It takes a fair amount of work to craft an engineering design challenge to teach science content, but it is ultimately doable, and the student learning outcomes can be very impressive.

Which Strategies Work for Teaching Engineering Design?

This section does not aim to be a comprehensive review of all the many engineering design teaching approaches that have been developed in the last decades by a multitude of engineering design instructors and researchers. Instead, what follows are some techniques that were compiled in a recent review paper (Crismond and Adams 2012; see right-most column of Table 1). These teaching strategies are organized around the three phases of doing engineering design described above: (1) Defining and Delimiting an Engineering Problem, (2) Developing Possible Solutions, and (3) Optimizing the Design Solution.

TEACHING STRATEGIES FOR DEFINING AND DELIMITING AN ENGINEERING PROBLEM

One teaching strategy that can be used is called PIES (Physical, Intellectual, Emotional, and Social). The PIES approach asks students to consider the physical, intellectual, emotional, and social needs of a product's intended users. Students can also be asked to do a product dissection, for which they take apart or reverse engineer an existing product that is similar to the one they are trying to develop so they can understand the challenges at hand. Finally, having students write a product history, in which they follow the evolution of a product

of interest can help them better understand some key ideas associated with the product's various forms and functions.

TEACHING STRATEGIES FOR DEVELOPING POSSIBLE SOLUTIONS

This phase of design work involves generating and considering a large number of possible solutions. In the popular press, there have been a host of approaches proposed to help people be more creative. However, beginning designers who are elementary and middle school age need convincing that such strategies can work because they often stop generating ideas once a viable one has been put forward. Some approaches to changing students' ways of seeing the problem and helping them generate a large number of possible solutions include reviewing catalogs (the internet can serve this purpose), using gestures and very rough sketches to get down ideas that come to mind, sketching, or having students rapidly make simple models from easily-shaped materials like clay or index cards and tape.

TEACHING STRATEGIES FOR OPTIMIZING THE DESIGN SOLUTION

Supporting beginning designers in optimizing a solution can hinge on whether those children have enough time to iteratively built, test, and improve on that design. Students need support with various aspects of time management, and teachers can help them set interim goals and "staging posts." Students can also be asked to produce a design storyboard of their project (Sadler, Coyle, and Schwartz 2000), which can show teachers if the performed iterations were helpful in improving the product. Teaching even younger students troubleshooting can help them optimize their prototypes while getting an opportunity to use science concepts during a meaningful moment of design work. Science concepts give traction to explanations of why failures occur (Crismond 2013). One model for such work has students ask three questions when testing a prototype: (1) What problems were noticed during testing? (2) Why did the problems occur? and (3) How might you fix the problem?

How Does Scientific Investigation Help Teach Engineering Design?

Another important idea about teaching engineering design in the science classroom is to recognize that science teachers are already starting with a deep knowledge of the science practices (as well as the science DCIs and crosscutting concepts) they need to know to teach engineering design.

For instance, science teachers already know the ropes when it comes to supporting students in the science practice of Obtaining, Evaluating, and Communicating Information. Applying this to teaching engineering design, science teachers can readily help students produce the kind of product history described above.

Science teachers who help their students make sense of natural phenomena are already expert at helping their students brainstorm, whether they know it or not. They regularly do this when engaging students in the practices of Analyzing and Interpreting Data and Constructing Explanations by asking students to generate many possible explanations (hypotheses) that account for what they've observed.

Science teachers who engage students in all the practices related to scientific investigation are also uniquely poised to support students in optimizing their design solutions by helping them create and interpret fair-test experiments. Such scientific experiments initially help students understand how their designs work and later help them ascertain the impact of changing product features on product performance. When students carry out investigations focused on a single design feature or variable, the interpretation of such investigations can be translated into design rules of thumb (Crismond 2011, pp. 244–246), that is, design recommendations that can be used by other classmates in their own work. The designing and interpreting of fair-test experiments is also used to compare one prototype with another and to diagnose problems with the prototype that can be fixed through iterative design.

Conclusion

We have outlined a number of difficulties faced by teachers trying to integrate teaching engineering design into their science classrooms, not the least of which being that engineering design may be unfamiliar to some science teachers. The authors hope this chapter has been a step forward in helping science teachers become more familiar with engineering design.

We have advocated that the best way to teach about the noun of the engineering design DCI is by involving students in doing the verb of engineering design and its related practices. If we focus on teaching only the engineering design DCI *separate* from the engineering practices, we run the risk that the engineering design DCI could be "safely overlooked" even while the *NGSS* are adopted (Cunningham 2014). It is both a workable and necessary approach that we integrate engineering design into the science classroom as both a DCI and a set of practices.

13

Both teaching about and doing engineering design seems as if it will take up class time that science teachers feel they do not have to spare. However, it is important to recognize that choosing a design challenge that requires students to learn and use science DCIs and science practices simultaneously can motivate students to learn these new science concepts and provide opportunities for them to apply and make meaningful connections among science ideas. As discussed in Chapter 1 of this book (p. 1), interweaving the three dimensions of DCIs, science and engineering practices, and crosscutting concepts to make sense of phenomena and design solutions to problems is what is unique about the *NGSS*. In this chapter, we have emphasized the additional opportunity that resides in carefully interweaving the science DCIs and practices with the engineering design DCI and practices. Students' motivation to learn science can be dramatically improved by connecting science to its real-world applications. Students can come to anticipate the practical utility of science ideas and practices. This understanding that science can be relevant to students' lives and goals for the future can help keep students involved with science as they go through their schooling. At the same time, teaching engineering design can deepen students' learning about the science DCIs themselves and enhance their skill with the various science and engineering practices.

For these reasons, we conclude that time spent on engineering design, if done well, can actually reinforce and amplify the goals of science education rather than being viewed as taking away from class time. We hope this chapter will serve as a useful resource to the science education community to make engineering design ideas and practices a cornerstone of the 21st-century science classroom.

REFERENCES

American Association for the Advancement of Science (AAAS). 1993. *Benchmarks for science literacy.* New York: Oxford University Press.

Adams, R. S., and B. Fralick. 2010. Work in progress: A conceptions of design instrument as an assessment tool. Proceedings of the Frontiers in Education Conference, Washington, DC.

Adams, R. S., J. Turns, and C. J. Atman. 2003. Educating effective engineering designers: The role of reflective practice. *Design Studies* 24 (3): 2752–2794.

Barlex, D., and N. P. Givens. 1995. The Nuffield approach to the teaching of mechanisms at key stage 3. Paper presented at the IDATER Conference, Loughborough, UK.

Benenson, G., and J. Neujahr. 2002. *Packaging and other structures.* Portsmouth, NH: Heinemann.

Carr, R. L., L. D. Bennett IV, and J. Strobel. 2012. Engineering in the K–12 STEM standards of the 50 U.S. States: An analysis of presence and extent. *Journal of Engineering Education* 101 (3): 539–564.

City Technology. 2013. Invent a wheel. *http://citytechnology.org/invent-wheel.*

Crismond, D. 1997. Investigate-and-redesign tasks as a context for learning and doing science and technology: A study of naive, novice and expert high school and adult designers doing product comparisons and redesign tasks. Unpublished doctoral dissertation.

Crismond, D. 2011. Scaffolding strategies that integrate engineering design and scientific inquiry in project-based learning environments. In *Fostering human development through engineering and technology education,* ed. M. Barak and M. Hacker, 235–256. Rotterdam, the Netherlands: Sense Publishers.

Crismond, D. 2013. Troubleshooting: A bridge that connects engineering design and scientific inquiry practices. *Science Scope* 36 (6): 74–79.

Crismond, D. P., and R. S. Adams. 2012. The informed design teaching and learning matrix. *Journal of Engineering Education* 101 (4): 738–797.

Crismond, D., M. Soobyian, and R. Cain. 2013. Taking engineering design out for a spin: How a simple whirligig design challenge can highlight both inquiry and design. *Science and Children* 50 (5): 34–39.

Cross, N. 2000. *Engineering design methods: Strategies for product design*. 3rd ed. New York: John Wiley & Sons.

Cunningham, C. 2014. Teaching engineering practices. *Journal of Science Teacher Education* 25 (2): 197–210.

Educational Development Center (EDC). 1976. *Teachers guide for clay boats: Experiments with floating, sinking, and simple volume relationships*. New York: McGraw-Hill.

Educational Development Center (EDC). 2002. *Design it! Projects*. Farmingdale, NY: Kelvin.

Engineering is Elementary (EiE). 2008. *Now you're cooking: Designing solar ovens*. Boston: Museum of Science.

Fischer, K. W. 1980. A theory of cognitive development: The control and construction of hierarchies of skills. *Psychological Review* 87 (6): 477–531.

Fischer, K. W., and T. R. Bidell. 1998. Dynamic development of psychological structures in action and thought. In *Handbook of child psychology: Volume 1, Theoretical models of human development*, 5th ed., ed. R. M. Lerner and W. Damon, 467–561. New York: Wiley.

Georgia Tech Research Corporation (GTRC). 2004. Design in the classroom: Cyclic design model. *http://designintheclassroom.com/designProcess/whatIsDesign/designStrategies.html*.

Georgia Tech Research Corporation (GTRC). 2009. *Project-based inquiry science: Vehicles in motion*. Armonk, NY: It's About Time, Herff Jones Educational Division.

Gero, J. S. 2011. Fixation and commitment while designing and its measurement. *Journal of Creative Behavior* 45 (2): 108–115.

Grillo, P. J. 1960. *Form, function and design*. New York: Dover Publications.

Jonassen, D. H. 2003. *Learning to solve problems: An instructional design guide*. San Francisco: Pfeiffer.

Kanter, D. 2010. Doing the project and learning the content: Designing project-based science curricula for meaningful understanding. *Science Education* 94 (3): 525–551.

Kolodner, J. L. 2002. Learning by design: Iterations of design challenges for better learning of science skills. *Bulleting of the Japanese Cognitive Science Society* 9 (3): 338–350.

Lawson, B. 1990. *How designers think: The design process demystified*. Oxford, UK: Butterworth Architecture.

Museum of Science, P. Y. Wong, and B. M. Brizuela. 2007. *Amazon mission*. Portland, ME: Walch Education.

National Academy of Engineering (NAE). 2010. *Standards for K–12 engineering education?* Washington, DC: National Academies Press.

National Academy of Engineering and National Research Council (NAE and NRC). 2009. *Engineering in K–12 education: Understanding the status and improving the prospects*. Washington, DC: National Academies Press.

National Research Council (NRC). 1996. *National science education standards.* Washington, DC: National Academies Press.

National Research Council (NRC). 2012. *A framework for K–12 science education: Practices, crosscutting concepts, and core ideas.* Washington, DC: National Academies Press.

Newstetter, W. C., and W. M. McCracken. 2001. Novice conceptions of design: Implications for the design of learning environments. In *Design knowing and learning: Cognition in design education*, ed. C. Eastman, M. McCracken, and W. Newstetter, 63–77. Amsterdam: Elsevier.

NGSS Lead States. 2013. *Next Generation Science Standards: For states, by states.* Washington, DC: National Academies Press. *www.nextgenscience. org/next-generation-science-standards.*

Purzer, S., J. Wang, D. Duncan-Wiles, and J. Strobel. 2013. Elementary students' abilities in engineering design: Optimization and tradeoff methods. Paper presented at the National Conference of Research in Science Teaching. Rio Grande, Puerto Rico.

Resnick, M. 2007. All I really need to know (about creative thinking) I learned (by studying how children learn) in kindergarten. Paper presented at the 6th Creativity and Cognition Conference, Washington, DC.

Sadler, P. M., H. P. Coyle, and M. Schwartz. 2000. Engineering competitions in the middle school classroom: Key elements in developing effective design challenges. *Journal of the Learning Sciences* 9 (3): 299–327.

Sneider, C. I., ed. 2014. *The go-to guide for engineering curricula, preK–5: Choosing and using the best instructional materials for your students.* Thousand Oaks, CA: Corwin Press.

Wedman, J., and M. Tessmer. 1991. Adapting instructional design to project circumstance: The layers of necessity model. *Educational Technology* 31 (7): 48–52.

CHAPTER 14

CORE IDEA ETS2

LINKS AMONG ENGINEERING, TECHNOLOGY, SCIENCE, AND SOCIETY

Cary Sneider

The inclusion of engineering in *A Framework for K–12 Science Education* (*Framework*; NRC 2012) introduces a fundamental change in the nature and spirit of science education. It is no longer sufficient for students to "know and understand" the core ideas in the science disciplines. Students are expected to be able to apply those core ideas to solve real problems that make a difference in people's lives.

Chapter 13 was concerned with the process of defining problems, generating and testing solutions, and optimizing the best solution to solve the problem. This chapter expands the field of view to encompass the broader context within which problems are defined and solved. The intent expressed in the *Framework* is to do more than impart information and develop skills. Rather, the essential goal is to engage students' interest, motivation, and commitment as they learn what engineering is all about and why it is important in people's lives.

The actual doing of science or engineering can also pique students' curiosity, capture their

interest, and motivate their continued study; the insights thus gained help them recognize that the work of scientists and engineers is a creative endeavor—one that has deeply affected the world they live in. Students may then recognize that science and engineering can contribute to meeting many of the major challenges that confront society today, such as generating sufficient energy, preventing and treating disease, maintaining supplies of fresh water and food, and addressing climate change. Any education that focuses predominantly on the detailed products of scientific labor—the facts of science—without developing an understanding of how those facts were established or that ignores the many important applications of science in the world misrepresents science and marginalizes the importance of engineering. (NRC 2012, pp. 42–43)

The engineering design process described in Chapter 13 is designated in the *Framework* as ETS1. The broader context described in this chapter concerns the disciplinary core idea (DCI) ETS2: Links Among Engineering, Technology,

Science, and Society. The ideas in ETS2 directly address the issues in the paragraph above: how science and engineering interact and their influence on society and the environment.

What Is This Disciplinary Core Idea, and Why Is It Important?

ETS2: Links Among Engineering, Technology, Science, and Society has two component ideas. The first is ETS2.A: Interdependence of Science, Engineering, and Technology. The second is ETS2.B: Influence of Engineering, Technology, and Science on Society and the Natural World. Neither of these two important ideas is entirely new to science education. What is new is the deep integration of these ideas into the fabric of new science standards.

These core ideas will enrich any science curriculum by injecting the human element—how teams of people with complementary skills work together on problems of great import and how the technological decisions we make as individuals affect society and the environment. It is the intention of the *Framework* authors that these ideas not be relegated to a chapter at the beginning of a textbook or left out because they are not thought to reflect the "hard science" expected in an advanced course. Like all of the other DCIs, these ideas are essential for all students to learn, and they are best learned in the context of the traditional science disciplines.

ETS2.A: Interdependence of Science, Engineering, and Technology

A BRIEF HISTORY

The notion that it is important for all students to learn how science and engineering move each other forward was first expressed as an important idea in *Science for All Americans* (Rutherford and Ahlgren 1990), the precursor to *Benchmarks for Science Literacy* (AAAS 1993), and arguably one of the first standards documents for science education in the United States. The idea was stated simply as follows: "Engineers use knowledge of science and technology, together with strategies of design, to solve practical problems. In return, technology provides the eyes and ears of science—and some of the muscle too" (Rutherford and Ahlgren 1990, p. 24).

Rutherford and Ahlgren are not just saying that technologies such as telescopes, microscopes, and computers have made it possible for scientists to make great discoveries. While that is certainly true, the desire to improve a practical technology has additionally often spurred the advancement of science. For example, the theory of conservation of energy owes much to the need to improve the efficiency of commercial steam engines; mapping the human genome has been stimulated by a desire to improve the technology of genetic engineering and cure inherited diseases.

The ideas expressed by Rutherford and Ahlgren in 1990 are not essentially different from the first component of the DCI in the *Framework*:

The fields of science and engineering are mutually supportive, and scientists and engineers often work together in teams, especially in fields at the borders of engineering. Advances in science offer new capabilities, new materials, or new understanding of processes that can be applied through engineering to produce advances in technology. Advances in technology, in turn, provide scientists with new capabilities to probe the natural world at larger or smaller scales; to record, manage, and analyze data; and to model ever more complex systems with greater precision. In addition, engineers' efforts to develop or improve technologies often raise new questions for scientists' investigation. (NRC 2012, pp. 210–211)

The first component of this DCI points toward a curriculm that integrates science, engineering, and technology and teaches that they are interdependent.

ETS2.B: The Influence of Engineering, Technology, and Science on Society and the Natural World

The second component of this DCI brings together two movements in science education: environmental education and science, technology, and society. Environmental education has roots in the broader movement to recognize the ways that human activities are affecting the environment. Some trace the rapid growth of the movement to Rachel Carson's seminal book, *Silent Spring* (Carson 1962). The environmental education movement has since matured, and publications such as *Excellence in Environmental Education: Guidelines for Learning* (NAAEE 2010), by the North American Association for Environmental Education, have provided helpful guidance for teachers and curriculum developers in how to support science standards through environmental education. The science, technology, and society movement in the United States owes much to Robert E. Yager, its most prominent spokesperson in the science education community (e.g., Yager 1996).

Learning about the Influence of Engineering, Technology, and Science on Society and the Natural World involves understanding the scientific questions and technologies that gave rise to the issues in the first place, and how they play out in human affairs. As examples, consider just two societal and environmental issues that are also two of the major DCIs: PS3: Energy (in the physical sciences discipline) and ESS3: Earth and Human Activity (in Earth and space sciences).

ENERGY

The use of energy resources to power industrial civilization takes a toll on the environment, in terms of air pollution, global warming, and loss of natural habitat when resources are extracted or as a result of oil spills or other energy-related catastrophes. To understand the causes of these problems, students need hands-on experiences in energy sources, forms, and transformations, along with the history of how our nation's energy infrastructure developed through a number of R & D cycles. Learning experiences that lead to a full understanding of this issue will likely take several years. Here are examples of curriculum materials that provide experiences related to energy, at the elementary, middle, and high school levels.

Upper elementary: "Whispers of Willing Wind" is a unit on energy for the upper elementary grades in the Invention, Innovation, Inquiry (I³) curriculum by the International Technology and Engineering Educators Association (*www.iteea.org/i3*). Student teams begin by researching the positive and negative impacts of the major energy sources, looking at fossil fuel power plants and solar and nuclear energy sources, and considering the differences between renewable and nonrenewable resources. Next, they study their family's energy use and consider ways to conserve energy. As a hands-on activity, the students

14

design and build a working wind turbine following given criteria and constraints. They test their turbines by using them to draw water from a simulated well, and they keep track of their work in engineering design journals. Since the heart of nearly all devices that generate electric power is a turbine, the hands-on activity helps students envision how a wide variety of power plants function.

Middle school: Investigating and Questioning our World through Science and Technology (IQWST; *www.activatelearning.com/iqwst*) is a middle school curriculum that emphasizes the big ideas in science. Each module is animated by a driving question to engage students in active inquiry and engineering. In a middle school unit on energy, the driving question is, "Why do some things stop and others keep going?" The module begins with a video of a complicated Rube Goldberg machine. As the students watch each part of the machine interact with the next, they begin to wonder if a machine could be constructed that goes on and on forever. Then they are given materials to design such a machine.

Rube Goldberg machines are a lot of fun for students because they are very creative. From an instructional point of view they are exciting because they provide rich illustrations of energy transfers and transformations and provide opportunities for students to consider factors such as friction and how friction might be reduced to enable the machine to go on longer.

High school: Curricula such as those mentioned above lay the foundation for later exploration of the physics of energy and the effects of energy generation on society and the natural world at the high school level. For example, Global Systems Science (*www.globalsystemsscience. org*) is a ninth-grade curriculum about major global challenges, including climate change,

ozone depletion, and loss of biodiversity. One of the units, "Energy Use," begins with inquiry activities concerning the use of electrical energy to support civilization. Students construct electric motors and test different types of lightbulbs to determine which are really more energy efficient. They follow the wires from electrical outlets to the power plants, and then to the sources of fuel to drive different kinds of power plants. They learn about the pros and cons of different sources of electrical power, and the effect of these different sources on the environment. They view a map of thousands of power plants that are joined together in the North American power grid. Finally, the students turn to the question of conservation when they design and construct model houses that are energy efficient.

EARTH AND HUMAN ACTIVITY

When Rachel Carson published *Silent Spring* in 1962, the global human population was 3.1 billion people. When *Science for All Americans* was published in 1990 the population had nearly doubled to 5.3 billion people. Now, in 2016, the global population stands at 7.3 billion, and the United Nations posits it may climb to as much as 9.5 billion in 2050. These vast numbers are hard to grasp, and the effect on natural environments around the world are enormous and include clearing forests for farms and cities, draining freshwater rivers and lakes, and air pollution. Here are a few examples that illustrate what teaching about the influence of engineering, technology, and science in this context may look like in the classroom.

Early elementary: The concept that humans extract natural resources to produce everything that we need to live is an essential idea in the *Framework* that is illustrated in classroom activities that engage students in creating materials that typically come in bottles and packages so they can understand the origin of these synthetic materials. Such an example is the "Designing Mixtures" unit from Seeds of Science/Roots of Reading (*http://scienceandliteracy.org*). This series of activities, which blends science and reading, begins with a reading about the choice of materials for various products. Students consider questions such as, "What if rain boots were made of paper?" They then experiment with a number of natural materials to produce their own glue recipes. To help them learn the process of designing mixtures, they read about a person who designs his own hair gel. Following the example, the students test their glues, take stock of the results, and then redesign their mixtures to improve them.

The "Designing Mixtures" unit provides experiences related to the expectations in DCI PS1: Matter and Its Interactions for the early elementary level: "Matter can be described and classified by its observable properties (e.g., visual, aural, textural), by its uses, and by whether it occurs naturally or is manufactured. Different properties are suited to different purposes" (NRC 2012, p. 108).

Middle school: Technology in Practice: Applications and Innovations (*www.bscs.org/technology-practice*) is a middle school curriculum that includes a module entitled "Designing Environmental Solutions." In this module, students develop technological solutions to environmental problems that have been caused by people. In the first chapter, "Garbage In, Garbage Out," students consider what happens to garbage that they put out on the curb once a week, learn about why many communities are turning to recycling to reduce the pressure on landfills, and think of things they can do to help reduce the problem. In the next chapter, "Air Pollution Solutions," students collect data on air pollution and consider costs and benefits of alternative technologies. In "Clean Up Your Spills!" students engage in a computer simulation to learn how to use different technologies to clean up oil spills.

Activities in this curriculum do not just build skills. They immerse students in the very problems that these students will face when they become adults. One of the science practices that students engage in is Obtaining, Evaluating, and Communicating Information about local environmental issues. They then turn to Defining Problems and Designing Solutions. Crosscutting concepts include Energy and Matter in Systems, Stability and Change of Systems, and Cause and Effect. The DCI for ESS3.C: Human Impacts on Earth Systems for the middle school level addressed by the curriculum is, "Human activities have significantly altered the biosphere, sometimes damaging or destroying natural habitats and causing the extinction of many other species. But changes to Earth's environments can have different impacts (negative and positive) for different living things. Typically, as human populations and per capita consumption of natural resources increase, so do the negative impacts on Earth unless the activities and technologies involved are engineered otherwise." (NRC 2012, p. 196).

High school: Engineering Projects in Community Service (EPICS; *https://engineering.purdue.edu/EPICSHS/About*) does not just teach high school students *about* environmental issues, it also engages them in actually working with local community groups to identify and solve problems through the engineering design process. Examples given on the website include restoration of a city park to a native riparian habitat, devising ways to protect the native cottonwood from the resident beaver population, the design of a

garden as a migration stop for Monarch butterflies, and the development of landscape and seating areas for park-goers. This curriculum fully embodies LS4: Biological Evolution: Unity and Diversity at the high school level in life sciences: "The sustainability of human societies and the biodiversity that supports them requires responsible management of natural resources. Scientists and engineers can make major contributions—for example, by developing technologies that produce less pollution and waste and that preclude ecosystem degradation" (NRC 2012, p. 196).

As with ETS2.A, the *Framework* provides specific core ideas for ETS2.B to illustrate how an understanding of the influence of Engineering, Technology, and Science on Society and the Natural World grows across the grades.

How Does Student Understanding of This Disciplinary Core Idea Develop Over Time?

At the early elementary level, students learn to think of situations that they want to change as problems that can be solved and realize that tools can sometimes help solve problems. Observations and measurements can also be used to refine ideas and test possible solutions. The "Best of Bugs" unit, described in the next section, is an example of how young children can answer an important question (how to help the plants produce fruit) by creating a tool that mimics the action of an insect to pollinate flowers.

At the upper elementary level, students learn that scientific discoveries can lead to new inventions and that engineers need to understand scientific concepts to improve existing technologies and invent new ways to accomplish their goals.

The revised FOSS (Full Option Science System; *http://lhsfoss.org*) curriculum unit in which students explore electrical phenomena and apply what they've learned to solve electrical lighting problems and design a telegraph key provides one possible model of what this may look like in an upper elementary classroom.

In middle school, students' notion of "technology" is to be expanded further. The goal is for students to learn how scientific discoveries in different fields have led to the development of entire industries, and how industrial development has, in many cases, provided motivation and funding for new scientific research. Similarly, the development of new technologies by engineers has supported the advancement of science by providing better ways to make observations and measurements, model and simulate natural processes, and conduct laboratory investigations that were previously impossible. Students' experiences in examining common technologies in the context of the curriculum from *Everyday Engineering* (Moyer and Everett 2012) can help them see examples of this two-way interaction between science and engineering, recognize that nearly *everything* around them has been engineered to solve a problem or meet a need, and gain insight into the needs of scientists to extend their research.

At the high school level, as students contemplate future careers, they are expected to differentiate a wide range of science, technology, engineering, and mathematics (STEM) careers, including the many different types of engineers and technologists. They are also expected to learn how people with a wide variety of backgrounds participate in research and development (R & D) cycles that drive the evolution of our technological world. For example, developing a means for safely and securely disposing of nuclear waste will require the participation of engineers with specialties in nuclear engineering, transportation, construction, and safety; it is likely to also require the contributions of scientists and other professionals from such diverse fields as physics, geology, economics, psychology, and sociology. The high school example for ETS2.B of biomedical engineering in the INSPIRES curriculum (p. 277) illustrates how engaging a unit on the R & D process in the medical field can be.

Teaching ETS2.A: Interdependence of Science, Engineering, and Technology
LOWER ELEMENTARY

What will characterize a curriculum that emphasizes the interdependence of science, engineering, and technology? Hopefully, many different models will be developed in the near future, but some guidelines follow directly from these ideas in the *Framework*, and a few curriculum materials have already been developed that combine science and engineering in the ways suggested in the *Framework*, although they were developed before the *Framework* was published. I've selected a few of these as examples of what this curriculum might look like in the classroom.

At the early elementary level, it will be important not only to teach students how to use tools for measuring and observing their world but also for them to become explicitly aware of the broader concept of a tool, including the idea that tools can be used to find things out (science) and to solve problems by designing and making things (engineering). Children can be encouraged to invent their own tools to accomplish a goal, such as opening a container, digging a hole, or displaying artwork. Emphasizing the utility of

tools is a different twist on the idea of hands-on and minds-on science.

One example of an instructional unit that revolves around development of a tool is the Engineering is Elementary unit "The Best of Bugs" (*www.eie.org*). The unit begins with a story about Mariana, a girl in the Dominican Republic, who is in a quandary because her raspberry plants will not produce fruit. Her aunt, who is an agricultural engineer, explains the scientific background that Mariana needs to understand the problem. It turns out that the plant is native to Hawaii, and there are no local insects that can pollinate it. The challenge for the students is to help Mariana out by creating a tool that she can use to artificially pollinate her raspberry plants (Martin 2005).

Once the students have the scientific background, they choose from a number of different materials to create a hand pollinator and simulate the pollination process in the classroom. They are taught to control variables to ensure that the different pollinators are given a fair test. The teachers guide offers suggestions to help the students process the story, learn about the role of agricultural engineers, and discover that hand pollination is actually used by real farmers. Like other units in the series, the students are given opportunities to reflect on the wide variety of technologies that surround them every day and the role that engineers play in creating and improving those technologies.

"The Best of Bugs" also illustrates an essential instructional goal described in the *Framework*—that learning experiences should include three dimensions: (DCIs, science and engineering practices, and crosscutting concepts). In this unit, plant pollination illustrates the DCI. It's part of a larger idea that plants have external parts with specific functions. This idea is described as one of

the endpoints of learning for the early elementary level of LS1: From Molecules to Organisms: Structures and Processes: "All organisms have external parts. Different animals use their body parts in different ways to see, hear, grasp objects, protect themselves, move from place to place, and seek, find, and take in food, water and air. Plants also have different parts (roots, stems, leaves, flowers, fruits) that help them survive, grow, and produce more plants" (NRC 2012, p. 144).

Although the activity of designing the hand pollinator involves several practices, including Developing and Using Models, and Designing Solutions, the practice in which students receive the most explicit instruction is in Planning and Carrying Out Investigations. While the children do not actually plan their investigations, they do learn that for the test of their pollinators to be fair, they must treat each one the same way and have a quantitative method for comparing the effectiveness of their pollinators to pick up and deposit "pollen." The best way to see this process is to observe one of the online videos of this class in action, such as the Engineering is Elementary video at *www.eie.org/eie-curriculum/resources/designing-hand-pollinator-grade-1-stillwater-mn*.

The third dimension of all learning experiences is that they should reflect one or more crosscutting concepts. Two of the crosscutting concepts seem most closely related to this activity: Cause and Effect (e.g., if the flowers are not pollinated they will not produce fruit) and Structure and Function (e.g., the ability of the hand pollinator to pick up and deposit pollen depends on its form). For the purpose of this chapter, however, the most important idea illustrated by this unit is that a scientific understanding of why the plants did not produce fruit was essential for engineering a solution. And the process of developing a tool

to pollinate the flowers prompts the students to investigate the flowers themselves more closely and to see the different structures that flowers develop to more easily deposit their pollen on visiting insects. In this way, science drives engineering, and engineering drives science. Science and engineering are interdependent.

UPPER ELEMENTARY

FOSS is a widely used hands-on curriculum that was redesigned when the *Framework* first came out. The "Energy and Electromagnetism" module begins with an engineering challenge. A fictitious lighting company is trying to figure out why an entire string of holiday lights fails when a single bulb burns out. As they solve this problem, the students learn about series and parallel circuits. Their investigations engage them in wiring the bulbs in a new way and also changing the arrangement of batteries to produce sufficient voltage to light the entire string and power an electric motor.

Students explore permanent magnets in the next part of the module, finding various ways to measure the strength of the magnetic field and determine how the magnetic force depends on distance from the magnets. They then extend the activity to examine what happens when different materials are placed between two magnets, including both magnetic and nonmagnetic materials. As the students' scientific understanding of magnetism grows, they engineer arrangements of magnets that can accomplish different functions.

In the third part of the module, students bring together their understanding of electricity and of magnets to construct and investigate electromagnets. The investigation begins by having the students observe that an electric current in a wire will deflect a nearby compass needle. They then construct electromagnets by winding insulated wire around an iron core and systematically investigating the factors that affect the strength of their electromagnets. With that scientific knowledge, they can then design an electromagnet of any given strength.

The unit culminates as the students read about the history of the electromagnetic telegraph key and are challenged to design, build, and test one based on their knowledge of electromagnetism. Once they have met the challenge the students wire together pairs of keys and establish long-distance communication. If there is time, the students can go on to design and build a doorbell, burglar alarm, or electric motor. PS2: Motion and Stability: Forces and Interactions is the DCI underlying this set of activities: "Electric and magnetic (electromagnetic) forces can be attractive or repulsive, and their sizes depend on the magnitude of the charges, currents, or magnetic strengths involved and on the distances between the interacting objects ... Forces that act at a distance (gravitational, electric, and magnetic) can be explained by force fields that extend through space and can be mapped by their effect on test objects (a ball, a charged object, or a magnet, respectively)" (NRC 2012, p. 118).

As in the elementary example above, when students transition from a science experience to an engineering design challenge, they are putting their understanding to work, which means they are more likely to remember the science and to learn how engineers use science to accomplish their goals. But the investigation does not stop when the engineering begins. Quite often the design does not work as expected, which forces students to go back and reconsider whether or not they fully understood the science. Once they do that, they can return to the engineering challenge with greater confidence and understanding. To quote Tom Kelly, founder of the design firm IDEO, "Fail Often to Succeed Sooner" (Fredman 2002, p. 56).

MIDDLE SCHOOL

The activities in *Everyday Engineering* (Moyer and Everett 2012) engage students in taking a close look at the technologies around them to discern the scientific principles on which they work and how these discoveries have been used in the products that make up our everyday experiences. For example, one of these technologies discussed is the turkey pop-up timer, which is a device inserted into a turkey just before it is put into the oven and that visibly pops up when the internal temperature of the meat has reached a safe-to-eat level. The students reverse engineer these efficient but inexpensive devices and locate the metal alloy that has been specially formulated to melt at just the right temperature to release a spring, which in turn pops up a small plastic signal indicating that the turkey is done. Students investigate many other technologies as well, from ballpoint pens to sealable plastic bags and toothbrushes.

Each of the investigations provides experience with DCIs from different disciplines. The pop-up turkey timer provides experiences that can address the DCI PS1: Matter and Its Interactions for the middle school level: "Solids may be formed from molecules, or they may be extended structures with repeating units (e.g., crystals.) The changes of state that occur with variations in temperature or pressure can be described and predicted using these models of matter" (NRC 2012, p. 109). Common to a great many of the experiences in this curriculum is the crosscutting concept Structure and Function and the practices of Asking Questions and Defining Problems as

well as Constructing Explanations and Designing Solutions.

In addition to hands-on activities that involve taking something apart and examining it closely to see how it functions, students are asked to read short historical summaries of earlier versions of the given technology. They read about the problems that engineers attempted to solve when coming up with the modern version and the assistance provided by scientists to better understand the phenomenon at the heart of the technology.

HIGH SCHOOL

Pasteur's Quadrant (1997) by Donald Stokes points out that for many scientists, solving a problem is not just the near-term goal of getting their equipment to work but also a long-term goal of value to society. The title of the book refers to Louis Pasteur, whose fundamental discoveries in microbiology were motivated by his desire to prevent disease, leading to such important technologies as pasteurization of milk and the first vaccine for rabies. The book points out that the distinction between "pure" and "applied" science makes very little sense, since a great many scientists conduct fundamental scientific research to solve an important problem that may affect society or the environment.

This close marriage between science and engineering is especially evident in the field of biomedical engineering. An excellent example of biomedical engineering is the learning module "Engineering in Healthcare: A Hemodialysis Case Study," which is part of the INSPIRES (INcreasing Student Participation, Interest, and

Recruitment in Engineering and Science) curriculum (*http://inspires.umbc.edu*). The module is introduced with a video about a teenage girl with kidney failure who must undergo hemodialysis on a frequent schedule. The video introduces her doctor, who explains that the purpose of a hemodialysis machine is to replace the function of the kidney by removing waste products from the blood. The challenge for the students is to design, build, test, and refine a system that mimics the function of a hemodialysis system.

A unit on biomedical engineering has great potential to engage students because it vividly illustrates the role of engineering in people's lives. By developing hemodialysis machines, artificial heart valves, and many other devices, teams of scientists and biomedical engineers have saved millions of lives. Such modules also provide a rationale for students to study biology, since without an understanding of how the body functions, it's not possible to correct problems or cure or prevent disease. This module illustrates a vivid example of the high school level expectations for LS1: From Molecules to Organisms: Structures and Processes: "Cellular division and differentiation produce and maintain a complex organism, composed of systems of tissues and organs that work together to meet the needs of the whole organism" (NRC 2012, p. 147).

The DCIs quoted above are from the three traditional disciplines of science: life sciences, physical sciences, and Earth and space sciences, illustrating that this core idea cuts across all of the disciplines. In fact, there is really no way to illustrate the interdependence of science and engineering without connecting it to one of the traditional fields of science.

Teaching ETS2.B: The Influence of Engineering, Technology, and Science on Society and the Natural World

ELEMENTARY SCHOOL

At the lower elementary level, students are expected to learn that their lives would be very different without technology. Technology is not only cell phones and computers, but also our clothes and what we eat. Furthermore, all technologies are composed of materials that came from nature—such as plant fibers woven into cloth or petroleum made into plastic. The unit "Designing Mixtures" from Seeds of Science/Roots of Reading helps students gain experience in this idea.

At the upper elementary level, the *Framework* emphasizes the role of engineers to improve existing technologies to increase their benefits while decreasing risks. Students in the upper elementary grades are also expected to learn how engineers improve technologies or invent new technologies to decrease known risks and meet societal demands, and how technological innovations can change how people live and interact with one another. In the unit "Whispers of Willing Wind" (listed on p. 277), the students construct and then improve on a wind turbine. They then apply the idea of technological improvement to think about our current sources of electrical energy, and how they might be improved to increase benefits and decrease risk.

MIDDLE SCHOOL

At the middle school level, the *Framework* emphasizes two major ideas. The first is that all human activity draws on natural resources, and the extraction of natural resources has consequences

for the health of both people and the natural environment. The second is that the uses of technologies—or in some cases limitations on their uses—are driven by people's desires and values, by scientific research, and by differences in such factors as climate, natural resources, and economic conditions. That is why people who live in different parts of the world use different technologies, and why the technologies of a given culture evolve over time. There are also many examples of technologies that appeared to have many advantages when they were introduced, but which are eventually found to have negative consequences. In these cases, society may impose regulations to reduce negative effects. In the unit "Designing Environmental Solutions" from the curriculum Technology in Practice: Applications and Innovations, the students consider ways to reduce the effects of garbage disposal, atmospheric pollution, and oil spills.

HIGH SCHOOL

At the high school level, students are expected to understand that civilization depends on major technological systems such as agriculture, health, water, energy, transportation, manufacturing, construction, and communications. Engineers apply scientific knowledge and engineering design practices to improve these systems. However, whether or not a given technological change is adopted depends on market forces, government regulation, or other societal demands. Since technological decisions can have profound effects on society and the natural world, they must be informed by thorough and thoughtful analyses of both costs and benefits. In the "Energy Use" unit from Global Systems Science, students examine the costs and benefits of our electrical power

14

FIGURE 14.1

The Two Related Components of the DCI ETS2: Links Among Engineering, Technology, Science, and Society

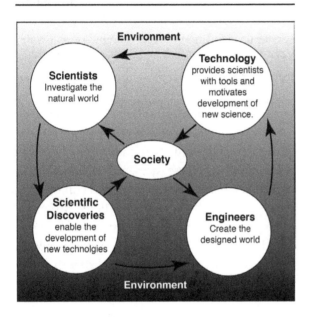

infrastructure, and examine ways to mitigate the most serious consequences. In the EPICS program, high school students work directly with individuals and organizations in their communities to solve a wide range of problems.

Connecting the Two Components of the Disciplinary Core Idea

Figure 14.1 illustrates the relationship between the two components of this DCI. First, consider the interdependence of science, technology, and engineering, starting at the upper left side of the diagram: When scientists investigate the natural world, they often make discoveries. In many cases, engineers apply these discoveries to develop new technologies. In some cases, new technologies

make possible entirely new scientific discoveries, which may lead to even better technologies, and so on. When these processes feed on each other, they become what is known as the R & D cycle.

Now consider the Influence of Engineering, Technology, and Science on Society and the Natural World. Remember, it goes both ways. As illustrated in Figure 14.1, society—in the form of voters, consumers, and their representatives—makes decisions that determine what scientists are allowed to study and what technologies engineers are allowed to create. Scientific discoveries and new technologies, in turn, powerfully influence people's lives. This dynamic interaction among scientists, engineers, and wider society plays out within the environment. And as the human population continues to expand, the environmental impact continues to increase at a rapid pace.

The implications of this for the classroom are that curriculum developers and teachers should consider both component ideas when planning their science units. Doing so will often involve a bit of history of science. As a concrete example, let's take a common topic in the science curriculum—Galileo and the first use of the telescope for astronomy. Such a unit might begin with the following quote and illustration (Figure 14.2) from Galileo's 1610 book *Sidereus Nuncius* (*The Starry Messenger*):

From observations of these spots [craters] repeated many times I have been led to the opinion and conviction that the surface of the Moon is not smooth, uniform, and precisely spherical as a great number of philosophers believe it (and the other heavenly bodies) to be, but is uneven, rough, and full of cavities and prominences, being not unlike the face of the Earth, relieved by chains of mountains and deep valleys. (Galilei 1610, quoted in Drake 1957, p. 31)

NATIONAL SCIENCE TEACHERS ASSOCIATION

FIGURE 14.2

Galileo's Drawing of the Moon as Viewed Through a Telescope

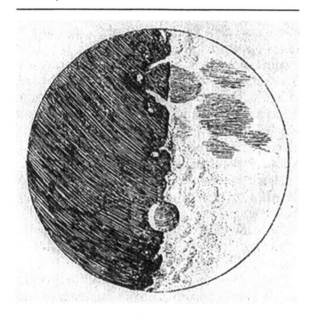

It is well known that Galileo did not invent the telescope. He learned about it from a Dutch lens grinder and then experimented with it himself for some time before he developed one that was good enough to see the surface of the Moon in great detail (see Figure 14.2.) That illustrates the value of technology in science. But a revised curriculum might go a step further and include the following quote from a few pages earlier in Galileo's book:

About 10 months ago a report reached my ears that a certain Fleming [Dutchman] had constructed a spyglass by means of which visible objects, though very distant from the eye of the observer, were distinctly seen as if nearby. Of this truly remarkable effect several experiences were related, to which some persons gave credence, while others denied them. A few days later the report was confirmed to me in a letter from a noble Frenchman at Paris, Jacques Badovere, which caused me to apply myself wholeheartedly to inquire into the means by which I might arrive at a similar invention. This I did shortly afterward, my basis being the theory of refraction. (Galilei 1610, quoted in Drake 1957, pp. 28–29)

This paragraph reveals the importance of international communication among scientists early in the 1600s. It also reveals that the story is not as simple as commonly taught, in which Galileo takes something made by a craftsman, improves it, and uses it for science. In the previous paragraph, Galileo refers to the theory of refraction, which implies an earlier scientific basis for his improvements. In fact, understanding of refraction can be traced back at least as far as 984 AD when the Persian mathematician Ibn Sahl wrote a treatise called *On Burning Mirrors and Lenses*, in which he described an accurate law of refraction that could be applied to lenses. More to the point, Johannes Kepler, who corresponded with Galileo, had recently completed a major book on optics, which it is very likely Galileo had read.

So the simple story of Galileo's use of the telescope to observe the Moon, planets, and stars was part of a long cycle of R & D that began with burning mirrors and lenses, which lead to the theory of refraction, which resulted in the development of an improved spyglass. The tradition of improved telescopes and new discoveries in optics and mechanical inventions to mount lenses and mirrors continues to this day, with the invention of adaptive optics for huge ground-based instruments and orbital telescopes that observe in a wide range of wavelengths.

Galileo is widely considered to be a scientist, but his work on the telescope can best be characterized as engineering design. This phenomenon is common today as a great many scientists spend much of their time designing, building, operating, and troubleshooting their equipment. There are also many instances in which engineers do science, sometimes conducting controlled experiments to test prototypes or to determine the properties of materials, often contributing new knowledge in the process. This history is a beautiful illustration of ETS2.A—the interdependence of science and engineering.

But there is a bit more to the story. Today we look back on Galileo's brilliant insights with admiration, but at the time, society frowned on the idea that Earth might not be the center of the universe. Galileo's observations of the Moon showed it to look much like Earth, and his further discovery that tiny moons circled the planet Jupiter suggested that Copernicus was right when he said Earth is not the center of the universe at all but just one of the planets with its own moon. The story of Galileo's detention, the threat of torture, and his house arrest toward his last years are an important lesson on the influence of society on science, and of science on society—a vivid illustration of ETS2.B.

The point of this is that instructional materials need to include at least occasional references to the history of science if students are to understand what it means for science and society to be closely linked. Such stories can be told in textbooks, videos, lectures, and literature. For example, a fascinating perspective on the Galileo story is provided in *Galileo's Daughter* (Sobel 2000), which offers deep insights into the human side of science and society of the seventeenth century.

The parallels to today's controversies at the interface of science, technology, and society may not be immediately obvious to students without a teacher's encouragement to consider the relationship between Galileo's struggle and such modern issues as the conspiracy theory that people did not actually travel to the Moon, controversy over the effects of human activities on Earth's climate, or the longstanding challenges to the theory of biological evolution. The *Framework* places the responsibility of engaging students in these difficult issues squarely on science teachers and curriculum developers.

Conclusion

The *Next Generation Science Standards* play an essential role in our science education system by specifying what all students should know and be able to do at specific levels of education. But the standards alone are not sufficient for planning curriculum. The *Framework* is a much richer document in that it describes in vivid detail the spirit of science and engineering and hints at the sorts of instructional practices that students will need to achieve in 13 years of schooling. These human issues at the intersection of science, society, and the environment can be tremendously motivating for students because they provide a reason for the students to care about what they are learning.

Curriculum Materials Mentioned in This Chapter

Elementary

- Seeds of Science/Roots of Reading: "Designing Mixtures": *www. scienceandliteracy.org*

- Engineering is Elementary: "The Best of Bugs": *www.eie.org*

- Invention, Innovation, Inquiry: "Whispers of Willing Wind": *www.iteea.org/i3*

Middle School

- FOSS: "Energy and Electromagnetism": *http://lhsfoss.org*

- Investigating and Questioning our World through Science and Technology (IQWST): *http://www.activatelearning.com/iqwst*

- Technology in Practice: Applications and Innovations: Designing Environmental Solutions: *www.bscs.org/technology-practice*

High School

- INSPIRES: "Engineering in Healthcare: A Hemodialysis Case Study": *http://inspires.umbc.edu*

- Global Systems Science: *www.globalsystemsscience.org*

- Engineering Projects in Community Service (EPICS): *https://engineering.purdue.edu/EPICSHS/About*

REFERENCES

American Association for the Advancement of Science (AAAS). 1993. *Benchmarks for science literacy.* New York: Oxford University Press.

Carson, R. 1962. *Silent spring.* Boston: Houghton Mifflin and Riverside Press.

Drake, S. 1957. *Discoveries and opinions of Galileo.* New York: Doubleday Anchor Books.

Fredman, C. 2002. The IDEO difference. Hemispheres, the Magazine of United Airlines. August. *www.ideo.com/images/uploads/news/PDFs/hemispheres_1.PDF.*

Galilei, G. 1610. *Sidereus nuncius (the starry messenger).* Venice, Italy: Thomas Baglioni.

Martin, J. 2005. Mariana becomes a butterfly: An agricultural engineering story. In *The Best of bugs: Designing hand pollinators*, Engineering is Elementary. Boston: Museum of Science.

Moyer, R. H., and S. A. Everett. 2012. *Everyday engineering: Putting the E in STEM teaching and learning.* Arlington, VA: NSTA Press.

National Research Council (NRC). 2012. *A framework for K–12 science education: Practices, crosscutting concepts, and core ideas.* Washington, DC: National Academies Press.

North American Association for Environmental Education (NAAEE). 2010. *Excellence in environmental education: Guidelines for learning.* Washington, DC: North American Association for Environmental Education.

Rutherford. F. J., and A. Ahlgren. 1990. *Science for all Americans: Project 2061.* New York: Oxford University Press.

Sobel, D. 2000. *Galileo's daughter: A historical memoir of science, faith, and love.* Middlesex, UK: Penguin.

Stokes, D. E. 1997. *Pasteur's quadrant: Basic science and technological innovation.* Washington, DC: Brookings Institution Press.

Yager, R. E. 1996. History of science/technology/society as reform in the United States. In *Science/technology/society as reform in the science education.* Albany, NY: State University of New York.

Ziman, J. 1980. *Teaching and learning about science and society.* New York: Cambridge University Press.

CHAPTER 15

CONCLUSION

Ann E. Rivet, Joseph Krajcik, and Ravit Golan Duncan

This book set out to discuss the disciplinary core ideas (DCIs) across life sciences, physical sciences, and Earth and space sciences in terms of their presentation in *A Framework for K–12 Science Education* (*Framework*; NRC 2012). The intent of this discussion was not just to reiterate the DCIs but to go further: to highlight why these ideas were identified as central to each of the disciplines, present the nuances of their constituent component ideas, and illustrate how understandings of these ideas develop across grade levels. The chapter authors have delved deep into these core ideas, framing the DCI's relationships to other concepts and their use in real-world contexts and providing some resources to support teachers and students in developing robust understandings of them. Importantly, a clear emphasis across the chapters is on how the development of science understanding is more than just "knowing" the concepts as things to memorize. Rather, the emphasis in understanding the DCIs is focused on knowledge-in-use: Science concepts are meaningful only in terms of how they are connected to, and used to explain, phenomena that exist in the real world.

Now we return to an idea that we presented at the beginning of the book, that the DCIs are a part

of the three interrelated dimensions—science practices, crosscutting concepts, and DCIs—that constitute scientific understanding. This is referred to as three-dimensional learning. These dimensions work together to explain phenomena in the world at increasing levels of complexity and sophistication. The *Next Generation Science Standards* (*NGSS*; NGSS Lead States 2013) are written using this architecture: They integrate a part of a practice, a part of a DCI, and an element of the crosscutting concept to form what are called *performance expectations*, illustrating ways that students may demonstrate three-dimensional understanding. This architecture also has implications for related assessments and instruction aligned with particular performance expectations. To show the connections between performance expectations, assessments, and instruction throughout this chapter, we draw from an example in Earth sciences. A middle school performance expectation for Earth's systems (MS-ESS2-4) states, "Develop a model to describe the cycling of water through Earth's systems driven by energy from the Sun and the force of gravity" (NGSS Lead States 2013, p. 80). In this performance expectation, students are demonstrating the ways that they understand the movement of matter through and across Earth's systems (the DCI) by

developing a model that shows this understanding (the practice) using the lens of energy and energy transfer (the crosscutting concept) to explain these processes. This demonstration of understanding is very different from the expectations of previous science standards, which were typically expressed in terms of students knowing a concept such as the water cycle. But what does knowing the water cycle actually mean? Earlier state and national standards did not clearly specify the level of detail, sophistication, or ways of understanding that were expected around this science idea. In contrast, as seen in the example above, the *NGSS* reflect current perspectives about science understanding as centrally focused on knowledge-in-use.

The three-dimensional architecture of the new standards has important implications for assessment and curriculum in science. First, with respect to assessment, it is important to keep in mind that the *NGSS* performance expectations are not prescriptions for assessment items. They are guides that explain the kinds of things that students should be able to do once they have developed a three-dimensional understanding. Assessments then follow from these performance expectations and should be designed to address and align with the learning performance, but they are *not the same* as the performance expectations. Assessment tasks are more specific and context bound, highlighting the ways that knowledge is used and applied in different settings. In that sense, assessments should involve more than students stating what they know about an idea, or even just finding a solution to a problem. Rather, assessment tasks need to embody the three dimensions of science understanding in the same way that the performance expectations do. They should focus on using the practices, crosscutting concepts, and DCIs to explain a range of different phenomena

or solve a set of related problems. Aligning with the Earth and space sciences performance expectation described earlier, an assessment task could have students using diagrams that they create to explain the paths by which water molecules travel through a forest ecosystem, with particular focus on the process by which the water moves (e.g., evaporation, condensation, and precipitation) and where the energy comes from to make those processes and movements happen. Students could also then be asked to compare this process to how water moves in a desert or arctic ecosystem, stressing similarities and differences in movement processes and energy sources that drive them.

The robustness of the *NGSS* performance expectations also means that they should be assessed at the end of a grade band or grade level. The expectations are substantial. These are not checks for understanding at the end of the week—or even after a chapter or unit—because the development of these kinds of understandings builds over time and across instruction as students engage with an array of practices and crosscutting concepts in learning about the core idea.

With respect to instruction, teachers should always be building toward the performance expectations but not teaching *to* a specific performance expectation. *No single lesson or unit should be considered as the sufficient end of teaching a particular performance expectation; the building of ideas toward a performance expectation should occur continuously across time.* Lessons can aim toward the performance expectation by combining different practices with the elements of the core ideas and crosscutting concepts described in the performance expectation. Even if a performance expectation explicitly cites a specific practice, building toward that performance expectation will likely involve instruction using multiple practices over a period of time. One cannot really teach a DCI or component of a DCI through only one practice. The resulting understanding would be limited and not robust in the way called for in the *Framework*.

Thus, the primary implication of this perspective for science classroom instruction is that the working together of the three dimensions of science understanding should be continuous. Instruction needs to focus on students figuring out phenomena or designing solutions to problems using DCIs, science practices, and crosscutting concepts on a consistent and regular basis, and this approach should serve as the bulk of the teaching and learning that takes place in science classrooms across grades K–12. For example, instruction that is aimed at the Earth science performance expectation described earlier should engage students with a variety of different thinking and reasoning about water in the Earth's systems, including exploring and explaining phase change of water, modeling states of matter and their characteristics, analyzing and interpreting data about the distribution of water at regional and global scales, designing and carrying out investigations about the relationship between light and heat energy and water movement, and communicating information about effects of the water cycle on other key Earth systems. Each of these learning experiences individually would not address the performance expectation, but together, students would be able to build and refine the understanding of water's role in Earth's systems that is dynamic, usable, and flexibly adaptive to a range of real-world contexts, which is the aim of the *NGSS* performance expectation.

The DCIs have a significant role in the *Framework* and the *NGSS*, which is an important consideration in policy measures related to implementation of these standards. Most significantly, these are DCIs for *all* students, developed across their whole K–12 learning trajectory. The concepts and processes encompassed by the DCIs are necessary understandings for everyone to become productive and contributing global citizens in the 21st century. It does not matter where the students are from or the prior experiences they have had or the abilities they bring to the classroom. It is the schools' and the teachers' duty to help them master these DCIs along with the science and engineering practices. Science is not optional or an elective, even in elementary school. Thus, policies at the school, district, state, and federal levels need to ensure that high-quality learning opportunities are provided to all students, regardless of age, background, or type of school attended.

And finally, we have a note for parents, teachers, and school leaders on the nature of this perspective on DCIs. We fully recognize that these new goals for science education are quite different from those that existed when we were students, and are even different from the goals for science learning 10 years ago. But we are in a different era, and our children need to use different ideas and have a more sophisticated understanding. New goals necessitate new instructional and assessment approaches. This means that the science classes that your children and students experience will be notably different from your experience, not only in structure but also in content. This is okay. Parents, school, and community members oftentimes are confused when classrooms look and sound different from their more "traditional" classroom experiences; yet this is exactly the kind of environment that results when students are fully engaged with science practices around DCIs. Thus, it is important

for teachers and school leaders to be able to not only implement the *NGSS*, but also to explain the nature and importance of the shifts in the new standards to their communities. Having everyone on board with these notable changes in science learning and teaching is critical to the success of developing robust science understandings for all students.

APPENDIX

DISCIPLINARY CORE IDEAS AND THEIR COMPONENTS

Physical Sciences Disciplinary Core Ideas and Component Ideas

PS1: MATTER AND ITS INTERACTIONS

- PS1.A: Structure and properties of matter
- PS1.B: Chemical reactions
- PS1.C: Nuclear processes

PS2: MOTION AND STABILITY: FORCES AND INTERACTIONS

- PS2.A: Forces and motion
- PS2.B: Types of interactions
- PS2.C: Stability and instability in physical systems

PS3: ENERGY

- PS3.A: Definitions of energy
- PS3.B: Conservation of energy and energy transfer
- PS3.C: Relationship between energy and forces
- PS3.D: Energy in chemical processes and everyday life

PS4: WAVES AND THEIR APPLICATIONS IN TECHNOLOGIES FOR INFORMATION TRANSFER

- PS4.A: Wave properties
- PS4.B: Electromagnetic radiation
- PS4.C: Information technologies and instrumentation

Life Sciences Disciplinary Core Ideas and Component Ideas

LS1: FROM MOLECULES TO ORGANISMS: STRUCTURES AND PROCESSES

- LS1.A: Structure and function
- LS1.B: Growth and development of organisms
- LS1.C: Organization for matter and energy flow in organisms
- LS1.D: Information processing

LS2: ECOSYSTEMS: INTERACTIONS, ENERGY, AND DYNAMICS

- LS2.A: Interdependent relationships in ecosystems

- LS2.B: Cycles of matter and energy transfer in ecosystems

- LS2.C: Ecosystem dynamics, functioning, and resilience

- LS2.D: Social interactions and group behavior

LS3: HEREDITY: INHERITANCE AND VARIATION OF TRAITS

- LS3.A: Inheritance of traits

- LS3.B: Variation of traits

LS4: BIOLOGICAL EVOLUTION: UNITY AND DIVERSITY

- LS4.A: Evidence of common ancestry and diversity

- LS4.B: Natural selection

- LS4.C: Adaptation

- LS4.D: Biodiversity and humans

Earth and Space Sciences Disciplinary Core Ideas and Component Ideas

ESS1: EARTH'S PLACE IN THE UNIVERSE

- ESS1.A: The universe and its stars

- ESS1.B: Earth and the solar system

- ESS1.C: The history of planet Earth

ESS2: EARTH'S SYSTEMS

- ESS2.A: Earth materials and systems

- ESS2.B: Plate tectonics and large-scale system interactions

- ESS2.C: The roles of water in Earth's surface processes

- ESS2.D: Weather and climate

- ESS2.E: Biogeology

ESS3: EARTH AND HUMAN ACTIVITY

- ESS3.A: Natural Resources

- ESS3.B: Natural Hazards

- ESS3.C: Human Impacts on Earth Systems

- ESS3.D: Global Climate Change

Engineering Disciplinary Core Ideas and Component Ideas

ETS1: ENGINEERING DESIGN

- ETS1.A: Defining and delimiting an engineering problem

- ETS1.B: Developing possible solutions

- ETS1.C: Optimizing the design solution

ETS2: LINKS AMONG ENGINEERING, TECHNOLOGY, SCIENCE, AND SOCIETY

- ETS2.A: Interdependence of science, engineering, and technology

- ETS2.B: Influence of engineering, technology, and science on society and the natural world

IMAGE CREDITS

Chapter 2

Figure 2.1: Joseph Krajcik

Figure 2.2: Kristin Mayer

Figure 2.3a: Concord Consortium (*http://concord.org*) and Concord Next-Generation Molecular Workbench website (*http://mw.concord.org*), used with permission. *http://mw.concord.org/nextgen/#interactives/chemistry/phase-change/molecular-view-gas*

Figure 2.3b: Concord Consortium (*http://concord.org*) and Concord Next-Generation Molecular Workbench website (*http://mw.concord.org*), used with permission. *http://mw.concord.org/nextgen/#interactives/chemistry/phase-change/molecular-view-liquid*

Figure 2.4: Concord Consortium (*http://concord.org*) and Concord Next-Generation Molecular Workbench website (*http://mw.concord.org*), used with permission. *http://mw.concord.org/nextgen/#interactives/chemistry/gas-laws/temperature-pressure-relationship*

Figure 2.5: Concord Consortium (*http://concord.org*), used with permission. *http://lab.concord.org/embeddable.html#interactives/interactions/forming-molecules-graph-no-axes.json*

Chapter 3

Figure 3.1: ThinkStock

Figure 3.2: Joseph Butera, NSTA Press

Figure 3.3: ThinkStock

Figure 3.4: ThinkStock

Figure 3.5: Joseph Butera, NSTA Press

Figure 3.6: Joseph Butera, NSTA Press

Figure 3.7: Concord Consortium (*http://concord.org*) and Concord Next-Generation Molecular Workbench website (*http://mw.concord.org*), used with permission. *http://authoring.concord.org/activities/4098/pages/54849/6923b4d4-75b4-4d59-b41a-b72065d85565*

Figure 3.8: Concord Consortium (*http://concord.org*) and Concord Next-Generation Molecular Workbench website (http://mw.concord.org), used with permission. *http://mw.concord.org/nextgen/#interactives/chemistry/intermolecular-attractions/boiling-point*

Chapter 4

Figure 4.1: Crissman, S., S. Lacy, J. C. Nordine, and R. Tobin. 2015. Looking through the energy lens. *Science and Children* 52 (6): 263–1. Used with permission.

Figure 4.2: IQWST (Investigating & Questioning our World Through Science & Technology) (*www.activatelearning.com*). Used with permission.

Figure 4.3: IQWST (Investigating & Questioning our World Through Science & Technology) (*www.activatelearning.com*). Used with permission.

IMAGE CREDITS

Chapter 5

Figure 5.1: ThinkStock

Figure 5.2a: ThinkStock

Figure 5.2b: dreamstime (*www.dreamstime.com/ royalty-free-stock-image-la-ola-applause-stadium-wave-frontal-applauding-colorful-line-people-figures-forming-perspective-d-rendering-image35053836*)

Figure 5.3: Joseph Butera, NSTA Press

Figure 5.4: User:Omegatron, Wikimedia Commons, CC BY-SA 3.0. *https://commons. wikimedia.org/wiki/File:Simple_sine_wave. svg?uselang=en-gb*

Figure 5.5: Joseph Butera, NSTA Press

Figure 5.6: User:Penubag, Wikimedia Commons, CC BY-SA 2.5. *http://commons.wikimedia.org/wiki/ File:Electromagnetic-Spectrum.png?uselang=en-gb*

Chapter 6

Figure 6.1: Hillary Lauren

Figure 6.2: Hillary Lauren

Figure 6.3: Hillary Lauren

Figure 6.4: Hillary Lauren

Figure 6.5: Hillary Lauren

Figure 6.6: Used with permission from SimScientists Assessment Systems: Life Science. Principle Investigator, Edys Quellmalz; Co-Principle Investigators, Barbara Buckley, Mark Loveland, Daniel Brenner, and Matt Silberglitt. IES R305A120390, *simscientists.org*.

Figure 6.7: Concord Consortium (*http://concord. org*), used with permission. *http://concord.org/ stem-resources/leaf-photosynthesis*

Chapter 7

Figure 7.1: Charles W. (Andy) Anderson and Jennifer H. Doherty

Figure 7.2: User:Delorme, Wikimedia Commons, GFDL and CC BY-SA 4.0. *https://commons. wikimedia.org/wiki/File:Mauna_Loa_CO2_monthly_ mean_concentration.svg*

Figure 7.3a: Yamina Pressler, used with permission.

Figure 7.3b: User: Hustvedt, Wikimedia Commons, CC-BY-SA-3.0. *https://commons. wikimedia.org/wiki/File:Beetle_kill_forest_colorado. jpg*

Figure 7.4: Parker, J. M., E. X. de L. Santos, and C. W. Anderson. 2015. Learning progressions and climate change. *The American Biology Teacher* 77 (4): 232–238. Used with permission.

Figure 7.5: Parker, J. M., E. X. de L. Santos, and C. W. Anderson. 2015. Learning progressions and climate change. *The American Biology Teacher* 77 (4): 232–238. Used with permission.

Chapter 8

Figure 8.1: The National Heart, Lung, and Blood Institute, public domain. *www.nhlbi.nih.gov/ health/health-topics/topics/sca*

Figure 8.2: Human Genome Project, Wikimedia Commons, public domain. *https://commons. wikimedia.org/wiki/File:Down_Syndrome_Karyotype. png*

Figure 8.3: User:Squidonius, Wikimedia Commons, public domain. *https://commons.wikimedia.org/wiki/File:Dolly_clone.svg*

Figure 8.4: PRACCIS, used with permission.

Chapter 9

Figure 9.1: ThinkStock

Figure 9.2: Cynthia Passmore, Julia Svoboda Gouvea, Candice Guy, Chris Griesemer

Figure 9.4: Petter Bøckman, Wikimedia Commons, CC BY-SA 3.0. *https://commons.wikimedia.org/wiki/File:Primate_cladogram.jpg*

Chapter 10

Figure 10.1: User:Fredrik, Wikimedia Commons, public domain. *https://commons.wikimedia.org/wiki/File:Universe_expansion.png*

Figure 10.2: user:Brian Brondel, Wikimedia Commons, GFDL and CC BY-SA 3.0. *http://commons.wikimedia.org/wiki/File:Newton_Cannon.svg*

Chapter 11

Figure 11.1: Jose F. Vigil. USGS ([1]), Wikimedia Commons, public domain. *https://commons.wikimedia.org/wiki/File:Tectonic_plate_boundaries.png*

Figure 11.2: US EPA, Wikimedia Commons, public domain. *https://commons.wikimedia.org/wiki/File:Earth%27s_greenhouse_effect_(US_EPA,_2012).png*

Chapter 13

Figure 13.1: NGSS Lead States. 2013. *Next Generation Science Standards: For states, by*

states. Vol. 2, 105. Washington, DC: National Academies Press. *www.nextgenscience.org/next-generation-science-standards.*

Figure 13.2: Kolodner, Gray, and Fasse 2003. Used with permission.

Figure 13.3a: Linear model: Lawson, B. 1990. *How designers think: The design process demystified.* Oxford, UK: Butterworth Architecture.

Figure 13.3b: Spiral model: Resnick, M. 2007. All I really need to know (about creative thinking) I learned (by studying how children learn) in kindergarten. Paper presented at the 6th Creativity and Cognition Conference, Washington, DC.

Figure 13.3c: Joseph Butera, NSTA Press; adapted from Georgia Tech Research Corporation (GTRC). 2004. Design in the classroom: Cyclic design model. *http://designintheclassroom.com/designProcess/whatIsDesign/designStrategies.html.*

Figure 13.4: Adapted from and printed with permission of Loughborough Design School, formerly the Department of Design and Technology at Loughborough University.

Chapter 14

Figure 14.1: Cary Sneider

Figure 14.2: Galileo Galilei. 1610. *Sidereus Nuncius.* Public domain.

INDEX

Page numbers in **boldface** type refer to tables or figures.

INDEX

Boiling of water, 2, 13, 24, 48
Boiling point, 13, 52, **52**
Bonding and energy, 15, 26–27
Brain, 103, 106, 107, 108, 117, 111, 114, 115
    of cloned sheep, 150
    hearing and, 82, 85
    vision and, 82, 86
BRCA genes and cancer, 145, 148, 153
Breast cancer, 145, 148, 153
Breathing, 97, 104, 111, 118, 121, 126, 135, 215
Brickhouse, Nancy, 183
Bromine, 18
Bubbles, 23–24
Butterfly life stages, 102

C

Calcium, 127
Calcium carbonate, 28
Calcium chloride, 28
Cancer-causing genes, 102, **102**, 114, 121, 145, 148, 153, 159
Cannibalism, 130
Car engines, 67, 68
Carbon, 14, 23, 68, 104, 115, 126, 127–128, **131**
Carbon cycle, 97, **127,** 127–128, 131, 133, 215, 229
    middle and high school students'
        understanding of, 133–134, **134**
Carbon dioxide, 20, 21, **21,** 24
    atmospheric, 126, **127,** 127–128, 220
        global climate change and, 226, 229, 232, 235
        greenhouse effect and, 212–213
        ocean acidification due to, 226
        on Venus, 212
    boiling point of, 13
    in photosynthesis, 105, **105,** 109, 113, 119, **120,** 126, 130, 135, 214
    produced by cellular respiration, 104, 135
    produced by light bulbs, 72
    released in combustion reactions, 14, 68
Carbon footprint calculator, 237
Careers in science, 3, 247, 268
Carson, Rachel, 265, 266
CD players, 81, 86, 87
Cell phones, 11, 43, 75, 83, 85, 86, 89, 92, 93, 94, 273
Cells, 99–103
    division of, 102–103, 272
    stem, 99, 103, 107, 114, 145, 150, 157
    structure and function of, 100–101
Cellular respiration, 69, 70, 104, **104,** 105, 107, 113, 115, 118, 120, 126, 128, 131, 133, 135
Center of gravity (center of mass), 36, 42
Chemical bonds, 26–27, 67
Chemical energy, 39, 57, 66, **104,** 105, 109, 127, 135
Chemical Reactions (PS1.B), **10,** 15, 283

development of understanding over time, 15
    grades K–2, 16, 17
    grades 3–5, 17, 20–21, **21**
    grades 6–8, 23–24
    grades 9–12, 25, 26–27
Chemotaxis, 106
Chlorine, 24
Chromosomes, 97, 147–148, 149–150, **150,** 151, 152, 155, 158, 160, 161, **161**
Cladogram of primates, **171,** 172
Climate change. *See* Global climate change; Weather and climate
Climate Change from Pole to Pole, 236
Cloning, 114, 150, **151,** 154
Coal, 53, 67, 68, 128, 208, 231
Cobalt chloride test paper, 24
Colliding objects, 34–35, 38, 45, 46, 51, 56, 57, 64, 65, 66, **70,** 71
Colors of light, 23, 82, 91, 93
Combustion reactions, 11, 14, 226, 233
Comets, 191, 192, 196
Community ecology, 125, 126, 128–130
    approaches to teaching about, 140–142
    development of understanding over time, 130, 135–140
        elementary school, 136–137
        middle and high school, 137–140
Compact fluorescent (CFL) bulbs, 72
Competition for food, 130
Components of disciplinary core ideas, 3, **3,** 283–284
    for Earth and space sciences, **182,** 182–183, 284
    for engineering, technology, and applications of science, **242,** 242–243, 284
    for life sciences, **96,** 283–284
    for physical sciences, **10,** 11–12, 283
Concord Consortium, 26, 28
    Boiling Point simulation, 52, **52**
    Electric Charge simulation, 50, **50**
    Interactions curriculum, 29, **30,** 50, 52–53
    Leaf Photosynthesis simulation, 119–120, **120**
    Molecular View of a Gas simulation, 28, **28**
    Molecular View of a Liquid simulation, 28, **28**
    Next-Generation Molecular Workbench, 28, 29, **30,** 52, **52**
    Temperature-Pressure Relationship simulation, 29
Condensation, 213, 217, 280
Conservation of energy, 11, 55–57, 217, 219, 264, 283
Conservation of Energy and Energy Transfer (PS3.B), **10,** 58, 61–64, 283
    common prior conceptions of, 61–62
    development of understanding over time, 61–63
        by end of grade 5, 64

        by end of grade 8, 64
        by end of grade 12, 64
    as a scientific idea, 62–63
    wave dimensionality and intensity resulting from, 79
Conservation of mass, 20, 21, **21,** 22
Conservation of matter, 128, 133
Contact forces, 40, 41–42, 52, 65, 66
Copernicus, 276
Copper sulfate, 23
Coulomb's law, 51–52
Crismond, David, 243
Crosscutting concepts, vii, 1–2, 3, 4–5, 7, 14, 279–281
    biological evolution, 176
    change, 206
    energy, 15, 19, 57, 58, 280
        in ecosystems, 123, 126, 143
    related to Earth and space sciences, 182, 186
    related to Earth's systems, 206, 217
        weather and climate, 211
    related to engineering design, 255, 259, 260
    related to links among engineering, technology, science, and society, 267, 269, 270, 271–272
    scale, proportion, and quantity, 22
    structure and function, 100, 107, 147, 154, 271
    systems, 44, 100
Cycles of Matter and Energy Transfer in Ecosystems (LS2.B), **96,** 126, 284

D

Darwin, Charles, 123–124, 125, 128, 140, 166–167, **167,** 168, **169,** 169–170
    On the Origin of Species, 123, 166
    studies of Galápagos finches, 168, 170, 179
Day–night cycle, 190, 198
DDT (pesticide), 102
Deep time, 190, 193, 227, 228
Defining and Delimiting an Engineering Problem (ETS1.A), **242,** 246, 248–249, 284
    teaching strategies for, 258
Definitions of Energy (PS3.A), **10,** 58, 283
    common prior conceptions of, 59
    development of understanding over time, 59–61
        by end of grade 5, 60
        by end of grade 8, 60
        by end of grade 12, 61
    energy as a scientific idea, 59–60
"Designing Environmental Solutions" module, 267, 273, 277
"Designing Mixtures" unit, 267, 273, 276
Developing Possible Solutions (ETS1.B), **242,** 246, 248, 249–251, 284
    teaching strategies for, 258